THE BANK

THE BANK

*The Birth of Europe's Central Bank and the
Rebirth of Europe's Power*

—————————— : ——————————

MATT MARSHALL

RANDOM HOUSE
——————————
BUSINESS BOOKS

First published in 1999 by Random House Business Books
Random House, 20 Vauxhall Bridge Road,
London SW1V 2SA

Random House Australia (Pty) Limited
20 Alfred Street, Milsons Point, Sydney,
New South Wales 2061, Australia

Random House New Zealand Limited
18 Poland Road, Glenfield,
Auckland 10, New Zealand

Random House South Africa (Pty) Limited
Endulini, 5a Jubilee Road, Parktown 2193, South Africa

Random House UK Limited Reg. No. 954009

Papers used by Random House UK Limited are natural,
recyclable products made from wood grown in sustainable forests.
The manufacturing processes conform to the environmental
regulations of the country of origin.

ISBN 0 7126 8070 5

Typeset in Sabon by MATS, Southend-on-Sea, Essex
Printed and bound in Great Britain by
Biddles Ltd, Guildford and King's Lynn

Companies, institutions and other organizations wishing to make bulk
purchases of any business books published by Random House should
contact their local bookstore or Random House direct:

Special Sales Director

Random House, 20 Vauxhall Bridge Road,
London SW1V 2SA

Tel 0171 840 8470   Fax 0171 828 6681

www.randomhouse.co.uk
businessbooks@randomhouse.co.uk

Contents

Preface

I first visited Lex Hoogduin, Wim Duisenberg's personal advisor, in late March 1998, to raise the idea of writing a book about the European Central Bank.

I told him that the only way I could write a reliable and accurate book about the ECB was if the bank gave me access to its board members and top-level executives. Already, the debate about the public accountability and transparency of Europe's central bankers had heated up, and they were being criticized for secretive practices. I suggested that giving me access could likewise help the bank's cause – that is, if it proved that the ECB's policies and structure were as sound and efficient as the bank's founders claimed. But I warned that the book would be fair. I had no private agenda, but admitted that as an American, I am basically pro-Europe, seeing the tremendous advantages that a federal system can bring under the right conditions – when member states can retain certain powers.

During that first meeting, Hoogduin couldn't promise me anything. The central bank was still in an embryonic form, and Duisenberg still hadn't been appointed president. Though he was president of the EMI (the ECB's predecessor), and presumed by most observers to be the lead candidate for the ECB presidency, the French were still trying to push their candidate, Jean-Claude Trichet.

But Hoogduin agreed that the book idea was a good one. Once Duisenberg was appointed in May 1998 and the ECB inaugurated in June, Hoogduin helped provide access to the entire ECB board and top-level executives. I was able to interview all of the people I chose to for this book, including the entire 17-member governing council. There are two exceptions. The first is Bernd Goos, the German head of the ECB's international relations. Goos fell sick for several months after the creation of the ECB, and time did not allow me to follow up on an interview after he returned. Talks with the ECB's public relations chief, Manfred Körber, and several other central bankers, helped me fill the gap to my satisfaction. The second is Antonio Fazio, the governor of the Banca d'Italia. Unfortunately, time again prohibited me from making the trip to Rome when an opening in his schedule finally did arise. However, Fazio was gracious enough to answer my questions in written form.

The debate about transparency and accountability at the ECB intensified in subsequent months, after the bank's controversial decision not to publish the protocol of its governing council meetings until 30 years had passed. In the March/April 1999 issue of *Foreign Affairs*, two Princeton University political scientists Sheri Berman and Kathleen R. McNamara called the ECB 'sinister' for its almost 'complete freedom from democratic oversight and control'. They echoed the criticisms made by others about the ECB, now one of the two most powerful financial institutions in the world.

This book makes no such critical conclusions. The central bank is Europe's first supranational institution, and as such, is being forced to bear the full weight of public scrutiny as a test case for a more politically integrated European Union. Yet this demand for transparency comes even despite no conclusive evidence that public scrutiny of central bank proceedings leads to better results. With most social questions, for example social security, democratic debate is desirable because there are inevitably winners and losers. Things are different in central banking. Low inflation is increasingly seen as a *neutral* policy, that is, one where no one loses. But the jury is still out on the extent of this neutrality, and the reader is left to make his own decision based on the summary of Europe's central banking history provided by this book in the first five chapters.

As the book explains, national sensitivities in Europe are such that an unfettered publication of the council's minutes is still not possible without the danger of creating national jealousies and serious inter-European conflict. Germany has laid down most of the central banking orthodoxy in Europe and continues to lead the way in a number of other fields in Europe's policy making. Its size and central position within Europe is evident within the ECB. This influence is to be expected, and other countries must reconcile themselves to this, given that unity of purpose is within Europe's economic and geo-political interests. Some national leaders, particularly in France, are wary about following Germany's lead, as displayed during the ECB presidential nomination in May 1998, recounted in chapter six.

These sorts of jealousies hamper the ECB's council members from being able to pursue Europe's interests objectively in public. If France's central bank governor Jean-Claude Trichet votes for an interest rate decision that clashes with France's interests, and the vote is publicized, the bank would come under withering criticism from the French public, throwing into doubt the legitimacy of the European project. This concern about conflict was behind Germany's three-decade fight to establish political union ahead of monetary union, a battle they lost. To them it would have guaranteed the solidarity needed to weather potential storms created by a single currency. For reasons explained in this book, the Germans relented on this demand during the negotiations over the single currency in 1991, but they still see the need for more political union in the future. This book, drawing from the views of the central bankers themselves, argues that such union is inevitable.

That said, the bank could be more open in publishing details on the arguments for and against specific policy decisions without revealing the names of council members. This would help quell criticisms of despotism and lack of transparency. The ECB could also announce the possibility of publishing more detailed minutes in several years' time – once a smooth start has been guaranteed. Alexandre Lamfalussy, the Belgian central banker who was president of the EMI before Duisenberg took over in July 1997, supports such disclosure. Duisenberg's leadership represents a continuation of Europe's tradition of élite, top-down government, a tradition characterized more by secrecy than that of the US system. It is a tradition that has become outdated, and may come back to haunt the ECB when the market begins to second-guess its announcements. (In the meantime, visitors to the bank's website at www.ecb.int will not find published minutes, but will find a useful and informative site.)

In recognition of the norm of secrecy on the part of most continental central bankers, I want to thank several people for their refreshingly frank observations: the Finnish board member Sirkka Hämäläinen, the Finnish governor Matti Vanhala, the Luxembourg governor Yves Mersch and the British general directors Jim Etherington and Peter Bull. Though some of them feared that their views could be construed as criticisms of particular nations, they all spoke without malice and in the interest of the greater good of the European project – which is admirable at a time when national taboos threaten to smother debate. It is also no coincidence that four of these five people are from Finland and Britain, the two countries that have been most free from the political baggage accrued on the continent after centuries of warfare.

The first five chapters of the book explain the history of the ECB's creation, and summarize the Dutch, German and French positions and the principal protagonists. I then outline the controversy surrounding the appointment of Duisenberg and introduce other aspects of the bank as it started operations in June 1998. Chapter seven is a summary of the bank's main responsibilities, followed by a summary of the reasoning behind the bank's monetary policy strategy and its first interest rate cut. Chapter nine explains why Europe will move towards greater political union. Chapter ten discusses the 'second wave' of likely ECB entrants, focusing on the British case. My conclusion is that Europe will become a strengthened pillar within the Atlantic hegemony during the 21st century.

Besides Lex Hoogduin, I am also deeply indebted to the ECB's Dirk Freytag, Manfred Körber, Christina Goodman, and Regina Schüller for their help. Thanks are also due to the governors and public relations officers of Europe's national central banks for their admirable patience in answering my badgering questions. I'd like to thank my family for helping me through the tough, lonely process of writing my first book, and for reading through the early drafts and providing endless comments. Eduard Bomhoff, André Szász, and Poilin Breathnach also deserve special thanks. Thanks also goes to Angelica Wagner and Dorte Huneke for invaluable assistance in transcribing scores of interviews. Special gratitude goes out to my editor at Random House, Simon Wilson, who showed unfathomable patience even as the book metamorphosed in unpredictable ways. Thanks too to the *Wall Street Journal*'s Peter Gumbel, who provided much guidance at the beginning of my stay in Germany and during my coverage of the Bundesbank and the German corporate world and economy since 1995.

CHAPTER ONE

The Showdown

There was a frosty edge to the evening air. It was Sunday, February 9 1997, and the world's most powerful central bankers gathered in the dining room on the top floor of the high-rise Bank for International Settlements in Basle, Switzerland.

The BIS, known as the 'central bank of central banks', was created in 1930, and had evolved into a forum where bankers could meet several times a year to discuss the financial world's most pressing problems. Under the agreed rules, the participants were not allowed to take notes, nor could they invite assistants in to join them. US Federal Reserve Chairman Alan Greenspan was permitted to bring the President of the New York Federal Reserve Bank, Bill McDonough – but that was part of the ritual. The other national central bankers, from Japan, Canada, and nine European countries, were to come alone. Finally, Alexandre Lamfalussy, president of the European Monetary Institute, the forerunner of the European Central Bank, and Andrew Crockett, the BIS's general manager, were also invited.[1]

---

[1] The BIS hosts the meetings of the so-called G-10, or Group of Ten, which assembles the day after the Sunday evening dinners. The G-10 is a misnomer, since it formally consists of the following eleven countries: Belgium, Canada, France, Germany, Italy, Japan, the Netherlands, Sweden, Switzerland, UK, and the US. The governors of the central banks of each of these countries are allowed to attend the evening dinners. Finally, the President of the European Central Bank (until mid-1998, the European Monetary Institute) and the General Manager of the Bank for International Settlements are also invited to the dinners. A formal meeting is held the next day, and a press conference follows.

Between them, the bankers control 95 per cent of the world's trillions of dollars of money in circulation.[2] All of them have the power to move currency and stock markets up or down. Alan Greenspan, with a few words spoken in public, could alarm the markets and, if he really wanted to, send the entire world into a recession. The meetings were much looked forward to by the bankers. With no cameras or aggressive reporters with notebooks on hand, they could drop their guard and speak their minds.

Wim Duisenberg, as president of the BIS at the time, was host of the dinner. Keeping to G-10 tradition, he sat at the centre on the north side of the large oval table, facing the window that looked out over the snow-capped Jura mountain range marking the French–Swiss border to the south – now shrouded in darkness. Opposite him was the seat of the G-10 chairman, which was filled by the German central bank president Hans Tietmeyer. Greenspan, though more powerful, sat off to Duisenberg's side. The BIS is the one important international financial organization that the Europeans truly control.

After the group had finished salad and the main course, Duisenberg tapped on a glass and announced that the evening discussion would begin. The subject of the evening would be announced by Eddie George, the governor of the Bank of England.

Eddie George cleared his throat, and proposed that they talk about European economic and monetary union. The European bankers drew breath. George was known for his publicly expressed doubt that Europe was ready for the single currency. To be sure, he was the central bank governor from a country that had decided not to participate. The bankers suspected that his desire for delay might actually veil a secret desire to have the project wait until Britain too was ready to join. Nevertheless, George's ensuing arguments forced them to confront the issue. George insisted that inflexible labour

---

[2] They directly control about 30 to 40 per cent of the world's reserves, but since their currencies are used as reserves by other central banks around the globe, the control of these reserves is actually only indirect (i.e., by changing interest rates.)

regulations in some countries had caused high unemployment. But a single currency would prohibit these countries from exercising an independent monetary policy, thereby removing the means for them to spark their economies into growth if unemployment reached intolerable levels. 'The unemployment problem is only getting worse,' he said. 'Introducing a single currency under such conditions, in my view, is a hazardous undertaking.'

Talk of any delay in achieving economic union had been taboo for the rest of the European bankers for the last half decade. Economic and monetary union (EMU) had been a vision in which many of them believed. They had all been working feverishly to prepare their countries for a switch to the new joint currency, due to be introduced in 1999. Stopping now would be a huge disappointment. Besides, if the project did begin on schedule, most of them would be members of the prestigious European Central Bank governing council, the select group which would govern the new currency.

That bank would be the most powerful institution in Europe, having the power to set interest rates, and with it, the power to move trillions of dollars of capital, and speed up or slow down the economy – in short, have more direct impact on the fortunes of more citizens around the world than any other institution apart from the US Federal Reserve. Unlike the European Commission, the ECB would not be a mere puppet institution, making proposals subject to government veto. The ECB would be fiercely independent, set the agenda and be accountable to no one. It would be supranational. It would enjoy raw power at its best. As members of the ECB's council, the central bankers would be masters of Europe's financial world.

Despite the taboo in discussing a delay, however, many of the bankers were relieved that George had brought up the issue. In recent weeks, the EMU project had been battered by a wave of pessimism and some of them were beginning to have their own doubts. In January, French finance minister Jean Arthuis had questioned whether France would be able to reduce its government deficit in time to meet the Maastricht limit for qualification in the single currency project.[3] The French government had already made deep budget cuts to meet the Maastricht conditions, and had run out of options. The public was exhausted, and with data showing rising unemployment, there were signs of a possible revolt. Protests had swept the country in late 1995, and fears of a repeat were growing. Legislative elections were only 14 months away, and the government was getting desperate. A public opinion survey that month showed that if a referendum was held on France's participation in the euro, 55 per cent of the French would say no. Without France, the bankers knew, the project would be doomed.

Meanwhile, the European bankers were also piqued about a challenge to their power by the European governments. For example, Arthuis had redoubled his efforts to create a 'stability council', a political counterpart to the European Central Bank that would make it more accountable to governments. Arthuis had managed to win the German, Belgian and Dutch finance ministers over to the idea, though they had insisted that it remain an informal body and not infringe upon the ECB's independence. But the bankers remained distrustful. They saw it as a veiled French effort to wield political influence over the bank. After all, even after the Maastricht Treaty had been signed, and the concept of ECB independence enshrined, president François Mitterrand had openly declared that the French wanted just that – political influence.

On a number of other fronts, the bankers had come to see the risks endemic in starting the EMU project on time in 1999. Even Germany, traditionally the most upright in its finances, was having difficulties. Tax receipts were shrivelling as more German investors shifted their money into Luxembourg accounts to avoid paying taxes, and – as a legacy of the high costs of German unification – Bonn's deficit was also set to overshoot the Maastricht ceiling. Unemployment had hit a

---

[3] Although the euro was scheduled for introduction in 1999, the deadline year for meeting the criteria was 1997. The Maastricht Treaty required that a country participating in the single currency project could not run up a public deficit equivalent to more than 3 per cent of its Gross Domestic Product, or the value of the sum of its goods and services.

post-war high in January, reaching levels not seen since Hitler came to power in 1933. Poll after poll showed a majority of the German population against the euro.

The French and German politicians were determined to meet the 1999 deadline. That was their job. But the German and French peoples weren't ready to make the sacrifices for further public-spending cuts. Would the eager politicians agree to fudge the deficit criteria to meet the deadlines? If so, what sort of signal would that send to Italy, Spain and Portugal? If rules were broken at the beginning, how could there be any hope of restoring discipline later? The Latin countries were already resorting to all sorts of budget gimmicks to lower their deficits. Italy had even raised a special 'euro' tax for the year. The bankers had an important role as honest brokers for the public. They could pull out a yellow warning flag if they wanted to. They respected the politicians' right to ignore it. But the public should be warned. The question was just how high they should wave that flag – and how directly they should confront the politicians.

George explained that a decision to delay now would be better than waiting until the last minute when the politicians would face overwhelming pressure to go ahead with the project. The financial markets might also accept a delay if it were announced now, but they might panic at a chaotic decision to delay later on. Better a late EMU than a badly timed one. Waiting would also help give Britain, Sweden and Denmark – the three countries which had decided to stay out of the project at the outset – time to consider joining. Even Greece, which had wanted to join, might be able to get its economic house in order to qualify. Meanwhile, the so-called 'club-med' countries – Italy, Spain and Portugal – would have more time to prove that their deficit cutting was sustainable, and not indicative of a frantic dash towards the finish line.

George looked round the table to see who wanted to begin. Wim Duisenberg, the craggy-faced president of the Dutch central bank, spoke up. 'Well, I haven't consulted with anyone about this, but I think a delay for two years would be a wise idea. Why not?' he asked, in his short and direct way. The words stunned the other Europeans. Duisenberg was the front-runner to become president of the European Central Bank,[4] and here he was throwing cold water on the project. Worse still, the Americans, Japanese and Canadians were looking on at this embarrassing faltering of confidence within Europe. The Swiss and Swedish bankers were also from countries outside EMU. Duisenberg was relaxed, enjoying a glass of wine and his usual cigarette with colleagues, but he was serious.

Privately Duisenberg had been busy debating the idea of a delay with colleagues at the Dutch central bank. He and the rest of the Dutch bank's board had commissioned a study from its economics department listing the pros and cons relating to a delay in the project. The report was so sensitive that it was kept top-secret, and wasn't even circulated inside the bank. It was positive, saying the benefits of a timely start were greater than the drawbacks.[5] But Duisenberg was sceptical. He'd been tacitly supporting a behind-the-scenes campaign by the Dutch government to push for delay among the other EU government leaders. The Dutch finance minister, Gerrit Zalm, was especially concerned about Italy. He made a series of trips to Germany to see if other leaders were ready to consider a delay, but had run into obstacles. Germany itself was in danger of not meeting the entry criteria, and was reluctant to take a hard line towards others. The German Chancellor, Helmut Kohl, even dispatched his foreign policy advisor, Karl Lamers, to try to persuade the Dutch leaders to take a more 'European attitude' towards the currency project, which only seemed to confirm the Dutch suspicions that the Germans were getting ready to weaken their stance – to allow the single currency project to begin even if some countries weren't ready. The Netherlands was alone in its

---

[4] Duisenberg had already been appointed president of the European Monetary Institute in July of that year. The EMI was the forerunner of the European Central Bank.

[5] The Dutch central bank report was commissioned in late 1996, and was linked with the publication of the first EMI convergence report at the same time, which had concluded that the fiscal conditions of European governments were so poor that there was no majority of member states ready to start EMU on January 1, 1997, the first possible start date nominated by the Treaty of Maastricht.

campaign. Zalm and Duisenberg consulted often, having weekly lunches at the 'Signpost' restaurant in the Hague, and while travelling together to regular European summit meetings. Now Duisenberg was away from the Hague, in the private company of his central bank colleagues in Basle, and he wanted their views.

Though Duisenberg had expressed doubt in the past, most of the five remaining European bankers from countries planning to participate in EMU had no inkling of the depth of his reservations. But two of them were also highly sceptical. Antonio Fazio, governor of the Banca d'Italia, a known euro-pessimist, harrumphed that he too supported the idea of delay. He'd watched his government create accounting methods that were innovative even by Italian standards. Added time would help ensure Italy's financial books were more sound.

German central bank chief Hans Tietmeyer had also waited for this moment. He too doubted the prudence of a punctual start, but as the most powerful central banker in Europe, had felt constrained in how much he could say in public. Any hint of hesitation and the markets would descend into chaos: investors would swiftly sell the Italian lira, Portuguese escudo and Spanish peseta, and pile into German marks. Before long, the currency links would be broken, and years of hard work dashed instantly. Tietmeyer had already made reference to delay in a speech the previous year. He had put it in the context of a preference for delay rather than a derailment once EMU began,[i] thereby shielding the degree of his doubt from the markets. He was debating whether he should come out and be more explicit.

Now his colleagues were discussing the issue in the open, and he was again faced with the dilemma of how much he could or should say. Tietmeyer didn't even like revealing his thoughts to his colleagues. On the one hand, he remained personally sceptical about the project's chances of success, and agreed with the risks outlined by George, Duisenberg and Fazio. But on the other, he was all too aware of the enormous weight of his words. In addition, he was reluctant to challenge a project that was the passion of the man to whom he owed his position, Chancellor Helmut Kohl.

Tietmeyer didn't speak as much as usual that evening. When he did, it was with doubt in his voice, and he was careful to avoid forceful conclusions. He bemoaned the lack of interest rate convergence in Europe, the huge problems countries were having in reducing their deficits, and the fact that a number of countries would not qualify at all if the debt criteria were to be taken seriously. These problems were increasing, not decreasing, he said. The debates in Italy, Portugal and Spain were 'verging on the hysterical.' Desperate to join in the first wave, they were resorting to an array of budgetary tricks. But also in the forefront of Tietmeyer's thoughts that evening, he would later reveal, were the questions he didn't dare utter at the time: 'Is the date really all that important; is it decisive? Could it be worth waiting a year or two to see how the situation develops?' It wasn't worth reaching the hundred-metre finishing line, only to then collapse. 'Tietmeyer, very conspicuously, sat on the fence', recalls one participant.

Tietmeyer was mulling over whether to express these questions out loud when his dilemma was resolved by a harsh riposte from Jean-Claude Trichet, governor of the Banque de France. Delay was a preposterous idea, he retorted, launching into a passionate defence of EMU. Certainly, the French were exhausted, but a delay would be even worse. The French might not have the stomach to rally behind the project a second time. 'Delaying would be against the spirit and the letter of the treaty,' Trichet told his colleagues. 'In my opinion, it will open up an enormous risk of not making it the next time. New pretexts would be created not to proceed,' he said. He cautioned that the markets could react violently. Public opinion could also turn against the project. In short, EMU would be consigned to the dustbin of history. Trichet spoke with the conviction of someone who could almost taste the power that he would soon be sharing with the Germans at the ECB. As the director of the Trésor, he had witnessed the agreement by Kohl, François Mitterrand and Italian prime minister Giulio Andreotti to set a deadline for EMU before 2000. For Trichet, the agreement had been a 'lucid vision' shared by Kohl and Mitterrand. He and his German counterpart at the time, Horst Köhler, had negotiated the treaty immediately. From that moment, he'd been an 'Ayatollah' in the service of that vision.[6]

Also hesitant to support a delay were the two Belgians, Alfons Verplaetse, governor of the Belgian central bank, and the EMI's Alexandre Lamfalussy. They backed Trichet. Verplaetse had recently turned against the idea of a 'core Europe', still supported by Duisenberg and Tietmeyer, which would comprise an élite group of northern European countries and exclude Italy, Spain and Portugal. In his habitually genial manner, Verplaestse said the bankers should wait to see if the other countries succeeded. Lamfalussy, who had thrown all his energies over the past four years into preparing the single currency as head of the EMI, not only had a personal stake in the project's success, but believed in it. 'A delay would be a significant loss of credibility,' he said, annoyed that George and Duisenberg had initiated the debate in front of outsiders. He urged Duisenberg: 'Don't base your views simply on public opinion. Let us see what is happening in the economy. Italy and the others could well have a reasonable chance of qualifying. With the degree of preparations that have been made, you can't just dismiss them out of hand.'

Lamfalussy had formed a new opinion of the Italians. Unlike his Dutch and German colleagues, he believed that they were making genuine progress. In 1993, Italian Finance Minister Carlo Ciampi had managed to persuade the Italians to break from wage indexation, and since then inflation had converged quickly with the rest of Europe. After the last significant depreciation of the lira in 1993, Italy's inflation had accelerated from 3.5 to only 5 per cent (moderate by Italian standards), made possible only because the trade unions had accepted a large cut in real wages. Since then, inflation had continued to fall. 'Nothing went haywire,' Lamfalussy explained. 'If they can

---

[6] See chapter 4.

succeed with the trade unions, they might even have a chance of getting their budget deficit down.'

Lamfalussy accepted Tietmeyer's argument that convergence needed to be proved as durable in the long run, but how strict did that test need to be? 'If you push that argument to the extreme,' he had told Tietmeyer, 'then you'll end up alone, because you won't even be able to trust the Dutch.' After all, the Dutch had devalued against the mark by 2 per cent in the early 1980s, yet they were the most prudent among Germany's neighbours in holding down inflation.

The G-10 debate in Basle revealed deep divisions of opinion, but they were left unresolved. Some in the room felt that they'd heard the beginning of the end. Andrew Crockett, the managing director of BIS, left the dinner with a sinking feeling, fearing EMU's days might be numbered. But Crockett wasn't certain how resolute the European bankers were. The Americans were bemused. 'We thought the best thing that we could do was to maintain an interested silence. It was very much an internal European debate,' McDonough recalls. 'My feeling was that Duisenberg was the learned professor running a seminar. Sometimes, by asking the difficult question, you get the students to say what they think . . . As I sat there, I was cheering on the side which was saying "Let's guts this through and make it work." I have the view that in anything, if there's a date, you're better off to try to meet it. Once you postpone, its difficult to gather the political will to seek to achieve it again.'

Trichet had saved the day.[7] He too had been influenced by his government's views. Paris was the only government which had ruled out a delay as a possible scenario at the time. The then German finance minister, Theo Waigel, recalls:

Not only in the Dutch central bank, but also in other circles

---

[7] It would be one of history's ironies that, when it came to the election of the first president of the ECB, Trichet would lose out to Duisenberg.

there were scenarios developed about what to do in case some countries didn't converge. We had always said that we would interpret the criteria strictly. But we realized that a continuous public discussion about a delay would have led to a catastrophic loss in public confidence. In fact, EMU would have been destroyed immediately. In 1996, a small group of us, including union representatives, gathered at the Chancellory's office. We agreed that the criteria must be fulfilled strictly, otherwise there would be no acceptance by the German population. We also agreed that Germany could not be the one to propose a delay. A couple of days later, someone in the circle leaked this to the media. From then on, we shut up. Internally, most countries were also preparing for various scenarios. There were discussions of one or two-year delays. However, the French never let themselves participate in this debate. They always said 'no, we're not going to discuss that'.

The following month, the bankers showed signs of having put the issue behind them. In a 'Banker of the Year' award ceremony in Frankfurt on March 3 (which Wim Duisenberg won), Tietmeyer, Duisenberg and Lamfalussy all came out forcefully against a delay in public. Their statements – at least those from Tietmeyer and Duisenberg – were more than an about-face. They derided the notion of a delay, even though they themselves had believed the issue serious enough to debate for hours in Basle. They knew that uncertainty had already given rise to turbulence in the markets. 'The fears and the rumours of the market about a delay of EMU are so ridiculous that I can't understand them,' stressed Tietmeyer. 'The rumours of delay are unfounded,' insisted Lamfalussy. 'They don't have any link to reality. EMU will start on January 1, 1999.' Duisenberg was the most emphatic: 'The start of the single currency has become a certainty, I repeat, a certainty, since the treaty of Maastricht was ratified.'[ii]

Later, Duisenberg would go as far to say that a delay would be a 'catastrophe'.

In an interview over a year later, Duisenberg said he had

difficulty remembering the event in Basle in February 1997, and denied that he had ever proposed a delay. Any proposal he had made in Basle would have been for 'academic reasons' only, he says. He argues that he had always considered a delay 'totally unrealistic and very dangerous'. He explains:

> I deliberately didn't take part in that discussion. That discussion was very much stimulated by the minister of finance, Mr. Zalm, and was meant to put national pressure on Italy to comply to the criteria. The attitude of Germany was much more important than that of the Netherlands, but in that respect, we had one line of thinking. So we joined forces . . . you might say the governments did . . . in maximizing the pressure on Italy. Both considered whether or not Italy should participate. But I personally never believed, not for one second, that we would start without Italy, but knew that we still had to keep up the pressure.[8]

A Frenchman had pleaded for EMU when the German camp, influenced by Tietmeyer and Duisenberg, had lost its nerve. It was a paradox, in many ways. The French had usually been the ones to come up with the ideas, and the Germans had shaped those ideas into rules and institutions. The Maastricht Treaty was a perfect example. In 1990, Mitterrand had wanted a single currency and had wanted it soon. He feared the financial and political power of the new reunified Germany, following absorption of the former Communist-led East Germany, and wanted to bind Germany irrevocably to the rest of Europe. Kohl, wanting to reassure his neighbour, agreed, but called for

---

[8] Duisenberg may have an intermittent problem with his memory. He also says he doesn't remember the classified research paper drawn up by the economics department which listed the pros and cons concerning a delay. Duisenberg's memory was also unreliable in the case of his 'voluntary' statement that he did not want to serve his full term as president of the ECB in May 1998. British Prime Minister Tony Blair had 'reminded' Duisenberg that the Dutchman had once earlier stated privately that he did not want to serve a full mandate. Duisenberg says he had forgotten that. But Blair's reminder later proved useful. See chapter 6.

a committee to be created to ensure that the institutions governing the new currency were agreed to by the central bankers. The Germans dictated much of what came out of the Delors committee, and had since finessed developments in their favour.

But in early 1997 support for the process was faltering. Part of the reason was the lack of political union. The Dutch and Germans knew that adherence to the rules for EMU by the French and others was crucial if the system was going to work, and that entailed trust. The French and others had resisted political union,[9] and so the best that could be done was to cobble together the Pact on Stability and Growth, which imposed fiscal limits and fined countries that breached them. But trust was continually being broken, for example by Mitterrand's declaration in 1992 that the ECB would be subject to government influence. This reflected the way Europe worked – in fits and starts.

But now that Trichet had convinced his colleagues to support a move toward EMU, the last bout of paranoia was over. In fact, the good times had begun to roll. Over the next twelve months, a pro-EMU euphoria swept over continental Europe. Economic growth accelerated, and tax receipts came pouring in, helping governments like Italy and Germany close their deficits. In the corporate sector, excitement mounted when it became clear that monetary union might start on time after all.

NOTES

[i] See author's article in *The Wall Street Journal Europe*, September 8, 1997. 'Germany Sets EMU Battle Lines – Debate Shifts to Consequences of Delay'.
[ii] Quotes from Gabriel Milesi, *Le Roman de l'Euro*, Hachette Littératures, 1998.

---

[9] See chapter 3.

CHAPTER TWO

The Dutchman's Restoration

When the facts change, I change my mind.
What do you do, sir?

John Maynard Keynes

On September 28, 1998 the day after his government was elected into office, then German finance minister Oskar Lafontaine held a press conference and called for lower interest rates across Europe. Wim Duisenberg, now president of the European Central Bank, responded coolly: 'It is normal for politicians to give their views, but it would be very abnormal if those suggestions are listened to.'

Wim Duisenberg is neither a German stooge nor a French one. But at the same time, he has a profound appreciation of the German central bank's record on low inflation. This buttresses his conviction that the bank should maintain its independence from outside influence. The independent German central bank, the Bundesbank, kept inflation low for decades, and thereby created conditions for lasting economic prosperity. In France, by contrast, political interference during the first few decades of the post-war period resulted in higher average inflation, a situation that changed only when leaders decided to peg the French franc to the German mark. During their negotiations to create a single currency in Maastricht in 1991, European countries acknowledged the strength of the German central banking model. They have since appointed Duisenberg and the ECB to introduce German monetary orthodoxy at the European level. As president of a central bank that closely resembles the Bundesbank in the way it operates, Duisenberg oversaw the smooth introduction of the single currency in January 1999 in the eleven participating countries: Austria, Belgium, Finland, France, Germany, Ireland, Italy, Luxembourg, the Netherlands, Portugal and Spain. Together with a group of like-minded bankers who sit with him in the ECB's governing council, he is now determined to keep the new single currency, the euro, as stable as the German mark had been.

Ultimately, however, Duisenberg is faced with a greater challenge. The single currency has set in motion a series of irresistible forces that are pushing European countries to more intense forms of coordination despite significant domestic resistance. Countries taking part in the single currency project realize that governments will have to cooperate more in tax and spending policies, and that an automatic transfer mechanism might be needed to balance out economic discrepancies across Europe.

On the one hand, this process of increased cooperation is welcomed. Only by harnessing the combined power – both economic and political – of its member states into a single, directed force can Europe hope to project itself in the world of international finance as powerfully as the United States. The discipline of increased cooperation on economic issues would also create a framework for better economic growth. On the other hand, the imperative to cooperate exposes national jealousies and infighting over the bank's policies. One problem is that economies still operate at different speeds, while the bank can only furnish a one-size-fits-all monetary policy. Duisenberg's decisions could become highly unpopular in a country that is in recession if the ECB is forced to make that situation worse by following policies tailored to the interests of Europe as a whole. A proud nation like France could lash out in protest against the European project if it is feels snubbed or overwhelmed by a single currency juggernaut that seems to be driven by Germany. The same is true of the smaller, weaker economies, especially if they are left to suffer with no financial palliative from more fortunate countries. Duisenberg's biggest challenge is to steer the ECB's policies through this minefield of national interests, a task that has been made more difficult by the impression in France that Duisenberg is 'a Bundesbank clone', and imposes 'a Germanic and orthodox colouring'.[i]

The makings of a president

Wim Duisenberg was born on July 9, 1935 in Heerenveen, a town of 40,000 residents on the western edge of Friesland, in the Netherlands.[1] While the Netherlands is one of the most densely populated countries in the world, the Friesland is far removed from the bulk of the Dutch population, most of which is packed into a region bounded by the Hague, Amsterdam, Utrecht and Rotterdam.

The son of a local government civil servant who managed the local waterworks, young Duisenberg enjoyed taking his boat out into the calm inland Frisian lakes, south of the Frisian Islands and protected from the aggressive North Sea. He first sailed when he was four – the same year, 1940, that the Germans invaded the Netherlands during the Second World War.

One of his most vivid memories, he says, is of the German arrival. 'It lasted three days and three nights. There was this eternal rumbling. They came on horses. I remember looking out and seeing them come with kitchen wagons, machinery . . .' he recalls.

---

[1] Judging by their history, the Friesians are tough people. They managed to fight off Roman invaders. Later, they killed the German apostle Bonifatius when he tried to convert them to Christianity. Fighting together, they fended off a Norman attack. It took Holland's rulers hundreds of years to conquer Friesland, and even then the region insisted on keeping its own legal system, language and culture. When the powerful Catholic Hapsburg Empire acquired Holland, Friesland thumbed its nose by warmly embracing Calvinist protestantism. Friesland became a bastion of continual rebellion. Today, it is the only Dutch region with its own language, Frisian, the Germanic language closest to English. Another reading of history is less complimentary. The region is mostly bog land, and so very difficult to penetrate and perhaps not even strategically important enough to occupy. The easy German invasion during the Second World War 'with horses', rather than the tanks which rolled over the rest of Europe, suggest the region isn't as tough as it's cracked up to be.

Willem F. Duisenberg, President of the European Central Bank

The Netherlands were occupied by the German Wehrmacht longer than many regions in western Europe, lasting from Germany's first *Blitzkrieg* in May 1940 until early 1945. This did not make for easy relations between the Dutch and the Germans after the war. During the occupation, the Dutch business community and political leadership were passive or even collaborationist, according to some accounts. While people in the Netherlands often talk about 'hate' when speaking of the Germans, the Dutch élite are more reserved, and since the war, have rarely engaged in anti-German diatribes.

The north, where Duisenberg lived, was especially passive. 'It was peaceful. Contrary to the west (of Holland), we had no hunger. It was a safe haven,' he recalls. The Dutch economy had been spared massive destruction, but there were serious hardships, and as late as 1948, the economy was still struggling to find its feet.

As a teenager, Duisenberg worked during summer vacations on several assembly lines, first for a cigarette company, then for a coffee company. He worked in a pig slaughterhouse, then for a bicycle manufacturer, pushing spokes into wheel rims.

Duisenberg left grammar school at 19, and began studying economics at the University of Groningen. Removed from the area in which he had grown up, Duisenberg's bond with his homeland deepened. Later, at the pinnacle of his career as a Dutch central banker, he won praise for organizing an annual trip to the Friesland region for under-privileged children. Hans Tietmeyer, the future chief of Germany's central bank and just four years older than Duisenberg, was attending school 100 kilometres away, across the border in the German town of Münster.[2] Their fates were going to become inextricably bound,

---

[2] At the Frankfurt 'Banker of the Year' ceremony in March, 1997, Hans Tietmeyer gave the speech honouring the winner, Wim Duisenberg. The award is made annually by a group of 21 financial publications from various countries. Tietmeyer stressed the common thinking and the culture that united the two men, who he said were born in villages only 50 kilometres apart. Perhaps this faulty geography – the towns are in fact 100 kilometres apart – reflects an unconscious exaggeration of the closeness between the two men.

and one was going to hand over the mantle of the most powerful man in Europe to the other.

By the time he was 26, Duisenberg had obtained a degree in economics, having specialized in international economic relations. His doctoral thesis was on the economic consequences of disarmament. Duisenberg was an assistant lecturer during these four years.

When Duisenberg received his doctorate in 1965, one newspaper *De Tijd*, remarked that he outwardly resembled the dashing American President John F. Kennedy: 'The likeness was more than obvious,' it read. 'The quiff of hair . . . an open face, jovial, youthful and charming, of the type that men say women fall for.'[ii] The only difference was that Duisenberg was taller: He stands at a towering 1.93 metres (6 feet 4 inches). Duisenberg possessed an air of calm confidence.

After he obtained his doctorate, he decided he wanted to go abroad for a few years. He saw an advertisement for a lecturing position in Dar es Salaam, Tanzania, and considered applying for it. But a professor friend had higher aspirations for Duisenberg, and warned him that the position wouldn't give him the experience he needed. So Duisenberg applied for a job at the International Monetary Fund in Washington DC, working on the European desk. Dutch influence within the IMF was strong at the time, with a disproportiate number of young Dutchmen seeking out careers as economists. The running joke among IMF staffers was that it was 'paid for by the Americans, intrigued by the Indians and run by the Dutch'.

Duisenberg worked there for four years until he was 34. Dirk Wolfson, another Dutchman already working at the IMF when Duisenberg arrived, recalls that there was something about him that turned heads:

He did very well at the IMF. He was a highly respected staff member. He had what the French would call *la manière*. When he enters the room, the room is full. He has a good voice, he talks well, he looks good. He was a bit of a prince charming. Americans always teased him about being the

'European Kennedy' for his good looks. I knew he would go far somehow. He had that all over him.

After the IMF, Duisenberg was hired by the Amsterdam-based Dutch central bank, De Nederlandsche Bank, to advise the bank's governing board. It was here, as a young advisor in charge of establishing a department for macroeconomic research, that he was first initiated into the culture of central banking. But he was still a low-ranking official in the bank unknown to many of the board members. Duisenberg struck his colleagues as sociable, with an easy way of dealing with people, but shy underneath. Somehow Duisenberg was able to gain the confidence of those he met. But Duisenberg can also be impatient, and at times doesn't converse, but merely makes statements. 'I've realized that in being direct and open – let me call it straightforward – I have to be very careful in what it is I am saying,' he says.

Duisenberg left his advisory position, which was only a one-year appointment, to become a professor at the University of Amsterdam. He taught macroeconomics for three years, but again kept a low profile. He didn't break any ground in economic theory, or belong to a particular school of thought. In fact, almost from the beginning, he was calculating his next move. Apart from a few articles for a weekly university journal, his published work was relatively scant.

Duisenberg, now a member of the social democratic party, made the giant leap from an obscure economics professor, of which there were hundreds in the Netherlands, to finance minister at the end of just three years. His colleagues say this was achieved on the strength of personal connections. The social democratic party was tiny, and Duisenberg happened to be part of a group of economists advising the party chairman, Joop den Uyl, who became prime minister in 1973.

According to University of Newfoundland Professor Steven Wolinetz, who has studied the Netherlands political scene in detail, the Dutch have a tradition of respect for people who are members of official boards, which partly explains their proliferation. In a sense then, Duisenberg had become 'legitimate' through his stint as professor, and had made the crucial contacts in the advisory board.

A journalist friend, Harry van Seumeren, of the *De Volkskrant*, agreed it was personal connections that catapulted Duisenberg upwards, but that this was normal in the Netherlands 'It's a very small country of 15 million people. The Social Democratic Party had 100,000 members. Of them, there was only a small proportion of educated professionals, economists, professors and lawyers. OK, so he wrote an article sometimes. But you know how it goes. You know someone. That someone knows another person . . .'

When Duisenberg became finance minister in 1973, he was part of an exceptionally young cabinet. Many ministers, including Duisenberg, were in their thirties, and this heralded a new era of openness in government. In The Hague, ministers visited a press club weekly and talked policy over beer. 'Occasionally, on sunny days, (Duisenberg) would make a trip down to the beach and drink a beer and snack with the press at a café,' recalls journalist van Seumeren.

But Duisenberg's dependence on those who appointed him plagued him in his new job as finance minister. The prime minister still called most of the shots on budget matters, and boosted government spending considerably that same year. 'That's when the real spending started,' says André Szász, a Dutch central bank board member of the time. Holland's major business newspaper, the *NRC Handelsblad*, called Den Uyl's government 'the most radically left government' in the history of the country.

The Keynesian

Even before he'd chalked up a personal record, the media had picked Duisenberg out to be a future leader. In 1974, after he'd become finance minister, *Time* magazine listed Duisenberg as one of 150 people under the age of 45 most likely to be leaders of tomorrow. At 31, he was the only Dutchman on the list. He had gained respect from those around him for the speed in which he tackled his work. Bert Groothof, Duisenberg's head of communications for eleven years at the Dutch central bank, noted his ability to grasp complex issues quickly and without much effort.

But the term of his watch at the finance ministry brought him no special kudos. His supporters say Duisenberg was personally against increased spending, even though he was officially responsible for forming the budget. They say he did what he could do to moderate this policy, but since he didn't have a political base of his own, he was forced to compromise. Indeed, as a professor, he had criticized the government's efforts at containing inflation for not being tough enough. Then, he had written an alternative election platform for his party. In it, he criticized the party's platform for getting too detailed, and therefore not giving itself enough room for manoeuvre. Second, he argued that its promises were not affordable. This would-be 'manifesto' was rejected by party authorities, and Duisenberg was forced to publish it independently in a newspaper. And, at a time of increased efforts by the Dutch left to put economic pressure on South Africa over apartheid, Duisenberg was the only minister supporting export credit guarantees for nuclear industry companies dealing with that country. He also refused to join his party's boycott of the Dutch AMRO-bank for doing business there.[iii]

However, Duisenberg's track record and statements once in office as minister show another side. They reveal that, far from being bullied into accepting these policies, Duisenberg embraced them, and though he made few public statements, what words he did speak were in defence of Keynesian economic theory. John Maynard Keynes was a British economist who had won widespread acclaim following his revolutionary General Theory of Employment, Interest and Money, published in 1936. Keynes formulated the concept of 'demand-led' economic growth, and believed that the government should manipulate its budget in order to manage growth in the economy and encourage demand. There were times when normal market forces didn't work correctly, and the government needed to step up public spending to help stimulate the economy. Increasing workers' disposable income, even at the cost of government borrowing, was necessary. Boosting 'demand' would spur companies to step up their 'supply' of goods, because they would be assured of more profits.

Franklin D. Roosevelt, looking for a way to put the US economy back on track after the 1930s depression, took Keynes' thinking as his ideological underpinning. The government injected billions of dollars into the economy, and it worked. Plunging prices and steep unemployment were gradually reversed, and the policy was acclaimed as an overwhelming success.

However, Duisenberg took longer to wake up to the dangers of deficit spending than he now likes to admit. Even as an independent economics professor, he had not acknowledged a connection between money supply and inflation, a relationship that was to become an essential part of German orthodoxy in creating the European Central Bank. Rather, as he argued in his last academic piece as a professor, worker wage increases and the rise of import prices to the small Dutch economy were the root of inflation. He makes no reference to increased money supply.[iv]

In 1973, Duisenberg's first year as minister, a severe oil crisis disrupted the international economy. The middle-eastern oil cartel OPEC increased oil prices and most European countries saw a major jump in inflation. In response, these countries sought to slow public spending in order to avoid inflating the economy even more. At the time, the Netherlands was relatively well off. It had its own energy supply, exporting more natural gas than it imported oil. With other countries cutting back spending, the IMF and the OECD encouraged the Netherlands to expand its economy aggressively in order to compensate. Dirk Wolfson, Duisenberg's acquaintance from the IMF who had since returned to the ministry to work for Duisenberg, recalls:

We were a sheikhdom. In 1973, the IMF and the OECD were telling us, begging us, to increase our budget. We had a very strong balance of payments at the time. The Germans also had a strong balance of payments, because they are Germans

. . . We were urged by the international community to pick up the slack that everyone else was creating. That year also coincided with the first left-wing government budget in the Netherlands for a very long time. There you had the recipe for a very expansive budget policy.

During his second year as minister, Duisenberg was still leading the Keynesian charge, pushing harder for spending programmes that some of his underlings thought so unfeasible and costly that they overruled him before the ideas got to the cabinet. Looking for a way to boost the economy, for example, Duisenberg decided to pump up the economy by giving money to workers. His reasoning was that lower income groups spend most of any additional money they get, rather than save it. Helping workers to spark economic activity would also champion the social democratic cause. Duisenberg even proposed to send a hundred-guilder cheque to every citizen. But Dik Wolfson, one of his chief aides, rejected the plan as too costly. Wolfson recalls:

He called me in early November on a Friday morning from the cabinet room at the beginning of the weekly cabinet meeting. He was looking for the quickest way to pump money into the economy. He said 'I have this crazy idea, but before I bring it into parliament, I need to know if we can deliver. Suppose I wanted to give one hundred guilders to each citizen to boost their purchasing power? Please find out over the course of the day if this will work, but call me before the end of the cabinet meeting'. I had to think it through very quickly. I called in the director of population registration, and umpteen other people. We quickly got mired in all kinds of problems. Should prisoners get 100 guilders? The idea finally broke down on the inability to reach people without fixed addresses, gypsies for example. I called him back. Duisenberg was still in the cabinet room, which looks out on to the parliamentary square of the prime minister's office. I said 'Look out of the window. How many gypsy trailers do you figure can fit into the parliamentary square?' I was trying to illustrate for him the sort of demonstrations that would take place, even if you can't reach one or two per cent of the population. He quickly acknowledged the problem. The idea was killed by lunchtime. It was one of Duisenberg's quirky brainwaves.

At the time, Duisenberg could argue that he was simply pursuing the same policies as other European finance ministers. After halcyon economic climates in the 1950s and 1960s, most western European countries were experiencing a gradual slow-down in economic growth and a rise in unemployment. In Germany, growth in GDP had averaged 7.8 per cent and 5.2 per cent annually in the 1950s and 1960s respectively. Over the 1970s, average annual growth was down to 3.1 per cent. France and Italy saw similar slowdowns. They were now trying to jump-start their economies with extra spending, even though it was more than governments could afford in relation to the tax income they received. They continued to borrow. In the short term, such borrowing was considered legitimate. Interest would have to be paid, but once the economy was up and running again, it would be affordable. The problem was that by the end of the 1970s, governments were still borrowing, and there was no end in sight.

Deficit spending had allowed Dutch and other European citizens to lead a lifestyle that was beyond their means, but to which they'd become accustomed. They wanted a Mercedes Benz when they could only afford a Volkswagen. Some governments, including the Dutch, had lost the ability to say no. But if Duisenberg was following a European-wide trend, he was pursuing it even more aggressively than the others. During his tenure as finance minister, Duisenberg was to be continually heckled by one critic in particular, Eduard Bomhoff, an economics professor who in many ways resembled the American economist Milton Friedman. He regularly claimed that such spending was disastrous. 'There was a lot of confusion all around. But the Netherlands went more strongly in the Keynesian direction than, for instance, Germany or Switzerland,' says Bomhoff. The Netherlands became known as 'the sick man of Europe,' a particularly worrying stigma given that Europe as a whole was already in poor health.

At first, Duisenberg held fast to his policies. Not only were other governments doing the same thing, he was backed by prevailing theory at the time. But Europe in the 1970s was different from the US in the 1930s. Unlike the US depression, which stemmed from international turmoil and falling prices, the 1970s developments stemmed from domestic inefficiencies and bloated governments. In the 1930s, European governments were small. In the 1970s, by contrast the public sector made up around 50 per cent of GDP. Expanding the public sector wasn't the answer.

In 1975, two journalists from the Dutch *Elseviers* magazine hounded Duisenberg about his record deficit at the time, underscoring how it threatened to increase inflation. Duisenberg rejected that logic. The deficit was a minor problem, he said dismissively. A government infusion of 7 billion guilders in increased spending and tax breaks would stimulate the economy, which would in turn bring in more tax receipts, and close the deficit, he said. The journalists pressed on, asking whether the government's share of GDP hadn't overstepped its limits. Duisenberg responded: 'I'm not one of those people who say the government's weight in the economy has reached its limit. I don't know if there is a limit. If there is, I find all this talking about limits so static – as if there's an end goal where the economy can't go any further,' he said. 'I don't see it that way.'[v]

Duisenberg saw no reason for painful government saving. Though he recognised that people might abuse the country's generous social welfare system, he showed little urgency in responding to reports that people were increasingly taking advantage of generous unemployment benefits even though they could find work, and staying home while receiving sick-leave payments even though they were healthy. When challenged on this by a journalist, he all but wiped his hands of the problem: 'There's always a small percentage of people who misuse the system,' he said. 'But it is impossible to measure.'[vi] Only after Duisenberg's departure, in the 1980s, was the Dutch social welfare system substantially slashed, and reformed to reduce abuse.

In 1977, Duisenberg was still an apologist for big spending. After national elections that year, the parties within the Den Uyl coalition divided over how to form a new cabinet. During this time, Duisenberg was criticised by Dutch employers for inflating the deficit even further. Duisenberg again insisted that it wasn't too large, and that it had been increased for a legitimate purpose: to reduce unemployment. He also defended a government law that gave subsidies to companies suffering losses as a result of the recession. 'To compensate companies for such losses, they are allowed to take a loan . . . That is being paid for by a growth in the deficit,' he said matter-of-factly. Again, he defended the right to increase the deficit in order to create jobs.[vii]

In a 1977 interview with the newspaper *Het Parool,* he defended the need for government spending of a additional 4 billion guilders, representing just over 1 per cent of GDP. Duisenberg was loath to concede that such a significant amount would lead to a cheapening of money's value, or inflation. Instead, the extra money would make it cheaper for companies to produce and invest, he said. The income from production of goods would more than compensate for any inflation. When a conservative economist, Pieter Korteweg of Rotterdam University, criticized him for this policy, Duisenberg lashed back, calling Korteweg a 'monetarist.'[3] Duisenberg criticized the monetarist logic, saying: 'I admit there is a link

---

3 Monetarism stems from the work of Milton Friedman, a professor at the University of Chicago. In 1963, together with Anna J. Schwartz, Friedman published his *magnum opus, A Monetary History of the United States, 1867-1960,* which argued that inflation had dire consequences for the economy. He argued that inflation was a monetary phenomenon, a sign that there was too much money in the economy. Banks, having too much money on their books, would lend the money on at cheaper rates than usual. Companies would step up economic activity, encouraged by lower rates of financing debt. They would bid up wages as they sought to hire workers from an ever scarcer labour pool. Workers would then demand more for their labour, thereby increasing their spending power. Finally, retailers would hike prices to exploit increased demand. Thus inflation would reverberate throughout the economy. Friedman argued that just as inflation was the result of a central bank's loose grip on money supply,

between budget deficits and inflation. Yet if economic growth is temporarily disappointing, we must stimulate the economy to bring it back to its earlier trend-line.'[viii]

Finally, Duisenberg also supported a law forcing companies to hand over 'above normal' profits to their workers by transferring to the workers portions of the company's shares. Companies criticized the policy, saying it did away with the profit incentive – essential for any free-market based economy. They said it also scared away foreign investors at a time when the Netherlands badly needed it because of growing unemployment. He said the companies' complaints were 'totally exaggerated.'[ix]

Duisenberg's conversion: 'Necessity is the mother of invention.'

The admission of a connection between deficits and inflation was the first step in a long transformation of Duisenberg from a convinced Keynesian to an economic conservative; from an activist to a minimalist. The catalyst was a combination of developments in 1975. By the autumn of that same year, Dutch policy had begun an about-face.

The catalyst came from Wolfson, the director of economic policy, and Nout Wellink, a deputy at the ministry. Wolfson had watched the state's finances deteriorate over the course of 1975, exacerbated by a drying up of northern Holland's reserves of natural gas. In late August, the OECD sent the Dutch an early draft of its annual Outlook report, which warned that Dutch unemployment would worsen and that

---

governments that run deficits by expanded state spending only added to the problem by injecting more money into the system. By running up their deficits in the 1970s, the Netherlands and other industrialized countries had effectively injected more money into the system than they had taken out in the form of taxes. The solution, said Friedman, was that central banks needed to rein in the money supply, by issuing less money, to tame inflation to a manageable rate. Less money made borrowing more expensive, thereby cooling inflation. Economic growth could therefore be moderated and remain sustainable. Friedman suggested a fixed rate of expansion for money supply of the order of about 3 per cent per year to break the inflation spiral and put the economy on a more stable footing.

economic growth would be only 3 per cent in 1976. Less than three weeks before, Duisenberg had drafted a budget that estimated 3.75 per cent growth. 'We suddenly had a big hole,' said Wolfson. Until then, the state had been increasing outlays even faster than the economy was growing, at a real increase of about 4.5 per cent per year compared to real GDP growth of 3.75 per cent. This couldn't last.[x] The public sector already consumed 50 per cent of output in the form of taxes. 'It was crazy. The public sector was taking over. It was going to take 52 per cent the next year, then 54 per cent the following year, and then keep going like that every year,' said Wellink. 'That's when we called Duisenberg.'

Duisenberg was sailing off the coast of Friesland taking a vacation like the rest of the cabinet. Wellink rang Duisenberg's beeper; soon Duisenberg called back. 'This is my holiday,' said Duisenberg gruffly. 'I don't want to come back to The Hague.'

'Minister,' Wellink responded, 'you have to present the new budget in a few weeks, and things are quickly turning into a disaster. We really think you should come back.'

'No, no, no. I'll stay here. You'd better come to Friesland. We'll do it here.'

Johannes Huijsman, secretary general of the ministry, and Wellink, travelled by helicopter to Duisenberg on his boat. There was a raging storm, and Wellink couldn't help drawing parallels. 'It was a disastrous time from both points of view.' After a good meal on the boat, 'we began our effort to convince him,' Wellink said.

They told him that a turnaround was crucial. Only a radical decision to limit spending would suffice. Duisenberg, having watched as his policies failed miserably over the past couple of years, had no alternative. Still on the boat, the trio drew up the so-called '1 per cent policy memorandum' which they planned to introduce to the cabinet for the following year's budget. The proposal would cap spending growth to 1 per cent of gross domestic product per year for the rest of the government's term. It was based on crude calculations on the back of an envelope. 'We couldn't do more than that in a few days,' said one participant.

Duisenberg would stay on his boat to finish his holiday while

Wellink and Huijsman went back and worked on the details, but they begged him to come back soon. Two days later, on a Friday, Duisenberg came back and told Wellink and Wolfson to rewrite his budget speech. Wolfson recalls:

> We rewrote it over the weekend. We worked our tails off, going through the whole damned thing, changing every turn of phrase where it was necessary to indicate that the government would shortly announce new numbers to make the budget fit into the new economic estimates. The cabinet would then have to decide on the final numbers. While we were doing the dirty work, Duisenberg was busy briefing the prime minister and calling back the other cabinet ministers so that they could crunch out a new budget.

Duisenberg recalls 'endless discussions' with his advisors over the following days about just how to rein in spending. When the budget was finished, Wellink submitted it to the cabinet. Meeting with his cabinet, Duisenberg insisted postponement of the plan wasn't possible. 'That summer [Duisenberg], was faced with a difficult challenge: How to become a Paul after being a Saul,' said Thijs Wöltgens, the financial spokesman of the Social Democratic Party, at the time.[xi] '[Duisenberg] became a conservative minister in the broadest sense of the word,' said Wellink, his successor at the bank, 'not only concerning monetary policy, but budgetary and economic policy in general. We realized that we had been on the wrong track for several years, and that we couldn't solve the problems by stimulating the economy.'[xii]

Duisenberg, now apparently a convert with conviction, battled for over a week to convince his cabinet of the policy. The left wing of the party reproached him for his 'rightist' policies. Seeing no way to convince his party, he took his cause to the nation's media, leaking his proposals strategically to get positive coverage. He made overtures to the country's business groups, unusual at the time for the social democrats, who had an antagonistic relationship with business. He pitched the policy as 'a bridge to new prosperity.' Business groups were far from impressed, but thought it was better than nothing. Finally, he met secretly with individual ministers of the cabinet, hoping to convince them that such a cap was in their interests. He tried to get them to see that for every guilder of economic growth, 82 cents went to fund the state's expensive spending projects. It was tough going. Once, he returned from a local meeting with constituents and reported: 'Nothing can be done. People keep staring at me with glazed eyes.'

But Duisenberg persevered. Finally the cabinet relented, and the policy was passed into law.

Still, the 1 per cent cap was not enough. The economy later dipped into recession. Unions, linking their wage demands more closely with state spending growth than economic growth, pushed the cost of labour to levels that became too exorbitant for companies to bear. The unemployment rate also shot up. Nevertheless, Duisenberg's cap was eventually hailed as the crucial juncture in the government's move to restore order to state finances.

By today's standards, the move was unimpressive, given the emphasis countries such as Germany and the Netherlands have put on erasing budget deficits altogether as a prerequisite to price stability and the success of Europe's single money project. Duisenberg's persistent critic; professor Eduard Bomhoff, now of the Forum for Economic Research at Nijenrode University, says: 'People sometimes forget that the rule called for spending to go up by one percentage point every year, not down. It was a crazy rule. It was just a way to tone down the extreme Keynesianism of his prime minister a little but still remain in the big-spending cabinet. It is not one of the monumental moments in the history of public finance.'

Looking back at his tenure at the finance ministry twenty years later, Duisenberg doesn't regret his Keynesian past. While Wellink admits that the government made mistakes, Duisenberg insists he changed his views as economic conditions demanded:

I don't like these labels – 'Keynesian' and 'monetarist' – very much. When I became minister of finance, the economy had just been jolted by the first oil shock of 1973. The Netherlands was hit badly by the oil boycott. We were suffering from a failure in total 'demand'. As minister, I helped compensate for that by increasing demand in a Keynesian way. We were rather successful in absorbing the oil shock, but then after a year and a half, it increasingly dawned on me and the others that this type of policy, if continued, would choke off investment and incentives for entrepreneurship, and burden the budget with interest payments to pay for the ever increasing finances. So I changed my mind. It was not a gradual process. It began in spring, 1975. By the fall, we announced a new direction in our policy, that is, we contained spending. The difficult part was trying to convince the country. I made a big mistake in that I thought it would take me six months. Instead, it took the country 15 years.

Duisenberg says he learned some lessons about the limits of government. He'd come to power believing in what the Dutch called *maakbare semenlering*, referring to the belief in the ability of government to manipulate society and the way it functions or performs. After his experience in power, Duisenberg's conception of the role of government changed. He came to believe that the government's main contribution was to create the 'climactic conditions of stability, continuity and confidence.'[xiii] With these basic conditions assured, the society and economy would thrive on their own – without government stimulation.

Wellink says: 'We were all Keynesians in those days. Duisenberg was one of the first in this country to realize that the Keynesian days were over. He had a real fight with the prime minister and the other ministers. They didn't like his conservative attitude on issues such as taxation, budget deficits, and the role of the economy.'

Duisenberg breaks with the social democrats

Slowly, Duisenberg changed his views further. He had 'outed' himself, and had gone too far to turn back. He drafted another budget-limiting programme for the 1977 elections. His party colleagues buckled and rejected it as too rightist. Relations with his prime minister, never ideal, deteriorated further, and Duisenberg was forced to seek refuge with the only minister at the time with any sympathy, Ruud Lubbers, the minister of economics. Lubbers was worried about the economy, and had requested a meeting with Duisenberg to discuss his concerns. 'Calm down,' Duisenberg told Lubbers. 'Let's go to Scheveningen [a seaside town close to The Hague], and have a beer at one of those terrace cafes.' After a few beers, Duisenberg broached the subject: 'So about that economy you were talking about?' It was Duisenberg's way of doing business; relaxed and almost nonchalant.[xiv]

He laid out a plan to Lubbers, and though he gained support from the minister, the alliance wasn't enough to calm the nerves of his party. Frustrated, Duisenberg announced he wouldn't seek office in the next government. After the 1977 elections, he retained his seat as a member of parliament, but he was discontent without the power to which he'd become accustomed. He was in the prime of his career and the *Time* magazine article had indicated he was destined for great things. For a time, Duisenberg had been heir apparent to the position of prime minister, but now he'd been pushed away from the party's mainstream, and his chances of making a comeback were slim. He hungered to move up, not down.

The allure of power

During his tenure as minister, he made great efforts to be elected chairman of the Interim Committee of the International Monetary Fund, one of the most powerful positions in international finance. The Interim Committee is an exclusive group of finance ministers belonging to the shareholder nations of the IMF, and their decisions affect the distribution of hundreds of billions of dollars of capital. It is the headquarters of global finance. The member nations lend their currencies to the IMF so that these funds can help countries in balance-of-payments difficulties. With the power to offer loans to indebted countries in exchange for promises from these countries to abide by stringent restructuring plans, the IMF can shape the fate of much of the developing world. The IMF spurs developing countries to open their markets and encourage economic modernization, thereby winning a lucrative opportunity for the industrialized countries to boost their exports and expand their own economic growth. The Netherlands, a 'nation of traders and priests', as the Dutch saying goes, depended on trade more than any other advanced industrialized country except for Belgium.[xv, 4] A lot was at stake, and leading this organization would bestow unprecedented status on a Dutch leader.

Having already shot to the peak of Dutch politics, Duisenberg realized he would have to move to the international arena if he wanted to move even higher. He was attracted to the power inherent in such a council, and the IMF interim committee. When Seumeren once asked him why he wanted the IMF job so badly, Duisenberg responded: 'It wields power. I like to have power.'

'But you have the finance ministry,' Seumeren responded. 'You can already order secretaries around.'

'Yes, I have power. But the IMF chairman has more,' Duisenberg told him.

Duisenberg failed to get the position. The opportunity might have come around again, but now he was no longer finance minister. There was one last alternative, however. The IMF meetings were not only attended by finance ministers; they were also attended by central bankers. If he became president of the Dutch central bank, this would be a sure way to reach the circles he'd admired. He had worked at the central bank for a year, but otherwise didn't have much banking experience. Yet as a former social democrat finance minister, he was the perfect candidate for an appointment to the central banking position by a social democratic government.

His chance came quickly enough. As finance minister, he had already made clear that he didn't want to remain a mere

---

[4] Belgium here includes Luxembourg, since the two are combined on OECD trade statistics. Belgium/Luxembourg surpassed the Netherlands in the 1970s. In the 1980s, Ireland would also surpass the Netherlands in dependence on trade.

parliamentarian after a change of government. Gerard Mertens, chairman of Rabobank Nederland B.V., the largest Dutch bank, approached him about a job as vice-chairman. Duisenberg accepted, and resigned his parliamentary post. The move was made specifically to gain the banking experience necessary to eventually earn the top position at the Dutch central bank.

In his resignation letter to former prime minister Joop den Uyl, he wrote that he had accepted a position at the Rabobank. Den Uyl wrote back: 'Dear Wim, I can't withhold my conviction that the transition from minister of finance to a private sector financial institution, however respectable, requires more distance than I observe in your behaviour.' He and others in the party saw Duisenberg's departure as a betrayal of the political vocation. Duisenberg had been elected by the people to represent them, and now he was forsaking his democratic responsibility. But den Uyl, in particular, saw the move as a professional conflict of interest, saying that, 'Someone who has just been elected to the chamber doesn't leave politics. And, as an ex-minister of finance, you certainly don't go to a bank.' The move was also seen as defection by Duisenberg to the other side of the political spectrum. Robobank, which had large agricultural interests, was seen as especially conservative. Later, den Uyl complained: 'I can hardly imagine that this man is still a party member of the social democratic party.'[xvi]

Those close to him said he was chafed by the criticism. 'Wim has found that embarrassing ever since,' says the socialist party's financial spokesman, Wöltgens, who sympathized with his colleague. 'Wim Duisenberg wants to lead. I think that, deep down in his heart, he found the parliamentary chamber to be a place for windbags.'

If Duisenberg had been bruised, he didn't let it show. 'Money is my profession,' he told an interviewer at the time. In fact, it wasn't money that he lusted after; it was status and power. His life in politics may have been brief, but his stint in the private sector was more so.

After two years, he'd announced he was leaving to join the central bank directorate, which had nominated him to be one of its members.

Duisenberg sees his vision bear fruit

In retrospect, Duisenberg's political career can be seen in a positive light. His ideas sparked an internal debate that was to modernize the party. Duisenberg had argued, among a small group of intimates in the 1970s, that the social democrats should form a coalition with the more free-market liberal party, a taboo at the time. It took the social democrats ten years to discuss openly the coalition option as a real possibility. In 1994, such a coalition became reality.

The anti-Keynesian debate he unleashed had international repercussions. The Dutch government's trimming back of spending in the 1980s, and a landmark agreement to keep wage rises at moderate levels, resulted in the country becoming the miracle of Europe by the mid-1990s, with unemployment halved and a robustly expanding economy. Germany's social democratic party chancellor Gerhard Schröder, France's socialist Lionel Jospin, and the UK's 'New Labour' prime minister Tony Blair, were all politicians who at the end of the 1990s were still trying to bring their parties to the position at which the Dutch social democrats had arrived a decade earlier.

On the central banking front, Duisenberg broke the mould by becoming the first social democrat to aspire to a central banking position. In an odd confession for the time, he argued that the institution was more powerful than the disparate individuals within it, not the other way around. The ideology of the individual no longer mattered, at least when it came to central banking, he said: 'People should get used to the idea that a social democrat is running the central bank, and that the function itself determines his behaviour.'

Similarities to the Bundesbank

Duisenberg did not have a smooth start at the central bank. Shortly after his arrival, Dutch mortgage banks suffered serious financial problems resulting from risky investments turned sour. The central bank was also the supervisor of the financial sector. Two banks were saved from brink of failure with rescue packages. Duisenberg and his team allowed a third bank, the Tilburgsche Hypotheekbank, to fail. At the time, many institutional investors blamed the failure on 'arrogant handling by the central bank.'[xvii] Critics blamed Duisenberg for being too harsh on the struggling banks, since mortgage banks had only come under the central bank's supervision the year before and were in the midst of a transitional period to meet tougher capital requirements.

Seventeen years later, Duisenberg calls the episode difficult, but one he doesn't regret. 'We had to make a decision whether or not to save the mortgage bank. We decided in the end not to save it, in order to let the market set the discipline.' But Duisenberg made another decision he was criticized for: appointing his best friend, real estate agent Cor van Zadelhoff, to a group of four people in charge of the bank's liquidation – a job usually reserved for lawyers. For a time, Zadelhoff and Duisenberg were inseparable on the international circuit, attending conferences together. At one point, Duisenberg even stayed in Zadelhoff's London apartment. Later, as part of an effort to save another ailing mortgage bank, Friesch Gro-ningsche, Zadelhoff arranged for the sale of a significant amount of the bank's real estate holdings at bargain prices to a Dutch pension fund, Algemeen Burgerlijk Pensioenfonds (ABP). It later emerged that Zadelhoff had good personal contacts with ABP.[xviii]

Asked about the Zadelhoff affair 17 years later, Duisenberg says that his selection of Zadelhoff came as a result of a series of coincidences. He says that during a late-night round of discussions after the central bank decision to let the bank go bankrupt, he called the chairman of the private banking federation to get a recommendation of who could be appointed to the group of liquidators, and the chairman had suggested Zadelhoff. Another coincidence the following morning led to Duisenberg's appointing Zadelhoff. Duisenberg recounts:

I was on my way to the bank, sometime before 8 a.m. I got a phone call in my car from [Zadelhoff] who said, 'I've just heard on the radio that the Tilburgsche Hypotheekbank is going into bankruptcy.' He happened to be my best friend, which is why I was so reluctant [to call on him]. He said: 'If I can do something to help, don't hesitate to call on me.' He was also in his car, and I asked: 'Which direction are you driving in?' He said: 'Away from Amsterdam.' I said: 'Turn around, make a U-turn and come to the central bank.' He was there in twenty minutes.

Within a year of joining the Dutch central bank in 1981, Duisenberg's transformation from Keynesian to monetarist was complete. He was promoted to bank president and soon began to criticize government spending policies publicly. It had become too difficult to fire workers, he complained. Though he held on to his party membership, he admitted past government practices were misguided: 'We've just stimulated the economy into a recession, so it's silly to try to stimulate our way out again,' he said in 1985.[xix]

Milton Friedman had been preaching the monetarist doctrine for decades, and it had appeared outmoded during the heyday of Keynes in the 1950s and 1960s. By the mid-1970s, he'd gained a substantial following, though his views still hadn't significantly influenced the thinking of the US Federal Reserve. Only in 1979 did a new Federal Reserve Chairman Paul Volcker start to implement them.

The first bank to adopt Friedman's views was the German Bundesbank. But the power yielded by the Bundesbank and the German mark prohibited the Netherlands and the other European countries from implementing a monetarist strategy of their own, even though the Dutch central bank had toyed with money supply strategies since the 1950s. The small size of the many European economies made them susceptible to shocks caused by currency fluctuations, especially against the mark. If the mark went up in value against the local currency, the cost of German imports increased, and these economies suffered inflation. The central banks were thus forced to abandon an independent monetary policy, and guide interest rates so as to keep their currencies tied to the mark.

The epitome of stability

By the time Duisenberg had become governor of the central bank and was preaching monetarism, the Dutch government had also realized that inflation needed to be combated. It therefore supported the bank's policy of tying the Dutch guilder to the mark.

Duisenberg was governor for 15 years. He did not clash often with government ministers in The Hague. His only real stand-off with the government came in his second year as governor, in 1983, when the government decided, against the central bank's advice, not to continue keeping the guilder pegged to the mark. A series of other currencies, including the Italian lira and the French franc, were being devalued against the mark in order to create some relief for their economies. Devaluation of their currencies made their goods cheaper in foreign markets, which boosted exports and therefore economic growth.[5] Despite the central bank's resistance, the government decided on a 2 per cent devaluation against the mark. This was not as large as that implemented by other European countries, but it was never-theless a blow to the credibility of the guilder.

Financial circles grumbled that Duisenberg hadn't resisted strongly enough. 'Duisenberg's love of golf doesn't work to his advantage,' said one commentary in the Dutch newspaper *Het Financieele Dagblad*.[xx] 'Word went out quickly that he is seen

---

[5] In the short term, this came at the expense of the German economy. In the long term, a devaluation harmed a country because the lower value of the country's currency meant that foreign goods became more expensive to import. This increased inflation. It also lowered the purchasing power of consumers. The competition between European states quickly led them to the realization that instability could be avoided by merging their currencies. This would also give countries outside Germany more control over their own destinies. To prepare a move to this stage, they had in the 1970s created a European Monetary System, a narrow band of 5 per cent within which the currency values would fluctuate against each other before making the final step towards unity (see Chapter 3). Ironically, the Netherlands and other countries had become even more dependent on the mark within this system than before they joined. Germany's economic clout and the credibility of its stability-oriented policies gave the mark special standing as the anchor currency in Europe, a reference value to which the other currencies were tied.

more often on the golfing green than at relevant financial symposia.'[6]

'The decision was extremely awkward for us, in particular for Duisenberg,' recounts former colleague André Szász. 'Duisenberg, as governor, was mentioned in the press as the one who had been overruled, even though the whole board had resisted the move. Duisenberg was very critical of the government.' He may have been critical, but he wasn't outspoken in public. He didn't air his disappointments in the press, but preferred to manœuvre behind the scenes. 'You won't find many public utterances [about the discussion],' Szász remarks. Duisenberg insists that he 'fought like a lion' within the cabinet against the devaluation, and threatened that his advice to the government, which would be made public in the form of published comments, 'would be negative, and it was'.[xxi] In reality, however, the central bank made no negative comments about the realignment, and its published letter on the matter was signed by a subordinate.[7]

Duisenberg revealed his keen political sense for central banking during the aftermath of the devaluation decision. The devaluation was made by heads of state as part of a EU-wide realignment decision during a summit in Brussels, and the haggling had continued all weekend. When the decision was finally reached late on Sunday, the central bankers braced themselves for the reaction when the markets opened on Monday morning. The response was fierce. The markets, faced with a breach of the prior Dutch commitment to keep the guilder tied to the mark, lost confidence in the guilder. Traders began selling guilders for marks in ever greater quantities. The

---

[6] To be sure, though he was an avid golfer during the 1980s, Duisenberg's colleagues say that he has rarely played since being appointed to the EMI in 1997. Some say this is because of his heavy workload. But his private doctor has expressed great concern for Duisenberg's health. Duisenberg smokes 'up to 40 cigarettes a day', and has recently been suffering from coughing fits.

[7] Letter from the Governing Board of De Nederlansche Bank N.V. to the Minister of Finance, Amsterdam, March 21, 1983. Signed by 'Director-acting Secretary'.

guilder would have plunged had it not been for the central bank's massive acquisitions of guilders in order to save it.

Szász argued immediately for an interest rate hike to stop the fall,[8] but says he was overruled by Duisenberg at the next board meeting later that week. 'I agree with you in substance, but if we do it now, everyone will accuse us of doing it merely to spite the government,' he told Szász. 'We should wait a week.'

'This will only make things worse,' insisted Szász. 'The markets will continue to place pressure on the guilder, and waiting a week will only mean that we will have to take an even more aggressive stance to stem the guilder's fall.'

Duisenberg was firm: 'Yes, but at least people will realize then why we are doing it.'

The bank left rates unchanged the first week, and Duisenberg calmly waited for the bank to publish its monthly foreign exchange figures. They revealed the massive depletion of reserves over the proceeding two weeks, the result of the central bank's attempt to prop up the guilder. 'It had the desired effect,' recalls Szász. 'The figures showed that we weren't just kids in a schoolyard brawl.' The media swung behind the central bank. 'The event showed Duisenberg has a feel for politics: he'd predicted the media's reaction,' said Szász.

It was the last time that Duisenberg allowed a devaluation. From 1983 on, he pegged the guilder tightly to the mark, and the Netherlands became the only country in Europe not to make another devaluation against the German anchor currency. Still, it took markets eight years to regain confidence in the Dutch determination to keep inflation low. Banks, fearful the inflation would eat away at the value of their loans, demanded higher interest rates in Holland than they did in Germany. 'It very much underscores my strong belief that you can lose confidence

---

[8] The logic of an interest rate hike is as follows: by lifting interest rates, assets denominated in guilders automatically become more valuable because they bear higher rates of return. This encourages investors to buy guilders in order to purchase these assets, thereby driving up the value of the guilder. A rise in Dutch interest rates also makes borrowing more expensive for Dutch companies, which means a slowdown in economic activity and thus subdues inflation. Investors are therefore also attracted to the guilder to avoid inflation eroding their assets.

in one day, but it takes years to build it back,' says Duisenberg of the experience.

Others have been impressed by Duisenberg's political instinct. Eduard Bomhoff, the economist, recalls visiting Duisenberg at the European Monetary Institute during the summer of 1997. Beforehand, Bomhoff had met a series of officials of lower rank, who all said it was too early to predict whether Italy would qualify for inclusion in the project. But Bomhoff found Duisenberg already knew the minds of the top central bankers. Since March 1997, after the fateful G-10 meeting in Basle, the bankers had resolved that a delay was no longer an option, and they had more or less accepted that Italy would be there at the start. 'Of course Italy will join,' he told Bomhoff. Bomhoff left that afternoon, surprised by Duisenberg's revelation. After Italy was officially accepted almost a year later, Bomhoff confided: 'I am impressed by his political antennae. The man had a much stronger political sense than any of the civil servants there.'

But Bomhoff's experience wasn't unique. Duisenberg talked more frankly away from of the public glare. He could not have said Italy would join in front of the media cameras; it would have been far too controversial. Officially, the decision would be made in May 1998, after a 'reasoned' review of the country's economic data. In reality, the political leaders and bankers agreed that it would not be a good idea to wait until that date to make the decision, and came to a consensus much earlier.[xxii]

Duisenberg's suggestion to delay EMU, made behind closed doors at the BIS in 1997, while at the same time denying it in public, is one instance of what seems to be a penchant for secrecy, which at times borders on duplicity. This raises questions about how much the financial markets will be able to rely on Duisenberg's public statements. The deal of May 1998 in Brussels, in which he won the nomination to the presidency of the ECB by making a gentlemen's agreement with Jacques Chirac to step down early, but which in public he denied he ever made, is another example. Upon initial consideration, the 1982 Zadelhoff affair might be forgiven as a mistake of a young central banker. But Duisenberg had already been finance minister for several years and should have been experienced enough to realize that appointing his best friend, a real estate agent, to manage the liquidation proceedings of hundreds of millions of guilders of real estate holdings, was politically questionable. At that time, Duisenberg refused to submit the central bank to parliamentary hearings about the supervision process, despite the crisis in the real estate sector, despite the call from a number of parliamentarians for just such a debate, and despite the fact that taxpayers' money was apparently being used to help some of these banks in crisis.

Later, the private contact between Duisenberg and Zadelhoff occured again in 1994, when the EMI was looking for a building to occupy. It was Zadelhoff who called the EMI's president, Alexandre Lamfalussy, to offer him help in finding a place for the bank. Zadelhoff was convinced that the EMI should not occupy the site on the edge of the downtown area of Frankfurt, but should look instead for a place in the banking district. Zadelhoff became personally engaged in guiding the project because it was 'an important and sensitive deal', he says. 'Of course, Duisenberg and I exchanged ideas about it,' says Zadelhoff. Mr. Lamfalussy was aware of Zadelhoff's connection with Duisenberg, but says he didn't know they were close friends.

Some Dutch central banking officials complained that Duisenberg sought to have the central bank pay for the costs of the wedding reception for his second marriage. Duisenberg says that's not true. In any event, he ended up paying for the reception himself. Some of these issues were made public, but caused little controversy in the small, close-knit establishment of the Netherlands (where the Queen officially appoints the central bank president).[9]

While most central banks publish their minutes, albeit some

---

[9] In 1998, the Dutch central bank, under Duisenberg's successor, Nout Wellink, decided to give 110 million guilders to the National Foundation of Art, which used the money to buy a painting, worth 80 million guilders, for display at the municipal museum in the Hague. It is another example of a decision taken without public input, this time with funds that are arguably public.

after several decades, the Dutch central bank's minutes are held secret forever.

As head of the ECB, Duisenberg has declared that transparency is one of the bank's most important goals. But, unlike the US Federal Reserve or the Bank of England's Monetary Policy Committee, the ECB refuses to release voting records and views of the decision-making members. Rather, the minutes are to be kept secret for 30 years, similar to the earlier practice of the Bundesbank and other continental European central banks. He and other board members based this decision on a fear that ECB council members won't be able to speak their minds freely if they know the media could report their every word. For example, board members would be reluctant to take on devil's advocate positions crucial in formulating the best possible policy, such as the role Duisenberg took in Basle, if their actions and views were then subject to public airing.

Duisenberg knows the danger first hand, since his role as governor pushed him into a dove-like stance in bank debates.[10] Publication of his views during these occasions – when he was taking a particular position to hone his negotiating skills – would have embarrassed the bank. Szász recalls:

> The government always pushed for lower interest rates, and Duisenberg always took the brunt of this in weekly meetings with the finance minister. They placed a lot of pressure on him. When we'd discuss interest rate policy on the board, Duisenberg would argue against us, because he knew he had to defend the move in public. It doesn't mean he's a dove. He just wanted us to convince him.

The Dutch-German camp

There was another reason for Duisenberg's wish to keep minutes secret: national sensitivity. Dutch monetary policy was

---

[10] In the arcane language of central banking, a *dove* – as peaceful bird – is someone who is more willing to lower interest rates in the interest of short-term economic growth. A *hawk* – a fierce bird – is someone who prefers to keep interest rates high to guard against rising inflation.

entirely dependent on German policy, and adjusting to it was often against the immediate interests of the Dutch economy. Knowing the truth might have been too painful for the Dutch population to bear. There is no relationship more schizo-phrenic in Europe than that between the Germans and the Dutch. On the one hand, the cultures and language are similar, while Germany's economic influence is enormous. The Dutch and German ties, mainly trade, are so interwoven that the Netherlands has been dubbed the 'seventeenth German state'[xxiii] by people on both sides of the border.[11] Both economies depend on a large export surplus for their prosperity. The German border with the Netherlands runs about two-thirds of the entire length of the Dutch land border.[12] In both societies, a consensus culture prevails, which has long provided an affinity between the two nations. Finally, there is the cherished tradition of a strong currency that binds them. 'Our tradition of a strong currency goes back longer than even the Germans,' says Szász.[13]

On the other hand, much of the Dutch population is still intensely anti-German. The country felt particularly betrayed during the Second World War, having again been one of the first countries to be invaded (they were first in World War I) and one of the last to be liberated. When asked his view of the Germans, a cab driver in Utrecht said simply 'It is hate.' Public opinion polls still show that, at least at the popular level, the German-Dutch relationship is one of the more troubled in Europe. Duisenberg's successor at the Dutch central bank, Nout Wellink, says these sensitivities made it tricky to sell the bank's policy to the public:

It was very sensitive in the past. Honestly speaking, when we

---

[11] In fact, the original borders of greater Friesland, 'Frisia Magna,' included territory that is now part of Germany.
[12] The southern Dutch border is with Belgium, but along the Dutch-speaking Flanders region. Thus Germany is really the only 'foreign' neighbour.
[13] Indeed, the Dutch florin (otherwise known as guilder) is the oldest of the disappearing European currencies, created in 1325. The German mark was created in 1876.

started to link our guilder to the German mark, we were very careful in selling this product. In the beginning, during the 1970s, we did not say we were 'linking' our currency to the mark, but that we were 'orienting' the guilder to the mark. We were careful to say we were 'correcting', not 'following'. And when you follow the history of our statements, you see that the wording became stronger and stronger over the years as political sensitivities died down.[xxiv]

One ramification of this Dutch dependence on the Germans is that Dutch central bankers have less experience in forging an independent monetary policy. With the Germans effectively setting European interest rates, other European banks were confined to pegging their currencies to the German mark within a small band of fluctuation. With the major exception of Britain, which stayed out of the European Monetary System until very late, the Germans were the only ones to have engaged in the great monetary policy strategy debates over the previous two decades.

Dutch co-operation, meanwhile, has been crucial to Germany's leadership role. Szász, as the board member responsible for international relations, was the Dutch central bank's envoy to EU negotiations on the EMS and the single currency project. He recalls his discussions with his German counterparts, first Leonhard Gleske in the 1980s, then Hans Tietmeyer in the early 1990s, and how they both expressed appreciation for Dutch support:

> Gleske told me that he preferred letting me have my say in the meetings. I would push the policy, and he would sit back and agree. That was better than having to argue the policy himself. We would actively support German policies in return for German support on issues that were important for us . . . We supported the Germans when they wanted to lift interest rates. They were able to say, 'Hey, it's not true that we're the only ones wanting to push up rates. Look at the Dutch!' . . . In 1993, when the EMS was widened to a band of 15 per cent, the French tried to get us to move away

from our policy of keeping within a 2.5 per cent band with the German mark. We made clear to the Germans that it was important for us. They supported us. Sure, there were limits. If the Germans weren't happy with a policy, and you tried to push it down their throats, they wouldn't put up with it, so we would give up. The French never thought of that.^{xxv}

One of the closest Dutch-German relationships that developed was between Duisenberg and Tietmeyer, and it became the cornerstone for the most important personnel decision for the ECB when it was created in 1998.[14]

Former German Chancellor Helmut Kohl said that achieving monetary union was 'the difference between war and peace in the 21st century.' Duisenberg says the words may 'sound exaggerated,' but he admits that the fear of a recurring war was the key motive behind the abolition of national control over the coal and steel industries in northern Europe. 'Underlying the push for free trade and an integrated Europe was a fear that reveals the truthfulness of (Kohl's) words,' he says. But for Duisenberg too, the single currency project has at its foundation an effort to deal with the German problem. 'As Thomas Mann asked fifty years ago: "Do we want to live in a German Europe or a European Germany?"'

---

[14] The two men also grew close during their terms at the BIS. Duisenberg served as chairman of the BIS for the three-year term, and then again from 1994 through 1997. It is one of the most respected jobs on the central banking circuit, and Duisenberg held it the longest, developing good relationships with other bankers. After one monthly meeting at the BIS, journalists waiting outside caught him stumbling out of the building at 2 a.m., arm in arm with Eddie George, both of them clearly having enjoyed a few drinks.

NOTES

i The *Frankfurter Allgemeine Zeitung* March 12, 1998, provides a good summary of French views of Duisenberg, including the view that he is a 'Bundesbank clone'. Meanwhile, the *Frankfurter Rundschau*, November 6, 1997, also has a good summary, including reference to 'a Germanic and orthodox colouring.'

ii Article written by Harry van Seumeren in the Dutch newspaper *Volkskrant* September 7, 1996. 'De Nederlandse Kennedy trekt Europa in'.

iii *De Tijd*. 'Duisenberg is nooit kroonprins geweest en zal het ook nooit worden.' September 24, 1976.

iv October 4, 1972.

v 'Potverteren? Erg goed dat we dat gedaan hebben,' by Cees Labeur and Onno Reitsma, in *Elseviers Magazine*, September 20, 1975.

vi Ibid.

vii *NRC*. May 6, 1977. 'Duisenberg kritiseert SER-economen.'

viii *Het Parool* 'Bezuinigen én stimuleren – hoe vertel je dat?', November 4, 1977.

ix *De Tijd* 'Duisenberg: "Wat werkgevers zeggen is volstrekt overtrokken",' September 24, 1976.

x Harry van Seumeren, 'De Nederlandse Kennedy trekt Europa in,' in *Volkskrant*. September 7, 1996.

xi Ibid.

xii Interview with author on September 28, 1998.

xiii Interview with author on November 25, 1998.

xiv Seumeren.

xv OECD statistics. Also see Willem Molle *The Economics of European Integration* (Dartmouth Publishing Company: Brookfield, USA 1990). P. 179

xvi Geert-Jan Laan and Rein Robijs in *Vrije Volk* 'Wim Duisenberg: de irritaties van een optimist,' September 1985.

xvii *Het Financeele Dagblad* 'Geld is mijn vak.' May 15, 1996.

xviii Laan and Robijs.

xix Laan and Robijs.

xx *Het Financeele Dagblad* 'Geld is mijn vak.' May 15, 1996.

xxi Interview with author, November 25, 1998.

xxii Based on interview with Juncker, November 6, 1998.

xxiii Germany has 16 states.

xxiv Interview with author, September 28, 1998.

xxv Interview with author in Amsterdam, June 24, 1998.

CHAPTER THREE

The Guardian of German Orthodoxy

Wim Duisenberg owes his election as president of the ECB in 1998 to one person above all: Hans Tietmeyer, president of the German central bank. The two met in 1983, after Duisenberg's conversion, when together they were forced to negotiate the terms of the guilder's last devaluation against the mark. France and other countries had become used to devaluing of their currencies against the mark. But it was humbling for Duisenberg and the Dutch, who prided themselves in having a currency as stable as Germany's. The devaluation was personally bitter for Duisenberg, who had just become governor of the Dutch central bank.

For Tietmeyer, it was one more confirmation of erring ways among even the closest of Germany's allies. In the 1970s, he had become an enthusiastic exponent of liberal economics. He and another high-level civil servant, Helmut Schlesinger of the Bundesbank, were pushing a new, more conservative monetary and fiscal policy mix. Tietmeyer had looked aghast at the expansive policies Duisenberg was implementing around the same time. Now, when asked about the Duisenberg of the mid-70s, Tietmeyer rolls back his head and laughs. 'That was when he was still an old Keynesianist. I still remember a visit to Holland in the late 1970s. Someone showed me a big hole in the street. "That's the Duisenberg hole," they said.'

After Duisenberg's conversion to more orthodox ways, their relationship improved. They travelled the European financial circuit together, visiting summits of European leaders and hobnobbing on the sidelines of central banker meetings. They pushed policies that were almost identical, their philosophy

49

summed up in one word: stability. They developed a trust in each other.

When it was time to announce a candidate for the presidency of the European Central Bank, Tietmeyer knew there was no-one else he could endorse for the job. In 1996, when Alexandre Lamfalussy, the president of the European Monetary Institute, was preparing to announce his successor – who under an implicit assumption would become the first president of the ECB when it began a year later – Tietmeyer met Lamfalussy privately and pushed Duisenberg for the job. He also encouraged Duisenberg to stand for the post. Duisenberg agreed.

The governor of the French Central bank Jean-Claude Trichet privately made it known that he would like the job, but Tietmeyer and Lamfalussy agreed that the nominee shouldn't come from Germany or France. Rivalry was so great that one of them would end up the loser. Tietmeyer also had doubts about Trichet. He'd confided privately to colleagues that Trichet could probably become 'too engaged'. His friend Duisenberg, the cool Dutchman, was 'smoother'.

Under the terms of the Maastricht Treaty, the heads of state appoint the president of the ECB. But Tietmeyer's endorsement, as president of Germany's respected central bank, the Bundesbank, was crucial. Tietmeyer's power and credibility on monetary issues was unmatched in Europe. Because the bank controlled interest rates and monetary developments throughout the region, Tietmeyer had become even more powerful than the formal trappings of his office implied. Next to Greenspan he was the most influential global power broker.

The anti-European proselytizer, Bernard Connolly, in his book *The Rotten Heart of Europe*, aptly described Tietmeyer's physical characteristics – though exaggerated the aggressiveness of Tietmeyer's personality – in the following sketch:

> He combined tremendous intellectual power with a fearsome physical presence and great ruthlessness in debate. He would give other speakers a remorseless hammering. Before the kill, he would arrange his features into a half-smile, half-snarl, his

bared upper gums looking for all the world like the gumshield of a heavyweight boxer about to deliver the knockout to an opponent trapped already near-senseless on the ropes.

British journalist David Marsh, in a book about the Bundesbank, writes: Tietmeyer 'combines missionary enthusiasm and formidable negotiating skills with the charm of a blunderbuss.'[i] On the eve of his retirement, at 69, Tietmeyer continued to show remarkable vigour. During a meeting with a visitor in his office at the Bundesbank, he gesticulated passionately on the edge of his black-leather couch (a staple of the Bundesbank board members) illustrating his arguments with sharp swipes through the air with taut, hands.

Tietmeyer was born on August 18, 1931 in the town of Metelen, in the Westfalen region not far from the city of Münster. It lies in the northwestern corner of Germany, almost touching the Dutch border. The history of the town, with a population of about 6,000, is typical of the history of the country as a whole. Like other German towns, it found itself in the path of almost every major war on the continent. The lessons of war, and the accompanying inflation, were forcibly inculcated into the town's collective psyche.[ii]

A convent was founded there in 889, and a small village grew up around it. The town was dependent on the textile business. It soon learned to specialize in military clothing, as minor and major wars engulfed it over the next 1,100 years. Spanish troops, seeking to maintain the subjection of the Spanish Netherlands in the late 1500s and early 1600s, often sought rest in Metelen. During the Thirty Years War across Europe, between 1618 and 1648, foreign invaders stole cattle and other livestock. Scarcity of food pushed up grain prices by 150 per cent. To meet the increased demand for money, the silver content of coins was diluted. The inflationary era became known in Metelen as the 'Kipper-Wipper' ('Seesaw') days. Accompanying the inflation, town historians recorded, was a decline in morals. Soldiers were often left unpaid by their troop leaders, and were forced to rob and steal. Brawls became common. The number of illegitimate children increased, as did

Hans Tietmeyer, President of the German Central Bank,
the Deutsche Bundesbank, until autumn 1999

the prevalence of gambling and alcoholism. 'This behaviour was transferred to the local population,' says one account. 'There was a general loosening of the social fibre.' Metelen was plundered again by French troops as they crossed over to Hannover to fight British troops during the Seven Years War beginning in 1756. Finally, realizing that additional fortifications they had installed in the early 1600s did not help, the townsmen of Metelen removed them, and planted gardens instead. Napoleon's occupation of Metelen in the early 1800s was peaceful, but when the Prussians repelled the French troops, the local townsmen were forced to pay heavy fines to avoid having to fight. Those who could not afford the fine fled to the Netherlands. It was only during World War I, and again in World War II, that the locals participated in the fighting themselves. After the first war, Germany experiended hyperinflation, and Metelen was hit hard. The worthless mark could not buy the foreign cotton needed for the town's textile industry, and between 1923 and 1925, textile production stopped. Unemployment soared.

Tietmeyer was born in the wake of these woes into a large Catholic family. Under the influence of the local convent, the town had remained strongly Catholic, and despite the rise of the Nazis elsewhere, had continued to vote for the Catholic-oriented 'Centre' party. Almost 80 per cent voted for the party during the elections of 1933, when Hitler came to power. Tietmeyer's family taught him to speak up for himself, and instilled in him Spartan ways: 'In our family, with eleven children, everyone had to assert themselves, but every one also had to be considerate. Not least, we were short of cash.'[iii] The son of a local government official, Tietmeyer recalls his fear of air-raids during the Second World War, the soldiers passing through the town and the food shortages, and the war victims among neighbouring families.

Tietmeyer's early interests gravitated toward Catholic social teaching, and he planned to become a priest. 'I'd been moulded by the village community where I grew up, a culture influenced by church and Catholicism, mixed with a bit of Prussian discipline.' His career was slow to take off for someone who was to reach such heights. He obtained his high school diploma at 21, and then attended a series of universities, including Münster, Bonn and Cologne, where he studied economics and social sciences. To finance his studies, he worked in coal mines in the industrialized Ruhr valley region just north of Cologne and south of Münster.

At first, he immersed himself in the works of Thomas Aquinas and St Augustine. But after a year of theology studies at Münster, he changed his mind. He began studying economics, first at Bonn, then in Cologne. When he was studying for his doctorate at Cologne, financed by the Catholic foundation Cusanus,[iv] he came under the influence of professor Alfred Mueller-Armack, a Protestant, and one of the fathers of the 'social market economy' – the concept behind Germany's post-war economic miracle. He was exposed first hand to arguments between Mueller-Armack and more free-market economists about just how much 'social' should be mixed in to tame the free-market. The synthesis in Germany was called Ordo-liberalism. The mix of Catholic social teaching and liberalism is reflected in Tietmeyer's degree thesis title: 'The Ordo-concept in catholic social doctrine.'

The founding fathers of Germany's post-war economy agreed that a flexible and dynamic market was crucial. A primary condition for its efficient functioning, however, was competition, which had been hampered during the planned economy of Hitler's National Socialists. Further, an economy could not be geared solely to expanding production. A strong state also had to ensure social welfare and an improved general standard of living, especially for the poor.

The leitmotif was the principle of *Ordnung*, or order. Stored up in the collective memory of Germans, and kept alive by the recounting of stories over the generations, were the experiences of centuries of war and trauma that towns like Tietmeyer's Metelen had suffered. Tietmeyer and his generation craved peace, and above all stability, instead of the inflation and disorder that had eaten away at Germany's social fibre. This obsession came to dominate Germany's political and economic diplomacy within Europe. Germany was to forge over the second half of the twentieth century a social and economic system that would become the model for the rest of Europe.

The 'social market economy', Tietmeyer soon learned, was a great catch-phrase, but it was short on details as to how to guide policy after the founding years of the 1940s and early 1950s. Tietmeyer was part of a generation forced to create the tools with which to apply these founding principles to the real world. 'The social market economy can never be fully realized,' Tietmeyer said. 'It is an ideal.'

Upon graduation, he still wasn't sure of his professional direction. The three posts he applied for were deputy director at the Volkswagen foundation; university teaching assistant; and, as Mueller-Armack had recommended, an entry-level job at the economics ministry. The economics ministry accepted his application first, in effect making the decision for him. He entered in 1962, at 31, and wasn't to leave until 20 years later.

First, he laboured for five years as a junior assistant in the 'Basic Economic Policy' division, the German government's 'think-tank' on economic strategy. It was where the ministry assigned young talent. He began work in a tiny room in the ministry's attic. His talent was rewarded with an appointment to head a sub-division in the department. It took several more years of serving in different capacities before he reached the position of department head and right-hand man to the deputy minister. It was the most influential civil servant position in the ministry. He stayed there for over a decade, until 1982, when he was 51.

It was at the economics ministry that Tietmeyer first travelled to Brussels and began to confront European monetary issues. He had some catching up to do. In fact, so lacking was the department in international expertise, that Otto Schlecht, the deputy minister and Tietmeyer's boss, sought to increase it by hiring Bernhard Molitor, the German representative in Brussels, to work under Tietmeyer. Molitor, a jovial character, says he was surprised when he arrived at the ministry by Tietmeyer's lack of familiarity with international institutions.[v]

Molitor understood Tietmeyer's handicap, having had a similar classical German education. It stressed Greek and Latin, but English was generally neglected. It was only during the second half of the 1970s that Tietmeyer began learning English intensively. He had witnessed the growing importance of English within Europe and knew he would need to speak it to operate in Europe. Molitor recommended that Tietmeyer chair the EU's Economic Policy Committee in Brussels.[1]

The idea of a European central bank

To understand the world that Tietmeyer was about to enter is to appreciate the history of German and European monetary relations. The first mention of a European central bank came in July 1940, when Hitler's economics ministry drew up detailed plans for a 'Bank of Europe' to govern the post-war monetary system based on the Reichsmark. The bank, to be based in Vienna, would be owned by individual governments and central banks, which would each pay in share capital. The 'Europabank', as it was called, would settle payments between member countries, and have the power to levy minimum reserves from the member central banks. Membership in the 'Central European Economic Union' would include Germany (which included Austria, Bohemia and Moravia), the Netherlands, Denmark, Slovakia, Romania, Bulgaria and Hungary. Belgium (and presumably Luxembourg, which had been in monetary union with Belgium since 1926), Norway and Sweden would have associate status, the ministry suggested. Special 'arrangements' would have to be made with Britain and France in a future peace treaty. The two other Axis powers,

---

[1] This committee was the light-weight sister to the powerful Monetary Committee. The Monetary Committee was specifically established by the Treaty of Rome, and comprised the EU's deputy economics and finance ministers and deputy central bankers. The economic policy committee was charged to co-ordinate economic policy among member states, and does not have a specific mention in the treaty. Rather, it obtained its mandate from a vague reference in the treaty, in Article 103, that called for the nations to co-ordinate their policies. With the introduction of the Euro, the more powerful Monetary Committee has been renamed the Economic and Finance Committee.

Italy and Japan, would have their own mini currency realms. Finally, the US would dominate the Americas. Aside from the dollar, the Reichsmark would become the world's leading currency. In his book about the Bundesbank David Marsh writes:

> In an intriguing foretaste of the Bundesbank's views half a century later on European monetary union the economics ministry added: 'For political reasons it could be undesirable to damage the self-esteem of member states by eliminating their currencies.' Initial plans were thus based on individual countries maintaining their own currencies, but agreeing to permanently fixed exchange rates against the Reichsmark.[vi]

Hitler's plans for domination of Europe were dashed, but the idea of a European central bank arose again during negotiations between Europe's post-war leaders to create the European economic community in the 1950s. The first concrete proposal for the creation of a bank, however, came on October 29, 1962, just after the young Tietmeyer arrived at the economics ministry. European parliamentarian Philippus van Campen, a Dutchman, called for currency union in a report that envisioned the central banks grouped together in a federal structure.[vii] It outlined nine developments required to achieve this goal, most of which were eventually adopted 30 years later in the Maastricht Treaty. The report prompted several initiatives over the next couple of years, but all made limited progress. For the Germans, especially, the timing was still too early. Obsessed with *Ordnung*, they didn't want to share a currency in the near term with countries which, like France, had different views about government intervention in the economy. Though they liked the idea of an eventual common currency, they first wanted progress on political union. Their core demand was agreement on economic organisation guidelines, which would prevent French-style political intervention in the economy.

But for the Germans, it was also essential that they did not come across as unfriendly. The foreign ministry requested that the Bundesbank – an independent institution – should not simply give a negative answer, but be on its best behaviour when negotiating with EU countries. The Bundesbank agreed.[viii]

In the following year, 1963, the European Council passed a resolution that appeared to bow to German demands. It said European countries should increase efforts to co-ordinate fiscal and economic policies so as to improve the conditions for currency integration. Then, in early 1964, it established the Committee of Central Bank Governors (CCG) as a formal committee of the European union, to help negotiate these matters.[2] It also directed the member states to prepare currency convergence within the EU's Monetary Committee.

Under German president Walter Hallstein, the European Commission (EC) then passed another initiative, again asking governments to come up with concrete proposals to pool their currency reserves into some sort of central organization. Proposals were drawn up by the German economics and finance ministries, both of which were rejected by the Bundesbank. The bank argued that if such proposals were implemented, it would hamper its ability to ensure price stability. It feared that pooling reserves could force an automatic extension of borrowing rights to other countries, probably at Germany's expense since its economy was Europe's strongest. The bank also argued that the plan would hamper its primary goal of ensuring price stability.

During this first flurry of proposals in the 1960s and early 1970s, the Bundesbank was the main obstacle to change. If the German central bank had not been independent, it would probably not have been able to resist the Chancellery office's passion for European integration. The German orthodoxy on money might have been sacrificed on an altar of Europe. It was the Americans who set up the German Bundesbank as an independent institution in Germany, on the model of the US Federal Reserve. This created a jealous guardian of sound monetary policy. In doing so, quite unawares, the Americans had effectively thwarted a speedy monetary union. The

---

[2] As its name suggests, the Committee consisted of the governors of the central banks of the EU's member states.

Bundesbank's delaying tactics were to give the US five decades to establish and consolidate the dollar's hegemonic position in the international financial system.

The Werner Report, 1968-1970

Tietmeyer had his first real crash course in European integration during a brief stint at the European affairs desk in the ministry. He accompanied the German representative, J. B. Schöllborn, to meetings of the so-called Werner Group to work through a proposal made in 1968 by Luxembourg Prime Minister Pierre Werner to create a single currency in Europe. The group, created in 1969, submitted its report in late 1970. Werner's proposal was a response to an international currency storm that was beginning to brew. After World War II, the Americans had created a series of institutions to stabilize the world financial system, the anchor of which was the pegging of global currencies to the dollar. In the late 1960s, the Bretton Woods system – as it was called, named after the conference location in the US where the system was conceived – had raised doubts as to whether the US could continue to back its dollars with gold reserves. The gold backing had been a key element of credibility behind the system, since each country was assured that it could trade its money in for gold. But if the dollar were set free from gold, this commitment would effectively be scrapped, and European currencies would be set free. The currencies would simply float against each other, with financial markets deciding their relative worth based on an unstable mix of speculation and how much they trusted the governments issuing the money. There was a general agreement among European countries that, to ensure stability, their currencies should stick to specific 'parities' in the event of a move to a global system of flexible exchange rates.

Werner's proposal called for the creation of a single European currency unit (ECU) for accounting, and the creation of a common fund to manage mutual support during balance of payment difficulties. He believed these steps would help reduce, even remove, the fluctuation of European currencies against each other. Concrete currency 'parities' could be set and changed only upon joint agreement. In effect, the currencies would be locked together. Ultimately, this would lead over time to a *de facto* common currency.

The proposal was discussed intensely within the CCG and the Monetary Committee. The Economics Ministry was responsible for German negotiations on European monetary issues at the time. It was Tietmeyer's first insight into the Bundesbank's obsession with the nation's money supply. Partly because of currency instability within Europe at the time, the Bundesbank dropped its earlier resistance to short-term credit aid to other countries wanting to support their currencies by borrowing funds.[3] But the Bundesbank wanted to limit such help. France planned to use the credit to sell marks and buy francs, in order to support its currency, but this would mean that the supply of marks would fluctuate. This troubled the Bundesbank. The amount of money in the economy influenced the amount of inflation, and Germany wanted to gauge it closely.

In the end, the Werner Group's work became mired in differences between the Dutch-German camp and the Franco-Belgian camps. The former believed that currency bands should be tightened, and a reserve currency band created, only after more harmonization in central banking and other laws. The latter called for an early move on both fronts. The president of the Bundesbank at the time, Karl Blessing, called the Franco-Belgian proposal 'extremely dangerous'.[ix] The two camps were to spar surprisingly often in the subsequent history of economic and currency issues.[x]

The stand-off over the Werner Plan was so heated that the Belgian prime minister sent a letter of complaint to German Chancellor Willy Brandt. Brandt ordered his economics minister to seek a compromise. He, in turn, put the pressure on his young workhorse, Tietmeyer. This was the first test of a

---

[3] After the devaluation of the French franc in August 1969, France received from its neighbours a credit of over $400 million. Belgium received a $100 million credit. The money was used to buy French and Belgian francs in order to boost the value of these currencies so that they stayed within the agreed ranges.

career that centred on managing the conflict between the chancellor's vision of European integration and the steadfast orthodoxy of the German economic establishment. During the first assignment, Tietmeyer achieved little more than some diplomatic finessing.

Tietmeyer prepared a parliamentary speech for his minister, Karl Schiller, in which the principle of 'parallelism', that is between political and monetary union, was declared as the foundation of Germany's European policy. Yet in the Werner Report, the Germans were forced into a compromise which suggested monetary union could come first, but on an understanding that it would be a catalyst for political union. Tietmeyer recalls:

> We were of the view that Europe could make a qualitative step toward tightening the currency bands only if there was first harmony in the entire economic policy area. This was the proposition of parallelism. Europe could only move in the direction of supranational monetary policy if it was ready to accept a supranational political framework, at first, by closer cooperation and, at a later stage, by transferring far-reaching responsibilities to supranational bodies. Therefore the Werner Report contained a famous clause about monetary union being a catalyst: 'monetary union appears as a leaven for the development of political union, which in the long run it will be unable to do without.' I wrote that sentence myself. I would have liked to write it differently, but that was the compromise at the end.

Interestingly, the report also called for the creation of a central decision-making body in which fiscal policies and general economic policy would be agreed. It is a reference that resembles very closely the concept of an 'economic government' the French government would resurrect in the 1990s when the single currency finally came into effect, but which the Germans would reject. Tietmeyer argues that the idea emerged during the 1970s because of the reigning economic philosophy at the time, which Germany also shared, which stressed a greater 'demand'

61

component. But the French were not ready to move away from de Gaulle's position that Europe should remain a group of fully autonomous nations, and would not agree to move toward a 'central state', though Tietmeyer's French counterparts Bernard Clappier and J. M. Bloch-Laine didn't rule it out for the future. 'They fought it out in Paris, and for the moment it was decided no: We're not going to go down that road,' Tietmeyer recalls.

Because of the differences, the two sides agreed on a first step: a relatively loose band within which the European currencies would fluctuate. The Germans demanded that any credits awarded to countries needing help to stay within the bands should be paid back immediately. After three years, the negotiators would review developments. If progress had been made in converging policies in other areas, the next step of monetary convergence could be made. 'We wanted to make it hard. Either economic convergence would be achieved, or the whole thing would collapse,' says Tietmeyer.

Werner presented his report on October 8, 1970, summarizing the state of unfinished work. The idealist European Commission (EC), however, pressed ahead with a more ambitious draft directive, calling for three steps towards of economic and monetary union without political union. By doing so, it ran roughshod over Germany's concerns, creating resentment in the Bundesbank and the economics ministry. At the European council meeting in November, 1970, the Germans criticized the plan. They also rejected a proposal that the Ecofin be given the power to formulate directives on monetary policy.[4] For the French, action through the Ecofin would keep national sovereignty intact, but at the same time enable them to influence German monetary policy and gain easier access to balance-of-payments aid. The Germans, however, argued that this would endanger the Bundesbank's independence, and thus its ability to maintain stability. The Bundesbank also argued that the Committee of Central Bank Governors should be made a

---

[4] Ecofin is the grouping of EU finance ministers which meets regularly to discuss European financial matters, and prepare for the European summits of heads of state (the grouping of the heads of state is called the European Council).

formal, independent body, not subject to Ecofin directives, since the committee was presumably the embryo of what would eventually become the European central bank. The economics ministry supported the Bundesbank, arguing that the independence of the Bundesbank must be upheld until at least the final stage of currency integration. The ministry added in secret correspondence with the Bundesbank that the German government intended to make an autonomous central bank the model for the European central bank.[xi]

As it happened, the next step in the Werner Report compromise was never carried out. 'It fell apart, basically because there was never a readiness on the French side for serious negotiations on the question of supranational central banking and political integration,' says Tietmeyer. The Werner Report fallout was a valuable lesson for Tietmeyer. He learned to develop a thick skin, especially in negotiations with the French.

It is a common misapprehension that the Germans did not want monetary union. Germany did want a single currency,[5] but only as a part of an overall move towards political union. Tietmeyer and the Bundesbank had fundamental fears about the French penchant for *dirigism*.[6] For political and economic union to come about, the Germans wanted France's acceptance of an agreed *Ordnung*. The Germans, led by Tietmeyer, would push through most of the basic tenets of the German 'social

---

[5] Germany, politically prostrate after the war, pursued a policy of integration with Europe, seeing in a unified Europe a new, progressive identity. When the German parliament first signed the Treaty of Rome in 1957, there were already critical voices within the governing coalition that the treaty had not gone far enough to create a single currency. Similar complaints were heard a year later, in December 1958, in the European parliament's committee for long-term economic policy on questions of finance and investment. The Dutch reporter, Philippus C.M. van Campen, said: 'The economic unity of Europe must be realized in all areas. Currency policy is one of the most important areas . . . It has been argued by all sides, that insufficient agreement on currency policy is one of the serious deficiencies of the Treaty.' Protocol of the 200th sitting of the Bundestag, on March 21, 1957, in Peter Bernholz, 'Die Bundesbank und die Waehrungsintegration in Europa,' in *Fuenfzig Jahre Deutsche Mark*, pp. 773-833.
[6] See Chapter 4.

market economy' by engaging in a three-decade battle of attrition against the French Colbertist tradition, which emphasized the importance of state control over other parts of the economy. There was a remarkable continuity in this German line of argument. A currency union can 'only come at the end of a development toward full integration, namely, after a common political and fiscal higher authority has been implemented,' said Otmar Emminger, a Bundesbank board member, in 1958. Monetary union 'is in the long term not conceivable without political union,' said Tietmeyer more than 30 years later, in 1990, after he too had moved to the Bundesbank.

The Bundesbank's dominion

Things changed after the breakup of the Bretton Woods system in 1971. The Americans abandoned their pledge to back the dollar with gold, and thereby its connection with European currencies. The dollar plunged in value. After continued currency turbulence, the Germans were willing in 1972 to agree to a tightening of currency bands within Europe, to a width of + or − 2.5 per cent and to short-term currency borrowing rights to help other countries support the so-called 'snake' band.[7] The new system was nominally supposed to treat each currency equally. But because of Germany's economic clout and low inflation, the German mark became the *de facto* 'anchor' currency to which other currencies were tied. When other currencies dropped to the low end of the band opposite the mark, it was expected that these currencies be brought back up, not that the mark move down. This forced Germany's neighbours to take action to adjust their currencies. They would have to hike interest rates, thereby attracting investors to buy their currency.[8] But higher interest rates encourage saving, not

---

[7] It was called a snake because of the shape in which the currencies progressed: they moved up and down together within a narrow band.
[8] Lifting rates increases the rate of return on assets denominated in these currencies. Investors, seeking to benefit from these rates, buy more of the currency in order to buy the assets.

spending. This slows economic activity, and hurts job growth. It was a tough policy for the Europeans to swallow. To their dismay, they were at the mercy of German policy.[xii]

Tensions heightened. Between 1972 and 1976, the UK, Italy and France were all forced to abort the mechanism, unable to keep up with Germany's low inflation ways. As inflation ate away at their currencies, they had been forced to the lower end of the band. Their governments didn't have the discipline to lift interest rates to bring the currencies back up. The alternative to raising rates was to call Germany to the bargaining table to negotiate a devaluation of the currency against the mark, so as to have a second life within the same band. But this was politically humbling, and always shunned near election time, since it demonstrated submission to Germany. France re-entered the system in 1975, but left again in disgrace in 1976. The first effort to move towards currency union had failed.[xiii] For Tietmeyer, the failure was to be blamed on the lack of convergence in economic policy.

During this phase of deteriorating exchange-rate co-operation, there was a spate of efforts to revive a commitment to European monetary union. In 1976, Wim Duisenberg was to appear on the European agenda for the first time with his 'Duisenberg proposal'. But it too failed to break new ground.[xiv]

Tietmeyer tightens his grip

Meanwhile, Tietmeyer was slowly taking over the reins of power at the economics ministry. He cut his teeth under some of Germany's most respected economic thinkers during his time at the ministry. His first minister was Ludwig Erhard, considered the architect of Germany's economic miracle. But Tietmeyer was not impressed by Erhard's intellect. He had greater respect for his second minister, Karl Schiller, whom he admired for both his intelligence and pragmatism. Schiller took over the ministry when the Social Democratic Party joined the CDU in a grand coalition in 1966. In 1969, the SPD formed a new government with the small Free Democratic Party, and soon Schiller had expanded his powers, merging the economics and finance ministries under his own leadership. Schiller once told his highest civil servants – Tietmeyer was one – that they were 'paid to say no'. It was a lesson Tietmeyer took to heart.

Although a CDU party member, Tietmeyer worked well with the new minister. He wrote many of Schiller's speeches, and helped create the Council of Economic Experts, which was modelled on the Council of Economic Advisors in the US and became one of the most respected institutions in the country.[9] Together with the deputy minister Schlecht, his immediate boss, Tietmeyer also developed the idea of a social dialogue between the government, employers and workers to agree on targets for wage increases. Tietmeyer was behind almost every major economic policy announcement, but for the time being remained out of the public eye.

As chief of the most important department in the Ministry, Tietmeyer had the right to 'review' any policy paper emerging from other departments. While he focused mainly on finding ways to modernize Germany's economy, he could also monitor European developments. His hawkish eye earned the respect of other departmental leaders. 'They always feared Tietmeyer,' recalls Bernd Pfaffenbach, who worked under Tietmeyer for seven years during this period. 'They knew he would find something wrong with their proposals, and criticize them. He almost always did.'

Tietmeyer's admonishments were all part of his search for a tenable order. He never relaxed. During office excursions, he invariably ended up at the ping-pong table, fiercely competitive even in informal settings. On vacation, he wouldn't lounge by the pool in a deck-chair to recover from his hard work at the ministry. Rather, he planned strenuous long-distance skiing marathons. Molitor, who worked in an office next to Tietmeyer's at the economics ministry during the mid-1970s, and one year Tietmeyer's junior, recounts:

While at the economics ministry, Tietmeyer worked 14 hours a day, from 8:30 pm until 10:30 pm, and went home to work

---

[9] Made up of five economists, the council is also known as the 'five wise men'.

more on the weekends. I never heard him swear or lose his temper. He never slammed his fist on his desk. But Tietmeyer can also be nit-picky. When he came back from vacation, he demanded that all the work done in his absence be reviewed again. Once, he read a paper of mine and handed it back to me, saying 'We've got to think this through from the beginning.' He always wanted to keep hold of the reins.

During this time Tietmeyer began to pull out all of the stops, say those who know him. There seemed to be a deeper determination, more personal, that was now driving him, colleagues recall. For a while, Tietmeyer turned into an intensely private man. He has never been known, even by those close to him at work, to open up about his private life, though it is more common in Germany to keep personal and professional lives strictly divided. A 'Red Army Faction' terrorist assassination attempt in 1988 didn't help matters, although acquaintances say Tietmeyer handled the event with remarkable clam. 'He is in control,' said one of his colleagues. 'He's not the type for going to balls,' says Pfaffenbach. 'He's the type to be scheming away on how to lead tomorrow's round table discussion at work. He always wants to be in charge.' Tietmeyer is also tough on himself. Once he was asked what he would like to become. 'Myself, only better.'[xv] Tietmeyer is also a voracious reader, and a formidably prepared during debates. One Italian central banker later worried that Tietmeyer's personality was too dominant:

> Tietmeyer works. He researches everything, even on the technical level. He knows the international financial institutions inside out, knows what their competencies are, and has an instinct for the diplomacy required for communicating with each of them. He knows which words and body language to use to his advantage. These sorts of people are dangerous. He's so arrogant that it doesn't make him a very likeable person. It's very difficult to have a discussion with him.

Tietmeyer demanded top form and sound logic from others.

Schlecht, who was the deputy minister at the time, recalls how Tietmeyer often had difficulty delegating work for fear that the quality wouldn't be good enough. 'He wasn't very good at team work. He always wanted to be the best,' says Schlecht.

Molitor remembers being one of the nervous department leaders. Tietmeyer would badger Molitor to take a tougher stance against industry demands for more subsidies. Molitor didn't like subsidies either, but powerful business lobbies made them difficult to reduce. 'But Tietmeyer kept attacking. He just wouldn't let go,' Molitor recalls.

Molitor and Pfaffenbach also recall ministry action in formulating a policy on energy prices after the second oil shock in the late 1970s. As prices began a return to normal, the Americans pushed for a floor 'safeguard price' for oil. Tietmeyer saw this as an American effort to protect themselves from European countries undercutting the cost of US production. When the Americans proposed the price floor in Paris, at the International Energy Agency, Tietmeyer rejected it forcefully. 'No, we can't do this. This would disrupt the forces of the free market,' he said. The Americans didn't get their way.

Tietmeyer was also hard on the French. He was especially bothered by the French refusal to enter joint EU negotiations with the Americans to reduce subsidies to national industries. And ass late as the 1960s, the French hadn't accepted the connection between money and inflation. This connection had long been regarded as fundamental for the Germans and Dutch, and it became the anchor of the Bundesbank's monetary policy strategy in the 1970s. 'Money as a concept was still an embarrassment to the French way of thinking,' says Molitor, recalling how the Germans had tried to teach the French the elements of monetary policy during negotiations in Brussels. Molitor still remembers the sense of victory the Germans felt when de Gaulle's chief economic policy minister Pierre Massé declared that the free market had irrevocably arrived in France. 'That was a key turn,' says Molitor.[10][xvi] Tietmeyer places the

---

[10] There were a number of other areas where Germany succeeded in pushing through in Europe its ideas on economic order. One major area was the introduction of German-style competition policy during the 1970s.

French acceptance of the money-inflation relationship as late as 1983. In any case, by the late 1980s, the French had fully accepted, at least officially, the main tenets of the German orthodoxy.

Banker power brings down politicians

The power of the independent Bundesbank to bring down even the most respected leaders of government over economically sensitive issues was brought home to Tietmeyer at an early stage. Events leading up to a showdown involving Schiller, head of the super-ministry of finance and economics, started after US President Nixon abolished the dollar-gold peg in 1971. Investors sold massive amounts of dollars to buy marks, fearing that the dollar was about to inflate. Schiller favoured floating exchange rates in Europe. This way, Germany could lower interest rates and make the mark less attractive. This would protect Germany from being swamped by currency fluctuations, and simultaneously boost the economy. The Bundesbank, seeking to avoid the responsibility of managing a world reserve currency, wanted to go even further. It proposed to limit the amount of capital inflows into the mark by setting currency controls. Schiller was against controls, saying they contradicted free market principles. But his cabinet sided with the Bundesbank, and Schiller, miffed by the rebuff, resigned. Ironically, his replacement, Helmut Schmidt, was forced to move to flexible exchange rates in 1973 anyway, after it became clear they were more efficient. It was a lesson for the young Tietmeyer. He would later argue vehemently for free-floating currencies at the ECB.

Several years later, Tietmeyer was partly instrumental in helping the Bundesbank bring about a fall of the SPD-led coalition itself.[11] The episode began when Tietmeyer started urging an early stop to prolific state domestic spending. Ludwig Erhard's implementation of social market policies in the late

---

[11] From 1969 to 1982, the SPD was the larger party in a coalition government shared with the small free-market oriented Free Democratic Party.

1940s had secured the basics of a market economy: competition, free prices and a minimum social safety net. However, beginning in 1977, spending began to slip out of control. Schiller had been swept up by the Keynesian policy of fine-tuning, which had worked for a while. State spending increased, and greater economic activity ensued. The practice was credited for pulling Germany out of a recession. But the social democrats failed to curtail spending once the recession was over. Inflation was the natural result. Tietmeyer led the charge against what he saw as short-term thinking. He also advocated supply-side economics, that is, improving the business conditions for companies (which 'supply' goods) by methods such as lowering corporate taxes. This de-emphasized the importance of the so-called 'demand' side, where Keynes had dwelt.

Tietmeyer was writing harsh supply-side memos long before US President-elect Ronald Reagan sat down at a restaurant table with Massachusetts Institute of Technology economist Arthur Laffer, and agreed on an ambitious tax cut plan that was to become known in the 1980s as 'Reaganomics.' Tietmeyer was also preaching tax cuts and privatization long before Margaret Thatcher was swept into power in 1979 and became known as the 'Iron Lady' for her ambitious privatization of state companies such as British Airways, British Rail, and the massive energy supply monopoly, the Central Electricity Generating Board. But it was several years before Tietmeyer could convince Bonn. Tietmeyer and his new economics minister and boss, Otto Lambsdorff, a member of the small free-market oriented Free Democratic Party, were members of a coalition government that was still dominated by social democrats. The FDP was too weak to push through many of its own ideas.

Lambsdorff had been badgering Helmut Schmidt, the new chancellor, to reduce spending. By 1978, the government deficit was larger than ever, and unemployment and inflation were both increasing. By 1979, the Bundesbank was itching to implement deflationary measures. It increased interest rates by half a percentage point. Immediately, government Finance Minister Manfred Lahnstein criticized the action publicly.

High rates worsened the government's finances, given that Bonn was borrowing heavily as a result of growing deficits. Unimpressed, the Bundesbank increased its rates yet again.

Meanwhile, Lambsdorff openly criticised Schmidt's budget policies in the cabinet. Schmidt, exasperated by both the Bundesbank and Lambsdorff, finally yelled at the economics minister: 'Why don't you put your proposals on paper?' Lambsdorff said he would be delighted to oblige. 'How long do you need?' Schmidt snapped. 'A fortnight,' said Lambsdorff. He counted upon Tietmeyer, his hard-working assistant, to help him grind out a scathing report within the deadline.

Tietmeyer drew up an audacious report. It started by criticizing labour policies, one of the most sensitive issues for the Social Democrats. Wages were too high, it said, and there were too many rigidities in the labour market. It was certain to anger the Social Democrats. 'It was tightly packaged and written so they couldn't avoid its message,' recalls Molitor.

The 'Lambsdorff memorandum', as it was to be called, was the catalyst for the Schmidt government's downfall. Schmidt had already begun to lose his party's support, not least because of its opposition to the stationing of US missiles on German soil. With his finances in disarray, Schmidt, desperate, lambasted the Bundesbank one last time in a parliamentary speech: 'This is a warning about the consequences of deflation,' he declared, saying the Bundesbank needed to lower rates significantly.[12] The Lambsdorff memo was the decisive blow. It divided the two coalition parties, and Lambsdorff and his FDP voted to link up with Helmut Kohl's Christian Democratic Party.

In his memoirs, Schmidt later fumed about his treatment by Tietmeyer. 'The economics ministry is rather like a habitat of an artist's hangout, its leading officials are highly intelligent, egocentric, full of antipathy against other schools of thought, indiscreet with the press, above all they hold as sacrosanct their near mystical concept of "Political Order".'[xvii] Schmidt was

---

[12] Speech in the Bundestag, October 1 1982.

partly right. The economics ministry was obsessed with order, but Tietmeyer and his colleagues didn't think it was especially mystical.

It was not the first time that the Bundesbank had caused the downfall of a Chancellor by siding with an opposition party over monetary policy. It had also been directly or indirectly involved in the fall of Ludwig Erhard in 1966 and Kurt-Georg Kiesinger in 1969.[13]

After Schmidt's fall in 1982, the Christian Democrats, led by Kohl, were ushered in with a programme similar to that advocated by Tietmeyer. Tietmeyer advanced to the most powerful position available to a civil servant. He wasn't eligible for a ministerial position, the preserve of political appointees. He was given the next best thing: deputy minister at the finance ministry, with a portfolio that included responsibility for currency issues. He toiled there for seven years, in charge of preparation of fiscal policy, currency strategy, EU issues, and preparation of global summits. He was Chancellor Helmut Kohl's 'sherpa' at such meetings. Here, at Kohl's side during the 1980s, Tietmeyer was swept up by Kohl's vision for European integration. He became Kohl's principal technician, accepting Kohl's agenda but making sure that he felt comfortable with the conditions on which the new European order would be achieved.

The new government quickly passed a significant tax cut, and started a spree of privatizations. Besides trimming government outlays and taxes, government policy was mid- to long-term oriented, not jumping from year to year in an effort to fine-tune the economy. These were all based on Tietmeyer's renowned '3 Cs' motto, that is, 'consistency, credibility and continuity'. It was a conservative discipline that resurfaced in

---

[13] As David Marsh, author of a book on the Bundesbank, noted, these examples showed how the greater the indecisiveness in Bonn, the more likely it was that the Bundesbank would enter the arena. With the entrance of the ECB in 1999, that lesson was to become even more important, since political forces across Euroland's 12 countries are more divided than those reflected by squabbles within the German government.

Tietmeyer's years at the Bundesbank, and then again as member of the governing council of the European Central Bank. The 3 Cs sounded similar to another Tietmeyer formula: 'Judgment, ability and personal responsibility,' he once said, are not only the motivating forces for a dynamic economy, but also the basis for personal behaviour.[xviii]

In interviews, Tietmeyer emphasized that verbal discipline is the most important trait of a central banker. Even Tietmeyer's iron discipline slipped occasionally – but only when the cameras weren't around. Intensely aware that the markets acted on his every word, Tietmeyer was primed for the sound bite when the media was present, but he could to lapse at the end of a long day. Once, after a press conference and after the cameras had been turned off, he turned to a group of journalists, and remarked 'the dollar is a piece of cheese'. The journalists were too baffled to respond. One of them finally asked what he meant. Did he mean that it was too weak? 'He looked at us with a big quirky grin on his face, and went on his way,' one of the journalists remembers.

European Monetary System 1978-1993

Meanwhile, the third concrete effort to create a single currency – and with it a European central bank – had been launched. It arose from a series of governmental talks in April and May 1978, but governments were becoming increasingly cautious about sharing their plans with the central bankers, whom they thought were too sceptical. In June, news was leaked about a secret initiative on a currency union being developed by Valéry Giscard d'Estaing and Helmut Schmidt, and their chief aids, Clappier and Schumann. A draft of the plan was distributed on the eve of a European Council meeting in Bremen on July 6 and 7. The Bundesbank president was informed at the same time.

This way government leaders hoped the Bundesbank wouldn't have time to mobilize effective opposition. In Giscard d'Estaing's view, the problems of the currency 'snake' had been caused by the stronger countries committing too few resources to support the system. The Bundesbank, he believed, had followed its own interests too egoistically, and should have been more ready to follow an expansive monetary policy to help the rest of Europe. Germany's high interest rates were attracting capital flows into marks, and thereby destabilizing the French franc.

Schmidt, meanwhile, was for obvious reasons anxious to secure good relations with the rest of the EU and the North Atlantic Treaty Organization (NATO). Western support for Germany's peculiar position at the centre of the cold-war divide was crucial: the nation itself was still divided in half, and Berlin was vulnerable. In his memoirs, Schmidt clarified his ambitions in drawing up the initiative with Giscard d'Estaing. He wanted to create a European currency as a counterweight to the dollar and the yen. To do this, Europe had to stabilize the fluctuations in its currencies and bring its economies further into convergence. In a passionate lecture to the Bundesbank's central council, Schmidt emphasized that such measures were needed to save the common market. Further, they were required for the successful execution of Germany's foreign relations.[xix]

It was the Schmidt-Giscard initiative that first created the European Currency Unit (ECU), a 'basket' of European currencies.[14] Several countries, again led by France, wanted national currencies to be freed from parity with other currencies, preferring instead that they be pegged directly to the ECU. The French saw this as a more manageable option: if the franc became weaker, so did the ECU (since the franc was contained in it), which meant stronger currencies would also have to become marginally weaker in order to stay in line with the ECU. The German-Dutch camp, however, insisted that every currency be forced to a keep parity with other currencies. This would make it more difficult for the individual currencies to inflate. In fact, under the German-

---

[14] The ECU consisted of fixed percentages of each participating national currency. In it, the mark was just one of many currencies.

Dutch plan, the new European Monetary System (EMS), as it was to be called, was just as biased as the original 'snake'. If the peseta weakened against the mark, there was an unwritten code that the peseta would have to move up to stay within the band. For lack of any other alternative, the mark was still the anchor currency.

The Bundesbank protested against additional French demands for currency market interventions by the central banks. The German bank's independence was still strongly supported by Tietmeyer and the economics ministry. Although the Bundesbank made some commitments to support the currency system, it was able to prevail upon the Chancellor to ensure the Bundesbank's autonomy. Otto Emminger, president from 1977 through 1979, wrote a confidential letter to Chancellor Schmidt, insisting that the Bundesbank be allowed to suspend any intervention commitment that interfered with price stability, and that the government be obligated to seek realignment with the EMS if the economic fundamentals of other European countries merited it. This 'Emminger Letter' was invoked several times over the 1980s and 1990s by Emminger's successors to warn the government against pressuring the Bundesbank to adjust its policy for the sake of upholding the EMS.

Retrospectively, the most far-reaching initiative struck between Schmidt and Giscard was made during a joint visit to the tomb of Charlemagne in Aachen: the establishment of a European central bank. The idea was to restructure the 'European fund' into a central banking structure, which would be a second step in the EMS plan. But it foundered on Bundesbank resistance. The other banks in the CCG supported the Bundesbank in its view that a change in the Treaty of Rome was required for such an institution. In November 1980, the finance ministry told the Bundesbank that the government had given up its effort to pursue the plan.

As for the EMS itself, things developed peaceably at first. Europe evolved into a zone of relative currency stability, at least until 1992. For the first few years, most countries – Belgium and the Netherlands excluded – had significantly higher inflation than Germany. This led to tensions with France. Part of the problem was that a new socialist government under Mitterrand had come to power in 1981 and was experimenting with expansive policies, lowering rates in order to fuel economic growth. This inflated the franc, and weakened it within the EMS. In April 1981 the French prime minister wrote to the chancellor to make clear his wish for a lowering of German interest rates. The Chancellery notified the Bundesbank of this correspondence and the Bundesbank immediately rejected the overture. A young reformer named Jacques Delors convinced Mitterrand to give up his policy in 1983, and stability was eventually restored. But at the height of the crisis, Delors and his aide, Michael Camdessus, flew to Bonn to seek permission from Kohl and his new finance minister, Gerhard Stoltenberg, for a revision in the parities. France needed a devaluation against the mark in order to give the economy some breathing room. Extra time would also give Delors the chance to convince Paris to commit to the new policy of a stable franc. No decision was reached, but a few days later, Stoltenberg flew to Paris, with Tietmeyer and another aide, to discuss the French situation in more depth. Delors pleaded with the Germans for understanding, saying the parity change was urgently necessary for domestic reasons, not least because of opposition to his stability measures within his own party. Indeed, some in France wanted to abort the EMS altogether. Finally, the Germans agreed to a parity change, but not a one-sided revaluation of the mark. On March 21, the mark was revalued 5.5 per cent and the franc devalued 2.5 per cent. The move ushered in a new phase of stability and convergence of interest rates in Europe.

The Genscher memorandum

The proposal that at last opened the way to monetary union had, at its heart, like the Werner proposal before it, a profound dissatisfaction with dependence on the United States. Until 1987, Germany had been relatively satisfied with the system of a German mark-dominated EMS. It was better than the old 'snake' arrangement, which had included too few countries, and much better than any free-floating system, which would cause the German economy to be buffeted by gyrating foreign currencies. Germany could focus on guiding monetary policy as it wished, pursuing its own interest. Only rarely did the rules of the system force Germany to adjust its policy or intervene when other countries screamed for relief.

But the arrangement was not to last. In January 1987, French workers protested against poor wage increases, a result of a return to lower inflation after France had entered the EMS. The dollar had also started a descent, which as always, sent new waves of dollar flows into German marks. To keep up with the mark, France was forced to hike rates further. It was a bitter pill for Jacques Chirac, the Gaullist prime minister who had just replaced a socialist regime. When the Germans refused to lower their rates, he was forced to negotiate a second devaluation against the mark – of 3 per cent – after only a year in office. 'Chirac and Balladur didn't want to play along any more,' recalls Tietmeyer. 'They felt their prestige was at stake, being solely dependent as they were on German monetary policy.'

The Germans complained that the French were not adjusting domestic policy early enough to avoid problems, seeking a parity change only when the franc first came under heavy pressure. The French, meanwhile, complained that the Germans were failing to co-operate. This wasn't justified. In the six weeks to the end of 1986, the Bundesbank intervened in currency markets by selling 36.1 billion marks. But the market pressures had become too great. The January devaluation of the franc would be the last ever. To save the French some injury to their pride, Germany and the Netherlands agreed to call the change a 'revaluation' of their currencies against the other European currencies.[xx] It was humbling for two Frenchmen who had just entered into such currency negotiations for the first time: Jean-Claude Trichet and his underling, Christian Noyer.

In February 1987, Chirac used the finance ministers' meeting of the G-7 countries at the Louvre to push an agreement to stabilize the falling dollar. He also began to push for an agreement in Europe for more resources to counter speculative attacks on currencies. Bundesbank President Karl Otto Pöhl agreed to such demands in the CCG in September 1987, but only on condition that France and other countries agreed to stick to the central parity rate and resort to movements within the band only when currencies came under speculative attack. Then interest rates could also be used to try to fend off the challenges. Finally, if both measures failed, joint intervention could be justified. This approach was expected to ensure more discipline.

The US Federal Reserve, seeking to fulfil the Louvre Accords, incorporated exchange rate considerations into its decision making. But the Bundesbank, under the leadership of its chief economist, Helmut Schlesinger, put exchange rate considerations aside and insisted on basing decisions on German money supply. With money supply growing faster than targeted, the Bundesbank hiked its interest rates in early October. The Louvre Accords had been weaker than the rules guiding the EMS obliging the Bundesbank to intervene, so the Bundesbank was legally free to chart its own course. However, its hike drew more investment into the mark, boosting its value further against the dollar and other currencies. US Treasury secretary, James Baker, publicly admonished Schlesinger, saying he was endangering the global economy. The recriminations only spooked US markets, leading to the crash of the New York Stock Exchange on October 17. US officials, furious at being let down by Germany, let the dollar float, pumping dollars into the market at a low rate to save its financial system. The Louvre Accords had to be scrapped.

This led to renewed speculation against the franc. In November, the Bundesbank, fearing the cost of massive intervention to save the franc, relented, and about-faced on interest rates. The speculation against the franc stopped.

Meanwhile, Wilhelm Schönfelder, a German foreign ministry official responsible for European affairs – a calm, courteous, pro-European – had increased contacts with his French counterparts over the course of 1987 to seek a solution to the turbulence. 'There was hardly a day that I didn't talk with them,' he recalls. In early 1987 Schönfelder and another colleague, Joachim Bitterlich, drafted a provocative speech for their minister, Hans-Dietrich Genscher. The speech called for an ambitious 'institutional' solution to the problems, hinting at the creation of a European central bank. It caused a small controversy in Germany, and Genscher realized he'd hit upon something. At the end of 1987, Genscher told Schönfelder to prepare a detailed memo outlining the need for a common currency and a European central bank to govern it. Schönfelder recalls:

> Genscher had indicated he wanted the memo at the end of June 1988. Of course, I leaned back and relaxed, as any civil servant would do, figuring I had six months to mull things over. Genscher called me on February 24. He said: 'I'm meeting the day after tomorrow with a group of journalists. You've had plenty of time to prepare the memo, and I want to have it ready before the meeting.' I didn't have it ready. I shut myself up in my office for a day and didn't take any calls. I'd already discussed the single currency issue intensely with Peter Schlüter, a friend at the Bundesbank and a true European, who was also the best mind on the topic. The memo contained many of his ideas. Genscher took the memo, culled it a little, and then told us to release it to the press. The reaction was overwhelmingly positive. From there, the way was clear for EMU.

There was a reason why Genscher had hurried. On February 6, 1988, Edward Balladur, Chirac's finance minister, presented Ecofin with a French proposal for a European Central Bank to control monetary policy. It resulted from a French belief that the Bundesbank and the German mark were simply too powerful. The pressure on the French franc after the US stock crash, and the two previous devaluations had hurt French pride considerably. Chirac wanted more say in running European monetary policy, and the Balladur proposal would ensure this.

Genscher's February 26 'Memorandum for the Creation of a European Monetary Area and a European Central Bank' was more extensive than Balladur's. Because of Schlüter's input, the memo was sophisticated in its description of the structure for the bank, stressing all the conditions the Bundesbank had long required: independence from national governments and the EC, monetary stability as a primary goal, and a prohibition against financing member state debts. The Bundesbank would be the model for the common central bank. Countries not prepared for the discipline necessary for joining such a venture would be allowed to join later. Genscher suggested that the European Council work through the idea at a scheduled meeting in Hanover on June 27.

In fact, Genscher considered the paper so controversial that he signed only his name to it, leaving out the foreign ministry's heading. He had given no advance notice to other German officials. Rather, he indicated that the paper was supposed to be for debate within his Free Democratic Party. Still, it was sent to the Bundesbank on the same day. Genscher knew he wouldn't have gained permission on the plan's details from his French colleagues, or even from his own government. He explains:

> It had to be a surprise. The French and the Chancellor's office were delaying on the issue. We still had to win over the French on many of the details. The Chancellor himself wasn't too sure about it. I had tried to bring up the idea in cabinet some months before. Jürgen Stark, the state secretary at the finance ministry, in particular, sought to hold it up. He always said: 'Yes, but . . .' I feared the progress we'd made within the European union could unravel if it lost its dynamism.[15] It was anachronistic to think that the single economic market didn't need a single currency. I knew that by proposing it this way, the Chancellor wouldn't be able to avoid dealing with it at Hanover. I warned [French foreign minister Roland] Dumas that it was coming, and told him that I thought it was important that we speak about EMU and agree on something.

---

[15] Indeed, Genscher feared that the European Union could unravel because of talks he had had with Mikhail Gorbachev in Davos, Switzerland in 1987, during which he had gained the impression that East and West relations were quickly thawing. He thought that an end to the Cold War would mean western Europe might lose the incentive to continue its ambitious integration project.

Genscher's memo was indeed a surprise – at the German finance ministry, responsible for currency issues, Stoltenberg and Tietmeyer scrambled to write up their own memo, which they published a few weeks later. The Bundesbank at first withheld judgment on Genscher's memo, accepting instead the 'Stoltenberg' memo, which Tietmeyer helped write. As Tietmeyer recalls: 'The Stoltenberg memo contained "the classical German position again: that is, first we must have economic convergence, then monetary union."' To this day, Stoltenberg hasn't forgiven Genscher for writing his memo. Its creation had escaped Tietmeyer's eagle eye, and it gained momentum before he could shape it in his favour.

Bundesbank President Pöhl was sceptical of the monetary union idea. When EC President Jacques Delors had declared before the parliament in 1985 that 'Europe must with all urgency endow itself with economic, technological, financial and monetary power,' Pöhl had derided 'those who waste their energy' dreaming about a European currency.

But events moved quickly, just as Genscher had hoped. Like Kohl, Genscher was a connoisseur of high politics. He dreamed of a greater Europe, and pushed Kohl towards its realization. Before the Hanover meeting, Mitterrand and Kohl agreed that Jacques Delors should head a committee to propose concrete steps necessary to reach the single currency objective. Because of his role in helping the French government embrace more conservative policies, Delors had gained respect among Germans and conservative central bankers. He also possessed the pro-European visionary requirements for such a job.

The only condition that Kohl demanded of Mitterrand for advancement toward a single currency was that France drop its controls on free capital movement in Europe, something that Mitterrand had been resisting for years. Mitterrand, now eager to push ahead, agreed to the demand.

Meanwhile, Delors' suggestion that the committee consist mainly of central bank governors impressed the bankers. The governors were the most sceptical about a single currency, and if they could be won over, the committee could succeed. The Delors group also met at the central banker's 'lair', the Bank for

International Settlements, in Basle, Switzerland, which was symbolically important because it was considered neutral territory for the various national central bankers. The Genscher memo dominated the debate; Stoltenberg's went unnoticed.

But Pöhl clashed with Delors on many of the ideas during the committee stage, especially regarding the latter's refusal to fully support an independent central bank.[xxi] Pöhl was resentful that a politician presided over the committee and he would later say it was 'one of the darkest moments in my life'. The Dutch central banker at the time, Wim Duisenberg intervened, to try to reconcile the two.

Meanwhile, Pierre Bérégovoy who had taken over as finance minister after Mitterrand's presidential re-election in May, expressed his concerns, sharing the view with the president of the Banque de France, Jacque de Larosière, that a new currency wasn't needed. They were closer to the view of Britain's John Major, who not only believed that the current basket of currencies, the ECU, could be expanded and supported with a common reserve fund, but also that this should compete with the national currencies, not replace them. If the ECU appealed enough to consumers and businesses, it would slowly replace the national currencies. But under pressure from Mitterrand, Bérégovoy and Larosière were forced into line. The Germans, meanwhile, were more divided. Kohl was strongly in favour of the project, but the finance ministry remained sceptical. At the Delors meetings, there were two main positions, as described by a witness to the negotiations, Italian central banker Tommaso Padoa-Schioppa:

There were two approaches. First, the approach of those who thought that the committee should propose one step forward towards monetary union; second, the approach of those who thought the committee should concentrate above all on the description of what the final state of monetary union should be. The first approach was that largely taken by the French, the second by the Germans. There was an attitude, which I call fundamentalist, on the part of the Germans which consisted of saying 'if we are talking about monetary union we must define exactly what the destination is, not what the next step should be.'

After several months of meetings, the committee drew up the Delors Report, which was signed by all of the governors and published in April 1989, and which described most of the measures needed to move toward a single currency. Because of his scepticism, Pöhl had gained the trust of the British. Geoffrey Howe, a senior British cabinet minister recalls: 'We had collective discussions, private discussions, and he'd clearly left us with the impression that he was not in favour of moving to a single currency. So he was, in effect, our anchorman.' Delors, realising that the plan needed Pöhl's approval, did his utmost to accommodate Pöhl, and gave in to all his demands. Pöhl had little other choice but to sign. With his signature, the others, even the British, felt comfortable signing. Later, Tietmeyer and the former Chancellor of the Exchequer Nigel Lawson would privately criticize Pöhl for signing the report. In his memoirs, Lawson expressed disgust with Pöhl, calling him a 'broken reed'.

Suddenly, events in eastern Europe gave the project new urgency. In November 1989, the Berlin Wall came down, and the two Germanys, east and west, quickly began negotiations for unification. Mitterrand, like other Europeans, was afraid of a new larger Germany, and desperately wanted to tie Germany inextricably into Europe. Before the Strasbourg European council summit in December 1989, Mitterrand pushed Kohl and his chief foreign policy aide, Joachim Bitterlich (who had now left the foreign ministry to join Kohl at the chancellery), to commit to monetary union in exchange for France's acceptance of Germany's unification. By the eve of the summit, Kohl had agreed, asserting that 'German unification and European unity are two sides of the same coin'. The two leaders decided to call an intergovernmental conference to meet before the end of 1990 to thrash out an agreement on monetary union, for which the Delors report would be the blueprint. Mitterrand announced the plans to the other European leaders during the summit. The lead negotiators would be the finance ministers. Kohl and

Mitterrand also agreed that a separate intergovernmental conference would be held to negotiate political union, to be led by the foreign ministers.[16]

These developments signified an important juncture for European integration. They were a departure from Tietmeyer's desire to keep monetary union connected with political union. From then on, European integration would develop more according to Schönfelder's vision of 'limping parallelism', according to which progress would be made toward either monetary or political union, depending on where steps were possible, with the assumption that progress in the lagging area would catch up.

Tietmeyer was taken off guard by the Genscher memorandum, and the quick progress of the Delors group. Before he could focus on them, he was diverted to another major project. In 1989, Kohl had appointed Tietmeyer to the Bundesbank directorate. He was to begin in 1990, and was responsible for international monetary affairs. But after unification talks began in 1990, Kohl called upon his trusted aide to negotiate the currency reform that year with eastern Germany. During the course of 1989, Tietmeyer had become increasingly persuaded by his chancellor's vision, and was even used as Kohl's special envoy to win support from other EU nations on the single currency idea. Kohl asked Tietmeyer to help him win over the British prime minister Margaret Thatcher – who was notoriously euro-sceptic – to the single-currency idea. While Tietmeyer held to his conviction that political union should come before monetary union, he supported, at least officially, the drive to realize the single currency project.

---

[16] There has been some speculation among German intellectuals about whether the German government ever sought to leverage 'politico-strategic' concessions from the French in return for a German willingness to proceed with monetary union. According to conjecture, the Germans might have found it in their interest to ask France to share with Germany its diplomatic and military might (and therefore nuclear capability) in return for Germany's relinquishment of monetary policy control over Europe. But in interviews, Genscher, Kohl advisor Horst Tietschik and several other officials have denied this was ever a consideration. Monetary union was always negotiated separately, and always considered in German interests if negotiated correctly.

During the reunification negotiations, Tietmeyer master-minded events behind the scenes. If the West Germans were going to be thrown together with the East Germans in a single currency zone, Tietmeyer wanted to ensure that West German order was installed in the East: 'It occurred to me to find a treaty concept (with East Germany) that didn't stop half-way, but went all the way, that is, to incorporate the economic and legal order.'[xxii] But in many respects, economic logic was left by the wayside. Though the market value of the East German mark was less than four to one West German mark, Kohl agreed to exchange them one for one. It was a tremendous cost for West Germany. In doing so, Kohl overruled objections from Pöhl and the Bundesbank that such a policy would be too costly.

By late summer of 1990, Tietmeyer was trying to catch up with the European single currency negotiations. He drew up a statement on EMU that was approved with few changes by the other members of the Bundesbank council: 'A monetary union is an irrevocably sworn co-fraternity – "all for one and one for all" – which, if it is to prove durable, requires, judging from past experience, even closer links in the form of a comprehensive political union.'[xxiii] Tietmeyer was merely echoing the words of the Bundesbank's first President, Karl Blessing, after the first proposal was made for a central bank by the EC in 1962:

> The final goal of the Commission is a European monetary union ... As a European, I would be ready to approve of European monetary union and to accept a centrally directed federal central banking system; as a responsible central banking practitioner, and a realist, I cannot however avoid pointing out the difficulties which stand in the way. A common currency and a federal central banking system are only feasible if, apart from a common trade policy, there is also a common finance and budget policy, a common economic policy, a common social and wage policy – a common policy all around. In brief, this would only happen if there was a [European] federal state with a European parliament with legislative powers in respect of all member states.[xxiv]

At the end of October 1990, the European Council, meeting in Rome, agreed to reject the British proposal, favouring instead a single currency governed by a European Central Bank. But the Council also agreed to push forward political union, calling for an intergovernmental conference which would culminate with the signing of a new Treaty enshrining the single currency accord. Bérégovoy, still not convinced, attempted one last time to keep the British within the project, saying the French would propose a plan that would reconcile the British and Delors proposals. He wanted to avoid what appeared to be a German vision of a two-speed Europe, which consisted of a core group of virtuous countries that would move to a common currency first, and a second group of stragglers which would qualify later. Pöhl, meanwhile, was still belittling the common currency idea: 'Why create a common currency? There is one: the mark!'

In France, Mitterrand finally put his foot down to quash Bérégovoy's complaints. In a meeting with his chief ministers in late January 1991, he declared: 'The policy of France is the single currency'. He conceded the danger of moving to a two-speed Europe, as Germany seemed to want. But he insisted that France would have to stay closely allied with Germany. The Germans, he pointed out, didn't have a seat at the United Nations Security Council. The mark was their only diplomatic weapon; they had a reason to insist on discipline, he stated. 'There will be no reconsideration of this alliance. Our ally is Germany. The British, they are allied with the United States.'[xxv]

The Bundesbank, believing that it had made some headway in obtaining a French concession on the independence of the bank, began to take the idea seriously, and drew up conditions for participation. They proposed the 'golden rule', which was already in play in Germany, which required the budget deficit not exceed the amount of public investments. The French agreed to the exclusion of those countries not meeting the strict criteria but found the 'golden rule' too nebulous. 'Public investment' was open to considerable interpretation, they felt, and could be manipulated at will by governments wanting to apply their own definitions. They proposed that public deficits not exceed 3 per cent of gross domestic product, and that debts not exceed 60 per cent. The 3 per cent rule came from a limit applied to the French budget set by Mitterrand in the early 1980s after a disastrous inflationary period.

Bérégevoy, finally persuaded to accept an independent central bank, proposed to counterbalance its influence by strengthening the finance ministers. He suggested creating an 'economic government' that would permit the finance ministers to consult each other on budget and fiscal policies. To the Germans, this looked like a French manœuvre to interfere with the bank's independence, and they rejected the idea.

In the middle of 1991, Pöhl resigned. He was weary of battle, having been overruled in his arguments about the costs of reunification. Replacing Pöhl was Helmut Schlesinger, one of the most experienced and respected of the Bundesbank council who had long been its chief economist, having introduced the money supply target at the bank in the late 1970s.[xxvi]

On 8 December, the eve of the European Council meeting in Maastricht, Mitterrand and Giulio Andreotti, the Italian prime minister, met for dinner at Mitterrand's out-of-town hotel. Their aides had wrapped up months of discussions that had brought the single currency project in reach of signing. One issue remained unresolved: a firm timetable. The Germans hadn't wanted to commit to a firm date, fearing that some countries wouldn't be ready. There had to be a way to divide the good performers from the laggards. Andreotti pulled out an idea conceived by Tommaso Padoa-Schioppa, his chief aide in the negotiations, and one of the four non-governors who had been part of the Delors Committee discussions.[xxvii] His idea was to come up with two dates – 1997 and 1999 – as deadlines. If a majority of the twelve did not meet the criteria by 1997, then the project would begin in 1999, even if only a minority of countries qualified. It was irresistible, an example of Italian innovation at its best.

Maastricht

The next day, 9 December, Mitterrand and Andreotti sprung the idea during the morning meeting of the Council. The

Germans had no alternative but to accept it. 'Kohl found the idea brilliant,' recalls a German negotiator at the time, Günter Grosche.

But most of the German delegation were more cautious. They were aware of the torrents of criticism being launched at the project in the German press back home. The upmarket news magazine, *Der Spiegel*, and the mass-market tabloid, *Bild*, both carried lead articles questioning why the cherished German mark was being sacrificed. It didn't help that the French wanted to make sure that the possibility of political fudging be kept open when it came to final selection of the participants. While the criteria were written explicitly into the treaty, they were weakened by the addition of the term 'approaching'.[xxviii] Selection would also be possible when a country was moving, or 'approaching', fulfilment of the criteria, thus opening up considerable room for manœuvre. Concern about public opinion at home made the German leaders consider demanding that Frankfurt be the seat of the European Central Bank. That decision was to come later.

There were several special concessions. The British were allowed an 'opt out' clause, which stipulated that they could forgo participation in the project but join if they changed their mind and met the criteria. A 'cohesion fund' was also created to help the EU's poorer countries, Spain, Portugal, Ireland and Greece, and modernize their economies. This help was considered essential for them to be able to catch up economically, and to qualify for and participate in monetary union.

On the mandate and the structure of the ECB, the Germans had achieved most of their aims. In fact, the European Central Bank would have an even clearer mandate than the Bundesbank. Its principle task was to maintain 'price stability'. The Bundesbank statute, by contrast, committed the German central bank to 'safeguarding the currency' – a vague expression which some could interpret as giving priority to its exchange rate value. As for its structure, the ECB would be a virtual clone of the Bundesbank. The ECB's main decision-making council would consist of an executive board plus the heads of the central banks of the participating member states. The executive board would have six members (including a president and vice president), and they would have the responsibility of executing the decisions made in the wider council. As the German central bank had originally been owned by central banks of the Deutsche Länder (states), the ECB would be owned by the national central banks. The EU's member states would have to change their banking laws to resemble those in Germany, to ensure that their central banks were also independent before the currency was introduced in 1999. Finally, the ECB would not be allowed to bail out any government with loans. Again, this was even tougher than the Bundesbank law, which allowed such loans within limits. In exchange rate policy, the EU council of ministers would have the final say, just as the German government could set exchange rate policy directives for the Bundesbank. New was that the ECB political counterpart would not be a single government, but a group of governments with no official way of co-ordinating budgetary or fiscal policy. That theoretically made the ECB more independent, since it would not be forced into regular contact with a single government or official: Only the minister of the country possessing the rotating six-month presidency would be allowed to attend the ECB governing council meetings. Conveniently, Germany would be taking over the presidency in the first six months of 1999.

*   *   *

There were two gaping holes in the Maastricht Treaty from Germany's point of view. The first was that it did not provide for any automatic sanctions against countries failing to meet the criteria once they entered the monetary union. This was later to haunt Germany as it tried to sell the project to the German population.[xxix] Second, Kohl had not made any progress towards the political union that he had told Mitterrand was the *quid pro quo* for agreeing to the single currency project, and which the Bundesbank had said was necessary. 'Political union and economic and monetary union are inseparably linked,' Kohl had said only ten days before the Maastricht conference. 'We can and will not give up sovereignty over monetary policies if political union remains a 'castle in the air".'[xxx] The Germans had pushed for agreements in fields such as foreign and security policy, social policy, immigration, and in increased powers for the EU parliament. But they had not been prepared or precise enough in their demands. 'It just wasn't thought through. The concepts were vague,' recalls Grosche, one of the negotiators.[17] Indeed, one of the main obstacles in Europe's subsequent push toward more unity over the 1990s and early 2000s was the lack of agreement in Germany and other countries about just what political unity meant.

The sanctions problem was subsequently addressed before the single currency's debut in 1999. But the political union which Tietmeyer had believed so necessary remained hauntingly neglected. 'The (monetary) union can only function if there exists unity over the general economic order,' Tietmeyer said.[xxxi] Günter Winkelmann, of the German economics

---

[17] The problem of having no political union will emerge in Chapter 9. Germany, tired of paying more into the EU coffers than they get back out again, is demanding a reduction of its contributions. Now that Spain and Portugal have qualified for monetary union, they no longer need special 'cohesion' funds, the German argument goes. This issue of transfers from richer to poorer countries will continue to haunt the single currency project. Just as the Maastricht Treaty was being signed, the dangers of introducing a single currency into economies of different speed and structure were being manifest in Germany. Germany's currency reform had hampered East Germany from adjusting to the huge shock it had received after reunification. It had received the German mark, but its workers and companies had been overwhelmed by its strength. They were still not as productive as their West German counterparts, and their goods in foreign markets priced in German marks had been rendered hopelessly noncompetitive. The result: Hundreds of thousands of companies went bankrupt, and millions of workers were thrown out of work. The German government, meanwhile, was forced to increase expensive money transfers to the east. The total cost of unification ten years after has been estimated at about one trillion marks. The German government vastly underestimated the cost of introducing the new currency. In the European case, a single currency would be simpler, since the individual currencies were already trading against each other at market rates, and would simply be merged into the euro at similar rates against each other. Transfers, though less important, are still necessary.

ministry, best summed up the lingering German suspicions: 'We feared that it [monetary union] would become a Trojan horse. Nice to look at, but suddenly soldiers jump out . . .'

In October 1993, two years after the Maastricht Treaty was signed, Tietmeyer became president of the Bundesbank. Soon, Tietmeyer came to personify the consummate central banker, and on the eve of his retirement in 1999, it was difficult to conceive that anyone could readily take his place. When he wanted a change in the mark's rate against the dollar, he steered the markets masterfully, crafting his words carefully for the desired affect. Domestically, he blasted government social policies and wage settlement agreements when he feared they could endanger stable money policy. Abroad, he was quick to tell countries to reform their economies in order to keep up with the fast-track European core, foremost of which was Germany. He skilfully kept alive the mythology that had come to surround the Bundesbank. On the eve of Tietmeyer's taking its helm David Marsh could write the following description of the Bundesbank, one which was all the more valid after six years of Tietmeyer's reign:

> It is deity and demon combined. The US Federal Reserve may be mightier, and the Bank of Japan more inscrutable. But neither matches the Bundesbank's independence, nor its pride, in taking unpopular decisions which can send financial tremor around the globe . . . At international monetary conferences, Bundesbank functionaries never look crumpled, like the French, or harassed, like the British, or out of their depth, like the Americans. The Bundesbankers are secure in the knowledge that, by defying inflation, they are pursuing the brightest and most meaningful lodestar in the sky.[xxxi]

The standing of Tietmeyer and his bank in Europe meant that his orthodoxy would live on, in the form of those colleagues steeped in the same German doctrine. Many of these colleagues sit on the governing council of the European Central Bank, the key decision-making council for governing Europe's new money. One of them is a hawkish Frenchman, who had riled the

French establishment for a decade by pushing for a franc that was more solid than even the almighty mark.

NOTES

[i] David Marsh, *The Bundesbank* (Heinemann: London, 1992.) p. 71.
[ii] *Metelen – Unsere Heimat*. Von Sigrid Howest. Gemeinde Metelen 1989.
[iii] *Koenner in Karos: Das Anti-Nietenbuch*. Heribert Klein. Koeln: Koelner Univ.-Verl., 1995. (pp. 11-29) p. 13.
[iv] Tietmeyer became the group's business director for three years, and today is still chairman of the foundation's scholarship association.
[v] Interview with Bernard Molitor, June 30, 1998.
[vi] Marsh, p. 133.
[vii] The Treaty of Rome in the 1950s called for three steps to monetary union. The second step had begun in January, 1962. The third had been scheduled for between 1966 and 1969.
[viii] Ibid., p. 787.
[ix] *The German Mark: 50 Years*, German Bundesbank. C.H. Beck. 1998, p. 791. The quote was contained in the Bundesbank's secret protocol, which was recently opened to a select group of academics who authored a fiftieth anniversary volume on the Bundesbank's policy. The access was granted as an exception for the anniversary event. Otherwise, the protocol stays secret for thirty years.
[x] To give another example, the two camps divided over the issue of whether to lengthen the time allowed for short-term settlement aid, again with Germany and the Netherlands vying for a more conservative time frame of less than 30 days, and France and Belgium pushing for at least 30 days or more. As usual, there was a compromise. Ibid., p. 798.
[xi] See German Bundesbank, p. 792.
[xii] The Bundesbank wanted to avoid the mark's becoming a reserve currency in Europe. So it forced an agreement that no country hold more than 10 per cent of its reserves in another member country's currency without permission from that country. Some other, smaller multilateral aid measures were also passed, including the funding of a European Fund for currency cooperation, which was to help countries in payment difficulties. It was to be directed by the central banks, but executed by the Bank for International Settlements in Basle.
[xiii] Accumulated inflation between 1971 and 1978 in Germany was only 42.14 per cent, compared to 145.96 per cent, 107.43 per cent and 89.47 per cent in the UK, Italy and France, respectively. It's no surprise that these countries left the mechanism in that order. Of the European countries, the Netherlands, once again, was the closest to Germany's inflation performance, registering 69.38 per cent inflation during the period.
[xiv] From the margins, the French kept firing off proposals, from a call to lift quotas for short-term payments aid, to a desire to pool a portion of the Fund's reserves. The Bundesbank resisted most of these efforts, although it did agree to some minor changes, including an increase in the short-term payments aid.
[xv] Frankfurter Allgemeine Zeitung questionnaire, cited in *Munzinger-Archiv/*

Internationales Biographisches Archiv. Infobase Personen. Anfrage: G 606856.

[xvi] Tietmeyer had been working on his French connections. He knew Michael Albert, a member of the French planning commission under Raymond Barre, through the Papal Academy for Social Science. It was to be a good contact. Albert is now a member of the council of the Bank of France, the French central bank.

[xvii] Klein, p. 21.

[xviii] Ibid., p. 16.

[xix] German Bundesbank, p. 798, taken from Deutsche Bundesbank historical archives not yet open to public scrutiny.

[xx] The Belgians also revalued, but only by 2 per cent.

[xxi] Interview with Karl-Otto Pöhl, 1997.

[xxii] Klein, p. 27.

[xxiii] Statement on monetary union. September 1990. Marsh. p. 243.

[xxiv] Remarks on *NDR* radio. January 27, 1963.

[xxv] Eric Aeschimann et Pascal Riche. *La Guerre de Sept Ans. Histoire Secrète du Franc Fort.* 1989-1996. Calmann-Lévy. 1996.

[xxvi] See Chapter 4.

[xxvii] See Chapter 7.

[xxviii] Besides the deficit and debt criteria, there were three others contained in the treaty. The level of inflation shall not exceed the average level of inflation of three countries with the lowest rate of inflation by 1.5 percentage points. The level of long-term interest rates shall not exceed the average level of long-term interest rates of those three countries with the lowest inflation rate by 2 percentage points. Finally, the currency must have participated successfully within the EMS for at least two years.

[xxix] See chapter 4.

[xxx] Kohl's speech in Jouy-en-Josas. December 3, 1991.

[xxxi] Klein, p. 29.

[xxxii] Marsh, p. 16.

CHAPTER FOUR

The French Surrender

No matter how much she tried, France couldn't fall in love with
Germany. But she respected him, and they began to think about
a marriage of convenience. They talked often. They began to
think it might work. The young Germany began to grow in
prestige and power, and soon he became impatient and more
insistent on marrying France. France knew she did not love
Germany, but realized she had better grab him while she could.
She consented to move in with him, but made it clear that she
didn't want marriage. After a while, Germany and France
talked of children. France liked the idea of a child, but proposed
that they adopt. Germany was upset. He refused, and decided
to let things be for a while. But then Germany and France began
to drift apart, and there were stormy confrontations. One day,
suffering financial woes, and fearing that Germany would stray,
France said she'd have children after all. At first, Germany
insisted that marriage would have to come first. Months went
by without any resolution. Suddenly, France declared she was
pregnant. In the rush to prepare for the child, the two decided
to hold off on marriage. The euro was born a bastard.

The proud history of the Banque de France

There are reasons the French have a problem with political
union, and were willing to have the euro out of wedlock. It has
to do with the long, grand tradition of the French nation. The
French have a highly developed sense of national identity. They
are proud of their country, its natural beauty, its history, its
language, the exploits of its monarchs and generals, its

intellectual achievements, its cuisine and its international influence. The tradition has helped shape the French central bank, the Banque de France.

The Banque de France itself has illegitimate associations. It was founded in 1803, by Napoleon,[1] and held its first shareholders' meeting in 1812. It is based in the majestic first *arrondissement*, a quarter in which many of the buildings are over three hundred years old. It resides in the Toulouse Mansion, named after the Count of Toulouse, who bought the building in 1713.[2] The Count was an illegitimate son of Louis XIV and Madame de Montespan. To visit the bank's governor, one must go through the Golden Gallery, a room as grand as its name, which stands as a shrine to the pomp and faded glory of French history. When the Count bought the mansion, he employed Louis XIV's architect, Robert de Cotte, to overhaul the gallery. Though the Count was 'legitimized', the scar of his heritage remains. At the end of the gallery, built into the hearth, is the original iron plate depicting the Count's coat of arms. Beside the fleur-de-lis escutcheon of France is a *bar sinister* symbolizing the Count's bastard origins.

The bank sits at the heart of Paris, adjacent to the Palais Royale, a few blocks south of the Paris stock exchange, and two blocks north of the Louvre Museum. This is the strategic centre: a focal point in Paris' triangle of political and financial power, delineated by the president's office at the Elysée Palace a few blocks to the north, the finance minister's office at Bercy three metro stops to the east, and the prime minister's office at Matignon just across the Seine to the south.

---

[1] In 1803, Napoleon demanded that private bankers create a central bank on the British model – a private company in which major banks would be the shareholders and charged with distributing bills. The 200 shareholders that made up the bank's general assembly elected an executive body, the fifteen-member general council.

[2] Built in 1635, the mansion was designed by François Mansard, the famous French architect. The mansion's vast collection of fine pictures and statutes once made it one of the most famous in Paris. By the time of the French Revolution, Toulouse and his successors had gone. During the revolution, the mansion's art treasures were moved to the National Museum, and the mansion temporarily became the centre of the government printing office.

For luminaries wanting to visit the governor, there is a special entrance on a small back road, 3 rue de La Vrillière. First the visitor identifies himself through a telecom system. A camera observes him from above. From a thick portal set in high stone walls, the door purrs open. One enters and finds oneself before another grated barrier. It is like taking a voyage back in time. Beyond there is a courtyard, and through a couple of wooden doors, one finally reaches the mansion, where governor Jean-Claude Trichet and his two vice governors are located.[3] Trichet himself sits in a magnificently stuccoed office at the back of the Mansion behind a mahogany Louis XIV desk. By a side-door in the office sits a pink seventeenth century armchair, oil paintings adorn the walls, polished floors are covered by a plush carpet. The only artefacts of the twentieth century are a brightly coloured painting directly behind Trichet, by Lahner, a Hungarian of the School of Paris, and two computer terminals on his desk.

Justix from St-Malo

Trichet was born in Lyons in 1942. He was the eldest son of a college professor of Latin, Greek and the arts from St-Malo, a proud port town in Brittany. His father died when Trichet was only 16, but he'd inherited his father's romantic nature, and soon fell in love with St-Malo, the home of his paternal ancestors. He spent time there as he grew up and today owns an apartment there. He would visit the town on his rare vacations, and recite the words of François-René Chateaubriand, the town's most famous son. Trichet's father and grandfather were both poets, and Trichet tried his hand too. He published poems in a student review at 19, and has remained an amateur poet. He has recited verses from St-John Perse, his favourite author, and Leopold Senghor, on French television.

One visitor to Trichet's holiday spot once discovered Trichet on the rampart of St-Malo reciting Chateaubriand's famous

---

[3] The other eight members of the bank's decision-making group, the Monetary Policy Council, have their offices in the Palais Royal.

verse: 'la meche battue par le vent'.[i] Trichet's father was also a friend of French President Georges Pompidou, who Trichet would personally encounter at university.[ii]

Trichet continued to dabble in poetry, but it wasn't enough to make a living. First, he attended France's state-run school for mine engineering in Nancy. Like Tietmeyer a few years before him, Trichet frequently went down into the mines. For three months, he worked in Auchel at mine No. 2 in the dark, dank, narrow shafts. Heat, high pressure and shifting draughts made the shifts physically exhausting. 'It was a cultural shock for me,' he says. The mines were part of the same large coal and steel belt that sprawled up into western Germany, where Tietmeyer had worked on the German side. The region still has dark memories of the war, having been the backbone of the two countries' military strength. So strategically important was the region, that it had been forced to integrate under the fist of the American allies who made Marshall Plan funding contingent on European co-operation. Thus the Coal and Steel Community was created, the first step towards European economic integration.

The director of the mine, Bertrand Schwartz, was like a second father to Trichet. Trichet made contacts with the labour movement, and joined the socialist party which was closely affiliated with the unions. But he remained a moderate. He graduated in 1965, and then did military service, but kept his union ties after he enrolled in the *Ecole Nationale d'Administration* (ENA), an élite school in Paris for state civil servants, by joining the local trade union branch. He remained a sympathizer with the left for many years.

He was 27 when he enrolled at ENA in 1969. The year before he arrived in Paris, the city had begun to boil over with street protests and government crackdowns on leftist and trade-union leaders. In 1969, President Charles de Gaulle had finally been forced to step down. In 1970, Trichet joined a group of 32 ENA students to sign a protest against the regime of de Gaulle's successor, President Georges Pompidou, for alleged repressive tactics.

Those who knew Trichet say he exhibits a missionary zeal –

searching out causes and stubbornly converting people to them. He is unflaggingly polite, almost saintly in his demeanour. But once he latches on to an interlocutor, he rarely lets go. His style is to seduce, usually through wordy arguments, rather than through exertion of authoritative power. A few years older than most of his student colleagues, his maturity gave him the edge in proselytizing. Trichet argued successfully for the only amendment in the students' protest declaration, insisting that it should refer to the 'forces of repression' instead of 'police forces'. This removed the blame from the police themselves – who were just puppets – and directed it at the regime. He was obsessed with fairness. But he was also loyal to authority. When the government threatened the students with exclusion from future public service, the students, led by Trichet, retracted their protest. Some of the more radical students criticized him as a moderate. He was always searching for compromises in the student general assembly. His friends nicknamed him 'Justix'. The nickname was appropriate, given Trichet's ties to the Brittany homeland of Asterix and Obelix, the Gaullish supermen who, fighting for the cause of justice, always won their battles. His graduation class collectively named itself 'Thomas More', for the moral authority expressed by the English author of *Utopia*.[iii]

Colbert's legacy

Trichet wanted to save his skin for government service for a reason. He graduated fifth in his class of 100 students, an impressive feat given the school's graduates were the pick of the crop. This meant he would be guaranteed a good job in the state's esteemed civil service system. ENA is the Harvard (or Oxbridge) of France. It is intensively competitive.[4] When it was

---

[4] Jacques Chirac, another alumnus, recalled that students, having read the key pages of a text for examination, tore them out so that none of their classmates could read them. Cited in Bernard Connolly, *The Rotten Heart of Europe*, page 295, quoted from Tony Allen-Mills, 'School for Scandal,' in *Sunday Times* magazine, 22 January 1995, p.24.

*Jean-Claude Trichet. Governor of the French central bank,
the Banque de France*

founded in 1945, it was placed directly under the authority of
the prime minister. Known as 'Enarques', the school's students
are trained in a mixture of practical and theoretical courses, in
a programme designed to produce leaders. In contrast to the
mass lecture system of most of France's prestigious *grandes
écoles*, ENA is based mostly on intimate seminars.[5] Enarques fill

---

[5] While Trichet was still sitting in his ENA seminars, Otmar Issing, the German
economist who would join Trichet in the ECB's governing council in 1998, was
already a professor, complaining about the mass education system in Germany.

the ranks of France's higher civil service, and tend to have overblown self-images. American political scientist William Safran writes:

> The social selectivity of Enarques has led to the impression that they share not only a high degree of intelligence and technical competence but also outlook and manners, and they feel a certain degree of contempt for other members of the political apparatus, if not for society at large ... Students learn above all to cultivate useful social relations and to become part of a tightly knit élite network. [iv]

The French civil service, led by the Enarques, enjoys a high regard, largely because of the legacy of Jean-Baptiste Colbert, a contemporary of the Count of Toulouse. Colbert, General Controller of finances and chief adviser to Louis XIV, was a mercantilist. He sought to speed up France's modernization with a new system of protective tariffs, taxes, subsidies and price controls, using some of the proceeds to fund massive spending on roads and canals. To help organize and execute his ambitious plans, Colbert centralized the French administration, extending the power of government over all fields including the management of money. His reforms contributed to making Louis XIV's empire the most powerful in Europe, and the era stands as France's most glorious. A by-product was a special élite group of technocrats, most with noble connections, charged with running the system. The civil servants were the proud upholders of the Colbertian tradition through the subsequent centuries. Both the right-wing Gaullists and the socialist parties believe in activist government – known as *dirigism*.

After the French Revolution in 1789, the hereditary system in the French bureaucracy was abolished and the power of parliament made supreme, at least on paper. In reality, parliament has remained disparate and disorganized, and civil servants as powerful as ever. Far from being considered a 'hired hand' as in the US federal bureaucracy, the French civil servant is seen as a member of a superior class. As Safran writes, French higher civil servants represent 'an awesome entity known as the State – at one time equated with the monarch and later with the republic'. They gained esteem abroad. When negotiations over the European Monetary Fund were conducted in the 1970s, Bundesbank President Karl Klasen warned that the Germans would have to make absolutely certain that 'Eurofanaticism'[6] did not lead to a loss of control over their own money. If the EMF were established, then 'we would not be dealing with [French President] Giscard d'Estaing but with the French bureaucracy. And if there is one thing I admire it is the French bureaucracy; it has been trained to the highest level by centuries of experience and is vastly superior to us in the diplomatic pursuit of national interest.'

The Enarques tend to despise Parliament, thinking of themselves as an 'objective' counterweight to a party-based parliamentary system. One observer of the selection process for ENA incoming students noted: 'In the spirit of the would-be énarque "the State is and always has been, like the Word in St. John's Gospel: "All that is made was made by it and without it nothing was made" . . . In their fetishistic attachment to the State and in their belief in its power and goodness, certain candidates are close to delirious.'[v]

Yet France's civil service is also aware of its vulnerability. Throughout the nation's long history, revolutions have frequently purged its ranks. Since 1789, France has had eleven different political regimes. Five were republics, three were monarchies, two empires and one a fascist puppet state. Despite their airs of superiority, therefore, the civil servants know their place, and tend to serve their governing ministers loyally.

In Trichet's year, the Enarques were again disillusioned with the regime. In 1948, just after the war, France boasted an economy larger than that of West Germany.[7] But within a few years, Germany had caught up and bounded ahead. French critics blamed the incompetence of the Paris government. From

---

[6] (Europa Begesiterung)

[7] The national social product of France was 178.9 billion, compared to Germany's 154.8 billion.

the end of the war until 1958, the first post-war government had poured money into social programmes and embarked on ambitious economic expansion, subjugating monetary policy to 'higher' political goals. This policy, together with France's protracted and costly war in Algeria, caused spiralling inflation. The government was eventually discredited and General Charles de Gaulle, a proud French nationalist, took power in 1958, founding a new constitution. De Gaulle was obsessed with restoring credibility to the franc. He introduced a currency reform, declaring: 'I will give France a model currency, its exchange rate won't change as long as I am here.' But his authoritarian style was unpopular on the left. He too was pushed aside, as a result of events in 1968.

Trichet begins his climb

The 1968 political unrest was badly timed. De Gaulle's departure came just as the Bretton Woods system was breaking down, and nervous financial markets feared a decline in the value of the dollar. They were nervously searching for safe haven currencies, and the troubles in Paris caused them to downgrade the franc in favour of the mark. The franc wasn't helped by the efforts of De Gaulle's successors, Georges Pompidou and Valéry Giscard d'Estaing, to catch up with Germany. Mammoth spending projects were launched as they sought to modernize the economy. But the projects did exactly what US economist Milton Friedman was arguing a government shouldn't do. They accelerated economic activity to a frenetic, unsustainable rate. The excess of money in circulation, fuelled by government spending, led to a decline in its worth. The result was inflation, as workers bid up their wages and businesses bid up their prices in response. It was a vicious circle.

Trichet graduated from ENA just when the inflation began in earnest under the regime of Pompidou. Despite his student protests against the Gaullist regime, he wasn't dissuaded from applying for the single slot the Finance Ministry offered once a year to the ENA graduating class. The position was one of the most coveted by ENA students. According to one of his classmates, Trichet talked a higher ranked member of his graduating class out of applying for the position, though Trichet now says the colleague had already decided to go elsewhere.[vi] He was awarded the place at the ministry, and became a member of the division that inspected the finances of the country's public institutions. Because of his college ranking, he was rewarded with the title of *inspecteur des finances*; it was an élite ranking, a sign that he was on the fast track to the top of France's commanding heights. It wasn't a mere title; it denoted the acquisition of an enormous amount of responsibility.

The job changed Trichet. As he gained expertise, he learned more about the economy, and noticed how much France's large national companies were struggling to make a profit. Their books only seemed to be getting worse. In 1973, Middle Eastern oil producing countries decided jointly to hike their prices and extract money from the rich industrialized west. The rise in oil prices quickly affected the entire French economy, first increasing the price of other goods, and then wages. Trichet witnessed first hand the evils of inflation and, though he hadn't studied economics, knew something was wrong with France's economy. He realized that companies should not be weighed down by burdensome taxes. As he moved up the ministry's hierarchy, he began overseeing the country's major industries: energy, telecommunications and aerospace. He encouraged the state-run companies to do their part in restructuring. But in 1975, France's inflation soared to 14 per cent, markedly worse than Germany's 7 per cent. France was not abnormal compared to other countries. The US faced 14 per cent inflation, and the UK and Italy had rates even higher.[vii] By 1976, Trichet was convinced change was necessary. 'The scales suddenly fell from my eyes,' he says, recalling his conversion to the idea that a market-based economy was the 'only possible model'.[viii]

He continued to keep a critical distance from the government, despite his position as a civil servant. He attended public meetings of the socialist party, and participated in debates about public finance. He even wrote papers for the opposition on how best to propose changes to the government's 'Plan' programmes.

In 1981, François Mitterrand and his socialist party came into power, and Trichet, 38, paid the price for having served the Gaullists. A victim of a general purge, Trichet was demoted. But he was transferred to the Trésor, the most prestigious division in the ministry. It was a blessing in disguise. He was young enough to resume his advance, and he soon became the Trésor's deputy director for bilateral affairs. This placed him on the international circuit, where he built up valuable contacts with bankers and other government officials. Soon Trichet was promoted to direct the Treasury's international affairs division, and, at 42, took over the chairmanship of the Paris Club, a body created by France and other advanced industrialized countries to arrange loans to developing countries. The appointment came just as the developing countries in Latin America began to face difficulties in paying off their loans. Trichet was forced to restructure the loans through a complex combination of absolving countries from part of their debt and demanding the rest be paid back. He travelled to the far ends of the globe to participate in the negotiations.

Trichet's humiliation

At home, meanwhile, Mitterrand's government hit a brick wall. It tried to follow the policies of its predecessor, declaring a massive spending programme to drive the country forward. It created more than 200,000 jobs by nationalizing companies. But while jobs were created, other economic developments slammed the country into reverse. Mitterrand was spending more than his tax income would allow, and soon the budget deficit ballooned, tripling within two years. Currency speculators, fearing a resumption of inflation, unloaded their holdings in francs to avoid being stuck with a devalued currency. The franc plummeted by more than 50 per cent against the dollar.

Stunned and left with little alternative, Mitterrand turned to the reformer in his cabinet, Jacques Delors, the finance minister who had warned all along of disaster. Delors suggested an austere programme of social cuts and wage moderation to save the country. He also prevailed upon Mitterrand to make greater efforts to defend the franc within the European monetary parity system. Thus began France's *franc fort* policy (maintaining a strong franc). Mitterrand also ruled that deficits should not exceed 3 per cent of gross domestic product.

Under Delors and his successors at the finance ministry, the new policy soon bore fruit. By 1986, the inflation rate had fallen to 2.7 per cent, and the franc, devalued once again to give France some breathing space during the reforms, stabilized against the mark. But other problems appeared. By taming the economy, the government's policy forced companies to cut back production plans, and this meant reducing the number of employees. Unemployment soared to nearly 10 per cent of the workforce. Predictably, the socialist government suffered at the polls, and though Mitterrand remained president, he was forced to share power with a Gaullist prime minister and cabinet in a so-called 'cohabitation'.

Edouard Balladur, the new conservative finance minister, gave Trichet the biggest break in his career. He appointed Trichet his chief of staff and his so-called sherpa, the deputy who accompanies the finance minister to the Group of Seven industrialized countries (G-7)[8] and other international meetings. It was a high profile job, but first, Trichet was humbled by his new bosses. Chirac, the new prime minister, wanted a devaluation of the franc as soon as he arrived in office. He introduced an ambitious liberalization plan, eliminating credit and price controls and implementing a vast privatization programme. But the franc had weakened further against the mark, and Chirac didn't want to push through the tough reforms with the usurious interest rates being used to defend the franc within the EMS. The franc was suffering from its past reputation and from speculation in the markets, which weren't convinced that France would hold to its low inflation policies.

---

[8] The G-7 consists of the seven largest industrialized countries in terms of Gross Domestic Product. They are the US, Japan, Germany, France, Italy, the UK and Canada. Government leaders, their finance ministers and the governors of their central banks meet to discuss issues on the global agenda. See Chapter 7.

As Balladur's right-hand man, Trichet was forced to prepare the devaluation negotiations. After devaluation, however, things got worse. In 1987, workers began to protest against lower wages. Then the dollar suddenly dropped in value, and investors, seeking refuge in a stable currency, shifted massive amounts of capital from dollars into marks. This boosted the mark to dangerously high levels against the franc. Chirac and Balladur forced Trichet to negotiate a second devaluation after only their second year in office. It proved to be a stain on Trichet' s career. Balladur's successor, Pierre Bérégovoy, in a heated discussion in 1989, told Trichet that he didn't trust him as a defender of the franc. 'I won't forgive you the devaluation of April 1986!' he said.[ix]

Devaluations were a double insult to Trichet's pride. It was humbling enough to have to seek a franc devaluation against the mark, but as a negotiator, Trichet was forced to beg the Germans to agree to such a move. Each time, the German team – led by Trichet's counterpart, Hans Tietmeyer – would preach to him the need to implement more economic reforms. The men became well acquainted with each other, but their positions made them into tough bargainers, and constantly forced them to come to terms with their differences. Their relationship, necessarily unequal, was cordial. Germany's economy was larger, and the mark stronger. Tietmeyer was a few years older, and correspondingly, a few steps ahead in his career. For his part, Trichet held the more powerful Tietmeyer in special regard. One high ranking French official who observed the two men together described Trichet as 'fascinated' by Tietmeyer. Trichet even adopting the same style of 'half-moon' glasses.[x]

A Belgian official at the time, Fernand Hermann, now a senior member of the EU parliament, recalls meeting Trichet during this time, when they were both members of the so-called Lyons Group, designed to promote the idea of the ECU. Hermann detected in the Frenchman an intense desire to match the Germans:

The problem for the French was that for many years they were paralysed by the Bundesbank, like the mouse is paralysed by the python. For them, the question was how can they share this power? That was Trichet's motivation. He came across as a convinced European, since he was defending the issuing of the ECU bond. But back then it was more a way to compensate for the power of the Bundesbank than a true European feeling. He was convinced that the way to produce European power was to do it at the European level rather than at the level of German–French relations.

Monetary union proposed

In 1987, Balladur promoted Trichet to be head of the Treasury, the most powerful civil service post in France. Under Trichet, the Trésor steadily expanded its jurisdiction in international affairs, and with it, Trichet's power grew. Trichet also gained control over monetary policy. As one senior Belgian central banker noted, 'Trichet has his fingers into everything.'

On February 6, 1988, Balladur announced on television that 'the time has come to examine the possibility of creating a European Central Bank that will govern a common currency.' The news came as a surprise to the public. Balladur said he was preparing to discuss the issue with his colleagues. A few days later, the German foreign minister, Genscher, sent his own memo to his chancellor, requesting that the project be discussed. It was the Genscher memo that formed the basis for discussion, in part because of the longevity of Kohl's government. In May, Balladur and the Gaullists were swept out of power.[9]

In June, Trichet witnessed the historical deal in Hannover between Mitterrand, Kohl and Delors to start the Delors group and move towards EMU. 'It was an enormous strategic move,' Trichet recalls. Mitterrand took his young aide aside afterwards and told him that he should heed the orders of Delors, the man charged with implementing the European vision. For Trichet, this

---

[9] While President Mitterrand was to stay in office for two terms, the prime ministers and their governments changed over the years. The strong relationship between Kohl and Mitterrand is one reason for the steady progress towards EMU from 1988 onward.

became his mandate, and he would pursue it zealously. Regardless of criticism or what his finance ministers told him, he stubbornly held his course, confident that he was serving a higher purpose. In 1991, he witnessed the decision by Mitterrand, Kohl, Delors and Andreotti to set the starting date for the single currency at 1999. All agreed that the importance of the project mandated its introduction before the turn of the century. Trichet immediately set about negotiating EMU with his German counterpart. It was one more reason why Trichet vehemently resisted a delay in the EMU project when Wim Duisenberg proposed the idea in the secretive bankers' meeting in Basle.

Despite his doubts about Trichet, when socialist Pierre Bérégovoy returned as finance minister in late 1988, he relied on Trichet more than ever. At Bérégovoy's request, Trichet looked into financial problems at the public company Société Générale. Within six months, Trichet had sorted it out.[xi] He continued to develop his negotiating skills with foreign partners, for instance, smoothing relations with an antagonistic Iran. His wife, an advisor to the minister of foreign affairs, and specialist in eastern Europe, helped him with his contacts. In short, he was the Henry Kissinger of finance.

Trichet was also successful in stabilizing the franc. Created in 1823 under Louis XVIII, the Trésor was charged with borrowing money from the financial markets to finance government spending. Trichet and his underlings talked regularly to private banks and traders, sounding out conditions in the market in order to get the best deal. They became intimate with the needs and concerns of the markets, and thus were the main channel of those needs into government decision-making. After his return to power in early 1988, Bérégovoy pushed rates down twice within two months. This was quicker than Trichet wanted. He knew the markets could become unsettled. A strengthening dollar made the Bundesbank worried that expensive American imports would cause inflation, and so the German central bank lifted rates three times during the summer.[10] Fearing the effect on the franc, Trichet convinced his minister to lift rates again. Those who know Trichet say that he hardened his views over the course of 1988. At first, he was an 'agnostic' about rate cuts.

But after the experience of that year, he became a believer in the *franc fort* policy.

He was encouraged by the most hawkish Frenchman of all, Bérégovoy's chief of staff Hervé Hannoun, a Jew of north African origin, and an advocate of an austere monetary policy that would outdo even the Germans. Hannoun was known as 'the diamond', for his untiring cajoling of other ministers to support sound fiscal policies. (Hannoun enjoys a particular mystique among the Parisian establishment, enhanced by word that he was only twelve when he first read Karl Marx's Manifesto of 1848.[xii]) 'His arrival changed the rules of the game,' said one French official at the time. Hannoun later became vice governor under Trichet at the Banque of France, and as such, Trichet's likely successor to governor around 2002.[11]

A stable franc brought down the costs for companies of financing their investments. Less fearful of inflation, investors became more willing to buy long-term bonds, and demanded lower interest rates on loans.[xiii] By the summer of 1991, the French 10-year bond rates, or 'yields', which had earlier been two percentage points more than German 10-year bonds, fell to just 0.5 per cent higher. They continued to drop.[12]

---

[10] When the Germans, concerned about rising prices, lifted rates three times within a month during the summer of 1988, French finance minister Bérégovoy complained about the Germans 'going it alone', and accused them of not consulting the French over that entire time. Karl Otto Pöhl rejected the complaint, saying that the Bundesbank had notified its partners about its policy, and that it was wrong to say that the Bundesbank had gone it alone. It was just one more example of the friction between the Germans and the French on interest rate policy. Aeschimann and Riché. P. 42.

[11] That is, if Duisenberg steps down in 2002, as indicated by his statement in Brussels in May 1998. Trichet will become President of the ECB. Hannoun, if made governor of the Banque de France, would then join Trichet on the ECB's governing council. But Duisenberg has not ruled out staying for a full eight-year term, ending in mid-2006 (see Chapter 6).

[12] The logic is as follows: If markets believe a currency is stable in the long term, they are more willing to invest in long-term assets, such as ten-year bonds, denominated in that currency. Increased demand for long-term bonds drives up their price. Take the example of a bond worth 1,000 francs with a set 6 per cent return, or 60 francs, upon maturity. The bonds are traded on the markets. If demand drives the bond's price up to 1,100, the set return (which remains 60 francs) corresponds to an ultimate yield for the investor of only 5.5 per cent. Thus more demand leads to lower long-term interest rates.

Drawing on his persuasive powers, Trichet used his credibility to win over minister after minister. He was a loyal civil servant, but he wanted to make his point heard. His motto: 'Absolute liberty in the role of counsellor; absolute loyalty in the execution of decisions.' Trichet directed the Trésor under five prime ministers. As new governments were elected into office, the jealous guardian was there to greet them. The French franc never again devalued against the mark. Even in 1993, when the policy threw France into recession, he held to a policy of *désinflation compétitive* (competitive disinflation). The idea was that by keeping inflation lower than other countries, France would outdo its neighbours in the achievement of lower rates of interest and be recognized as the most favoured place to invest. It could also gain a competitive advantage abroad, the price of its export goods increasing more moderately than those of its competitors. The term was coined by another French official, Jean-Baptiste de Foucault. But Foucault was more moderate than Trichet. Trichet, with moral support from Hannoun, became its most ardent adherent and marketer.

Under Trichet's reign, the Trésor maximized its power. Ironically, with Trichet still at the helm, it now began to relinquish layer after layer of that power. In an effort to modernize the economy, he accelerated the privatization programme. By spinning off state-run companies, his bailiwick became smaller and smaller. He slimmed down state regulations, modernized the banking system, and created the French futures exchange, the 'Matif,' through which the treasury could more efficiently sell government bonds. With each step, it seemed, he moved France closer to the German and Anglo-American models. He criticized what he called French 'inferiority' and 'fundamental psychological problems' which he said were keeping the country from modernizing.[xiv] At the same time, his crusade became ever more controversial within the French establishment. They didn't believe a civil servant should be making the decisions that (they felt) a politician should be making.[13]

Obsession with Germany

After 1990, German unification handed Trichet an opportunity to step up progress on *désinflation compétitive*. The German government introduced a massive Keynesian-style boom, raising taxes in order to invest hundreds of billions of marks into East Germany each year. It was similar to the Keynesian policies France had so often launched in the past, and predictably, inflation began to spiral upward. Trichet tried to bring French inflation below that of Germany for the first time in two decades. He dreamt of making the franc even stronger than the mark. The Germans were struggling, and it was time for France to score some credibility points against her larger neighbour. Trichet had never accepted the mark as the anchor. In May, 1990 he declared *'L'ancre du système, c'est le système lui-même'* ('The anchor of the system is the system itself').[14]

Instead, France found the currency seas choppier than ever. To tame inflation, Germany's Bundesbank hiked interest rates to record levels,[xv] forcing France to lift rates to keep the franc tied to the mark. This threatened to throw the French economy into recession, but Trichet's hunch was that if he could only keep interest rates lower than those in Germany, the advantages would eventually kick in, and France's economic expansion could surge ahead of Germany's. By 1991, French inflation had dipped lower than German inflation. But its long-term interest rates, though they had decreased, were still higher than Germany's. That was because France was still paying the price

---

[13] 'The parliamentarians have the impression that it is the superstructure which is imposing its choices,' said one parliamentarian of a party within the ruling majority. 'The budget minister's budget is nothing other than the plan of Trichet', complained another. Aeschimann and Riché. p. 197.

[14] Trichet continues to argue, even today, that the mark was never the anchor of the system. (Interview with author, August, 1998). But his statements often implied that the mark had enjoyed that status. On February 13, 1990, in a note to his minister, Trichet wrote: 'As much as Germany doesn't merit (or no longer merits) being the anchor of the EMS, our country must do everything to convince international investors that we are ourselves candidates to be the anchor . . . that the Franc is a candidate for revaluation against the mark . . . and that it will have the right one day – as soon as possible – of having long-term rates lower than German long-term rates.' Aeschimann and Riché. p. 117.

for past sins. Long-term interest rates were decided purely by the financial markets, and they were still punishing France with a so-called risk premium. By the end of 1992, France was entering its deepest recession in fifty years. With opposition parties increasing their criticism of his government's, Bérégovoy looked to Trichet to deliver the benefits he'd promised. Trichet was in a dilemma. To maintain support for his policies, he needed to provide results. But he had underestimated the stubborn memory of the markets.

In a note to his minister on April 10, 1992, Trichet pleaded that, despite the economic pain France was suffering, a tight hold be kept on the *franc fort* policy:

> Our grand objective is to follow a policy of controlling inflation with the intentions – ambitious as they may seem – first, of holding French inflation below that of Germany; and second, as consequence of the first objective, of endowing the franc with the potential to revalue against the German mark; and third, as a consequence of the second objective, of reducing, and then reversing, the 'risk premium' between the franc and the German mark, and therefore to eventually obtain long-term interest rates that are lower in France than they are in Germany.[xvi]

The key term was 'eventually'. Trichet, was thinking of the long term. However, his memo, and its implications, excited the national pride within the French establishment. Bérégovoy and his successors, being politicians, wanted results immediately in order to pacify increasing outrage on the home front. Instead of garnering respect, Trichet was showered with derision. Critics named him the 'Ayatollah of the franc'. Other nicknames were 'monetary megalomaniac' and 'the gnome of all gnomes'.[xvii] ('Gnome' is a popular insult among the conspiracy-prone French, meaning a person with sinister influence, especially financial, as in 'gnomes of Zürich'.) Jean-Marie Colombani, editor in chief of *Le Monde*, once asked Trichet: 'Are you sure you don't work for the King of Prussia?'[xviii] French sociologist Pierre Bourdieu called him the 'henchman' of the German Bundesbank.[15]

In fact, domestic distress was worsened by an attempt by Bérégevoy to bring French rates below German rates prematurely. It was a year in which the economy had been slowing. The number of jobless had increased by over 200,000. By October, street protests by angry workers pushed Bérégovoy to manœuvre behind the scenes to lower French short-term interest rates – without Trichet's permission – lower than those of Germany's for the first time since the 1970s. He'd seen the Dutch do the same, and he believed it would work for the French, despite what the markets believed. He rallied a close circle of advisers to support a cut of 0.25 per cent percentage points, with only Hannoun opposing the move. He then took the decision to Trichet as a *fait accompli*. But within two weeks, Bérégovoy's designs were dashed. The Bundesbank, following its own agenda, raised rates, which again put immediate pressure on the French franc. By November 18, the French were forced not only to cancel their rate cut, but to increase the main rate by 0.5 per cent percentage points – to even higher than it had been before. Bérégovoy decried the injustice of the EMS: 'The virtuous countries are penalized,' he complained.

1992: Mitterrand's statement

In September 1992, on the eve of a French referendum on monetary union, Mitterrand made a statement on the ECB that was to stay emblazoned in German memories. Mitterrand was debating with the Gaullist leader, Philippe Séguin, the leading opponent of EMU. Séguin criticized Maastricht for handing over control of monetary policy to an unelected, democratically unaccountable group of 'technocrats' in the ECB. Mitterrand scoffed at Séguin's statement. He said that 'the technicians of the [European] Central Bank are charged with applying in the

---

[15] Trichet was offended, but undeterred. In 1991, Bérégovoy had offered Trichet the chairmanship of a major French bank, BNP, a chance to enter a high-profile, well-paid job in the private sector, and safely away from controversy. But Trichet turned it down. He already had his eyes on another prize: the European Central Bank.

monetary domain the decisions of the European Council . . . It's been said that the European Central Bank will be the master of decisions. It's not true! Economic policy belongs to the European Council and the application of monetary policy is the task of the [European] Central Bank . . . The people who decide economic policy, of which monetary policy is no more than a means of implementation, are the politicians . . . [The members of the ECB would be like members of the Commission who] no doubt cannot help feeling a certain tenderness for the interests of their individual countries.'[xix]

Mitterrand's assertion confirmed what the Germans feared: that the French, with their tradition of political subordination of economic and monetary policy, would not swallow the concept of an independent central bank. It was also a worrying sign of French fickleness. The independence of the ECB had been accepted after long, exhausting years of negotiation, and enshrined in the signing of the Maastricht Treaty. German students of French history noted that the French took contractual commitments less seriously than other nations, in particular the Germans. The French had regularly scrapped constitutional orders – almost every generation since 1789 has witnessed a revolution. French constitutions had been revised so frequently that French citizens had difficulty identifying with a particular regime's norms or principles. This contrasted with Germany, where a particular system and order is given priority over the whims of public opinion. The German constitution prohibits referenda, for example. The French tradition held that legitimacy is vested in the Rousseauist notion of the 'general will'. If the nation revolts against a specific order, all contradictory legal norms and contracts are considered annulled. France was the first major European country to produce a revolution. Germany, by contrast, has never had a revolution.[xx]

These differences gave rise in Germany to an instinctual mistrust of the French. Alexandre Lamfalussy, the Belgian banker who was president of the European Monetary Institute before Wim Duisenberg took over, recalls a conversation he had with one of his German assistants after he came out of an EMI meeting in 1996. She had spent all of her vacations in France, but was still deeply distrustful of the franc. 'Do we really have to give up our mark for the euro?' she asked. 'This is terrible. Why, it will be the same as the French franc,' she said.

'Why do you say that?' Lamfalussy responded.

'Because there's always inflation in France.'

'Now look,' Lamfalussy answered. 'Think back over the last five years. Did you not notice that French inflation was less than that in Germany?'

The woman thought about it for a moment and said: 'Yes, you're right.'

In fact, Trichet's policy had made the franc stronger than the mark. The woman's distrust was 'typical of the German instinctual suspicion of other countries,' says Lamfalussy. But the Germans weren't alone in their suspicion of the French. American social scientists, confounded by the French tendency towards revolution, crisis and dissent, talked of France's reluctance to 'marry the twentieth century'. Others talked of a 'delinquent society' that makes incessant demands on the state for benefits but refuses to accept the necessary social and political obligations.[xxi]

Various public opinion surveys have been conducted within the two nations that purport to show that the French and Germans consider themselves strong partners and allies within Europe. But detailed studies suggest the relationship at the popular level isn't especially strong.[xxii] Surveys show that 60 per cent of Germans view the German-French friendship as 'something that exists only in the heads of politicians'. Only 28 per cent said that there is a 'real connection between the people in both countries'. Erwin Teufel, the prime minister of the German state of Baden-Württemberg and former German representative for German-French cultural affairs, described his own experience in meetings between Germans and French administrators. 'The Germans bring a well-prepared pile of papers to the table, while the French partners prefer an initial exchange of ideas. The result: the Germans find the French frivolous, and the French feel overwhelmed by the German approach of using structured concepts and organizational charts.'[xxiii]

Mythologies from the past

The differences between the two nations are rooted in hundreds of years of history. The French have become accustomed over the centuries to large-scale, centralized Colbertist state interventionism. They also had radically different experiences with money. The lessons they learned were the opposite of Germany's.

The franc was the brainchild of Oresme, one of the earliest known advocates of monetary stability in history. Oresme, the fourteenth century monetary councillor of Charles V, had looked on in dismay as the king devalued the state currency by reducing its precious metal content 71 times over two decades. Oresme acknowledged that the devaluations had been profitable for members of the king's court, since they would be the first to find out about them. But regular citizens suffered, he argued. He persuaded the king to introduce a new currency, the franc, in 1360, and obtained the king's promise to keep it stable. But to the consternation of monetary historians studying the period, the economy plunged into a depression, and prices actually began to sink. Deflation, not inflation, ravaged the French economy. The second wave of the plague (1360-1363) broke out. As for Oresme, he disappears from the history books, not surprising given that the king was likely to have been quite upset. The birth of the franc has been shrouded in controversy ever since, with economic historians still arguing heatedly over the cause of France's woes at the time. Tietmeyer himself has been an enthusiastic participant.[xxiv]

How different it was for the birth of the mark in 1948. The Germans began with a broken national spirit, having nothing but a worthless Reichsmark and Lucky Strike cigarettes to barter. But quickly, the Americans helped introduce a new currency, the mark, in the form of notes freshly printed and shipped from the US. As the Germans rolled up their sleeves and rebuilt the nation, the new mark was the embodiment of stability at a time when so much was in flux. The association between the mark and stability became deeply embedded in the collective German psyche. The German economy boomed. Not unexpectedly, the French lack the same attachment to their currency. German economists see the currency as the cardinal factor underpinning the post-war economy: it mirrors the country, its society, its people and morals. Germany no longer defines itself by its military strength or by the size of its land mass, but by its currency. True, the French give importance to their currency, but it is treated as one factor among many. 'A country is a territory, an army and a currency,' Charles de Gaulle once declared.

Unlike the Germans, the French have never experienced hyperinflation. And, there are other events in French history which have created doubt about the merits of a strong currency.[xxv] The relatively strong economic growth of the late 1920s during the regime of Raymond Poincaré can be attributed to a devaluation, not to a policy of *franc fort*: in 1928, Poincaré fixed the franc to a parity of 65.5 milligrams of gold, or a rate of 124 francs to the British pound, a significant dilution when compared to the rate of 25 francs per pound before the First World War.

Likewise, negative experiences have resulted from a policy of *franc fort*. In the early 1930s, France held to its parity with gold, even though other major currencies, including the British pound and US dollar devalued. France's exports became prohibitively expensive, and the economy deteriorated. Between 1933 and 1936, ignoring the problems, the government of Pierre Laval held stubbornly to the parity. In 1933, in a diplomatic effort to win prestige, France even masterminded a gold-bloc alliance with Belgium, Luxembourg, the Netherlands, Switzerland and Poland, in which each country pledged to help the others defend their gold parities. But by 1935, the French government could no longer afford it. Desperate, Laval was forced to slash state spending by 10 per cent. The following year, the left-wing Front Populaire was elected into office and finally devalued.

Because France's civil servants rarely study economics, in contrast to their German colleagues, they tend more often to cite such historical references in their debates. The analogy between the 1930s and the early 1990s was inescapable. Despite multiple attempts by French businessmen to persuade

Bérégovoy to abandon the *franc fort*, however, Trichet always managed to repulse them.

The currency markets attack

Seeing Mitterrand's referendum-eve ECB statement as a threat to its negotiated *Ordnung*, the Bundesbank went on the offensive in the next edition of its *Auszüge*, a bulletin of press articles published regularly.[xxvi] The Bundesbank underscored its reproach by printing eight, mostly negative, articles about Mitterrand's comments.

Mitterrand's statement, and the ensuing recriminations between the German and French leaders,[xxvii] undercut Trichet's efforts to restore credibility to the franc. The franc had not devalued for five years, a record since Europe's currency coordination began in the 1970s. In the view of the financial markets, however, the mark played the anchor role. Regardless of the challenges posed to the German economy by unification, the mark enjoyed a premium of stability. The only difference was that the ties securing the anchor to the other currencies were fraying badly. Markets started to speculate against currencies at the lower end of their permitted bands, sensing that European economies were on their last legs – battered by the high German rates – and would soon be forced to devalue.

The attacks had started ahead of Mitterrand's ECB statement and began with the weaker currencies. By July 1992, pressure had already built up on the lira and sterling. Rumours of a US Federal Reserve cut in interest rates brought a flow of capital into the German mark from the dollar, placing more pressure on other European currencies, especially the lira.[16] Doubts

---

[16] Desperate, the Italians hiked their discount rate to 15 per cent. They knew that if they devalued, they could be disqualified from participation in the EMU. But with the latest move, short-term market rates rose to 18 per cent, bringing squeals of pain from Italian industry. Tommaso Padoa-Schioppa, the Italian economist who worked on the Delors report, and who was at the time number two at the Banca d'Italia, put in a call to Delors, telling him that a 'political' solution was needed for the lira crisis. He urged Delors to put pressure on Mitterrand to find

about the outcome of the upcoming French referendum had increased, which also placed the franc under speculative pressure. This allowed the Italians to argue that any devaluation should include the French. Trichet rejected a devaluation: it would be too much of a blow to French credibility.[17] But with the lira still falling, the Italians were desperate. Carlo Ciampi, governor of Banca d'Italia, in a newspaper interview on 11 September, declared that the Bundesbank's interest rates were 'excessively high and needed to be brought down'.[xxviii]

The Germans, meanwhile, were pushing for a realignment. In a single week in September, they had been forced to buy DM 24 billion in foreign currency.[18] But by selling marks for these other currencies, the Bundesbank had injected billions of new marks into the economy. These waves of new marks interfered with the Bundesbank's monitoring mechanism. Bundesbank President Helmut Schlesinger, a polite but unfailingly conservative Bavarian, worried that the Bundesbank might lose control of its money supply rudder.[19] He defused the threat by declaring that the Bundesbank's obligation to intervene in the currency markets had been met. He suggested that Britain, France and Italy adjust their parities so that the Bundesbank would not be forced to protect them, but they rejected the proposal. Alarmed, Schlesinger called for a meeting with chancellor Kohl and finance minister Theo Waigel. Kohl hesitated about taking action to push his neighbours for a realignment, fearing negative repercussions on the Maastricht

a solution with Chancellor Kohl. It wasn't the last time that Padoa-Schioppa resorted to politics. Later, in the ECB governing council meetings, his tendency in this direction rubbed many of his ECB colleagues the wrong way. See Connolly, p. 144. To be sure, Padoa-Schioppa says he does not recall making the phone call, though he does not deny making it. In an interview with the author on November 27, 1998.

[17] Trichet was chairman of the Monetary Committee in Brussels, which prepared the European Council and the Ecofin meetings for discussions on monetary issues. He used his power to reject all talk of realignment.

[18] European central banks, led by the Bundesbank, sold a stunning 87.2 billion marks during the third quarter of the year.

[19] See chapter 5.

Treaty. But when Schlesinger revealed the Bundesbank's alarming currency intervention figures, Kohl relented.

A realignment was now required. In mid-September, deputy finance minister Köhler and Tietmeyer flew to Paris to meet Michel Sapin, the new French finance minister, and Trichet, at the French finance ministry. Behind closed doors, the French and the Germans ironed out an agreement. They decided to sacrifice the lira in what Irish Finance Minister Bertie Ahern termed a 'sweetheart deal' between Germany and France.[xxvii] Trichet managed to convince them that France was determined to stay in. Tietmeyer and Köhler flew on to Rome, and forced the Italians to agree to a 7.1 per cent devaluation on September 13. To formalize the agreement, Trichet didn't call for a meeting of the Monetary Committee. Rather, he contacted the other partners via telephone and fax. This was unexpected for the British and the formal-minded Germans. It proved just how powerful the Germans had become: both Trichet and the Italians, having reached an agreement with Bonn, considered the informal agreement a done deal and neglected formal notification of other member states. After all, if the Germans had decided, and the French had agreed, what could the other countries really say against it? Publicly, it was announced that the lira would devalue by 3.5 per cent and Europe's other currencies would revalue by 3.5 per cent. On Monday, September 14, the Bundesbank cut its discount and Lombard rates by half a percentage point, a move that was supposed to help.

But the actions failed to ease market fears. Schlesinger gave a newspaper interview on September 15 in which he said the situation was not yet resolved and a more extensive realignment would have been better. The markets then attacked the pound and the lira, eventually forcing the two currencies out of the EMS altogether that same day, later dubbed 'Black Wednesday'. The lira plunged an additional 5 per cent. The peseta and the escudo fell 6 per cent a few weeks later, and more devaluations took place in these and other currencies over the following months. Trying to avoid ejection, the Bank of England had lifted its minimum lending rate to 12 per cent, but the markets, led by financier George Soros, did not relent. They continued to borrow billions of pounds, and then turn round and sell them for marks. Pounds flooded the market, and it became increasingly expensive for the Bank of England to buy them back again. Despite an afternoon announcement that interest rates would be lifted to 15 per cent the next day, the markets continued their attack. They knew that Britain, a nation of home owners – with mortgages set at variable interest rates – would not be able to tolerate such pain. They were right. Finally, the British gave up. The pound plunged. George Soros was reported to have grossed $1 billion speculating against the pound. Suddenly, the markets turned on the French franc. It sent shudders through the French. The event roused the historical fear that the Anglo-Saxons were out to get the French, an obsession documented by Keynes as early as 1924:[xxviii]

> Each time the franc loses value, the minister of finance is convinced that the fact arises from everything but economic causes. He attributes it to the presence of foreigners in the corridors of the Bourse, to unwholesome and malign forces of speculation. The attitude is rather close to that of the witch doctor who attributes the illness of cattle to the 'evil eye', and the storm to an insufficient quantity of sacrifices made before some idol.

A bridge too far?

The French referendum on EMU on Sunday, September 20, 1992, was decided by the slimmest of majorities: 51 per cent to 49 per cent in favour. While it was an endorsement, it was much feebler than expected. On Monday morning, the markets attacked the franc with full force. They were questioning French commitment to Maastricht, and by early morning the franc was in free-fall as investors bet that Paris didn't have the nerve to defend it after such a narrow endorsement for EMU. Sapin and Trichet were in Washington, attending an IMF meeting. Spending billions of francs within a few hours of opening, the Banque de France officials panicked. They called Sapin and Trichet, waking them in Washington, where it was 3 a.m., and asked them for directions.

After managing things over the phone until the markets closed in Europe, the two Frenchman met the German delegation at the Four Seasons Hotel, where they tried to convince Schlesinger, his deputy Hans Tietmeyer, Finance Minister Theo Waigel, and Waigel's state secretary, Horst Köhler, to publicly declare unlimited support for the franc. But Schlesinger resisted, arguing that the Germans were already fighting their own war against inflation. As it was, the Banque de France was intervening, selling German marks for francs, and this contributed to Germany's surging money supply problem, Schlesinger pointed out.[20] He cited the famous 'Emminger Letter', which the former Bundesbank president Emminger had sent to the Chancellor declaring that he would agree to help support the European currencies, but only as long as it didn't threaten the stability of the mark. There was no reason why the Bundesbank should intervene, Schlesinger said. Trichet persisted, arguing that a public commitment from the Germans would actually obviate the need for intervention, since it would scare off the speculators. Schlesinger, finding Trichet's argument too much of a gamble, did not budge. On Tuesday, Sapin returned to Paris, leaving Trichet alone to bargain against the four-man German delegation.

On Tuesday morning, the Germans prepared to force a devaluation of the franc. But two events saved the franc. Coincidentally, Kohl met Mitterrand the same day, and Mitterrand explained the gravity of the situation. He told Kohl that France would not devalue. If necessary, France would leave the EMS. Kohl did not understand the workings of the markets, but his overriding political passion was European unity, and the German–French relationship was the cornerstone to that unity. He called his former aide, Hans Tietmeyer, and demanded a compromise statement by the two central banks on the mark-franc parity 'within the hour'.[21] xxix

---

[20] In August, Germany's broad indicator for money, M3, had already grown by 9 per cent compared with the previous year, much more than the target set by the Bundesbank.
[21] Later, writing in his memoirs about the meeting with Kohl, Mitterrand talked about 'the attacks which were totally artificial, it was speculation . . . There are a certain number of specialists who are able to move considerable masses of money

The second event was the arrival in Washington of Otmar Issing, the Bundesbank's chief economist, to assist Tietmeyer in convincing the flustered Schlesinger. With their two votes against Schlesinger's, they prevailed on him to accept a public statement of support. At last, the two sides reached a compromise. The Banque de France raised its rates and, simultaneously, the Bundesbank trimmed its rates. On Wednesday, the two sides issued a communiqué saying that the parity rates between the two currencies reflected economic fundamentals and that no changes in that parity were justified. At first, the markets didn't let up.[xxx] Finance minister Michel Sapin warned the speculators that they would be defeated, recalling that during the French Revolution, 'heads had rolled'.[xxxi] Finally, on Thursday, just when the French were on the verge of giving up, the markets relented. News had leaked that the French-German political commitment had impressed George Soros, and that he was now betting against a devaluation.[xxxii]

Over the next month, the markets calmed. But fears about whether the system could hold were enough for politicians and bankers alike to start supporting the idea of a 'core Europe.' Alfons Verplaetse, Governor of the National Bank of Belgium, in a statement that few took seriously, suggested that Germany, the Benelux and France should form a monetary union immediately.[xxxiii] Later in the year, the franc again began to come under pressure. The French economy, battered by high interest rates, was in deep recession.[xxxiv] The markets slowly began taking out loans to buy francs for sale later when the time was ripe.

---

and therefore decide the politics of the world, simply to be able at the end of the day to count their money bags and benefits, which are often considerable.' See Aeschimann and Riché, p. 172. This suspicion of the markets has been a common theme in France. In 1995, prime minister Alain Juppé criticized what he called the 'gnomes of London', after currency markets began speculating against the franc. The speculation came after signs that Juppé would not hold to promises to cut the budget deficit. The *Wall Street Journal Europe* responded in an editorial, saying the minister had shown his dirigiste reflexes by criticizing the way the markets judge 'that which is good and that which isn't.' [It is interesting to note the parallels between the French views and those expressed by Asian leaders, particularly in Malaysia, during the Asian crisis in 1997 and 1998.]

Meanwhile, Trichet was losing control on another front. The recession hit the French banking system hard. High interest rates scared away property investors from buying land with correspondingly high mortgage rates. Property prices fell. This hurt banks which had lent money to the developers. Obtaining lower prices for their property sales, the developers began to default on their loans. Trichet, as head of the Trésor, was responsible for banking supervision, along with the governor of the Banque de France. With no personal banking experience, Trichet was dependent on his subordinates. The problems had a direct effect on the state's revenues. In particular, the state-owned Crédit Lyonnais announced mounting losses. Public documents showed later that Trichet had given an early warning about the banking problems to his minister. But he failed to sound the full alarm, and appeared to underestimate the magnitude of the crisis.[xxxvii] The banks, though warned, did little to clean up their books. Over the next few years, Crédit Lyonnais ran up 100 billion francs in losses from bad debt, making it one of the greatest financial debacles in history involving a single company.[xxxviii] The Trésor was tarnished by other problems. Crédit Foncier de France SA, a state-owned mortgage lender, also ran into trouble under Trichet's watch. Losses reached 10.8 billion francs (1.8 billion dollars) in 1995, forcing the state to bail it out in 1996. Comptoir des Entrepreneurs, another real estate financing company in which the state held a stake, ran up over a billion francs in losses in 1992 and 1993, also requiring a bail-out. These débâcles damaged the reputation of Paris as a financial centre just at the time when the single currency project was increasing competition between it and other centres, including Frankfurt and London. Some critics blamed Trichet for being too preoccupied with EMU to devote attention to the banking sector.[22, xxxix]

---

[22] Christian Noyer, Trichet's protegé, was left to deal with many of the problems. See Chapter 6. Besides the financial problems mentioned above, there were a series of other difficulties. Thomson SA, the state-owned company which holds shares in electronics company Thomson-CSF suffered losses for four years in a row between 1993 and 1996. It was a recipient of billions of francs in subsidies.

Gaffe Alphandéry

Though the Bundesbank began to speed up interest rate cuts in early 1993 to counter a German recession, they weren't fast enough for France. France shadowed the Bundesbank's cuts, but its own economic contraction only worsened. It didn't help that a new Gaullist government had just been elected, led by prime minister Edouard Balladur, with a politically naïve finance minister Edmond Alphandéry. Desperate, they tried to duplicate Bérégovoy's manœuvre of the year before, and they lowered rates on June 21 to slightly below those in Germany. As daring as the rate cuts were, they weren't deep enough for critics. In mid-June, rightist politicians derided what they called the 'social Munich' of the new Gaullist government's *franc fort* policy, blaming it for doing nothing to solve unemployment.[23]

In 1996, the government said that after 15 years under state management, Thomson had accumulated debts of 25 billion francs and had a negative net worth of 6 billion francs. In December 1996, its sale to Lagardere and Daewoo Electronics Corp (a Korean conglomerate) was suspended after an 'independent' privatization committee rejected the terms. The cancellation was justified on the basis that advanced technologies, partly funded by the state, would be passed on to the Koreans, and that the deal did not guarantee enough jobs in France. It was widely seen as a sign of French national prejudice against foreigners, especially Asians. Thomson-CSF, today Europe's biggest defence electronics maker, went on to lose 1.5 billion francs more in 1998. The French state owns 40 per cent of the company, down from 58 per cent in 1997.

---

[23] The term 'social Munich' was clearly carefully chosen. Munich was the location of the meeting at which the Allied powers appeased Hitler over Czechoslavakia. It was marked by historians as a crucial juncture in Hitler's war designs. Encouraged by the appeasement, Hitler became more ambitious. The term, as used by Philippe Séguin, president of the French parliament, the National Assembly, (a gaullist, but outside the government) thus referred to the French government's appeasement, and blind following of, the Bundesbank's policy of high interest rates, conjuring up the shadow of German dominance. It was no coincidence that shortly after Séguin's statement, the leftist politician Jean-Pierre Chevènement conjured up similar images, denouncing the government as the 'Vichyssois of our time'. The fascist Vichy regime which ruled in Paris during World War II collaborated with Hitler. Quotes cited from Aeschimann and Riché. p. 206-207.) The government's monetary policy as forged by Trichet would continue to be criticized from politicians by the left and the right.

Alphandéry reacted defensively. On the eve of a bilateral meeting with the Germans scheduled in Paris on June 25, he appeared to call on the Germans to lower interest rates, saying in a radio interview that reducing unemployment in France depended on rate cuts in Germany. He added that he had arranged a meeting with the Germans to discuss this (in fact, the meeting he referred to had been scheduled for quite some time, and the Germans hadn't planned to discuss rate cuts). For the Germans, it was heresy. Tietmeyer and Waigel cancelled their visit. The markets, already nervous, became more jumpy when negative data on the French economy was released on July 6.[24] On July 7, the franc plunged. The Banque de France intervened on a mammoth scale, but managed to stabilize the franc only for a few days.

On Friday, July 30, with funds still haemorrhaging out of the franc, Trichet's strategy was to hold on at least until the markets closed for the weekend when he could hold an emergency meeting with the Germans.[25] He knew the franc wouldn't be able to hold, and badly needed a deal. He had recently participated in secret meetings with the Germans to try to find a solution, but Schlesinger had blocked any agreement.[26] Kohl, too, had told Balladur that he could not intervene any

---

[24] The data, released by INSEE, predicted decline in GDP of 1.2 per cent for the year.

[25] Intervention by the Banque de France by the end of Thursday reached 27.5 billion dollars, or 150 billion francs, twice the amount that the Bank of England had spent in its failed effort on 'Black Wednesday' the year before to save the pound.

[26] Aeschimann and Riché (pp. 216-225) report an amusing secret meeting in Munich at this time between the French and the Germans. Trichet, Alphandéry, Noyer (Alphandéry's chief of staff), and de Larosière (Banque de France) show up in Munich, but the Germans refuse to meet them at the airport. Not having any marks on them, the French officials were forced to scramble to find a way to exchange francs for marks. The symbolism didn't escape them. 'The Germans are mocking us,' complained de Larosière.

more in what he said were the affairs of the Bundesbank.[27] The best Trichet was able to do was to get the Germans to agree to announce a meeting of the EU's Monetary Committee for that weekend. There, Trichet could meet with Tietmeyer, Schlesinger's more forthcoming deputy. Tietmeyer would also have more power to negotiate a deal, since he was scheduled to replace Schlesinger the following month as president. Traditionally, a meeting of the finance ministers followed Monetary Committee meetings. If only Trichet could work out a deal with Tietmeyer, the ministers would be sure to approve.

During the sitting, Tietmeyer proposed that the EMS band be widened to 6 per cent. But the French delegation, led by Trichet, who presided as Chairman of the committee, refused. They believed this would signify a French defeat. They made three demands. First, the Bundesbank should cut rates. Second, it should intervene without limit to buy the franc. Finally, it should actually keep the francs it acquired through intervention on its balance sheet – and not demand that France buy them back later. 'The fourth demand, Mr. Chairman,' replied Tietmeyer sarcastically, before he rejected them, 'is that Germany must immediately abandon its monetary sovereignty.'[xl]

On Saturday afternoon, bilateral talks between the Germans and French continued. By that evening, Trichet made another proposal: that Germany temporarily leave the EMS. This was justified, he argued, because Germany's unification had caused unusually high interest rates. The other countries shouldn't be made to suffer. The Germans would have accepted this. But then the Dutch, who considered their guilder irrevocably linked to the German currency, said that if the German mark left the system, the guilder would too. They also let slip a secret: that

---

[27] Balladur responded: 'I consider that the German right is the same as the French right, and that in Germany too, exchange rate policy depends on the government, not on the central bank.' Balladur was technically correct. Exchange rate policy did still rest with the government. But the Bundesbank's 'Emminger brief' had established a policy that the Bundesbank could reject any agreement that it felt endangered inflation.

they already had a special agreement with the Germans to keep the two currencies tied to a 1 per cent band of fluctuation – even tighter than the normal 2.5 per cent called for by the EMS. This surprised the other central bankers. If the Dutch and Germans were keeping little secrets of this sort behind the backs of the others, one French commentator asked, what would be happening at the European Central Bank?[xli]

The Belgians, meanwhile, showed themselves open to supporting the French idea that the German mark – and if need be, the guilder too – be cut temporarily from the EMS. But when the Luxembourgers caught wind of this, they also insisted on staying with the Germans, even threatening to break away from their currency union with Belgium if need be. Belgium, not wanting to lose Luxembourg, gave in and said it too would refuse a break with the mark. The Spanish then proposed that France and the other southern European countries form a Latin monetary union. It was an embarrassment to the French, who quickly rejected it.[28]

Trichet's manœuvring had failed. By the end of the meeting, it was obvious that there was no alternative to Tietmeyer's proposal of widening the band. The Germans had suggested a 6 per cent band. But the French were forced to ask for 15 per cent, wide enough so that speculation could not force them out of the band. The currencies could now fluctuate by 30 per cent against each other – 15 per cent on either side of the parity rate – so widely that the system was effectively meaningless. The proposal was accepted. It was a blow to the EMS system, and to French pride. The band remained as wide as this until 1999.

After the decision, speculation against the franc ended, but Trichet persuaded Balladur not to cut rates immediately. That would only increase nervousness in the markets again. On the other hand, Trichet pointed out that long-term interest rates had remained low during the entire débâcle. This indicated the

---

[28] In fact, there were a number of proposals. Trichet, for example, proposed the idea of creating two EMS zones, one around the mark and the other around the franc. This quickly started to look too similar to the Spanish idea, and was dropped.

markets believed the franc enjoyed long-term credibility.[29] That meant that short-term rates should be allowed to come down as well, but he recommended a policy of 'small steps'. In 1994, the economy began to grow again, as did jobs, and much-needed stability settled upon France.

The monetary conversion

In September 1993, Trichet was appointed to become governor of the Banque de France. The Maastricht Treaty contained a German demand that central banks be made independent, and Trichet's task was to manage the bank's transition, by 1994, to independent status. In doing so, he confronted centuries of tradition. Unlike Germany, where the central bank had gone from a government agency during the Nazi regime to a fully independent institution under American occupation forces, the French central bank had gone the other way. In 1806, just three years after he founded the Banque de France, Napoleon had second thoughts about allowing private bankers to control money supply, and wanted government also to have a say. He appointed a governor and two deputy governors to head the bank's governing council.[30] In 1936, the Popular Front extended state control over the bank, ruling that the government would appoint a majority of the governing council members. Finally, in 1945, General de Gaulle nationalized the bank outright. Governors were puppets of the government. Once, in 1984, governor Renaud de la Génière said publicly that France concerned itself 'too rarely' with monetary issues. He was promptly dismissed.[xlii]

Trichet, as director of Trésor, had himself been sceptical of the idea of making the bank independent, since it was the most powerful tool within his department's portfolio. But at Maastricht, he had been forced to assure the Germans that the French would live up to its commitment, and Trichet had been

---

[29] See footnote 12.
[30] See footnote 1.

one of the few in the French delegation that accepted the idea.
The legislative debate on the bank's independence was heated.
Parliamentarians from the left and right denounced the
'denationalization of monetary power'. Even within the ruling
majority, 50 abstained from the final vote for independence, 40
of them Gaullists.

Trichet took the Bundesbank as his prototype. First, he
wanted to change the way the French thought about money,
and move the debate closer to German lines. The Bundesbank
was so strongly supported by the population that it could
actually face down the Bonn government.[31] One of Trichet's
first moves was to create an independent communication
policy. The nine-member Monetary Policy Council (CPM)
divided France into regions for which they would be
responsible – similar to the Bundesbank's decentralized
structure. The members then launched a public offensive,
touring their regions and giving speeches at city halls, union
groups, universities and other constituencies. Trichet began
taking public opinion surveys about the franc and the Banque
de France. With help of a new press department, he scoured the
French media, and personally phoned journalists or editorialists
believed to have misunderstood the bank's policy. He also
organized five-day seminars to help journalists and other
professionals penetrate the complex jargon of the central
banking world – again similar to Bundesbank practice. As at
the Bundesbank, one member of the council was designated
'chief economist', charged with discussing the economy and
the state of the financial markets, and generally instigating
proposals about interest rates.[xliii] In this case, it was Trichet's
loyal deputy governor, Hervé Hannoun.[xliv]

Like Tietmeyer, Trichet gives interviews in which he argues
that government reform, not a change in monetary policy, is the
only way to create more jobs. He advocates free market policies
such as allowing more part-time work and increasing the
flexibility of the labour market.[xlv] Finally, Trichet even tried to
implement a monetary policy strategy based partly on money

---

[31] See chapter 5.

supply targeting – duplicating the Bundesbank's cherished tradition. However, the money supply figures were never reliable enough to guide policy with, a fact Trichet doesn't like to admit. In reality, France was as dependent as ever on the Bundesbank and the franc's exchange rate with the mark in guiding its policy.[32]

The gnome of all gnomes

While at the bank, Trichet continually battled with the political powers. In 1994, Trichet was able to cut rates considerably, and criticism subsided temporarily. But things soon turned sour. In early 1995, Trichet wrote an open letter to Mitterrand requesting that the president moderate public sector wage increases. Chirac, who was running as the opposition candidate for president that year, attacked Trichet, saying 'the governor of the Banque de France is not there to indicate to the government what economic policy it should follow, nor to tell the social partners what they have to do.'[xlvi]

Chirac went on to win the campaign, based on a platform that called into question Trichet's *franc fort* policy. Though he never rejected the policy explicitly, Chirac criticized the powerful 'technicians' who appeared to be ruling the state, and stressed the need for the 'primacy of politics'. Several 'anti-*franc fort*' ideologues had inspired Chirac's campaign. One was Emmanuel Todd, a demographics expert who believed that lower interest rates, and thus higher inflation, were favourable to the youthful and poor sectors of the population because these favoured immediate spending and borrowing, and that the *franc fort* policy was causing a fracture between these disadvantaged portions of society and the more wealthy, élite

---

[32] After the bank's first year of operations, Trichet himself called a fixed growth of money supply an 'internal' objective, adding that uncertainties in the economic cycle and statistical aberrations had made the M3 data 'hardly readable'. M3 supply could oscillate between 0 and 5 per cent over the next four years, he said. But such a wide range effectively includes most of the possibilities of money supply growth, and therefore has little explanatory, or 'targeting' value. M3 as a concept was essentially worthless in the French case. See chapters 5 and 8.

portions of society who favoured low inflation.[33] Chirac emphasized this theme of 'fracture' during his campaign, implying several times that he would seek to temper Trichet's *franc fort* policy. In the end he scored an upset victory against his party rival, Edouard Balladur, who touted Trichet's orthodoxy.

After the new government failed to cut spending in 1995, Trichet was forced to push interest rates up again to stave off speculation against the franc. Though the government eventually about-faced on its budget plans, the high rates depressed business sentiment and growth slowed. Several days before announcing major cuts in the social security system on November 20, finance minister Alain Juppé called Trichet to communicate the details of the ambitious policy. Juppé's hope was that by promising cuts in government spending, Trichet and the Banque de France would keep their side of the bargain by cutting rates. Trichet and the bank complied. Three days before the announcement, they cut rates. Unfortunately, the cut wasn't enough to avoid one of the biggest strikes in France's post-war history. Millions of people took to the streets in Paris to protest the government cuts. Union leaders denounced the government for 'imposing without debate the verdicts of a new Leviathan – the financial markets'.[xlvii]

By January 1996, the economy was deteriorating further, and Trichet and the bank lowered rates sharply. Under constant attack, Trichet again launched a public relations offensive. Seeking to boost a more humanist profile among his compatriots, he even appeared on a poetry programme on television, where he talked of his passion for literature and of his youth when the Senegalese writer and statesman Léopold Sédar Senghor would pay visits to his family in St-Malo. Trichet proceeded to read an extract of a poem by St-Perse.

---

[33] According to Todd's theory, high interest rates and low inflation protected the savings and assets of the aged and more wealthy. Thus, lower rates and higher inflation are considered 'redistributive'. The problem with this theory is that it is very short-term oriented (and thus all the more attractive to politicians). In the long term, of course, higher inflation causes interest rates to go up as lenders become accustomed to the inflation. The wealthy, in turn, will demand a higher return for their assets. The advantages of inflation thus disappear over time.

But by mid-1996, Trichet became even more of a Gaullist whipping boy. On television on July 14, 1996, Chirac blamed Trichet for the Credit Lyonnais' losses. 'There was the director of the Trésor, and there was the Banque de France, which were charged with assuring control. I regret to say that this control wasn't exercised well,' Chirac said. It was a frontal attack on Trichet, who was director of the Trésor at the time when Crédit Lyonnais first ran into trouble. The same evening, Chirac also blasted Trichet for keeping 'interest rates much too high'. Prime minister Juppé joined in, complaining that Trichet's 'policy of small steps' destroyed any jump-start effect that a bigger rate cut might have achieved. 'Economic agents remain expectant, always waiting for the next lowering,' he complained. Juppé wanted Trichet to use the full margin of 15 per cent against the mark, but Trichet held stubbornly to the parity rate. On August 8, the finance minister Jean Arthuis fired another salvo at the banker. He announced the discovery of new material in the Crédit Lyonnais débâcle, and demanded that an investigation be launched. One Gaullist parliamentarian, Philippe Briand, said he 'regretted' having voted for the independence of the bank because 'the economy's vigour depends on the good will of a sovereign banker and his private counsel.'[xlviii]

The markets, seeing Trichet beleaguered with criticism, started selling francs again, worried about Paris' commitment to the Trichet orthodoxy. The government quickly retreated. Juppé declared there was no conflict between the government and Trichet over the goal of a stable currency. Similarly, Arthuis said he had not meant to target Trichet. They had given him his beating; they would now leave him alone. The franc stabilized. By 1997, interest rates on ten-year French bonds moved lower than those of similar US bonds, for the first time in 77 years, and have stayed lower, something Trichet never tires of pointing out. In other words, French companies are enjoying better finance conditions than the US.

What ensued was a period of relative peace. Most of France's mainstream politicians, realizing that Trichet had the power of the markets behind him, finally accepted their defeat. His chief critic, Gaullist leader Philippe Séguin, also seemed to relent.

Indeed, by late 1997, events were to force Chirac and a new socialist government to put aside their differences with Trichet. Just like Louis XIV and his adviser Colbert more than four centuries before, who had used the fiercely independent corsairs from St-Malo to help them in their attack against the Dutch,[34] Chirac's government would now turn to Trichet to help them fight one of their biggest battles yet in the single currency drama – also against the Dutch.

NOTES

[i] *L'Express*. September 16 1993.
[ii] *L'Express*. November 15 1995.
[iii] *Echos*. September 13 1993.
[iv] William Safran, *The French Policy*. Longman, New York: 1991. p. 201, 202.
[v] Philippe Meyer, *Dans mon pays lui-même* (Paris: 1994) cited in Connolly, p. 295.
[vi] *Institutional Investor*, May 1997: Rick Butler, *The Trials of Trichet*.
[vii] While France differed from Germany on its inflation performance, it was closer to the performance of US and Japan. The same can be said of exchange rate developments. In 1998, the franc was at the same level with the dollar as it was thirty years before, despite short-term fluctuations. The mark meanwhile, has steadily increased significantly in value against both currencies.
[viii] Éric Aeschimann and Pascal Riché. *La Guerre de Sept ans*. Calmann-Lévy, 1996: Paris. p. 34-39.
[ix] This was less than fair to Trichet. Indeed, when Bérégovoy took office in May, 1988, he pushed for a rate cut within a week of taking office. The central bank, under Jacques de Larosière, had opposed the move. In July, Bérégovoy bullied through another cut of .25 per cent. Trichet had argued for a cut more modest, of an eighth of a percentage point. Aeschimann and Riché. pp. 34-39.
[x] Philippe Bauchard, *Deux ministres trop tranquilles* (Paris, 1994). p. 152. Cited in Connolly, p. 306. Bauchard also writes: 'Trichet obeys Tietmeyer – quite simply, he obeys him.'
[xi] See also *Le Monde*. January 13 1990. Trichet was also one of those behind the creation of the European Bank for Reconstruction and Development in 1990.

---

[34] Colbert used St-Malo as the focus of his efforts to build up a great fleet for France which would help defend French interests abroad. In 1655, it was even decided that the crew for the king's flotille du Ponant should be made up entirely of 'Malouins', as the corsairs from St-Malo were known, since they were the most tried and tested sailors. The government encouraged them in their pirate raids on foreign vessels, with the Dutch as one of the principal targets. But the Malouins, like Trichet, were fiercely independent, and were often the cause of great hand-wringing in Paris.

[xii] Aeschimann and Riché, p. 59-63.

[xiii] The spread between ten-year German and French bond yields began to close in 1990. It closed altogether for most of 1993, but then opened again between 1994 and 1995. It closed again in 1996.

[xiv] Aeschimann and Riché, pp. 59-63.

[xv] In 1991, German inflation had reached 4 per cent. On August 15, led by its hawkish new president Helmut Schlesinger, the Bundesbank began to raise interest rates steadily.

[xvi] Aeschimann and Riché, p. 59-63.

[xvii] See *Die Zeit*. December 12, 1996. 'Frank und fröhlich'.

[xviii] *Die Woche*. November 14, 1997.

[xix] Aeschimann & Riché, p. 104.

[xx] Remarks in televised referendum debate, 'Aujourd'hui l'Europe', TF 1, 3 September 1992. Cited with help from Connolly, p. 141-2.

[xxi] Even during the post-WWII era, the Germans hadn't elected a Chancellor directly out of office until Helmut Kohl's defeat in 1998. Until Gerhard Schröder, all new chancellors had been brought to power by a mere reshuffling in the governing coalition, independent of the results of popular elections.

[xxii] Though a bit outdated, Safran's book also provides an excellent overview of the French political system and national identity. He cites political scientists Gabriel Almond and Sidney Verba, who refer to France's refusal to 'marry' the 20th century, and Jesse R. Pitts, who writes of France's 'dilinquent society'.

[xxiii] Forsa survey, April 1997.

[xxiv] *Frankfurter Allgemeine Zeeitung*. April 24. 'Ein Land wie jedes andere in Europa.'

[xxv] Hans Tietmeyer und Dieter Lindenlaub. 'Nicolaus Oresme und die geldpolitischen Probleme von heute,' in *Die Handeslblatt-Bibliothek 'Klassiker der Nationalökonomie.'* (Verlag Wirtschaft und Finanzen GmbH, 1996).

[xxvi] Connolly, p. 409, cites *FAZ* 4 September 1992 article. 'Deflation – eine Chieffre der Besorgnis: Zur Wirtschaftsdebatte in Frankreich'.

[xxvii] Ulrich Schneider, economist at Deutsche Bank and head of the bank's shadow committee of the ECB – created specifically with the goal of debating and criticizing decisions made by the ECB – calls it the Bundesbank's *Pravda*, after the official newspaper of the Soviet government. 'You have to read between the lines to understand what it is really trying to say.'

[xxviii] French criticism of statements by leading politicians, see Eric le Boucher, 'Bonn: l'exploitation de la 'peur l'Alemagne' dans la campagne irrite beaucoup . . .', in *Le Monde*, 4 September 1992. Cited in Connolly, p. 407, along with other sources, including WSJ, Brussels 2 September 1992 'With Friends Like These.'

[xxix] *Financial Times*, 11 September 1992.

[xxx] *Financial Times*, 6 January 1992.

[xxxi] Cited in Connolly: p. 170: Preface to French edition of 'A Tract on Monetary Reform' (London, 1924).

[xxxii] Aeschimann and Riché, p. 151.

[xxxiii] Gabriel Milesi. *Le Roman de l'Euro*, p. 42-45.

[xxxiv] Cited in Connolly, p. 179. *Financial Times*, 24 September 1992.

xxxv Connolly, p. 181. Cites market sources that estimated that the Bundesbank had loaned 130-140 billion francs, out of a total intervention of 160 billion francs. That was much more than the 10 billion pounds of intervention in favour of the sterling the week before.

xxxvi *Financial Times*, 26/27 September (again cited in Connolly).

xxxvii This was the tragedy of Connolly's argument in 'The Rotten Heart of Europe'. Because of his rigidly euro-sceptic views, he blasted anyone who supported EMU. His criticism of Trichet, one of EMU's most passionate supporters, was among the harshest. But as future events were to show, Trichet's franc fort policy was right. French growth picked up and would indeed be among the strongest within core Europe in the late 1990s. France would also benefit from lower interest rates. Unemployment would stay high, but Trichet has argued continually that this is due to the inflexibility of the labour force – a view widely held by establishment economists.

xxxviii Le Nouvel Economiste, No. 1063, September 20, 1996.

xxxix See *Le Nouvel Observateur*. August 15-21, 1996, Le Nouvel Economiste. No. 1063. September 20, 1996. See Le Figaro, 16 March 1995, and Connolly, p. 216. Between 1988 and 1993, Jean-Yves Haberer, president of Crédit Lyonnais and his aides pursued an adventurous policy of massive growth in order to make the bank the largest in the world. It was another example of the French drive for prestige. They had bet that interest rates would come down and the economy would accelerate, and prepared balances in 1991, 1992 and 1993 that did not properly reflect the huge risks undertaken.

In 1994, parliamentary investigations began into the activities of Jean-Yves Haberer, the bank's president and a friend of Mitterrand. In 1995, massive losses were discovered, and the government announced a 50 billion franc rescue plan. Alain Juppé, foreign minister in the Balladur government, said: 'You have a mighty department in the finance ministry – La direction du Trésor – that propels its best officials to the head of our big nationalized banks. How do you imagine that the controller can control someone who has emerged from its own ranks?' A number of other sources blamed the close ties between Haberer, Bérégovoy, and other Énarques, for example Trichet, as being the true cause of the problem.

xl *La Tribune*, Wednesday, April 3, 1996.

xli This quote, first cited by Connolly, was confirmed by some of those present at the meeting.

xlii Milesi, p. 64.

xliii Aeschimann and Riché, p. 199.

xliv Hannoun refused to comment on a question in an interview about whether he was offered the directorate job that Christian Noyer was eventually assigned. French officials say he was offered the job first, but refused because he did not want to go to Frankfurt. A *Le Monde* journalist contends it is because he is Jewish. Strauss-Kahn said it was because of 'family reasons'.

xlv The two deputy governors are absolved of 'regional responsibilities'.

xlvi *Le Monde*, April 30, 1996.

xlvii Option Finance No. 411 July 8, 1996.

xlviii Pierre Bourdieu. 12 September, during a protest at the Paris train station, Gare de Lyon.

xlix Miles, p. 129.

CHAPTER FIVE

The Monetary Jesuit

On the eastern edge of the southern German city of Würzburg sits the magnificent palace of the Würzburg bishops, the Residenz. At the time of its construction, it was supposed to symbolize the wealth of the German bishops and prove that they could hold their own with Versailles and Vienna. Though Würzburg remains less famous, it succeeded. It boasts the world's largest fresco, in which Europe is represented by a Greek goddess enthroned above a globe to symbolize the continent's status as ruler of the world.

In 1945, an Allied aerial attack on Würzburg destroyed much of the old city. A major rail junction in Germany, Würzburg had been targeted for obliteration. But the fresco withstood the tremors. Painted on a large, vaulted ceiling, the fresco defied the critics who had claimed that it would one day collapse, because of its lack of underpinning. The architect was Balthasar Neumann, once an unknown, humble craftsman of church bells and weapons, who developed into one of the most accomplished architects of eighteenth century Europe. Neumann was so confident of his vault's stability that he offered to fire a battery of artillery under it.

A shy, nine-year-old boy named Otmar Issing had looked on at the Allied bombing at the time, and had marvelled at the vault's survival despite the destruction of one of the palace's wings. The son of a restaurant owner who fought first in France, then in Russia, during the Second World War, Issing remains proud of the Residenz. 'I'm a local patriot. The older I get, the more I love it,' he says, referring to the splendour of the emperor's room with the fresco by one of the greatest artists of the age, the Venetian Giovanni Battista Tiepolo. After the War, Issing's high-school and college years in Würzburg were notable only for their tranquillity. He started his career as an unknown economist, but within a few decades he too would be given an architectural assignment as challenging as Neumann's: in June 1998, shortly after the ECB took up operations, Issing was appointed its chief economist, thereby becoming the lead architect of a monetary policy superstructure that would challenge the Federal Reserve's role as the most powerful bank in the world.

Though it has never been made explicit, the ECB is Europe's only hope of dethroning the Americans from their place as rulers of the financial world. Issing's job was to restore the Greek goddess Europa to her rightful place, just as she sits in the fresco in Würzburg. In many ways, the single currency project was being painted on an audacious, unsupported vault – and there were plenty of critics predicting its downfall. Issing's job was to make sure that the euro could withstand the tremors caused by potential conflict – even if it meant firing a battery of cannons beneath it.

Issing's first major assignment: governing money in unified Germany

Issing has become accustomed to the role of architect. Back in 1990, as an economics professor at the University of Würzburg, the Bundesbank directorate appointed him chief economist, replacing Helmut Schlesinger, who had been appointed vice president of the bank. Schlesinger and Hans Tietmeyer were impressed by Issing's work at one of Germany's most important think-tanks, the Council of Economic Experts, and had lobbied him to take the job.

The chief economist's job was to assess the economy, check for signs of looming inflation and propose countermeasures. As such, the position was also known as 'chief navigator'. At his disposal was an impressive team of economists who made up the bank's research division. Like the council's other members, the chief economist had only one vote on policy decisions, but he had special power because he set the agenda in the council debates. He was *de facto* the most influential member of the council. Although relatively unknown, Issing had published a standard textbook on economics which was used throughout Germany. He seemed to share the orthodoxy of the Bundesbank – to guard the mark's stability hawkishly by stamping out inflation. The council therefore entrusted him with the task.

In the early 1990s, the bank's chief navigator was like the captain of an ocean-liner in treacherous waters. Germany was as sturdy and secure a ship as they come. But it had taken on board a heavy burden – East Germany and its economy of 16 million people, more than 30 per cent of whom had lost their jobs. Far from being the strong economy that Soviet propaganda had boasted – sixth largest in the world – the East German economy collapsed like a house of cards. With few alternatives, Issing, supported by Schlesinger, decided to hold a steady course dictated by previous Bundesbank policy. A policy based on gauging money supply had served the Bundesbank well in the past. It could do so again, they agreed.

A rocky boat ride

As the 1991 Maastricht negotiations were being wrapped up, the German economy was quickly slipping out of control. Germany's unification the year before had incurred tremendous costs. Early wage agreements with eastern German workers were negotiated to match levels in western Germany, even though east German workers were only half as productive as their west German counterparts.[1] Instead of saving their money, they spent it on expensive consumer goods in an effort to catch up with their western compatriots. This spending spree sparked an economic boom in Germany. It also drove up prices. Inflation jumped to 4 per cent by early 1992, double the Bundesbank's preferred ceiling of 2 per cent.

---

[1] Productivity = the value of goods produced per hour.

Alarm bells rang for the Germans. They had suffered under the high inflation of the 1920s, and they were determined to avoid a repetition. During the First World War, Germany ran up an enormous debt to finance its war on the European continent. After being defeated, it was shouldered with weighty 'reparations'. The Weimar Republic began printing reams of Reichsmarks in order to pay off the debt, but inflated the mark to disastrous levels. The value of savings held by millions of German families were eroded. Wheelbarrows full of banknotes were required to afford a loaf of bread. Frustration and disillusionment helped pave the way for Hitler's National Socialists.[2] But the Nazis led Germany into a second expensive war. After 1945, the mark was again worthless, to the point where American cigarettes became a major form of exchange. Fear of inflation was therefore deeply ingrained in the German psyche. Since the currency reform of 1948, a steady mark had been serving the Germans well. In the 1950s, economic growth was so robust that the era became known as the 'economic miracle'. Soon German society was to become as prosperous as any western nation. With inflation suddenly on the increase again in 1990, the Bundesbank came under domestic pressure to stamp it out.

The Bundesbank's strategy since the 1970s had been based on monetarism. Like Friedman, its economists believed that price developments depended on the amount of money in circulation. The danger of inflation grew when money supply increased too much. To reduce the money supply, the Bundesbank raised the interest rates it charged to private banks wanting to take out loans. As the cost of borrowing became more expensive, the banks borrowed less. The banks, in turn, had less to lend to businesses. The banks preferred to deposit money with the central bank, not borrow it. This funnelled money out of the economy.

Higher interest rates also discouraged companies and con-

---

[2] 'Nothing made the German people – this must always be called into memory – so embittered, so filled with hatred, so ripe for Hitler, as inflation,' Issing has said.

sumers planning to borrow money to finance production or take out a mortgage on a new home. Some would decide the cost of borrowing wasn't worth it. In sum, economic activity cooled down. Inflation was kept under control.

The practice of controlling the amount of money circulating in the economy, though simple in its logic, was revolutionary when Schlesinger first introduced it in 1974. Milton Friedman had been preaching this creed in the US for decades, but the US Federal Reserve mistrusted the Chicago economist. His views were unconventional for the era, which was still dominated by Keynesian adherents. Helmut Schlesinger, while chief economist of the Bundesbank, was the first to transform Friedman's theory into practice.

Friedman had argued that money supply should grow at a certain rate per year, depending on how much the economy demanded. He even argued that a central bank wasn't really needed. Rather, the government only needed to pass a 'rule' which would adjust the money supply accordingly every year. But Friedman was thinking of an economist's 'perfect world'. In reality, any economy is imperfect, its momentum always fluctuating. Sometimes this is due to human unpredictability, sometimes to other, natural factors. When OPEC hiked the price of oil in the 1970s, inflation swept the industrialized world, sparking a temporary demand for *more* money. Nations going to war see the disappearance of large sections of their male workforce, as men move to the battlefront. The economy shrinks, and requires *less* money to manage its transactions. If governments step up spending to finance the war, the economy requires *more* money.

Adjusting Friedman's policy to the real world, Schlesinger knew a central bank was necessary to make rational decisions on how much the money supply needed to grow per year. According to his plan, the Bundesbank would assess the economy's performance each December, and decide how much the money supply should increase the following year. The policy was immediately successful when implemented in 1974. By stamping out inflation, the Bundesbank ensured that the mark held on to its purchasing power longer than other currencies.

Investors were willing to pay more for the mark, and therefore its value continued to rise against that of other currencies. But because the mark was tied to other currencies within the 'snake', Germany was forced to revalue the currency several times – by adjusting the parity rate at which it traded against other European currencies. German monetary policy became the model for the world.

For twenty-five years, Schlesinger's strategy remained intact, albeit with some minor technical changes. For example, as the financial sector grew more complex, he recognized that a broader definition of money supply was needed for his compass. He therefore introduced what he called 'M3', which consisted of cash in circulation, the money in checking deposit accounts, and in other types of short-term deposit accounts.[3] Additionally, in 1979, he decided that a specific monetary target was too confining, given unpredictable factors that might slow down or speed up an economy's need for money, and introduced a money growth 'corridor', usually in the order of 4 to 6 per cent a year.

Issing holds tight

When Issing took over in 1990 and needed to restrain sudden inflationary pressures and calm domestic alarm, he followed Schlesinger's rigid targeting of money supply. Unification was his first challenge. To rein in the soaring money supply it had caused, Issing, supported by Schlesinger, kept pushing the Bundesbank council to hike up interest rates. By July 1992 the council had pushed up its Lombard rate[i] to 9.5 per cent, a record, and was still raising the bank's 'Repo' rate.[4]

---

[3] In 1999, the ECB would widen the definition of Europe's M3 to include deposits in money market funds. In its first annual report, the ECB published a breakdown of the value of Europe's M3 in November, 1998, as follows: Currency (7 per cent), overnight deposits (32 per cent), deposits redeemable at notice of up to three months (27 per cent), deposits with an agreed maturity of up to two years (20 per cent) and money market fund shares and money market paper (7 per cent), repurchase agreements (5 per cent) and debt securities with a maturity of up to two years (2 per cent).

But money supply kept climbing. In July, the rate of annual inflation moderated to 3.3 per cent from 4.0 per cent, letting Issing and his colleagues hold off on hiking interest rates again. As late as August, Issing suspected that the increasing money supply meant that the economy was about to witness a boom, although data was now showing it was in fact slowing markedly. 'I don't see a recession,' he said in mid-August, 1992. 'I see a good chance of a lasting recovery,'[ii] Issing explains why the Bundesbank kept rates so high despite the sluggish economy:

> The inflation rate was more than the Germans and the Bundesbank could tolerate. You've got to see things in the perspective of Germany's experience and priorities of the population. Our job was first of all to stop the inflation rate from rising further. There were many critics who said [the effects of reunification] were exceptional and that we should forget about inflation for a while. But that is not acceptable for a central bank. The Bundesbank fought for credibility over decades, and we saw that this credibility helped us very much during reunification. Despite the huge debt that the German government took on, investors didn't lose trust in the Bundesbank, and we were able to achieve low long-term interest rates again.

---

[4] The *Securities Repurchase* rate ('repo') was the rate used by the Bundesbank in providing credit to financial institutions. The Bundesbank would demand this rate from banks borrowing money from it, and the rate generally guided overall market rates. The *Lombard* rate was awarded by the central banks to institutions seeking to deposit funds at the bank, and generally set a ceiling for interest rates. The *discount* rate was the interest rate charged on overnight loans to financial institutions, and set a floor for interest rates. The ECB would later be based on this model. Its main rate would be called the 'refinancing' rate, its ceiling rate the 'marginal lending facility' and its floor rate the 'deposit facility.' By this time, Issing had been able to gauge how money circulated in the East German economy. The problem wasn't too vexing, however, given that the East German economy was barely a tenth the size of the West German economy, and thus money developments in the region only modestly affected the overall German money supply. Problems would occur later, however, as investment streamed into the East German economy to take advantage of government sanctioned tax write-off privileges (to lure investors east).

By September, however, Germany's rates had become intolerable for the rest of Europe. Unable to bear the economic consequences of such high interest rates, Italy and Britain, the third and fourth largest European economies, faltered. They fell out of the EMS, and sharply devalued their currencies. Italy's lira dropped by 30 per cent against the German mark. The lower prices of imports from Italy and Britain helped reduce inflation danger in Germany, but at a tremendous price. German companies were hopelessly underpriced by British and Italian competitors, and exports to these countries plunged almost overnight. 'From one day to the next, the Italian market, which for many German firms was decisive, just fell apart. This left deep scars in the German economy, there is no question,' Issing says. Just as Schlesinger's German-focused policies had caused chaos in New York and Europe during the 1980s, and had eventually forced an about-face in the Bundesbank's policies, now Issing too was forced to pay the price of narrowly following Germany's self interest. The cost of not taking foreign conditions into account was a recession. The reason for keeping rates high – inflationary fears – disappeared, and Issing had no choice but to abandon his high interest rate policy.

Issing reasoned that inflation and money supply were both likely to decline sharply in the coming months, and so aggressively pushed the Bundesbank to lower rates. By October, however, money supply was still growing by 10 per cent compared to the same month a year before. The economy had, meanwhile, descended into ther deepest recession in Germany's post-war history. It was the opposite of what was supposed to happen. Economic activity was contracting, and by rights, money supply should be decreasing. But it wasn't.

With money supply still rising, the Bundesbank council abandoned the Bundesbank's discredited money supply strategy, and voted to cut interest rates anyway. In February 1993, it cut rates again. Various theories, most without backing, began to circulate about what was influencing the money growth. Some speculated that marks were increasing their circulation in Eastern Europe. But the money supply data for January, published after the Bundesbank's February decision, suddenly contracted by 2.4 per cent, undershooting the Bundesbank's new goal for the year of 4.5 per cent to 6.5 per cent. Confusion grew.

Predictably, many German economists heaped criticism on Issing and his money targeting strategy. Issing conceded that it had suffered a loss of credibility, but insisted there was no alternative. With his eyes already set on European monetary union, he said the same would be true for monetary policy conducted by the future ECB.[iii] The alternative, Issing said, was for the Bundesbank to give up tracking money supply altogether: But 'this would be like a sea voyage without a compass. No one would be able to identify an appropriate level of interest rates,' he said. In a given year, the money supply might not be linked with inflation, but over a course of several years, it would be, he maintained.

The problem, of course, was that money supply had effectively become useless for guiding interest rate policy. Controlling money supply was more vexing than it first appeared. Lenders and borrowers of money can suddenly be fickle. They can burst with confidence or flee in panic, often irrationally. For example, Christoph Zwermann, a trader at Sal. Oppenheim, a bank that has offices just a few blocks away from the ECB, keeps a calendar pinned up by his desk listing the dates of full moons. A computer analysis based on past financial data reveals a negative correlation between the mark and the yen on full moons. His computer graphic shows how the market can be consistently traded accordingly. He and thousands of other traders have determined that it works. The markets, constantly on the search for 'trends', find the most bizarre reasons to turn from optimist to pessimist within minutes. They can speed up or slow down their lending or borrowing habits at whim. None of this can be detected by the central bank, at least immediately. If data reveals that money is growing faster or circulating more quickly than expected, the central bank isn't told why. Thus the faster circulation could be a temporary phenomenon, or could be one for the mid-term, or for several years. Money can be leaked abroad, or come cascading in from other countries, attracted by higher interest rates or scared away by the fear of inflation. Even if the Bundesbank knew what sort of money supply development would be best for the German economy, these outside factors made it increasingly difficult to stick to its targets. Since the Bundesbank had introduced its money targeting system, it had missed its goals at least 50 per cent of the time, sometimes considerably.

The US abandons money supply targeting

Keynes, in his *Treatise on Money*, likened the central bank's task of controlling money supply to keeping the water in a reservoir at a steady level. Besides the water that the central bank poured into it, there was an array of other factors disrupting the water level, for example, natural rainfall, evaporation, leakage and the habits of the users of the system.[iv] As William Greider wrote in a book on the US Federal Reserve: 'In Keynes's reservoir, the waters were always roiled and choppy, giving off confusing signals. Sometimes, the water level heaved and tossed so violently that not even the reservoir keepers were sure what was happening.'[v] By the mid-1980s, a confused and queasy US Federal Reserve abandoned strict monetarism as practised by the Bundesbank. Implemented by Chairman Paul Volcker in the early 1980s, the strategy had proved unworkable. At the beginning of the 1980s, the US underwent substantial deregulation in the financial sector. Fewer controls on money investments meant that the various valves in the reservoir – through which money was pumped in or drained out – were constantly changing in size and number. The US economy was also more diverse and dynamic than Germany's. It could adjust to the global economy more quickly, as attested by its transformation over a decade from reliance on industrial machinery and manufacturing to concentration on computers, software, telecommunications and financial services. Money flowed quickly from one industry to another, and circulated at various speeds depending on industry's needs. Financial services, such as banking and fund management, were also becoming more complex. All of this made the connection between money supply and inflation increasingly tenuous.

While Volcker maintained that money supply was a key aggregate to watch, he was forced to incorporate other economic indicators, too. Data such as housing starts, industrial production and the consumer price index, were quicker gauges of how the real economy and inflation were developing.

It was an eclectic approach, but one that the Federal Reserve was well equipped to handle. The Fed was the only other central bank that could serve as an alternative model for the Bundesbank (indeed, after World War II, US occupying forces had constructed the Bundesbank in the image of the Federal Reserve) and the Fed's relinquishing of money supply targeting left the Bundesbank alone in its practice.

The other powerful central bank of the world, that of Japan, was also reeling under the impact of uncontrollable events. In the early 1990s, the economy entered a deep recession. After years of booming growth, the economy's so-called bubble finally burst. Regardless of the bank's policy, the Japanese economy would not be able to climb out of the doldrums. Most other central banks in the world were merely glorified exchange boards. Whether in Europe or elsewhere, they usually pegged their currencies to the mark or the US dollar, and were reluctant to pursue an independent monetary course.

But the Bundesbank didn't want to admit that it, the emperor of European monetary practice, had no clothes. The bank knew that if it admitted that it was moving to an eclectic approach, its prestige both at home and in Europe would take a beating. By renouncing money supply, the Bundesbank would renounce the cover it had used to justify its policies to its population and other nations, and which protected it from criticism when its policies caused suffering. That cover was one reason why the Federal Reserve Chairman Paul Volcker introduced money supply targeting in 1979 to control rampant inflation. As Charles Schultze, the chairman of the President's Council of Economic Advisors, noted at the time:

In theory, the Fed could have kept on raising the bejesus out of the interest rates, but that's what it couldn't do politically. The beautiful thing about this new policy was that as interest rates kept going up, the Fed could say, 'Hey, ain't nobody here but us chickens. We're not raising interest rates, we're only targeting the money supply.' This way they could raise the rates and nobody could blame them.[vi]

A deeper truth was that although Issing had demonstrably backed the money supply strategy, he had already been incorporating other factors in pursuance of a much more pragmatic approach. Indeed, Issing was considered, and admired for being more of a pragmatist than Schlesinger. He gained such credibility during his tenure as chief economist at the Bundesbank that he was never outvoted, and in 1993 even led the Bundesbank majority to vote for rate cuts despite president Schlesinger's reluctance. Issing's role as internal leader of the Bundesbank on monetary policy was, for him. crucial:

> It is the function of the chief economist, whoever it is, to pre-pare the decisions and to present the analysis so that there is an accord within the council. It is a continuous process. He has to present the analysis twice a month, and he has to stay credible the whole time. There are many meetings, many clever people who confront him, and in the end they each have one vote. We're not talking about winning a one-time vote. It is about the development of a common thought process. Let me put it this way: If someone is in this position, and he's not developing a line of thought, not convincing in his arguments, not providing the substance needed, and not portraying them in a consistent way over time, then he's the wrong person.

But the Bundesbank's secretive approach to its policy making gave it a mystical air. If private banks, which had developed large research teams, caught on that the Bundesbank was moving to an eclectic approach, they could issue their own forecasts of economic growth and inflation, challenging the Bundesbank's own estimates.[5] The markets could 'know' as much as the Bundesbank, which would be a fatal blow to its credibility.

Issing also had an ulterior motive for his obsession with hiking rates. He wanted to compensate for what he saw as irresponsible government and wage policy. The government and employers' federations had been generous in East Germany, allowing wage rates to increase by 4 to 5 per cent per year. Deficit spending had increased considerably, and value added taxes were being increased to finance even more spending in 1993. The government was also subsidizing investments in Eastern Germany by offering to waive interest payments on borrowing, meaning that high interest rates were not scaring away investors as intended. This was all tampering with the Bundesbank's desire for a smooth link between money and inflation. Developments in the East German economy were already unpredictable enough. Such incentives made assumptions about the appropriate level of money supply even more difficult.

Olaf Sievert, a former member of the Bundesbank central council, says that Issing was the most adamant on the Bundesbank council about countering wage hikes and other inflationary policies pursued by Bonn, such as tax rises. Sievert, a strict monetarist, argued in council meetings that money growth should be kept constant – even if a high wage settlement would soak up part of the nation's money supply, leaving less money over for other purposes such as investment. Keeping money supply constant could mean slower growth, but Sievert – a self-declared monetarist 'hawk' – was determined to make these economic actors pay the price of their inflationary actions. Issing, however, was even tougher, Sievert recalls. Issing would seek to *reduce* money supply in an attempt to punish the actors for their inflationary actions. This way, even less money would be left over after a high wage round, meaning that a recession was almost pre-programmed. 'I assumed that economic actors,

---

[5] Private banks do not have the expertise to analyse the Bundesbank's complex money supply data as efficiently as the Bundesbank's hundreds of statisticians and economists. But other economic data is easier to access and analyse, and private banks and institutions could arguably synthesize these into general predictions of inflation just as efficiently.

such as labour unions and government were free to make their own decisions,' says Sievert. 'Issing wanted to counter those decisions.'

In short, Issing was launching a central bank crusade against government policies he personally opposed. Instead of accommodating government policies by funnelling the economy more money, he actually tightened the money tap. These policies did not merely cancel each other out, they were counter-productive.

For many European critics at the time, a booming economy, which created jobs, albeit at the cost of slightly higher than desirable inflation, would have been preferable to the recession initiated by Issing. Jean-Claude Juncker, prime minister of Luxembourg, called Issing's actions at the time 'a grave mistake'.

But the Bundesbank's strategy was written in stone. What's more, empirical research had convinced Issing that low inflation in the long term was the best guarantor of economic growth.

The economic success of Germany in the post-war era reveals the economic logic behind low inflation. Price stability helped German businesses gain confidence in the future. They were able to plan better, and could make efficient decisions about what sort of investments to make. If they wanted to build a factory or design a car, they knew that costs of production would not increase significantly over the long term, which helped them specialize in goods that enjoyed a quality edge against their competitors. In other countries, higher inflation forced companies to think more short-term. Fearing that the value of their investments could be reduced considerably over time, they were more reluctant to invest. If they did invest, they were more likely to demand immediate returns. Cars and factories would be built, but they would be built more cheaply. The low inflation also helped lower the cost of borrowing for German companies. German and foreign investors were keen to invest their money in German assets, because they knew inflation would not eat away at their value. They were willing to invest in such assets even at lower rates of interest. Thus, a major German company could issue bonds, or borrow money from the bank, at lower rates of interest than its foreign competitors.

The Bundesbank's independence was a key factor in its succesful fight against inflation. Other central banks were influenced by their governments and could be bullied into accepting higher inflation. Governments, wanting to boost economic growth before elections, put a premium on short-term policies. They could pressure their central bank to lower interest rates and inject vast amounts of money into the economy to stimulate growth and job creation. But this created inflation.

For Issing, no conditions warranted that interest rates be lowered simply to improve economic growth. That, in his view, would be short-term thinking. Labour unions and businesses would soon catch on, and link their wage and prices accordingly, expecting not only more economic growth, but inflation along with it. A vicious spiral of inflation would begin. Like Friedman, Issing believed economic growth could be best sustained in the long run by a moderate pace dictated by low-inflation.

To this day, Issing stands by his policy. He underscores that inflation rates in 1995 were reduced to 2 per cent from about 5 per cent in 1992. Issing knew that as long as inflation was running higher than the Bundesbank's desired ceiling of 2 per cent, he would maintain popular German support for higher interest rates. True, other countries might be fuming, but Germany's interests were being served.

However, the Issing-led Bundesbank policy also dealt a lethal blow to the European Monetary System. After the rate increases in 1992, Italy and Britain had been forced out. France also tottered, managed to stay within the band for another year, but was ultimately also defeated. Schlesinger, who had since become president of the Bundesbank, became weary of intervening in the currency markets to support other currencies. The Bundesbank sold tens of billions of marks of its reserves over the third quarter of 1992 alone to support the EMS. By 1993, pressure increased again on the Irish pound, the British pound, and the French franc. Finally, as discussed in the previous chapter, Germany and its neighbours agreed to increase the EMS band to 15 per cent.

Otmar Issing, member of the Executive Board of the European Central Bank

These were tough times for Issing. In the ensuing years, the question of money supply would continue to bedevil the Bundesbank. During his ECB confirmation hearings in May 1998, Issing was asked which decisions in his career had been the most important. Notably, he shied away from drawing attention to the controversial policy that had so alarmed Europe in 1992. Rather, he chose to elaborate on a more mundane year, 1996. German money supply had expanded quickly in the first months of 1996, widely overshooting the corridor of 4 per cent to 7 per cent growth. But all the other indicators showed low inflation and weak economic growth. Again, Issing was forced to abandon Bundesbank tradition. Seeing no way to reconcile the contradictions, the Bundesbank cut the Discount and Lombard rates by 50 basis points.[6] The Bundesbank's reasoning for its move – an expectation that monetary expansion would weaken in the near future – managed to convince both the public and the financial markets that the Bundesbank was holding to its traditional line.

In reality, it marked another retreat from the monetarist method. Under Issing's theory, monetary expansion should have been a warning of upcoming inflation, a so-called *leading* indicator. But now, in effect, Issing had conceded that money supply could be dependent on economic developments 'a *trailing* indicator: if the economy was in the dumps, it meant that money supply would begin deflating. It eventually did. In other words, targeting the money supply was the exact opposite of what was required.[7] Though Issing remained faithful to

---

[6] 100 basis points = one percentage point.
[7] With the accelerated deregulation of financial services in Europe during the early and mid-1990s, money supply developments became even more unpredictable than before. Consumers and businesses were constantly changing the way they used their money. If the Bundesbank lowered short-term interest rates, in the hope of sparking more lending, economic actors could switch their savings into long-term savings accounts where rates of return were relatively high. This would move more money out of the short-term accounts that the Bundesbank considered in its money supply measurement. If the bank raised rates, economic actors could decide to move this money back. In other words, money supply could either expand or decrease in the opposite direction to the one that the Bundesbank wanted.

money supply targeting, he admits he swallowed a dose of hard reality:

> I won't say it was a watershed, because then it would make me seem like a Saul who transformed into Paul when he finally saw the light. That wasn't the case. Rather, it was a continuation of a process that began when I first entered the bank. Reality is so multifaceted that it can't be captured in academic illustrations on a blackboard. In the classroom, you can control things, and enter data into formulas. Unfortunately, reality isn't like that. On the other hand, the Bundesbank chose a money supply strategy in 1975 and did well with it. Her credibility was in large part connected with it. So the problem was explaining to the public why we were deviating from that strategy, although we weren't giving it up and didn't want to give it up. I was convinced that the money supply development should come back under control, that it would come back into our estimates of where it should be. But I will never forget the first few months of that year, how the money supply outgrew our corridor by 20 per cent. Many people didn't take me seriously. They smiled at me when I said, no, I'm convinced that it will come back down. By the end of the year, the money supply had approached the corridor and in 1997 we met our target.[8]

Despite the contradictions in his method, and the ever increasing number of hoops he was having to jump through in order to justify his stand to the German nation, Issing remained true to money supply. But alternative methods popped up elsewhere on the continent. The Bank of England introduced a system of direct inflation targeting, and a growing number of economists were saying this was a more efficient way of taming inflation. Like the Americans, the

---

[8] In fact, developments were less clear than Issing makes them out to be. Although money supply did not continue growing at 20 per cent over the target, by the end of the year it was still far above the Bundesbank's corridor.

Bank of England looked at developments such as wage agreements, import prices, prices of raw materials and government tax polices to estimate in which direction overall inflation was headed. Money supply would also be reviewed, but since the link between money and inflation had become vague and fleeting, it was relegated to one factor among many. For the Germans, this allowed too much discretion in interpretation. Indeed, as the Bank of England published monetary policy debates showed, individual central bank members were more apt to disagree with each other, and interest rates were more likely to swing up and down. The discretionary, eclectic approach bothered the Germans. 'It's like John Wayne riding through the prairie, having to draw his gun on every rabbit that pokes his head up from the grass,' complains Jürgen von Hagen, a German economist, and one of the most vocal supporters of monetarism.

But for Issing, there was another reason to resist change. Money supply strategy had long been the hallmark of the strongest currency in Europe, and therefore its credibility counted for a lot. After the euro was introduced, other countries might be more tolerant of inflation than the Germans. Money supply could be a veil behind which he and other central bankers could hide – removing attention from inflation and economic growth, and keep public debate focused on the difficult-to-understand money supply strategy. But the best way to prevent tension over differences, Issing believed, was to achieve political union first.

Issing's ivory tower

When Issing was a boy, he used to run races with his brothers. As a sprinter in the 100 and 200 metres, he became the Bavarian 'Meister'. Even on the national level, he was among the leading runners. Later, after he joined the Bundesbank, it was said that he would warm up for the central council's fortnightly meetings by swimming in the bank's pool.

Issing is good looking, well-built, a little shy, never arrogant, and has a mischievous smile and deep blue eyes. He is also a family man. 'The thinking girl's crumpet,' according to a female journalist in Frankfurt with an American news agency. Issing is also unpretentious. Before he got to the Bundesbank he only owned a couple of suits.

Issing is a philosopher by nature. He first studied philology at Würzburg University, where became enthralled by the classics and developed a special admiration for Aristotle. In contrast to Plato, Aristotle was a practician. Aristotle may have doodled away much of his time thinking, but it wasn't to dream up the perfect order of the world, as Plato tended to do. Aristotle was concerned with creating the best order that would match real conditions.

Issing took this to heart. Like Tietmeyer, he eventually switched to economics, and obtained his doctorate at 26. Colleagues were impressed by his broad grasp of theory and history. Bernhard Molitor, the German economics ministry official, met Issing during the early Würzburg days, and was fascinated by an academic paper Issing wrote about Aristotle. Molitor still keeps the paper on his living room bookshelves, three decades later. 'It's a highly philosophical treatise,' he says. Issing spent much of his time in Würzburg ruminating on Germany and Europe's future economic and monetary order, and how they might best be merged. It was almost as if he spent his whole time preparing for the job he would later take up at the ECB. His doctoral thesis was on 'Problems of Economic Policy with Fixed- and Free-floating Exchange Rates. Example: the European Economic Community'. His post-doctoral thesis was on 'Key Currencies and the International Monetary System'. He stayed on at the university until 1990, except for two brief one-year stints at neighbouring Bavarian universities. Issing impressed his students by using lively and practical examples to illustrate economic principles. One of their favorites was the fictive debate Issing would carry on with Socrates in the 1980s, under the pseudonym Sigmar Otis, about the woes of the rising and falling dollar for Europe. During this debate, Issing expressed his own consternation about the wildly swinging dollar at the time. Socrates, when asked why the dollar rose even though the US had a widening budget deficit, shrugged his shoulders, saying he'd never seen anything like it in his day. It was Issing's way of explaining that money can behave in strange ways, often not according to economic theory.

Meanwhile, Issing became the most prominent flag bearer for German orthodoxy on money issues.[vii] In 1988, he was appointed to the most respected body of government advisors in the country, the so-called 'Five Wise Men', which issues an annual report that is considered Germany's mainstream economic bible. Here he began to criticize Bundesbank policy, vocally opposing the bank's minimum reserve and discount rate policies, which he believed created unnecessary costs and subsidies for German banks. An avid believer in free-market principles, he once said he is driven by a 'conviction that the market economy as a principle of order is always threatened.'[viii] But above all, Issing had become known as 'Mr Money Supply'.[ix]

Like many Germans, Issing was tied to his *Heimat*.[9] When the Bundesbank nominated him to the Bundesbank council in 1990, he was 54. It was the first time he had left Bavaria, or academia, for any length of time. 'This happened with a great inner hesitation. I was leaving the world where I felt I belonged, in which I knew I was at home, and from where nothing else could have lured me away,' he said. At the Bundesbank, he retained a position as honorary professor at Würzburg. Like Tietmeyer, and most of the ECB central bankers, he has had no private sector banking experience. 'As an investor, I'm more conservative than most housewives,' he says.[x]

Issing's *Ordnung*

Issing's biggest misgiving about the European project was the lack of political union. Without it, two crucial areas of the economy – the regulation of the labour market, on the one hand, and government tax and spending, on the other – had been left to the jurisdiction of national governments. These areas 'are the

---

[9] There is no satisfactory translation for this German word. Broadly, it means 'homeland.'

biggest potential risk for the success of the currency union,'[xi] Issing declared in July 1998. If government wage, income tax, social security contributions and other regulations make the cost of hiring a worker more expensive in France than in Ireland, companies will create jobs in Ireland at France's expense, and thus cause political unrest in France. Before monetary union, countries could adjust to these problems by adjusting their exchange rates. But a monetary union would make such adjustments impossible. For Issing, political union – which could include fiscal transfers from wealthy regions to those that suffered more unemployment, for example – was a missing piece in the European integration puzzle.[10]

Over the decade between Genscher's memo in 1988 proposing the creation of a single currency and the final decision in 1998 to go ahead with EMU, Issing grappled with this theme with no apparent resolution.

In 1988, Issing stated outright that monetary union was not possible without political union. 'Member states will hardly fully give up their sovereignty in the monetary field and transfer it to a European central bank, as long as national governments insist on independent fiscal policies,' he said. He added that an ECB cannot be erected in isolation from political institutions,

---

[10] The economic logic is as follows: before monetary union, France could lower the franc to help boost its exports, with the effect that added economic growth would create more jobs. Under a united monetary policy, that right would disappear. Countries would no longer be able to react to sudden outside shocks to their economy by raising or lowering interest rates. If a sudden surplus of paper on the world market drove down paper prices in Finland, then that country's economy – which is very dependent on paper production – would be negatively affected. It wouldn't be able to lower interest rates. But if unemployment were to rise, neither could it increase spending on benefits, because it is obliged by the Maastricht Treaty to stay within a 3 per cent deficit limit. It could create resentment against Europe. The Finns could also increase demands for temporary compensatory transfers from other European countries. A single currency would also make differences in wages more transparent, which would be another reason why poorer countries would cry out for compensation from richer, less indebted countries. 'All experience shows that an unavoidable pressure would be created for compensation via transfer payments from the rich and less indebted countries to the poorer regions,' said Issing in July 1995. See Otmar Issing, 'Geld Stiftet noch keine Staatlichkeit,' *Frankfurter Allgemeine Zeitung*, July 15, 1995. Introducing transfer payments, for Issing, would be a way to create a stable political order in Europe.

and therefore a European government is the necessary counter-part.'[xii] In subsequent years, in speech after speech, Issing would pound out a similar message.[11]

Issing rejected the views of those, who, like France's Banque de France official, Jacques Rueff, believed monetary union would be a frontrunner, or catalyst, of more political union: 'L'Europe se fera par la monnaie, ou ne se fera pas', Rueff had said in 1950. (Europe will be made by money, or won't be made.) Issing believed that Europe's nations weren't ready to give up their monetary sovereignty without first agreeing on a political order that would create the necessary solidarity. In *Politics*, Aristotle asserted unequivocally that the *polis*, or the public arena, was the most important area of human affairs. If the polis was out of order, every thing else would be too.[12]

By rejecting Rueff's views, Issing also took an indirect shot at the French. At first glance, it might seem ironic that Issing and other Germans had such a difficult time in dealing with French philosophy on EMU. For the French, politics were also primary. But there the parallel ends. In France, monetary policy took a backseat to a regime's overall political vision and was therefore subject to government control. As a result the French had major problems accepting an independent central bank during the Maastricht Treaty negotiations. In the German system, monetary policy was independent from government influence. It was the disciplined economic behaviour by governments in response to such independence that the Germans wanted to disseminate. Any attempt at unilateral political intervention would in their view be dangerous.

For Issing the EMS had given politicians a useful political cover to keep monetary policy disciplined. But what would it

---

[11] Issing kept contrasting Maastricht with what he called the 'normal case' of having a state's area of jurisdiction match its currency's area of jurisdiction. 'Because of grave holes in the Maastricht Treaty, we must fear developments that will weigh upon Europe's sense of unity.' (*Zusammengehoerigkeitsgefühl*)

[12] 'The German position was always that the currency union must stand at the end, that it must be the crowning conclusion . . . The desire to use currency union as a way to usher in political union is putting the cart before the horse,' Issing said in 1996. (Interview with *Der Spiegel*, January 15, 1996.)

mean if the mark – the anchor of the system – was suddenly replaced by a single currency? Would the discipline disappear as well?

Issing's scepticism on this point has led some German and foreign observers to mistake him for a closet nationalist.[13] That is a misrepresentation. Issing now speaks favourably of the European project, and agrees that it is advantageous to Germany. He has said the European Central Bank itself must bridge national differences, and those working in it must serve European, not national interests. Competence is not the only prerequisite for members on the bank's board, he says: You must also 'think European'. Issing also has high ambitions for the euro. He often recounts a history lesson that taught him the advantages of monetary union at an early age: In the first century AD, a business man travelled from Rome to Colonia Claudia Ara Agrippinensis, today's Cologne. 'During his whole journey, he could reckon on the right to pay his bills with the same currency, the denarius,' Issing says.

Money – The source of Freudian eroticism or religious schizophrenia?

At the heart of Issing's obsession with political unity is his belief that a society's relationship with money is a profoundly complex one. In an article written in April 1996, he traces the meaning of money through history and ranges from Freudian psychoanalysis to religious metaphors to underscore how money reflects the psychological makeup of a nation.[xiii] Once

---

[13] Issing admitted he was a sceptic for a long time. He recalled in 1990: For a long period, we said nothing will come of EMU. We have the better monetary policies. Why should we take over a worse currency? Then we saw that if we remained on the sidelines, we would be confronted with difficulties. So we decided to advance to the head of the movement, with the aim of making the Bundesbank's position clear at a European level.
Interview with Marsh, April 15, 1991. See Marsh, p. 245. Issing went on to say: The Bundesbank made its decision to 'participate constructively' in the monetary union campaign following the EC summit in Hanover in June 1988.

European currencies were merged, the psychological relationships between the populations and their money would be forced to confront each other, he inferred. His conclusion was that the currency would have to stay – as in Germany – strong and respected. In other words, other nations must converge with Germany's psyche, not the other way round.[14]

He starts his thesis with examples of universal and age-old tension between the world of art and the world of money. The German composer Richard Wagner, who associated with German revolutionaries in the late 1840s, enjoyed blasting his audiences with tales of the demonic side of money, from speculation to swindling. As Issing tells it, much as Wagner professed a hatred of the capitalist world, he also knew how to enjoy it. He ran up huge debts to those around him, who justified giving him material support on the grounds of his talent. He then fled to Dresden, his debts unresolved. Even artists who are financially well off may prefer to give the opposite impression, such as the wealthy German poet Heinrich Heine, who managed to convince those around him that he was 'as poor as a church mouse'.

For Issing, this hostile attitude toward money on the part of intellectuals mirrors a tradition of social tension between the opposites, 'spirit' and 'money'. This tension has roots in religion. In both the Old and the New Testaments, Issing points out, there are warnings of the dangers of letting money affect one's relationship with God and one's own character. As outmoded as these admonishments may seem today, Issing argues that they are still part of society's deeply schizophrenic

---

[14] Indeed, Issing would later boast, in March, 1998, that the German mark and the Bundesbank had won the 'competition' to become the most successful currency and central bank system in Europe, and therefore are the unchallenged models for Europe's monetary constitution. 'The European Central Bank as a new institution and the problem of accountability', paper by Issing at the Symposium on 'Challenges for Highly Developed Countries in the Global Economy', in Kiel, on March 20, 1998.

relationship with money. This is where Issing brings in psycho-analysis. Issing writes:

> Intellectually, it is not much further from here to psycho-analysis, and as expected, we land in anal eroticism. According to Freud, as a child grows into an adult, his original eroticism in defecation is replaced by an interest in money. From a psychological point of view, money replaces the function of excrement. Freud writes: 'We have got used to explaining an interest in money – insofar as it is of a libidinous nature, and not rational nature – as the desire to excrete . . .' In this view, money embodies the opposite to everything that is noble and distinguished. Money is not only an object – the goal of lower motives – it is also the measure of all things. In the end, even the individual's value is expressed purely in money terms. In short: money debases. This general, single measure of all things removes differences of class and occupation. The person's value is determined solely by his listing in the yearly income tables.

From a particular European perspective, the powerful dollar is the real culprit, Issing writes. The US exports its money values, along with 'hamburgers, soul music and management culture', to Europe and then to the rest of the world. 'Money is destructive and has proved that nothing can stand in its way, not even one's relationship with God . . .' he writes.

But despite its demonization over the centuries, Issing says, money has survived, and can also be seen as serving a higher purpose than merely a functional means for trade. Indeed, it created the means for individual emancipation and independence.

In Issing's view, currency has now become a sort of reflection of the entire economy. He cites Walter Eucken, a famous twentieth century German economist:

> The sort of money that a nation (Volk) has mirrors everything about that nation: what it wants, does, suffers, is. The nation's money also has significant influence on its economy and its fate. The condition of a nation's money is a

symptom of all of its conditions . . . Nothing says so much about the sort of wood from which a people is cut, as what it does in currency policy.[15]

In his essay, Issing notes that André Glucksmann, the French philosopher, goes even further, lifting the German preference for monetary stability to the order of a 'currency religion'. Issing says that the religious metaphor element was aptly captured in a statement by Portuguese prime minister, António Guterres, during a summit in Madrid: 'As Jesus Christ decided to build a church, he said to Peter: "You are Peter, the rock, and on this rock I will build my church." Today we could say "You are Euro, and on this new currency euro, we will build our new Europe."'

If it is true that a new, more powerful Europe is being hewn, and that the single currency is being used as its symbolic foundation, Issing says, 'then all the more reason for a stable euro' and 'all the more threatening every doubt about its strength'.

His analysis is provocative for two reasons. First, it highlights Germany's peculiar obsession with its currency. When the German media erupted in criticism of the new (and short-lived) German finance minister Oskar Lafontaine for his calls upon the Bundesbank in late autumn 1998 to lower its interest rates, thereby interfering with the Bundesbank's independence, the Luxembourg prime minister, Jean-Claude Juncker, was horrified. He called the German media reaction 'totally hysterical'. Though Lafontaine's statements had been directed as much at the new ECB as they were at the Bundesbank, no similar signs of neurosis over Lafontaine's remarks had been exhibited by France.

But second, and more important, Issing implies that a society's relationship with money is so profound that a single

---

[15] One of the most quoted economists in Germany is Joseph Schumpeter, who worked at the turn of the century. Schumpeter talked of the 'primacy of currency policy'. This view challenges French President Jacques Chirac's conviction that there is a need for 'primacy of politics'. See chapter 4.

currency project, almost by definition, requires political union. If a currency's strength symbolizes the character of its population, the very notion of a 'single' currency implies a 'single' people standing behind it. According to Issing's thinking, if France and Germany were to introduce a single currency, the currency would reflect a mix of those two cultures, which in the long-term at least, would be weaker than the mark but stronger than the franc. But a weak currency is unacceptable to the Germans, which is why the German negotiators insisted on creating a bank and reaching fiscal agreements that would reflect those of Germany. Because money goes deeper than mere institutions – Issing argues it gets to the foundation of a society's very psyche – the Germans wanted more than mere institutional quick-fixes.[16] They wanted the French to prove that their political economy had so transformed itself that it too could sustain a currency as strong as Germany's.

For this reason Germany had insisted for decades that political union be realised before currency union. It was only during the heat of the Maastricht negotiations that Kohl brushed aside these demands. The lack of political union is why Issing was not entirely satisfied with the Growth and Stability Pact solution agreed upon at Dublin in 1996. The pact, designed to allay German concerns about whether other countries would hold to the fiscal criteria in the treaty, created sanctions to be imposed on countries not holding their deficits to the limits required under the Maastricht Treaty. But it stopped short of a push for political union, as have all subsequent proposals.

---

[16] An example of Issing's view that changes in institutions weren't enough: 'The importance of legal independence (of the ECB) may have been overstated,' Issing said in a speech in early 1998. 'Not even an independent central bank can lastingly defend monetary stability against a "society of excessive demands" – in other words, every society gets the rate of inflation it deserves and basically wants.' Issing was concerned, for example, that member states would fail to cut back on 'the dense jungle of over-regulation' of labour markets. He cites the IMF's negative scenario for Europe that, if reforms aren't made, unemployment could soar and cause economic output to shrink by 2.5 per cent a year. (Issing speech in Kiel, March 20, 1998)

Following Issing's logic, divided societies imply a weakening in the firmament of the single currency project itself. Less unity at home meant less of an ability to project a unity of power abroad. Even in 1998, after EMU was a sure thing, and he'd taken up his seat at the ECB, Issing spoke of increasing 'centrifugal forces'.[xiv] In March, he fretted about whether Europe would be able to reach a consensus on an acceptable or optimal rate of inflation.[xv] As he said in his ECB confirmation hearings in Brussels in May, 1998:

> I don't want to cover up the fact that I was much more hesitant on the question of European currency union . . . Standing before the great leap, I'm not without worries. Worries, because I understand the consequences of a common currency. These worries have been reduced with impressive advances in convergence, but they haven't been totally put to rest . . . I admit, a few years ago I would have ruled out the possibility of reaching price stability in the EU, and that Germany with its lowest inflation rates in many years, would find itself only in the middle field of the member states . . . Unfortunately, similar convincing progress in other areas hasn't been achieved.[xvi]

Germany's gold scandal

The 1997 debacle over gold reserves provides perhaps the best illustration of both German monetary obsession and Bundesbank strength and prudence. In spring 1997, Kohl's government surprised Europe by producing a plan to revalue – almost immediately – the Bundesbank's gold and currency reserves. These reserves were being held at values far below market rates – a sign of the Bundesbank's conservative policies – and their revaluation could boost the bank's balance nicely, and allow a transfer of billions of marks to Bonn's coffers. Bonn was in dire need of help to close what seemed to be a dangerously high budget deficit. Economists were predicting the deficit would surpass the 3 per cent of gross domestic product limit stipulated in the Maastricht Treaty for participation in EMU. Yet 1997 was the deadline to meet this limit, and Bonn was in danger of being embarrassed, especially after preaching to its neighbours to put their own finances in order.

Followed by live television cameras, finance minister Theo Waigel flew by helicopter to Frankfurt from Bonn to meet with the Bundesbank, and handed it an ultimatum that the policy be implemented. The Bundesbank sat tight. Its members wanted to regroup in secret before they responded. Issing drew up a draft statement, blasting the government's plan as an attack on the bank's independence and a blow to the credibility of the EMU project. While Issing agreed that there was, in principle, nothing wrong with revaluing the reserves, he wanted to avoid this happening in the crucial year of 1997, since it could damage the credibility of the euro project. After so many years of preaching to the French that they should become more stringent with their finances, he feared that all this work could suddenly be for naught. Budgetary tricks in Bonn would send a very bad message to Europe's neighbours. The Bundesbank council endorsed Issing's memo, and after a week of silence, fired it off.

In the end, the Bundesbank won the showdown, albeit at the cost of significant damage to Bonn's credibility. The Bundesbank had appeared to be at the mercy of Bonn, since the government had threatened to change the Bundesbank law at its discretion. The blast of publicity in response to Issing's memo generated a popular revolt around Germany. Parliamentary representatives, who returned home to their constituencies that weekend, noticed the negative sentiment. On Monday, they returned and deputies within Kohl's own party openly threatened revolt if Kohl and Waigel didn't relent. The next day, Kohl and Waigel did just that. They abandoned the policy, saying they would take it up the following year, and then only partially. The Bundesbank had won with a deft handling of public relations. Kohl and Waigel, meanwhile, were the subject of scorn in Italy and other countries. Italian prime minister Romano Prodi, in a burst of *shadenfreude*, wondered aloud whether Germany would be able to qualify for monetary union.

It was a woeful sign of what even the German government could do when desperate. If the German government was capable of breaking the spirit (and arguably, even the letter) of the Maastricht Treaty, the Bundesbankers wondered what the other countries were capable of. Indeed, even before the euro's launch in January, the Italian prime minister, Massimo d'Alema was arguing that an 'interpretation' of the stability pact was necessary, specifically that the 3 per cent limit on budgets should exclude spending on infrastructure projects.

With German credibility damaged by Issing's resistance to the gold plan, the nomination of Issing as the ECB's chief economist would be a bitter pill to swallow for Kohl's government. Germany's leading financial newspaper, the *Frankfurter Allgemeine Zeitung*, published a column supporting Issing. Other publications ran articles speculating whether the government would punish Issing by instead appointing Waigel's deputy, Jürgen Stark, who had actually been the originator of the gold plan in early 1997.[17] The government finally conceded that Issing would be the better choice, if only to maintain the credibility of Germany's demand for an independent central bank. 'We are dealing with a credibility issue. That's why we've got to go with Issing,' said Bernd Pfaffenbach, counsellor to Kohl, before the official appointment.[xvii]

Taking up his role at the ECB in mid-1998, Issing agreed to build an outrageous vault, but for now he wasn't worrying about restoring the goddess Europa to her throne on top of the world. Neither was he guaranteeing the ECB would withstand a battery of political guns. 'The dollar, overnight, will get a competitor. But its leadership – at least at the beginning – won't be endangered,' Issing says.

*   *   *

---

[17] Stark was appointed to the Bundesbank directorate in 1998, and was given the international relations portfolio. That means he accompanies the president to ECB governing council meetings. Stark ordered the money and credit experts in the finance ministry's Section VII to draw up the plan for using revaluation of Bundesbank gold reserves for filling Bonn's budget deficit in April 1997. One of the section's leaders, Peter Japcke, who worked out the plan, said Stark overruled the section's objections. 'We civil servants are like harem ladies,' Japcke complained. 'We're well-fed and well-dressed, but at decisive moments we have to be quiet and do what we're told.' (See author's article in *The Wall Street Journal Europe*, Monday August 4, 1997.)

Frankfurt: The Secret Capital

Issing says he found it difficult to leave the cosy academic confines of Würzburg, his *Heimat*, to join the cool, impersonal world of central banking in Frankfurt. Indeed, though small by the standards of Paris, New York and London, Frankfurt was still the most cosmopolitan city in Germany.

Frankfurt was a top candidate for the new capital of West Germany after World War II, but lost out to Bonn, which was the favourite of Chancellor Konrad Adenauer. Berliners had also vetoed the decision, fearing that in the event of a long-term division of the country, Frankfurt would be big enough to dash Berlin's hopes of regaining the status of capital.

In industrialized, modern Germany, Frankfurt finds itself at the midpoint of Germany's dynamic western economic strip stretching from the Ruhr Valley in the north to the manufacturing centre in Baden-Württemburg. It is the communications and transport centre for the whole of Germany. With a quarter of a million passengers arriving each day, the Frankfurt train station has more visitors than any other station in Europe. Today, Frankfurt airport is the most frequently visited airport on the continent.

Frankfurt is best known as headquarters of the Bundesbank. By the end of WWII, Berlin and Hamburg had become rival banking centres. Frankfurt's position was re-established when American occupation forces co-operated with German officials to erect the new German central bank system with its headquarters in Frankfurt. They insisted on a decentralized banking system, which meant that there was no major banking centre in Germany for many years. Slowly, however, Frankfurt won influence. On June 20 1948 the Americans delivered to the Frankfurt headquarters some 10.7 billion marks worth of newly printed Deutschmark notes under armed guard, to replace the Reichsmarks. In 1984, Deutsche Bank moved its headquarters to Frankfurt, and today its sleek twin towers are the city's most impressive skyscrapers. The move was a sign that Frankfurt had won back its status as the centre of German banking. Today, Frankfurt is home to over 400 banks.

The choice of Frankfurt

With hindsight, the choice of Frankfurt for the seat of the ECB was surprisingly uncontroversial. In 1992, when the decision was made, the introduction of the single currency was so far off and accompanied by so much uncertainty that politicians didn't put up too much of a fight over where the bank should be located. When the Maastricht Treaty was signed in 1991, the German media had reacted negatively, questioning the sense in giving up a currency that had served the nation so well. Reacting to domestic pressure, the German delegation in Maastricht argued that the ECB should be based in Frankfurt in order to help Bonn sell the project to the sceptical German population. After all, the Bundesbank was based in Frankfurt, and so the city would symbolize continuity of that tradition.

The French foreign minister Hubert Védrine acknowledged later that Mitterrand didn't object to the choice of Frankfurt, assuming that it was part of the price to pay to get the Germans to accept EMU.[xviii] In hindsight, this was a very large concession. Other countries had expressed interest. In mid-1992, as talks concerning the ECB's headquarters picked up, the cities of London, Frankfurt, Amsterdam, Barcelona, Lyon, Lille and Strasbourg had all declared themselves candidates. The German government pushed Frankfurt aggressively. Meanwhile the French government didn't even have its own proposal.[xix] With the French ready to accept Germany's wishes, there was little hope that one of the other cities would win, and Frankfurt was only chosen at the European Council meeting in Brussels in October, 1993.

The Maastricht Treaty called for the creation of a European Monetary Institute (EMI) in 1994 as a forerunner to the ECB, which would draft up statutes, monetary policy instruments and strategy for the future. Its decision making body – named the EMI council – consisted of the of EU central bank governors and the EMI president. As president, the governors chose the Belgian Alexandre Lamfalussy, who was general director of the Bank for International Settlements (BIS). For years, the EU central bank governors had gathered regularly under the auspices of the Committee of Central Bank Governors (CCG),[18] and had formed a small secretariat at the BIS to manage their affairs, in the belief that the BIS headquarters in Basle, Switzerland represented 'neutral' territory. By the end of 1993, the group had expanded to about 30, including lawyers and economists, and it became the embryo for the EMI, which was founded in January, 1994.

From the beginning, the German influence was strong. Hanspeter Scheller, an ex-Bundesbanker, who had joined the BIS in 1973 to work for the CCG, was appointed the EMI's secretary general. Under Lamfalussy, he was in charge of overseeing the most important preparatory work for the move to the single currency, including formulating the draft of monetary policy strategy. It was P.W. Schlüter, another German, who moved from the Bundesbank to take over the EMI 'administration' division, and arranged for the choice of the 'Eurotower' skyscraper to be the EMI headquarters. The 35-storey building on the south side of the city was at first considered temporary lodgings, since only a few floors of the building were available. But in early 1998, the location was made permanent. It is in the midst of the city's banking quarter, unlike the fortress-like Bundesbank, which is based on an autobahn junction outside the city.

Kaiserstrasse 29 and the tie to the central bankers of Charlemagne

The site of Eurotower, at Kaiserstrasse 29, has a mixed and interesting history. Like the rest of the immediate area, the street was only built and developed after the German empire was founded in 1871, relatively late in Frankfurt's history. In the late 1880s, Kaiserstrasse 29 was the site of a building named after the Prussian royal family: the 'Hollenzollern Haus,' a major attraction at the time. The building was at first owned by a

---

[18] See chapter 3.

Jewish real estate company named Oppenheim & Weill.ˣˣ One
of the partners was Simon E. M. Oppenheim, a banker and
businessman related to the famous Jewish Oppenheim banking
house. Also in the building were the offices of a Jewish banker,
Jacob Sichel. The city archives show that in 1933, the year when
Hitler grabbed power, Sichel's name suddenly disappeared from
the city's register. Besides Sichel's departure, there was another
foreboding change in the neighbourhood: the street running
north from the Hollenzollern Haus changed its name to 'Adolf
Hitler Strasse,' and stayed that way until the end of the war.[19]

During the Second World War, the Hollenzollern Haus was
bombed to ruins – and was considered too much of a shambles
to restore. But a Dresden restaurateur, known as Hans Arnold,
arrived looking for a place to start a new business. Arnold was
a family well known for its cuisine for generations. In Dresden,
it had served Germany's kings, Wilhelm I, Wilhelm II, and then
later President Friedrich Ebert and Reich Chancellor Adolf
Hitler. The entire city of Dresden had been levelled, and to
Arnold, the largely intact walls of Hollenzollern Haus were
enough to make do with. He cordoned off a small section of the
ruins, and rebuilt and reopened the 'Kaiserkeller' restaurant.
The rest of the lot remained in ruins. At one point, a bank
robber took refuge in the ruins, and while being hunted by the
police, shot and killed a German shepherd search dog. The city
newspapers were outraged at the killing, caring more, it seemed,
about the dog than about the robbed bank.

In 1970, the Hollenzollern ruins were swept away, and the

---

[19] The Oppenheims, meanwhile, were either forced into exile or received
protection, helped by having converted from Judaism to Christianity. It is
noteworthy that at least one member of the Oppenheim banking family would
serve continuously on the central executive of the German central bank, the
Reichsbank, from the time it was created in 1876 until 1932, when Simon Alfred
Oppenheim was forced to resign. (Michael Stürmer, Gabriele Teichmann,
Wilhelm Treue *Striking the Balance* Weidenfeld and Nicholson, London 1994
p. 194.) The Oppenheim bank (Sal. Oppenheim jr. & Cie.) is still operating from
its Cologne headquarters, and maintains a large branch in Frankfurt, only a few
blocks away from the 'Eurotower.'

restaurant closed, to make way for the construction of a skyscraper, beginning in 1971. The new building's first occupant was the Bank für Gemeinwirtschaft (BfG), a trade-union bank. The tower was bought recently by a real estate subsidiary of Dresner Bank. The ECB is negotiating to take over the whole building. Only the American investment bank, Salomon Brothers, which occupies the first floor, and the German bank, Commerzbank, still rent some office space there. In the meantime, the ECB rents out meeting rooms across the street in the Frankfurt branch of the Italian bank, Monte dei Paschi di Siena, the oldest bank in the world.

Bahnhof Viertel

The Eurotower's entrance is decidedly nondescript. There is no sign outside, nor even inside the main lobby, that indicates the building houses the ECB – 'for security reasons', according to the bank's chief security guard. Outside of the building, life is a bit less glamorous. Kaiserstrasse is located on the southwest fringe of Frankfurt in an area named the 'Railway station quarter' (*Bahnhof Viertel*), after its most notable feature.

The street is the city's most seedy. Along the four blocks running eastward from the station to the Eurotower is Frankfurt's red-light district, home to an estimated 1,500 prostitutes and 20 bordellos.[xxi] To the unsuspecting new arrival, a trip down Kaiserstrasse can be jarring. Junkies with visibly scabbed arms and legs loiter there. It is not uncommon to see drug addicts injecting themselves on the sidewalks, with regular police patrols apparently oblivious. The oversupply of prostitutes has been accompanied by an influx of criminal elements and drug dealers,[xxii] an embarrassing stain that the city has been fighting for years to clean up and transform into a posh sector attractive to global corporations and banks. On a cross street just around the corner from the ECB is a drug clinic. Police regularly round up drunkards who become too loud while loitering around the Willy-Brandt-Platz subway located just behind the bank, to the south. A good number of the city's approximately 100,000 illegal aliens work in the quarter, at poorly paid, often black-market, jobs. Of the 3,300 residents in the quarter, about 70 per cent are of foreign origin.

Though the area to the bank's east is an eyesore, the region to the west is among the city's most posh. Just behind the ECB is the city's main theatre and a few blocks further west is Frankfurt's expensive shopping district. There are ambitious plans to develop a series of further skyscrapers; part of an effort to push Frankfurt into the ranks of the world's leading financial centres. Over half the city, including almost all of the centre, was destroyed during the war. But rather than restore the city to its former self, the rebuilders decided to allow the creation of a sky-line filled with skyscrapers. It has become known as the most Americanized city in Europe.

The roots of Europe's central banking

Frankfurt's history of creating money began when the Holy Roman Emperors were elected and crowned there between 1562 and 1792. Just a few blocks east of the Eurotower is the Römerberg, or 'Roman hill', the historical and geographical centre of the city. It is where Charlemagne built his fort and where the Imperial coronations took place. Underground pathways still exist from the days when the Emperors used them to escape the masses while moving to the town hall from the thirteenth-century Gothic cathedral, St. Bartholomaeus, after being crowned. There, at the town hall, the Emperors would reappear and distribute freshly minted money, bearing their own portraits, to the citizens.

There is no other city in Europe that owes its importance to money as much as does the city of Frankfurt. Over the centuries, its relative liberalism towards Jews helped it become a major financial capital. The early modern state, beginning with the Holy Roman Empire and its city states, had continually failed to establish an efficient bank to handle money circulation.

Jews were exempt from the general prohibition against the taking of interest, and so they became the indispensable bearers of credit.[20] Frankfurt developed into an international trading crossroads toward the end of the eighth century, when Charlemagne stayed there during the winter of 793, and records showed that he engaged Jews as commercial agents.[xxiii]

During the Thirty Years War (1618-1648), the Jews were fought over by the political powers that be. In an attempt to gain control of their resources the Frankfurt Municipal Council claimed that the Jews owed allegiance to the Council, not to the Emperor. Moreover, the Council, in a display of anti-semitism typical of Europe at the time, demanded that Jews live under special city laws restricting their movement. The Emperors fought to ease these restrictions. Escutcheons with the inscription 'Protection of the Imperial Roman Majesty and the Holy Reich' were affixed to the three gates of the Jewish ghetto. The Emperors, after all, were highly indebted to the Jewish Oppenheim family. It was the court-purveyor, or 'Court Jew', Samuel Oppenheim who procured loans for Leopold I for his war with Turkey.[xxiv]

The city became so wealthy that Goethe, Germany's favourite poet, called it Germany's 'secret capital'. Goethe was born and brought up in Frankfurt, and today his statue stands across the road from the 'Eurotower'.

Frankfurt's political lessons

Symbolically, Frankfurt has an unfortunate political history. When Austria and Prussia began rolling back the French forces in 1813, Germany's romantic writers reawakened interest in the glories of the Holy Roman Empire. Frankfurt's socially liberal

---

[20] The Frankfurt Jewish Rothschild family became a world leader in state loans. It was the Rothschilds who, in 1861, enabled Abraham Lincoln to finance his Civil War. It was Jewish Frankfurt bankers, Erlanger & Sons, who helped raise funds for the Southern states. Frankfurt's Jewish families have also funded the movement to construct the land of Israel since the middle of the nineteenth century, including paying for building the Israeli parliament, the Knesset.

attitude made Frankfurt the centre of a movement for the creation of a powerful German nation based on civil and democratic rights. But the movement crumbled after making only preliminary progress. The failure, historians say, lay in the lack of the liberal movement's democratic foundations. Today, as European nations try to build acceptance for a more politically unified Europe in the twenty-first century, the history of the Frankfurt rebellion might provide some useful lessons.

NOTES

[i] The Lombard rate is the interest rate which the Bundesbank set on deposits. It set the 'ceiling' for interest rates.

[ii] *Welt am Sonntag*, August 16 1992. Page 23. 'Ich sehe gute Chancen fuer einen anhaltenden Aufschwung.'

[iii] *Die Zeit*, March 19, 1993. 'Tueckische Trichter.'

[ivi] John Maynard Keynes, *A Treatise on Money*, Macmillan, 1930.

[v] Greider, William. *Secrets of the Temple; How the Federal Reserve Runs the Country*. Simon & Schuster. New York: 1987. p. 197.

[vi] Cited from Greider, p. 120.

[vii] He has also been a long-standing member of the so-called Kronberger Kreis, an élite group of German economists who meet regularly and who share a belief in free-market principles.

[viii] Issing speech in March 1998, cited in 'Garant fuer eine Geldpolitik im Sinne der Bundesbank-Tradition,' *Frankfurter Rundshau*, May 4, 1998.

[ix] Issing was known for his regular public support of money aggregates. In 1988, for example, Issing joined six other economists in a call on the Bundesbank to set a monetary goal for that year.

[x] *Wirtschaftswoche*, July 5, 1998. p. 18-19. 'Stabilitaetswaechter.' Though Issing is on the free-market side of the German spectrum, Issing shares the overall desire for 'order' that prevails in German economic and monetary thought. As for other German economists, the word 'order' has a prominent place in Issing's vocabulary. It was Issing's dedication to a 'firm political order', for instance, that won him an endorsement by the élite German newspaper *Frankfurt Allgemeine Zeitung* for the ECB position.

[xi] Issing speech in Konstanz on July 4 1998 'Von der D-Mark zum Euro.'

[xii] Issing, Otmar. 'Europaeische Notenbank – in Phantom,' in *Frankfurter Allgemeine Zeitung*. March 12, 1988.

[xiii] 'Wider die Papiergaunerein' by Otmar Issing, *Frankfurter Allgemeine Zeitung*, April 6 1996.

[xiv] Issing speech in Konstanz. July 4, 1998.

[xv] Issing Speech in Kiel. March 20, 1998.

[xvi] Europaisches Parliament Sitzungsdokumente. DOC–DE/RR/353/353488. May 11, 1988. p. 22-23.

[xvii] Author's interview with Pfaffenbach.

[xviii] *Nouvel Observateur*. November 13-19, 1997. See Hubert Védrine, *Les Mondes de Françoise Mitterrand: à l'Elysée 1981-1995*. Fayard.

xix *Le Monde*. 7-8 June, 1992. 'Jean-Claude Trichet est élu président du comité monétaire européen'.

xx Michael Strümer, Gabriele Teichmann, Wilhelm Treue. *Striking the Balance. Sal. Oppenheim jr. & Cie. A Family and Bank*. (Weidenfeld & Nicolson: London, 1994.)

xxi There are no official numbers on prostitution in the area. In her essay, 'Das Frankfurter Bahnhofsviertel – Kosmopolitisch – international – multinational,' Irene Hübner estimates that 2,350 prostitutes and 26 bordellos operate in the Bahnhof Viertel. In Hübner, *Mehr als Milieu – ein literarisch-politisches Lesebuch der Schreibwerkstatt Leben im Bahnhofsviertel Frankfurt* (Brandes & Apsel: Frankfurt, 1987). The city's police department says the figures have decreased slightly in recent years. It estimates about 1,000 prostitutes and 14 bordellos now operate there. But it admits that half of the prostitutes are illegal aliens, and therefore its estimates are probably on the low side because of the difficulty of keeping count.

xxii See *Mehr als Milieu*. Ein literarisch-politicsches Lesebuch der Schreibwerkstatt Leben im Bahnhofsviertel Frankfurt. Brandes & Apsel: Frankfurt, 1987.

xxiii Eugen Mayer. *The Jews of Frankfurt*. Verlag Waldemar Kramer: Frankfurt am main, 1990.

xxiv Frankfurt city archives. See also Eugen Mayer. *The Jews of Frankfurt*. Verlag Waldemar Kramer: Frankfurt am Main, 1990. Pages 22-24, 25.

CHAPTER SIX

The Coronation

The most controversial event in the birth of the ECB came on May 2, 1998, when the president of the bank was selected. French president Jacques Chirac had long been irked by the Netherlands. The Dutch were long-time allies of the Germans in monetary policy issues, and their special tie with Germany had perturbed France, especially when it appeared to be collusive in nature, for example when the Dutch and Germans revealed in 1993 that they had secretly agreed to tie their currencies in an even narrower range within the European Monetary System than the range held to by the other participating countries. Of all European countries, the Netherlands had held its currency tied directly to the mark the longest, and thus was considered too close to the German camp for France's liking. The Netherlands had often been the only country arguing alongside Germany, a key psychological support without which Germany might have been forced to give in over many of its most passionate demands. Wim Duisenberg, as the Dutch central bank governor, embodied that closeness.

Chirac was therefore perturbed by a unilateral proposal from the central bankers that Duisenberg be president of the EMI. On May 14, 1996, Belgium's Alexandre Lamfalussy, president of the European Monetary Institute, had met with the European central bankers during a regular meeting at the EMI council in Frankfurt and proposed that Duisenberg be his successor. The appointment was important because there was a growing assumption that the person who got the job would also become the first president of the ECB in mid-1999. For Lamfalussy, Duisenberg seemed to be a natural choice. As chairman of the

EU central bank governors committee, Duisenberg had been the first to be considered for the EMI presidency in 1993, but he declined the position, preferring to stay at the Dutch central bank. In early 1996, Tietmeyer had approached Dusienberg and encouraged him to run for the position. By the spring of 1996, Duisenberg made clear to Lamfalussy and the other bankers that he was interested. On February 4, Duisenberg told a German newspaper, the *Börsen Zeitung*, that he wanted to head the ECB, just days before he was to attend the BIS meeting in Basle and suggest to his fellow bankers that a delay be considered.

Duisenberg explains: 'At that time, I accepted to do it if I had a reasonable political certainty that I would also be appointed president of the ECB.' The bankers agreed on Duisenberg in a unanimous decision, and also let it be known that they assumed it was logical that Duisenberg, as the president of the EMI, would become the ECB's first president. The French were furious. They contended that the French central banker, Trichet, was given a fait accompli and had no other choice but to vote with his colleagues. But it wasn't as if the French were ready with their own candidate. In fact, Chirac was still openly attacking Trichet on television in July with apparently little awareness that Trichet would turn out to be his only viable candidate.[1]

The Germans meanwhile, took an early stance that Duisenberg was the natural candidate for the ECB. Waigel explains:

> It was clear to everyone that Duisenberg would be the candidate for the first president of the ECB. Chirac made clear that the vote was valid only for the presidency of EMI, but wasn't valid for the presidency of the ECB. This way, he'd indicated his reluctance to accept Duisenberg. We recognized that France, true to its tradition, would probably propose its

[1] Chirac's preferred candidate, Michel Camdessus, the head of the International Monetary Fund, was not well liked by the Germans and other countries, and was dropped.

own candidate, just like it does for every position that opens up in the world, whether it be the position of managing director at the IMF, general secretary of the OECD, EU Commission presidency, secretary of the European council of ministers, or chairman of the Monetary Committee – there is no position that the French don't find it perfectly natural to apply for. They've had some success in this, so it's to be understood. But naturally, everyone hoped that a solution would be found in favour of Duisenberg, especially if all of us were in favour of him. Duisenberg was the choice of the stable countries of Europe, not only of Germany and the Benelux, but of other countries too. Besides, we believed that it was best that the candidate come from a small country. We knew that other countries would find it difficult to support a German candidate.[i]

Belgian prime minister Jean-Luc Dehaene later said that he too had sensed Chirac's growing opposition to a Dutch candidate. The Dutch government had initiated a short-lived campaign in early 1997 to delay EMU, fearing that Italy wasn't ready to participate, and complaining in general about the budgetary manœuvres that Europe's southern countries performed in order to qualify for monetary union. The Netherlands had also consistently demonstrated a permissive attitude toward drugs. Because of the elimination of border controls between many EU countries, these drugs were finding their way into France, a considerable provocation given that Chirac had made internal security one of his campaign issues.

In late 1997, Chirac was still pondering what to do about the ECB presidency. Earlier in the year, he'd sought to propose Camdessus, leader of the IMF, for the position, but the Germans, who had complained about his leadership of the IMF, rejected the idea.[ii] In October, Chirac became impatient and put in a call to the new socialist prime minister, Lionel Jospin. He pressed him into agreeing that they appoint a French man to the bank. He wanted to know whom Jospin would support. Jospin hesitated, knowing full well that most of the other European countries and bankers were already agreed on

Duisenberg's candidature. But he couldn't refuse Chirac's overture. There was no alternative other than Trichet. As Waigel explains:

> Jospin and French finance minister Dominique Strauss-Kahn were in a very difficult position. The proposal to nominate Trichet came from Chirac himself. Jospin and Strauss-Kahn, as socialists, didn't have anything against Duisenberg, who is a social democrat. Rather, they supported Trichet out of solidarity with the president, because the state president gave them the alternative of 'either you go along with this or I tell the nation that the French government isn't ready to support a French candidate.'

Neither Chirac nor Jospin wanted to announce the decision alone, so they did it jointly. First, however, they assigned Strauss-Kahn to inform Ecofin. Chirac called Kohl and informed him of the impending announcement. Kohl said that he did not have anything against a French candidature, but that he believed Duisenberg was a strong candidate, and that the announcement would make things difficult. He said that the Germans would not reject the nomination if the French were able to come up with a compromise solution with the Dutch. Word quickly travelled to the Dutch, who were furious. Strauss-Kahn explains that the French manœuvre was more than merely pursuit of national interests:

> Chirac decided he wanted to act. He asked Jospin if he agreed with the idea that we should not let Duisenberg become the president just as it had been decided by the central bankers, and whether Jospin didn't agree that the politicians should have the say on such matters. Jospin said that he agreed, and added that I would have to tell the Ecofin that we finally had our own candidate. It was lunch time at the meeting, and I was getting ready to announce it. Before I could say a word, my Dutch colleague (Gerrit) Zalm broke in. 'It's a scandal. Those Frenchmen want a different sort of monetary policy. That's the reason why they don't want Duisenberg. They're

having problems accepting all this.' He was wrong. Duisenberg wasn't the problem. If the central bankers hadn't said before that they wanted Duisenberg, and had just been silent, there wouldn't have been any problem with the nomination of Duisenberg. The real point was a question of principle. Who's going to decide? My colleague from the Netherlands, Jean-Claude Juncker, supported this idea.

Chirac and Jospin publicly proposed Trichet on November 4. German officials, on hearing of the French announcement, suspected the French were suffering an internal crisis about having accepted so many of the German proposals during the construction of the Maastricht orthodoxy. Germans Hans Tietmeyer and finance minister Theo Waigel warned that dissension over the ECB nomination would weaken the central bank and the euro's credibility. They had also endorsed Duisenberg several times. 'I know of only one candidate: Duisenberg. And I don't know a better one,' Waigel told his EU colleagues.[iii] In June, Tietmeyer had said Duisenberg 'incarnates total stability', adding that he had complete confidence in 'Wim'. Helmut Hesse, a member of Bundesbank council, said: 'One thing is for sure, the president of the European Central Bank will not be a Frenchman.'[iv]

But the French lined up behind Trichet. An economist at the Banque de France, Philippe Weber, told the French media that the nomination of Trichet was justified because 'the ECB had been placed in Frankfurt, its statutes were a carbon copy of those of the Bundesbank, the "ECU" had been re-baptized "euro" to please the Germans, and the Euro-11 council will be informal.'[v] Karl Lammers, a foreign policy expert in the German parliament, and close adviser to Kohl, appeared to sympathize: 'In light of French tradition, we must understand that eventually they'd also like to score a point.'[vi] Pierre Moscovi, France's minister for European affairs, and Paul Marchelli, a Banque de France council member, both said that an 'implicit accord' had been made between Mitterrand and Kohl on October 30, 1993. In return for a French concession that the ECB be based in Frankfurt, the Germans would agree that the first president would be French. But Kohl acknowledged no such deal and Mitterrand had since died. Nowhere had such an understanding been written down. Indeed, such a deal was highly unlikely, given that other French officials say there was little disagreement about the need for the ECB to be situated in Frankfurt. For example, Hervé de Charrette, a former foreign minister, told a radio interviewer on November 5:

> When the central bank's foundation was agreed on in Maastricht, a decision was made simultaneously on the seat of the bank. The Germans, namely Chancellor Kohl and his government, used strong pressure and with extreme prodding requested that the seat should be in Germany. At the time, we said the mark is the strongest European currency, the Germans are having difficulty warming to the euro-project, in short, on basic and formal grounds, the seat must, without question, be in Frankfurt.[vii]

But de Charrette instead this didn't make the French proposal of Trichet any less legitimate: 'There are two important currencies in Europe . . . it is self-evident that if the seat is based in the country of one of those, the governor should come from the country of the second,' he said.

Pre-summit talks

Preliminary talks about how to find a compromise on the ECB nomination between the French and the Dutch were fruitless. Soon, other European leaders were offering their services to help find a compromise. They included Jean-Claude Juncker, who was president of the rotating European Council. Juncker proposed splitting the term between the two sides. According to Chirac's finance adviser, Jean-François Cirelli:

> By the end of 1997, we had the feeling that a deal could be struck, in which the term would be divided into two four-year mandates. The idea was obvious. All of our friends on the

outside said it was so simple. But it was also clear that the
suggestion couldn't come from the Dutch or the French
because neither side wanted to give up any ground. Nobody
wanted to make the first step. The Germans came very late
into the discussion saying a split in the mandate would be a
problem for legal reasons. This was only three or four weeks
before the meeting in May. For us, it seemed more of a
Bundesbank position than a government position.

Cirelli noticed the opposition within the German camp from the
German media, which were filled with accounts of 'background' comments by German finance officials who were
against splitting the term. It is true that the comments came late,
and there was confusion on the German side. Even within the
Chancellor's office, there was division. Joachim Bitterlich,
Kohl's closest diplomatic adviser, was known to be close to the
French – his wife is French – and did not want to shoot down
the French proposal prematurely. He launched an intensive
round of negotiations between Kohl and himself on the one
side, and Chirac and his diplomatic advisor, Jean-David Levitte,
on the other, amounting to more than thirty conversations in
the five months leading up to May. His goal was to engage the
French, and to slowly win them over step-by-step. The French
remained set on the idea of splitting the term in two four-year
terms. Kohl's finance advisors, meanwhile, had balked, arguing
that a split would be perceived badly by the markets and would
violate the spirit of the treaty. Waigel had also fought the
proposal, saying it contradicted the statutory independence of
the ECB as laid down in the treaty. He had held this line for
months:

> Not for a moment did the Chancellor or myself drop our
> support for Duisenberg. We clearly told Duisenberg and the
> Dutch 'we're standing by your side.' But we obviously had to
> recognize the French wish, and so after their proposal, we
> began to consider what chances there were to find a
> compromise solution. We considered other positions which
> might be part of a trade-off, for example, the ECB vice

president slot, or chief of the European Bank for Reconstruction and Development in London, which was also open. There were also considerations as to whether the mandate could be split, for example in two four-year terms. We realized that this wouldn't work for legal reasons. The only thing that was compatible with the Treaty was if the chosen candidate says 'I'm now 63, but in eight years, I'll be 71. I've been voted for eight years, but I don't want to fulfill the full term.' But it had to be his voluntary statement, not under pressure, and to which he wouldn't be legally bound.

Alas, Duisenberg didn't seem ready to make such a concession. On March 25, having had plenty of time to think about making such a statement, Duisenberg rejected the idea of cutting his term short. During a press conference at the EMI, a journalist asked: 'Are you still aiming for a period of eight years for the presidency of the ECB?' Duisenberg responded: 'As far as the terms of the office of the presidency of the ECB are concerned, the Treaty is unambiguous in stating that the term will be eight years.' In other newspaper interviews, Duisenberg also indicated he would not accept a splitting of the term.

Bitterlich and the Chancellor held their cards close to their chest, and did not include Waigel or other ministers in their preparation for the Brussels summit on May 1–2. A week before the summit, on April 23, Bitterlich forwarded some discussion points to the Elysée, including a sketch of a possible deal. Chirac's office circulated the notes, interpreting them as an official memo. According to Bitterlich's scribbled notes, the mandate could be offered to Duisenberg, but Duisenberg would offer to step down for four years, after which France would be ready to propose a successor for an eight-year term. Bitterlich later claimed that the note was misinterpreted.

Klaus Regling, the chief of European negotiations at the finance ministry, recalls how his ministry was kept out of the dealmaking:

This question was taken care of by the Chancellor's office. We weren't included in the discussions as we usually were on

EMU issues. We made our position clear to the Chancellor from the beginning. But we weren't informed of the Bitterlich memo. I only heard about it afterwards.[viii]

Waigel, foreign minister Klaus Kinkel and Hans Tietmeyer had not seen the memo.[ix] Kohl's failing to round up his troops came back to haunt him a few days later.

In early 1998, the rotating EU presidency had switched to Britain. British prime minister Tony Blair, who was to chair the Brussels European council meeting on May 1-2, met the Dutch a day before the summit. Blair reported to Chirac that the Dutch were ready for a compromise on splitting the mandate. But they needed a way to save face, Blair warned Chirac. Earlier, Chirac had threatened the Dutch prime minister Wim Kok that he would veto Duisenberg if no solution was found, which had aggravated Dutch sensitivities. The Dutch knew how credible that threat was. The Dutch had – over the previous few years – seen the French push out Dutch candidates for the top spots at the IMF, the European Bank for Reconstruction and Development and the European Commission.[2] As France's Cirelli recalls:

We heard from intermediaries – the British and the Germans – that the Dutch could agree. We hadn't heard it directly from the Dutch. Everyone else said it would be OK. Just a day before, there had been an Anglo-Dutch meeting in Brussels, and Blair had said it would be a little more difficult for the Dutch, that it was a question of face saving. But at least when we entered the room, we knew that we had the Germans with us. There was an agreement in principle. So we came to Brussels with only one question unanswered: no one had spoken to Duisenberg himself.

It had seemed trifling at the time, but in hindsight, it was a major error. It underscored what had become the *leitmotif* of

---

[2] For Theo Waigel's remarks on the French enthusiasm for filling high-ranking international positions, see earlier in this chapter (p. 181–2).

the whole debacle: the French misperception of their place in the world. The French civil service and political élite had taken it for granted that their right to nominate their own candidate was on a par with the Duisenberg proposal. Believing in the primacy of politics, they had assumed that Kohl's neutrality was sufficient to come to a political arrangement in the end. They discounted the fact that the majority of European countries was behind Duisenberg. If the euro was supposed to signify any-thing, it was new European unity. But the French still seemed to be engaging in power politics. Everyone had agreed that splitting the term, if it were done voluntarily by Duisenberg, would be consistent with the treaty. But the fatal flaw of the French was assuming Duisenberg would accept this, that he would agree on a specific date, and that this could be specially codified.

On Thursday, Jean-Claude Juncker, well known for broker-ing deals between Germany and France, called Duisenberg to ask him how far he was prepared to go in agreeing to a division in the term. 'I'd realized,' said Juncker, 'that, besides [Dutch prime minister] Wim Kok, no one had actually talked to Duisenberg.'

Duisenberg told Juncker that he was ready to accept a splitting of the term, but that 'I must be able to announce that I will resign out of my own free will. I'm not going to sign on to a particular date.'ˣ Juncker, delighted, informed the other players: Kohl, Jospin, Kok and Blair. Chirac, in Japan at the time, was also informed. The split, Juncker and Duisenberg agreed, could be justified to the public if Duisenberg gave a statement, that in view of his age he did not want to serve his whole term. Of course, this wasn't entirely true. Duisenberg had not been concerned enough about his age to consider cutting his term before the Dutch-French stand-off forced him to. He had, years before, thought of not serving a full term if he got the ECB job, and had mentioned this in an interview. Duisenberg recalls how Blair conveniently reminded him of the interview:

Apparently, I had mentioned this one year before I was

appointed to the EMI in 1996. Of course, I had forgotten. It was discovered by the staff of Mr Blair. The staff dug up an interview that I gave to a Dutch feminist monthly magazine where the question was asked: Will you do the job for eight years? My answer was: 'I do not regard it as very likely.'

The sentence was enough to supply other leaders with proof that a statement by Duisenberg that he wanted to step down early would indeed be 'voluntary'. Jean-Claude Juncker and Blair began circulating the information that Duisenberg had told them too that he had not wanted to fill the full term. The agreement, as Juncker understood it, followed the rough guidelines of Bitterlich's misunderstood 'memo'. A division of the term would not be formally agreed, since this would be in danger of violating the treaty's stipulation that terms were for eight years. But Duisenberg would voluntarily agree to step down. Everyone seemed to be on board. The problem lay in the fact that the two sides hadn't agreed to the exact date on which Duisenberg would step down. The French were ready to let Duisenberg make that decision voluntarily as long as he stated it clearly. They assumed this wouldn't be a hitch, since Juncker and others had already said Duisenberg agreed to a voluntary departure half-way through his term. For the French, a four-year term beginning on July 1, 1998 would mean that Duisenberg would stay no longer than July 1, 2002. In addition, the French planned to appoint the next president, who would stay for the full eight years. The problem was that, within the German camp, Waigel was pushing for less explicit terms. 'The day before the summit, I telephoned the Chancellor. I said that whatever happens, nowhere, not even in an informal agreement, should a date be set.'

Brussels

When Chirac arrived in Brussels on May 1, he was confident that a compromise could be reached. He was ready to veto any alternative, even if that were to deal a blow to the growing credibility that the euro project was enjoying witnessed by soaring stock exchange prices and bullish comments from economic analysts about the euro's likely strength. Chirac had been hardened by some recent defeats. In one of the greatest defeats of modern French politics, he'd called elections in 1997 in an effort to regain support for his Gaullist prime minister and government, but the Socialists won a stunning surprise victory. As president, he was having to share power under a 'cohabitation' arrangement. It meant that his influence was now limited, mainly to foreign affairs. He was also facing domestic criticism that the Maastricht Treaty had placed monetary policy under control of a bank and system that was modelled entirely after Germany. He was ready to go to the wall.

For tactical reasons, Blair had not discussed the compromise with other European leaders. Bitterlich's scribbled memo had been loosely circulated among the French, but otherwise only Blair, Jospin, Kok and Kohl were privy to the script. When the luncheon began at 1 pm, Blair told the leaders of a compromise agreement that Duisenberg would be appointed to a full eight-year term, and added that Trichet would succeed him. Blair then announced he was going to speak to Duisenberg about the appointment. According to the script, Duisenberg was expected to tell Blair in their one-on-one that he did not want to stay the full eight years, and that he would like to leave at some point in 2002. Then Duisenberg was expected to make that statement before the heads of state. But in his meeting with Blair, Duisenberg didn't bite.

Instead, he asked Blair to get the heads of state to ask him in writing to stay 'at least until January 1, 2002'. Duisenberg would then make a statement agreeing to the request.

Slightly bewildered, Blair went back to the room where the heads of state had gathered, and took Chirac and Jospin aside to ask them if they agreed. The French found Duisenberg's proposal unacceptable, since it meant that Duisenberg's term was still not limited. 'Chirac came to me and started arguing,' says Duisenberg. 'That is how I was drawn into negotiating.'

The misunderstanding created chaos. From 1 pm until 7 pm, there was a whirlwind of diplomacy, with the four main leaders

– Chirac, Kok, Blair and Kohl – engaged in bilateral talks and internal talks with their own delegations, trying to find a solution. The other leaders were left waiting in the dining room, increasingly impatient. 'Lunch' which had been scheduled to last until 3 pm, still hadn't been served. For hours, the debate became bogged down over Duisenberg's demand for the clause 'at least until' on the one hand, and the French desire for a definite date of departure on the other. Duisenberg recalls: 'He kept trying to force me to declare that I would step down soon, very soon, after the national banknotes had been removed after four years. I kept on refusing.'

Slowly, however, Chirac began to whittle down Duisenberg's resistance to agreeing to a vague date of departure. As Waigel explains:

It was difficult for Duisenberg, because he had to decide on this alone. His own side, the Dutch, were determined to have a success, whatever the conditions, especially after failed bids for international positions in the past. I don't know how far they discussed the splitting internally. But if Duisenberg had suddenly said, 'I'm not going to do this,' and another candidate was selected, the Dutch would have been devastated. At the same time, he was determined to hold on to his personal integrity and independence. He told me he didn't want to accept a specific date.

Finally, at around 7.30 pm, the French managed to win an agreement that Duisenberg would voluntarily announce he would depart after the euro money was distributed in the euro area, which was scheduled for completion at some point in the first half of 2002. This was sufficiently binding for the French, yet left open the precise date of his departure. Kohl, negotiating with just a couple of his closest advisors, agreed that such a vague reference to departure date could be agreed to. Finally, it seemed, all the major players, even Duisenberg, were on board.

But when Kohl took the agreement back to finance minister Theo Waigel, foreign minister Klaus Kinkel, and Bundesbank president Hans Tietmeyer, for approval, they rejected it. With federal elections only months away, Waigel and Kinkel warned Kohl that the German public wouldn't accept such a compromise and that Kohl would lose the elections if he accepted it. It was also the wrong signal to financial markets. Besides, Tietmeyer was dead set against it. The Bundesbank had humiliated Kohl and Waigel only less than a year before, when it skilfully mobilized the public against Bonn's plan to revalue the central bank's gold reserves. So close to the elections, Kohl wasn't ready to cross Tietmeyer again. Waigel insisted that any declaration leave the decision to Duisenberg to choose his date of departure. Appointing Duisenberg's successor, moreover, would have to take the form of an informal, 'gentlemen's' agreement, and would have to remain unwritten. If the French didn't agree, the Germans should pack their bags and go home, Waigel told Kohl. As Regling recalls: 'The Chancellor thought that he'd found an agreement that was acceptable. But we kept telling him that it wasn't going to work. This happened over and over again. That's why we were there until early the next morning. There were constantly new efforts, and new problems.'

Around 8 pm, exhausted, the four sides regrouped. After a short break, they began negotiations that would last over four more hours. Jospin had pre-scheduled a trip to New Caledonia, and had taken his leave at 7 pm, leaving French finance minister Dominique Strauss Kahn to negotiate in his stead. Frustrated, Chirac and Strauss-Kahn fell upon another strategy. They approached Blair and Kohl and suggested that they agree on a third candidate for the presidency. In recent months, Sirkka Hämäläinen, the Finnish central bank governor, had been mentioned as a possible compromise candidate: Finland was neutral territory, and Hämäläinen – known as the 'iron lady' in the German press – had kept inflation down to impressively low levels throughout tough economic times. Now her name was brought up again. But Kohl, shaken by the rebuff from his ministers, had hardened. He rejected a compromise, insisting Duisenberg was the right candidate. Finally, after hours of discussion, the French relented. Strauss-Kahn recalls: 'Someone proposed a solution. If it was not possible for the heads of state to declare that Mr Duisenberg will not stay for more than four years, then Mr Duisenberg must say in his own words, that for personal reasons he agrees not to stay later.' But as Strauss-Kahn knew all too well, the solution was nothing more than what the Germans, and especially Waigel, had been insisting on the entire time. The trick was finding a statement to which the French would agree. Blair and Kohl finally told Chirac that it was time for him to iron out a statement with Duisenberg that would be acceptable to both of them. 'The break-through came with this *tête-à-tête* between Chirac and Duisenberg,' recalls Cirelli. 'I don't know exactly what they said to each other, but it worked.'

The exact details of this night of intrigue will remain unclear, since the bilateral talks were numerous and the principal actors remember events differently, each coloured by their own inter-pretations. In the end, only Duisenberg knows just how much he promised verbally, and to whom he promised it. Duisenberg, for his part, said in an interview that he purposefully made sure that Blair was constantly by his side during the discussion with Chirac, so that no misunderstandings would arise later. 'At no single moment was I alone with anyone – neither with Chirac, nor Kohl nor Blair.' And no one-on-one talk with Chirac ever happened, he insists, not even in the presence of Blair.

Duisenberg sat at a table and wrote out a statement. He showed it to Chirac and Kohl, and they approved. It looked remarkably close to the statement that had been agreed to at 7.30 pm, but there was an added emphasis that the final decision would be Duisenberg's alone. Within ten minutes, at a few minutes before midnight, Duisenberg's statement was agreed to by the other leaders. By 12.30, the final press con-ference had begun, and Duisenberg's statement was announced:

I want to thank you for the honour of nominating me for the function of President of the ECB on this historic occasion. I explained to the President of the European Council that I will, in view of my age, not want to serve the full term.

On the other hand it is my intention to stay at least to see through the transitional arrangements for the introduction of the euro notes and coin and the withdrawal of the national notes and coin, in accordance with the arrangements as agreed at Madrid.

I wish to emphasize that this is my decision and my decision alone and it is entirely of my own free will and mine alone and not under pressure from anyone that I have decided not to serve the full term. Also in the future the decision to resign will be my decision alone.

During the press conference, Chirac was his usual bulldozer self. Announcing the deal, he insisted Duisenberg's statement had been voluntary. But journalists in the audience broke into derisive laughter. They had been aware for months of the plan for a split term and of how Duisenberg had repeated privately that he was opposed to such a solution.[3] Chirac bristled. He retorted that such an agreement was appropriate since it is normal for countries to represent their own interests, and that this is exactly what France had done by pushing for Trichet. Strauss-Kahn, worried about the reference to national 'interests', scribbled Chirac a note, warning him that his statement would be misunderstood. Chirac promptly corrected himself, saying that he had not meant to use the term 'interests'. Blair made a good effort to put a positive gloss on things. Speaking after Chirac's confident statement, Blair declared repeatedly that Duisenberg had made his decision of his own free will.

Two other decisions were announced. First, the other ECB board members were named. Second, the finance ministers and central bankers announced that they would use the existing central rates in the European Monetary System as the value of the national currencies when they converted to the euro on January 1, 1999.

The aftermath

After the summit, other European leaders were despondent. 'It's

---

[3] In April, Duisenberg's chief aide at the EMI, Lex Hoogduin, also told journalists that Duisenberg would not accept a split in his mandate.

not at all good for the European Central Bank to begin in this way,' said José Maria Gil-Robles, president of the European Parliament. 'Let us hope that a baby born in such a bad form can recover and be strong in the future.'

One lesson that can be learnt from the May summit is that the real decision-makers were the German and French leaders, symbolic of what had long become obvious to any observer in Europe: that the European currency project was always a French-German driven project. Blair was a marginal figure, and he was made into a scapegoat for the all-night blunder. Prime Minister Romano Prodi of Italy called Blair 'ill-prepared'. Other EU leaders criticized him for making them swelter in the lunch room for a full twelve hours, with no change of scenery. Cirelli, recalling the British attempt to help during the late negotiations, said: 'The Brits tried to intervene, saying "can we help?" The Germans, the Dutch and the French told them, in so many words: "It's none of your business, stay out. This is a euro question."'

The same evening, Austrian prime minister Viktor Klima said that European leaders 'had never seen anything like it'.[xi] Klima announced that his government would immediately take control of the regular inter-EU discussions about the single currency preparations, as Austria was the next country to hold the EU rotating presidency, and unlike the UK, it was a fully-fledged euro member. It was to become the first diplomatic brush-off for Blair, who had been basking in wide international approval for a recent agreement he'd signed with Northern Ireland. Klima's compatriot, foreign minister Wolfgang Schüssel, was more negative than most other leaders about the Brussels meeting. 'If you had experienced the events of today, you would not have got the impression that this had anything to do with creating a union,' he said.[xii] 'It was an unusually hard wrestling match,' Kohl said later that evening. 'In my experience – and I have been present at many milestones – it was one of the most difficult hours.'

But the British lack of preparation for, and sensitivity about, euro issues, has been evident on other occasions. One German leader complained of Blair's last-minute preparation for the ECB's inauguration on June 30 at Frankfurt's old opera house, the *Alte Oper*. Blair had prepared the keynote speech, the last during Britain's EU presidency, on the plane journey over. Malcolm Bruce, a senior member of Britain's Liberal Democratic Party, complained about Blair's performance and the apparent exclusion of Britain from any serious brokerage of the deal. 'Other people formulate the rules; we join later and complain about it,' he said.

Dominique Moisi, a French analyst at the French Institute for International Relations, said the dispute symbolized a major transition in European politics. 'It's the last gasp of nations as they are giving up something they no longer control. This is a symbolic moment of transition between two worlds,' he said.[xiii]

But another question, not posed by the media or other commentators at the time, was how the agreement reflected on Duisenberg's character. The immediate media attention focused on Chirac's arrogance. But splitting the term wouldn't have been possible if Duisenberg had simply resisted getting caught up in the game in the first place. Why did Duisenberg, who had professed that he would not stand for a splitting of the term, finally agree to issue a statement that clearly alluded to a compromise? He knew that the Maastricht Treaty called for a term of eight years, and so if he believed that the ECB should be truly independent, why didn't he insist that it was to be eight years or nothing? Could Duisenberg have returned to the Dutch central bank or to Dutch politics? Duisenberg says not. A year before, he had moved to the EMI after receiving a pledge of support from all EU governments, except for France, for the ECB job. A successor was now firmly in place at the Dutch Central bank, and it was too late to return to politics. The truth was that he badly wanted, and needed, the ECB job, and let himself get pulled into the debate with Chirac in order to save his candidature. Moreover, Blair's reminder that he had earlier indicated he might not wish to serve the whole term gave him independent justification for accepting an early departure.

When will Duisenberg step down?

Since the meeting, Duisenberg has been cagey about his true

intent. The real meaning of his statement, however, seems to point in the direction of a willingness to hold to his agreement with Chirac to step down. Yet the more the controversy grows around the date of his departure, the firmer Duisenberg seems to get about not leaving.

He has had support from other political leaders. After the Brussels agreement, Waigel insisted that there is no legal reason to prevent Duisenberg from serving the full eight years. Waigel, when asked what would happen if Duisenberg changed his mind and wanted to stay on for eight years, said: 'Then no one would be able to stop him.' Dutch finance minister Gerrit Zalm and Belgian central bank governor Alfons Verplaetse have made similar statements.

But the most credible reason to believe that Duisenberg had made no commitment to step down came from Blair. Duisenberg explains:

A few days after the summit, I was on my way from the Netherlands to the European parliament for the confirmation hearing. In my car, I got a phone call from Blair. He said: 'I know you are on your way to the European parliament. Maybe it would be of interest to you to read the declaration which I gave to the House of Commons during the question and answer time. I said: 'What did you say?' He said: 'It's better if you see it in writing, because then you have it in official form.' He faxed the minutes of the British parliament to my hotel in Brussels, where I was stopping off before going to parliament. The minutes showed that Blair was asked the question: 'Mr. Prime Minister, if Mr. Duisenberg were to decide to fulfill his full eight-year term, can he do so?' And then they showed that the prime minister said 'Yes.'

Within a few weeks, in an effort to counter such statements, Chirac said that Duisenberg had promised him privately he would retire by July 1, 2002. But questioned on November 25, more than six months after the May decision, Duisenberg admitted that the controversy was making him more stubborn:

Well, today I still don't think I bowed. I said nothing more than I had always said, that it would only be my decision, it was not likely that I would stay the whole eight-year term. But the moment when I step down is only up to me and no one else. So of course, afterwards, in all honesty, this has all increased my determination to stay as long as I can.

Explaining why he let himself make the statement – which appeared to allude to an agreement – in the first place, Duisenberg states:

I was unwillingly drawn into a negotiating process in which I didn't want to participate. But so it happened. I was drawn into it. And I knew what the views of the various players were. It was part of the game. One thing that one shouldn't be sur- prised about is how politicized the process was. Any inter- national appointment is a political process. It's the outcome of political struggle and debate, whether it be the secretary gen- eral of the OECD, the president of the European Commission, or managing director of the IMF. In the 1960s and the 1970s the bigger countries could never agree among themselves on who to appoint, and countries like the Netherlands and Sweden benefited from that as the bigger countries tried to find a solution. Since the mid-1970s and early 1980s, the big countries have been much more likely, or keen, to agree among themselves, to more or less impose on the world their decision. But this time, it didn't work. The central bankers were unanimous in their recommendation. Some leaders, including Mr Chirac, were not prepared to accept what they saw as a 'diktat' from the technocrats – the central bankers.

Thus, when pushed, Duisenberg makes it clear that his position is hardening. In an interview with *Le Monde* on December 30, 1998, Duisenberg responded again to a question about whether he would quit after four years: 'The answer is no.' The remark caused an uproar in France, and immediately thereafter, he took a step backward again: He began telling interviewers that he would no longer comment on the issue, and that the markets would have to get used to living with the uncertainty. In other words, it *was* still an open question.

In some ways, Duisenberg's response to the mandate issue resembles his response to pressure placed on him by European governments to lower rates in late 1998. In both instances, he was personally prepared to follow a policy that the political powers desired of him. But the more it looked as if he was being politically coerced into the decision, the more he resisted agreeing to that policy.

A separate argument in support of Duisenberg's decision to make the 'voluntary' statement, of course, is that his decision in the end saved the project from disgrace. The markets had expected Duisenberg would be appointed president, and a rejection of Duisenberg would have given them serious shivers. The character question, at least then, was not an issue. The result was summarized best by Portugal's prime minister, António Guterres, who empathized with Duisenberg's move, having himself experienced the insult of being shut out of the talks between the Germans, French and the British: 'I accepted the feeling of humiliation, because the euro is more important.'

On the day of the agreement, European currency traders were mixed in their evaluations of the Brussels outcome. Some feared the decision dealt a blow to EMU's credibility, and expected a sale of Eurozone currencies for dollars. Sal. Oppenheim was one such bank and hedged its positions respectively.

But others conceded that while a splitting of the term was bothersome, the monetary policy result would be no worse, given Trichet's reputation as a monetary hawk. It was, as Moisi said, a last gasp by political forces for autonomy. From now on, interference with the ECB would be like tampering with a hornets' nest. Infuriate the bankers, and they were likely to sting back in the form of tighter monetary policy to prove their independence.

The European media was highly critical of Chirac. The German mass-circulation *Bild* called him 'Rambo', and described him as having 'rammed his head through a brick wall . . . In the decision over the head of the European Central Bank, Chirac got his way, regardless of the cost, and almost wrecked the introduction of the euro.'

The French, meanwhile, were also left feeling bitter. When Duisenberg took he helm at the ECB, and made the preliminary decisions about personnel, the French started complaining that there were too many Germans in top management. In June, Duisenberg announced that the ECB's top 'management' positions would be filled almost entirely with those workers who had been at the EMI. But in addition, he selected Manfred Körber, the 'Prussian' director of public relations of the Deutsche Bundesbank, to be chief of the ECB's public relations. Körber ran the Bundesbank's public communications efficiently, but on a tight rein. Though board members ultimately decide when and to whom they gave interviews, Körber was the gatekeeper in deciding which journalists gained access, and was known to be obsessed with control, becoming furious if journalists held on to interview notes for a few days without publishing an article – since each interview with a board member was timed precisely to feed markets a particular signal. But with Körber, the ECB was in solid and safe hands. Ultimately, the choice reflected another characteristic of Duisenberg: the ability to pick good people and delegate work to them. For example, at the Dutch central bank, he brought over his trusted former finance ministry aide, Nout Wellink, and groomed him as his successor. Wellink is now a key ally of his in the ECB governing council. At the Dutch central bank, Duisenberg also hired a personal assistant as a gatekeeper for all his activities, allowing him to withdraw from direct relations with the bank's director of communications, Bert Groothof. Groothof contrasts this with the style of Duisenberg's successor, Wellink, who prefers to be immersed in day-to-day details. At the ECB, Duisenberg has also brought in a capable assistant, the former chief of economics at the Dutch bank, Lex Hoogduin, to manage his office. Duisenberg's style has bothered some at the bank, who criticize it as too aloof. One high-ranking ECB staff member says:

> Duisenberg is someone who tries to minimize conflicts. I think he's doing a good job trying. But [Duisenberg's

predecessor, president of the EMI Alexandre] Lamfalussy was more concerned with the details. He was more present, visiting offices and giving you feedback. He was more popular with the rank-and-file. Duisenberg, he's sitting somewhere at the top of the bank. He's more distant.

The other new addition was the chief of the ECB's international relations division, Bernd Goos, also from the Bundesbank. The French also began to notice how Duisenberg travelled freely in Germany, speaking the language fluently. He didn't need his public relations assistant to accompany him around, as did Lamfalussy. *Le Monde*, describing Duisenberg, wasn't exactly complimentary: 'He has a disjointed air. He likes classical music, and has a false air of an ageing playboy – part of the well-heeled *caviar gauche*.'

Duisenberg also reportedly decided that the board would operate according to the more collegial 'ministerial' system common in the Netherlands and Germany, in which board members keep their portfolios unless an unusual situation requires a change. He reportedly decided against the more absolutist 'cabinet' system common to France, under which the president is free to shuffle portfolios at his own discretion, for example giving Issing the cherished chief economist title for one year, and then handing it to someone else.

At a ceremony in Bonn marking the 50th anniversary of the German mark, Duisenberg gave a speech in fluent German. 'See,' Waigel declared triumphantly. 'The euro speaks German.' (Duisenberg has since taken up French lessons. He also bought a holiday home in southern France in late 1995.)

France's Christian Noyer, as chief of ECB personnel, shrugs off these complaints. 'People in France are complaining about Körber and Goos, but what they don't understand is that these guys don't have anything to do with policy making.' But then Noyer's position as the highest-ranking Frenchman at the ECB was the result of another controversial push by the French.

Noyer: France's default

Christian Noyer, 48, is the youngest of the European board members. With dark brown eyes and smoothly clipped salt and pepper hair, Noyer is cherubically good-looking. Soft-spoken, with a placid tone, he can be wooden in front of larger audiences, but has charm and a ready smile in smaller groups. For most of his career, he has had the good fortune of being in the right place at the right time. Loyal and reliable, he was often the default candidate for a job the next step up the ladder. His sky-rocketing career has also been propelled by his mentor, Jean-Claude Trichet.

However, in 1995, after reaching the pinnacle of his career in the French civil service, events in Paris suddenly derailed him. Noyer became an unsuspecting victim of partisan politics. Earlier, he'd loyally served the right-wing Gaullist finance minister Edouard Balladur. In a newspaper interview, he had talked of the 'harmony' of political views between himself and Balladur, a *faux-pas* for a civil servant who was expected to stay neutral if he was to avoid being purged after a change in government. In 1995, Balladur ran for the presidency and was the early favourite to win the elections. Had he won, Noyer might have been able to secure his own position at the top of government. But at the end of the campaign, Jacques Chirac, stressing social and solidarity policies in order to gain the vote of French workers who had been unsettled by the rapid changes in society, produced an upset. Noyer's primary mentor, Jean-Claude Trichet, had departed to the Banque de France in 1993. Without his two guardians, Noyer's fortunes soured.

Until then, his life had resembled a 'long river of tranquillity'.[xiv] He was born in the nondescript Paris outer suburb of Soisy. His father was a government functionary, a real estate manager in the city of Rennes, known as a bastion of conservative Gaullism and Catholicism. Noyer studied law at the University of Rennes, which is not far from the Brittany coast, where he liked to go sailing, a hobby he had in common with Wim Duisenberg and one reason Noyer says the two have hit it off so well together since their arrival at the ECB. 'Sailing is something we can talk about together; we share adventures,' he says. A law professor gave him a taste for public life and he developed a belief in free market principles. But having Gaullist leanings, Noyer was also fiercely proud of his nation, and saw the need for a strong state. He once said that France couldn't be 'overestimated', either politically and diplomatically. Its rich culture and its history, he said, permits France to continue speaking loud and strong.[xv]

Noyer graduated from Rennes at 21, and then went to Paris, where he pursued advanced degrees in law and political science and then enrolled in the Ecole Nationale d'Adminstration (ENA). After ENA, he went straight to the Trésor, following in the footsteps of Jean-Claude Trichet. Noyer spent a good part of the next two decades at the Trésor, dealing mostly with banking and financial issues. He was seconded to Brussels, where he was the financial attaché to the French delegation. There he represented French interests in negotiations over the Common Agricultural Policy, which despite growing criticism recently for cost and distortion of agricultural prices, Noyer praises as Europe's 'only real common policy'. Unlike other programmes, which are largely redistributive, the CAP helps all countries through the support of prices in all EU-member states.

On his return to the Trésor in 1982, he helped implement a new bank law, and after three years, began work in the Trésor's international division. It was then that he began working directly for Trichet. In 1986, when Trichet had moved from the Trésor to become chief of staff to finance minister Edouard Balladur, Trichet took Noyer with him, and appointed him a senior adviser to Balladur, where he helped abolish exchange and credit controls. Later, he was put in charge of privatizing Société Générale. For the next several years, Noyer held on to Trichet's coat tails. Whenever Trichet made a move, Noyer would follow. When Trichet was appointed to direct the Trésor in 1987, he brought Noyer in to work as his deputy. First, Noyer was in charge of 'international multilateral issues' where he handled the IMF, the European monetary system and currency market portfolios. Then he directed debt management and banking issues. Finally, in 1992 and 1993, he oversaw the

Christian Noyer, Vice-President of the European Central Bank

state's industrial public holdings and managed their financing.

In 1993, at 42, Noyer had his big break. Finance minister Edmond Alphandéry appointed Noyer his chief of staff – yet another slot that Trichet had once filled. Later that year, when Trichet left to go to the Banque de France, Noyer took over Trichet's position in charge of the Trésor. It was one of the most influential administrative position in the republic. Unfortunately, Noyer was not able to enjoy the prestige for long. Within a year, things began to go wrong, and his two-year tenure was rocked by bad publicity. His key contribution on the European level was to push the French to accept a widening of the bands to 15 per cent during the 1993 crisis in order to save the EMS.

Trichet had managed to turn his Trésor position into an internal pulpit from which to rally government support behind stability oriented policies. But in the process, the policies had caused economic contraction, and with it, domestic resentment. Critical politicians, both within and without the government, turned Trichet into a whipping boy for the country's woes, but Trichet had a stubborn character that could withstand such public battering, and, remarkably, even thrive on it. Trichet stayed on to direct the Trésor under several ministers, over a course of five years. Each minister became indebted to him for taking such a hard line; it saved them from doing it themselves.

Noyer, by contrast, was soft-spoken, even bashful, prone to search for compromise rather than holding to a specific policy line. He was used to being the 'nice guy', as most ECB council members were later to describe him. As one French commentator put it, he was 'a discreet man, accepting opposing points of views as something the most natural in the world'. Worse, the economy plunged into full recession, and Noyer was forced to bear the resulting opprobrium, both from within government and from the public at large.

Finally, during a staff reshuffle, Noyer was forced out. He was appointed chief of staff to finance minister Jean Arthuis, since there was supposedly no alternative candidate for the job. Again, it was Noyer's 'by default'.[xvi] He regretted having to take a step backward. 'I accepted it. But I had already done the job,' he says.

Things didn't get better. Noyer did not get along with the

minister, despite the fact that the two shared Gaullist leanings. Jean Arthuis had wanted someone else for his chief of staff, but had been overruled by the prime minister. Noyer lasted there only two years, and in 1997, when the socialists swept the Gaullists out of power, Noyer was left looking for a job. The four years – two at the Trésor and two as chief of staff for Arthuis – had been marked by a number of débâcles, some of which were clearly beyond Noyer's ability to control or influence. They ranged from financial problems within the state company, Crédit Foncier, to gaffes over the privatisation of two other companies, CIC and Thomson. But the worst, most costly mishap was at the publicly-run Crédit Lyonnais.[xvii] The chairman of that bank was given a free-hand to pursue his ambitious goal of making the bank the largest in the world, but in the process, he ran up a series of risky debts, though much of the bad debt first became apparent when Noyer arrived in 1993. As director of the Trésor, Noyer was a key supervising official. Trichet, was at the helm of the other supervisory institution, the Banque de France, and had earlier been head of the Trésor when the bad debts began mounting. After 1993, Credit Lyonnais's bad debts increased, but state aid kept being funnelled in. Again, accusatory fingers (albeit politically motivated) began to point in the direction of Noyer and Trichet. Noyer defends himself, saying he and other civil servants had pushed for reform in the financial sector, but that ministers had not had the political will to push it through. He also said that such failures 'unfortunately arrive from time to time,' and compares the Credit Lyonnais crisis to the US savings and loan crisis in the 1980s, when the US government had also underestimated the problem at the beginning.

In 1997, with no godfathers feeling indebted to him, Noyer's options were limited. He was offered a position as financial counsellor in the French embassy in Washington, and as French executive director at the IMF, but these were steps-backward and he turned them both down. For months, however, he remained a 'director' working on 'various assignments'. Disillusioned, he began looking for a job in the private sector.

Saved

On Monday April 27, 1998 Noyer received an unexpected call from the Elyseé. On the line were Chirac and his finance minister Dominique Strauss-Kahn; they wanted his view about a possible job opening. It was less than a week before the May 1-2 European Council summit in Brussels, where the two French leaders would decide with other leaders who was to be appointed to the ECB's six-man directorate. There would be a few other decisions to make that weekend. For example, they would also give their final blessing to accepting eleven EU member states to participate in the single currency. But none were as controversial as the one surrounding the slot of the ECB presidency.

Chirac and Strauss-Kahn were publicly insisting that their candidate for the position, Jean-Claude Trichet, was the right man for the job. The German Bundesbank and the Dutch were standing firmly behind their candidate, Wim Duisenberg. A majority of the other member state leaders also seemed to be supporting Duisenberg before the Brussels summit. However, a few months earlier, the French had begun to believe that a compromise could be found, and the week before they received apparent confirmation in the form of the memo from Chancellor Helmut Kohl's diplomatic advisor, Joachim Bitterlich, that gave the green light to the plan to divide the eight-year presidency. In addition, to sweeten the deal for the French, the Germans would support a French candidate for vice president.

The two French leaders had already approached a deputy at the Banque de France, Hervé Hannoun with the offer of the vice presidency, but he had turned it down. Now time was of the essence and, with few alternatives left, they had settled upon the loyal and dependable civil servant Noyer. As Noyer himself says, 'The list of candidates wasn't that large' because of the experience and qualifications required.

'In the eventuality that Duisenberg is chosen as president of the ECB, would you agree to be nominated as vice president?' Chirac asked him. Noyer, surprised by the offer, was pleased that it came from both leaders. It meant he would be in no one's debt. Chirac was of the rightist Gaullist party, and Strauss-Kahn of the socialist party. In Noyer's words, it meant that 'there was complete consensus. It was not a purely political appointment after which there could be expectations.'[xviii] For Noyer, it was a dream come true. Long before his summons to the Elyseé, he'd pondered the possibility of an ECB appointment, but had put it out of his mind, believing that his chances were too slim.

It didn't take long for him to accept: he agreed within 48 hours. The decision came just in time. The French failed to push through Trichet, and so Noyer was appointed vice president. In addition to Duisenberg and Noyer, the six-man directorate was also to include the Bundesbank directorate member Otmar Issing, the Finish central bank governor, Sirkka Hämäläinen, Spanish central bank board member Eugenio Domingo Solans, and chairman of Italian stock exchange and former Italian central banker, Tommaso Padoa-Schioppa – all of whom had been nominated by their national governments. When the directorate met in mid-1998, and divided areas of responsibility among its members, Noyer was awarded jurisdiction over personnel and legal issues – again, more or less by default, since he was a trained lawyer and the only member on the directorate not experienced in central banking.[4] Other board members took on the responsibilities that required more technical and policy-related knowledge of central banking.

Most of the work in the personnel and legal areas had been completed before Noyer arrived in June. The ECB carried over almost without exception all of its staff from the EMI, and so by June, when the ECB officially started operations, it already employed 540 people.

Of those jobs, 310 were considered 'professional', meaning they demanded an advanced university degree and were in some way linked to policy research or policy execution. The rest were

---

[4] In fact, Noyer is the only one of the entire 17-member ECB governing council (which is the key decision-making body, and consists of the six directorate members plus the eleven governors of the national central banks) who does not have central banking experience.

secretaries, mail messengers, security guards, truck drivers and janitors.

Noyer's conversion

As vice president of the ECB, Noyer is the No. 2 at the bank. As a graduate of ENA with close ties to the Paris government establishment, his biggest challenge is to demonstrate support of the ECB's independence and that he is not going to bow to pressures from the Elyseé or Bercy. The élite of the ENA, like the generation before them, had become accustomed to parachuting into cosy jobs with state-controlled companies. Their futures appeared secured by the benefits of high-level public service. But as the state contemplated spinning off its public holdings – banks, telecommunications, airlines – ENA's élite found themselves under threat. As Noyer looked around the world in the 1970s and early 1980s, he saw examples of how the state still appeared successful in conducting monetary policy. The United States, which had an independent central bank, for example, had higher inflation than Japan, where the bank was fully dependent.

But by the 1990s, Japan had stumbled upon hard times. The Tokyo stock market crashed, and the economy screeched to a halt. Suddenly, the Japanese central bank looked capable of failure after all. Seeking to keep its currency at a low exchange rate, it had held interest rates low. But this had caused unsustainable growth in the stock market – the so-called 'bubble' economy, which then finally burst. In contrast, back in Europe, the Bundesbank had continued to show good results. It kept inflation low, and at the same time, during the late 1980s, economic growth was creating hundreds of thousands of jobs. France and other countries were now keeping their currencies closely in line with the German mark, thereby also experiencing the beneficiary effects. 'I was initially puzzled by the variety of results,' said Noyer. It did not take him long, however, to decide there was little alternative but to support the idea of an independent central bank. 'Now, with hindsight, the Japanese case turned out to be particularly complicated,' he says. He is now certain that, given the average performance in terms of economic growth and stability, 'Europe has one of the best results, globally, if not the best.'

He says he also shares the 'political vision' of his German colleagues, Otmar Issing and Hans Tietmeyer, that the two countries are ready to forge ahead on more aspects of political union. The euro can only help that process, he says. The rhetoric of his youth, of France's right to speak loud and strong, has been moderated into more co-operative language.

My father was a prisoner of war for four years in what was Germany at the time. He was held in Pomerania (currently Poland). It was a cold place. Many other members of the family had to fight during the first and second world wars against Germany. So when I was young, I was taught to have a cultural bias against Germany. On the other hand, my parents had always been convinced that you could only get rid of the demons of the past by unifying Europe. It has been a major achievement that we have been able to build on the personal experience of our forefathers in the second World War . . . When you start to operate policies of major importance which can only be implemented while considering the eurozone as a single country, this is consistent with more political union, simply because the people need to start to think more about a common destiny. The euro, for the first time, will give European societies a concrete sign of European identity. They will hold Europe in their hands.

Noyer is careful how he expresses his vision of this closer union. He doesn't see the need for centralization, since technology has made it more possible for decentralized execution. The European Central Bank's organization is a good example. Decisions are made in Frankfurt, but they are executed separately, via the various national banks. Noyer rejects the notion that there needs to be a concentration of power.

Technology has changed a lot of things. Today you can operate a network where any decision made at a given point in the network can be implemented almost simultaneously in decentralized financial centres. A need to concentrate business at one given financial centre doesn't exist anymore. These technological capabilities are improving year after year. This means that other factors for attracting people to a particular city are of major importance. Is the city aesthetically pleasing, is it open to new ideas; is it multicultural? These become the decisive questions. The fact that the ECB is based in Frankfurt does not have any influence on the overall network. We at the ECB are totally neutral on these things, not only because we want to be neutral, but because the needs of the institution are such that they don't preclude anything.

At home at the ECB

Noyer sits comfortably on the 35th floor of the Eurotower building, looking over the beautiful vista of the Main river. He tells visitors that it reminds him of his days at Bercy – at the finance ministry in Paris – when he enjoyed the view of the Seine winding into the sunset towards Notre Dame. It is the best view at the ECB. Wim Duisenberg has taken an adjacent office, which had been occupied by the EMI president before him, Alexandre Lamfalussy. But during Lamfalussy's tenure, Commerzbank decided to build the tallest office tower in Europe right across the road. It now looms outside Duisenberg's windows. To the north are the towers of the other banks that make up Frankfurt's impressive skyline. These are Germany's banking establishment: Deutsche Bank, Dresdner Bank, and DG Bank. Behind the towers are the rolling hills that encircle Frankfurt in a bowl shape, and which are the location of Frankfurt's wealthy suburbs.

Noyer says Frankfurt has a more liberal and international atmosphere than other German cities. 'For Latin people, this region, along the Rhine, is much easier to adjust to than Bavaria, or north Germany.' Nevertheless, compared with Paris, New York and London, Frankfurt is a very 'regional' city, he says, choosing a politer phrase than 'provincial'. Noyer still often travels home at weekends, but now has an apartment in the Westend, a wealthy quarter bordering the banking centre and a few blocks away from the ECB. Like all the board members, he drives a German car, a BMW. He has also started meeting Frankfurt's commercial bankers. He gave one of his first speeches in Frankfurt at Dresdner Bank, with which he had developed ties during his days negotiating at the club of Paris, when Dresdner board member Ernst-Moritz Lipp represented the private banks during some of the negotiations.

Life at the ECB

The ECB is Europe's most 'supranational' institution so far. At the ECB, employees are not considered representatives from their own countries, following national self-interests, as is the case within the European Commission in Brussels and other international organizations. Rather, at the ECB, workers are implementing policy independently, as individuals and for the interests of Europe, no longer trying to find compromises between national interests – at least in theory. 'The difference is that you have to think European,' says Noyer.[xix]

As of December 1998, of 57 leadership positions at the ECB, 11, or 19 per cent, are German, which corresponds almost exactly to Germany's population as a proportion of the EU total (21 per cent). This is not a coincidence; it is carefully planned. For example, on another measurement, Germany possesses three of the 14 top 'directorate' positions, or 21 per cent. Scheller, a dry, pipe-smoking ex-Bundesbanker, is one of them,[5] the general director of personnel and administration.

Scheller likes to keep count. He knows the figures of each nationality off the top of his head. Of the 310 total professional workers at the ECB, about 70, or 22.5 per cent, are German. Second and third are France and Italy with 40 each. Only under the professional level – messengers, truckers, security guards, and janitors, and other support staff – do the Germans show up in much higher proportions (after all, it's difficult to invite a Frenchman to work as a trucker in Frankfurt). But even here,

---

[5] The other two are Bernd Goos and Manfred Körber.

the foreign presence is impressive. For example, Scheller hired a French janitor who has worked for years at a German bank in Frankfurt. Many of the 'foreign' recruitments were people already working in Germany. Though the house language is English, the German connection is strong. In the protocol section, for example, there are two women working together, one who is French, the other Irish, who speak German together because they have both lived in German-speaking cities for several years.

The Dutch-German camp revisited

But perhaps the most subtle power network within the ECB is that of the Dutch-German camp that seems to spread its influence throughout the organisation. On the 35th floor, next to Duisenberg's office, is 'the assistant to the advisor', Lex Hoogduin, whom Duisenberg brought with him from the Dutch central bank. Then there is Frank Moss, the Dutch-speaking (Flemish) Belgian chief of the 'protocol' division. He has direct access to Duisenberg. Moss is the official who sits in on the governing council policy meetings and takes minutes. He has the power of the pen; it is he who decides what is written and recorded for the history books. He writes the minutes in English, and releases them to the national central banks for translation. A Dutchman, Van Baak, is head of the personnel directorate under Scheller.

But nowhere is the Dutch-German influence more evident than in the economics directorate, which is the most important force within the ECB for formulating monetary policy. Dutchman Gert Jan Hogeweg heads the directorate and also chairs the committee for monetary policy which includes other national bank representatives. Under Hogeweg, the directorate is split into three divisions. By far the most influential is the 'monetary policy' division, headed by a young and energetic ex-Bundesbanker Hans-Joachim Klöckers, considered a rising star at the ECB by his colleagues. During the important post-unification years of 1991 and 1992, Klöckers wrote speeches for Hans Tietmeyer.

Though Klöckers is not a council member, and thus does not have a vote, he is personally in control of the way monetary policy is debated within the bank. As head of the monetary policy division, he is the funnel for the flow of debate that emerges among the rank-and-file researchers and which then passes up to the council, and also of policy shifts and demands from the council being passed down again to the researchers. Klöckers, 37, made his mark as an assistant to Jean-Jacques Rey, the Belgian EMI official charged with preparing the groundwork for monetary policy strategy for the ECB. Under Rey, Klöckers churned out over 30 reports on monetary policy strategy. From mid-1998 until Spring 1999, he was putting in 14-hour days. Rey says of Klöckers:

> He's the one with an overall view. If you say something that is inconsistent with what was already agreed upon six months ago, he immediately alerts you. He's the conductor of the orchestra, the one keeping the various instruments in harmony. He has a strong point of view, but at the same time, he is fair and balanced with those he talks with.

Under Klöckers, in turn, are three sub-divisions. One of them deals with monetary policy strategy, which is led by a German Issing acolyte, Klaus Masuch, who studied with Issing at Würzburg, and who worked under him at the Bundesbank for several years before leaving for the BIS to start with the original team that was to develop into the EMI. Masuch's division, along with the 'monetary policy stance' division, are the two key divisions. Finally, Wolfgang Shill, another German ex-Bundesbanker, heads the 'economics developments' division, which is also under Hogeweg.

Not counting the Flemings, the Dutch have 9 per cent of the ECB's management positions, even though they form only 4 per cent of the EU population. Their two seats amount to the most powerful representation on the 17-member governing council, given that one of them, Duisenberg is president.

The French meanwhile are strewn throughout the ECB in various capacities, and dominate no one particular division. It is the Italians that we turn to in the next chapter, who dominate the bread and butter of the central bank's work: 'market operations'.

Better Paid than the Bundesbank

Like the central banks in Germany and some other European countries, the ECB has shrouded its wage policies in secrecy. Scheller reveals only that the wages compare with those of the European Commission. But the job descriptions of the ECB are hardly comparable to those of the Commission, so there is substantial discretion among the ECB's management in setting salary. It is an open secret that a banking job at the ECB is much better paid than the equivalent at the Bundesbank or most other central banks.[6] One high-ranking ECB official reported that his salary is 40 per cent more than his former salary at the Bundesbank. Other reports have estimated salaries as much as 80 per cent more than the Bundesbank, though the accuracy of these reports is questionable.[7] xx ECB workers argue that they merit the pay difference. First, they consider themselves the 'élite' of the central banks. Most of those who came to the EMI originally did so upon recommendation of their national banks. They are also required to be able to write and 'negotiate' in the house language, English, which means that, on average, they have better language skills. Finally, at least so far, they are working much longer hours.

Like the corps of 'Eurocrats' who work at the European Community headquarters in Brussels, ECB workers have a

---

[6] One difficulty that Scheller has faced in setting wages is caused by the very different pay scales within the various national central banks. The Bundesbank pays its workers rather low salaries compared to the private sector. Its top managers also make much less than those at the Banque de France, for example. Most of the banks are public institutions, but some are privately organized. The Austrian bank, for example, is a private shareholder company.

[7] For example, *Der Spiegel* reported that the ECB's chief economist, Otmar Issing, earned an annual salary of DM 545,000 in 1998 while he was still at the Bundesbank. In an interview, Issing would not comment on his current salary, but said it is lower than DM 500,000, and that it wasn't any higher while he was at the Bundesbank.

range of benefits. Those who are hired from other countries earn, in addition to regular salaries, an 'expatriate' supplement of 16 per cent of their salaries. If they have already worked in Germany for five or more years, then they receive only a 4 per cent supplement. All ECB workers earn a 'household' supplement of 5 per cent of their wages. They also benefit from special EU tax levels, and other favourable social insurance schemes.

Most German employees have to contribute 50 per cent of their social security payments (the other 50 per cent being paid by their employers), but ECB employees contribute a minimum of 4 per cent of their salaries to social security. For health insurance, they also contribute far less than their employer – only 1 per cent of their salaries – again, much lower than the 6 per cent or more typically paid by most workers in Germany. They don't pay any unemployment insurance, but they enjoy unemployment benefits for a year in the rare event that they do lose their job. The contracts are special to the ECB, and any legal recourse by the staff is to be taken directly at the European level.

The salaries of the board members are set by a committee comprised of three outside appointees of the Governing Council and three appointees of the Council of Ministers. The committee decided to take as its yardstick the salaries paid by the European Commission. According to that measure, Duisenberg makes the same as the President of the European Commission, which was 553,372 marks in 1999. This includes a basic salary of 449,257 marks, plus a 15 per cent residential allowance, a 5 per cent house allowance and a 14,263 mark entertainment allowance. The board members make 20 per cent less, or 442,698 a year. For seven of the eleven governors of national central banks, salaries are not public information. But based on tax returns and available information, it appears that the Banca d'Italia's, Antonio Fazio, makes the most of them all. These reveal that Mr. Fazio earned about $600,000 in 1995 (the latest figure available). The salary reflects the prestige that the central bank enjoys in Italy, though some government officials are critical of the bank's lack of transparency. 'Fazio acts like the emperor, emerging out of his palace twice a year to speak to the people, and then going back in again,' said one diplomat. The range of governor salaries decreases from there. But most, if not all, appear to make considerably more than Alan Greenspan's salary of $137,000.[xxi]

Below the 35th floor, where Duisenberg and Noyer have their offices, on the 34th floor, are the offices of the four other board members. The carpets are a warm beige, unlike the lower floors, which have plainer, grey carpets. On the east side of the 34th floor reception area is a seven-foot tall wooden pyramid, the pink surface of which is dotted with black-painted squares. The guards said it came from Finland, but no one knows how it got there. On the west side, there is a bronze sculpture from the Dutch central bank of 'Claus, the defender of the euro,' a mounted armoured knight leaping over what looks like a wall. No one except for the board members and their secretaries work on the floor. Like the 35th floor, the 34th floor has its own security guards, who watch the area with video screens that are linked to with cameras. Except for the occasional ring of their mobile phones, and their quiet conversation, the floor is otherwise blanketed in silence. The hallways are painted a conservative white, with wainscoting below.

The other floors host a mish-mash of departments. Until December 1998, operations and some other divisions were scattered on several floors. On the second floor is a euro-modish cafeteria and separate coffee area; but here, the centre of Europe's new currency, no cash is accepted – only smart cards. On the fifth floor are the ECB's library and archives. ECB documents are top secret. Those not cleared for release to the public are held closed for 30 years, just like the minutes of the ECB's governing council. The floors are decorated with spartan sterility, sprinkled with modern art on loan from a local Frankfurt museum. The bathrooms sport slick steel pedestal wash basins, and politically correct hand-towel dispensers – instructions are written in German, English and French.

The staff is allowed to use the Bundesbank's swimming pool and gymnasium free of charge. The ECB also has teams that compete in soccer, tennis and swimming against the other national banks. And, after all that, should any of Europe's most powerful bankers have energy to spare, the Bank organizes golf, biking and skiing activities.

NOTES

i Interview with author, January 21, 1999.
ii *Nouvel Observateur*. November 13-19, 1997.
iii *Neue Zürcher Zeitung*. November 5, 1997.
iv *Le Monde*, November 6, 1997.
v *Valuers Actuelles*. 15 November 1997. P. 45.
vi *DLF*. November 5, 1997. Noon.
vii *RTL* (French) November 5, 1997. 6pm.
viii Interview with author, December 16, 1998.
ix Interview with Waigel, January 21, 1999.
x Juncker interview with author, November 6, 1998.
xi *International Herald Tribune*, Monday, May 4, 1998. 'Blair's Role in Bank Deal Fails to Clarify Country's Position in EU.' p. 11
xii *The Wall Street Journal Europe*, Monday, May 4, 1998. 'As Europe Launches New Currency, Summit Battle Casts a Shadow,' p. 6.
xiii Ibid.
xiv '. . . tranquility' Description of Noyer contained in the French newspaper. *Echoes*. December 13, 1993. 'Complèment Trésor'. 'Harmony' is a quotation attributed to Noyer in the same article.
xv 'Christian Noyer, l'empirique,' *Le Monde*, September 14, 1993.
xvi *Le Monde*, January 3, 1997. 'Le malaise de la direction du Trésor après l'échec des dernières privatisations.' Here, too, his appointment was described as a 'default'.
xvii *Le Monde*. January 3, 1997.
xviii Interview with the author, November 26, 1998.
xix Interview with the author, November 27, 1998.
xx *Der Spiegel* 34/1998. Pp. 86-90.
xxi 'For sale: central banking, low mileage, high running-costs' *The Economist*, January 30, 1999.

CHAPTER SEVEN

The Bank's Operations

As underscored in Keynes' reservoir analogy, the central bank is like an operator of a reservoir, regulating the water level so that the community linked with it can enjoy an adequate supply.

In constructing the new euro money zone, Europe's leaders implemented a series of directives designed to harmonize financial service laws. These have helped break down the barriers between the ten individual reservoirs of the member countries,[1] and Europe's money supply has now accumulated into one large pool. According to the pool's user habits, the money travels freely across EU borders with almost no regulation.

On the one hand this larger pool has positive effects. Bottlenecks in supply of money are discarded, money flows more quickly to those regions and businesses that demand it, and the costs of obtaining money are thereby reduced. Businesses prosper as the cost of financing is brought down. On the other hand, keeping order, once quite easy in a tiny reservoir with barriers preventing major leaks, has now become more difficult. A storm within the large EU reservoir can now whip up more aggressive waves, causing havoc as they slosh about Europe in ways that society may not be equipped to handle. Money will abandon less efficient regions. Starved of capital, unemployment will rise, and governments will come under domestic pressure to find remedies.

---

[1] Luxembourg already had a monetary union with Belgium, so there were only ten monetary zones, not eleven, before 1999.

The tool kit

During the construction of the large reservoir, some regulatory differences between member states were left intact, however. These act as underwater barriers in the Euroland reservoir, essentially reefs that generate eddies and undercurrents. Odd, unpredictable things can happen. If the general money level falls, money might stay welled up in specific, controlled sectors of the Euroland economy. In less controlled sectors, it might haemorrhage out. No one knows how faithfully the overall money supply level reflects the reality underneath the surface. When the money level rises, some remote sectors protected by regulatory walls might find themselves flooded once the walls are breached.[2]

At no other time in history has a central bank been charged with controlling such a potentially large and complex reservoir. In 1999, the eleven countries making up the euro area produced $6.9 trillion in goods and services per year, compared to $7.2 trillion in the United States. In the next few years, other countries in western and eastern Europe are scheduled to join, which will make the eurozone the largest economy in the world, surpassing even that of the United States. Scores of other countries are indirectly attached to the European reservoir. Many African countries, for example, have linked their currencies directly to the euro, having previously been tied to the French franc. When the central bank adjusts the water level in the reservoir, therefore, it will also be affecting an increasingly extended area.

The Fed's power, until now, has been so dominant that it has

---

[2] An example is France's Crédit Lyonnais. The French government has infused it with massive amounts of aid after the bank began running up major losses in the mid-1990s. But the aid was agreed by EU authorities on condition that the bank's activities be curtailed to operations within France only. The billions of euros being pumped into the bank by the state means that money supply must be reduced somewhere else in Europe in order to keep the overall supply level constant. Thus, indirectly, member state economies can be made to suffer by the activities of other countries. Take housing. Some countries rely more on variable interest rates on mortgages than in others. If interest rates go up, some consumers are faced with higher mortgage payments. They inject more money into the economy than in those countries where mortgage rates are fixed. Again, money is flowing into the Euroland reservoir through a mixture of arcane and complex valves.

been expected to operate its reservoir with an eye on making sure that the global irrigation system is kept stable. The emergence of the ECB means there will be two main operators, perhaps with vastly different views about the desirable level of the world's reservoir system.[3]

At the same time, Europe's tax laws are still the most complex in the world. Each country has its own laws regulating corporate taxes, income taxes, capital gains taxes, value-added taxes, not to mention taxes (or in some countries, contributions) for social security, health insurance and unemployment insurance. Each country allows its own exceptions and loopholes. There are other distortions. Some countries, for example, have housing markets that are based on fixed-rate mortgages, others on variable-rate mortgages. All these factors cause distortions in the way money flows through the economy.

Like the Fed, the ECB has a diverse set of plumbing tools to adjust the money supply. Its main method is buying and selling government bonds and other financial instruments.[4] If the ECB believes that the money supply is too low, for example, it injects more money into the system by buying government bonds.[5] It usually does so through intermediate players, for example private banks. The ECB transfers cash to the private bank, and puts the government bonds on its balance sheet. The private bank, which has sold the bonds, pumps the received cash into the economy, usually in the form of loans to clients who need the funds to finance projects. Overall, the money in the economy rises by the amount of the bond value. The ECB does

---

[3] In January 1998, Argentina announced that it was pegging its peso to the dollar so tightly that it would guarantee to exchange each peso for a dollar, and dollars could be used by companies to pay taxes and by consumers buying goods. In other words, it was legal tender. Its central bank became an 'Exchange Board', possessing no independent policy of its own. Many other countries peg their currency to the dollar, but most maintain their independence, and have the discretion to devalue or revalue if they so decide.

[4] All of the European governments issue bonds regularly to raise the money needed to pay for spending projects. Besides the central bank, other actors, for example private banks, can buy these bonds.

[5] When the ECB buys bonds from private banks, it usually sets a date at which it demands a resale.

this in such massive quantities that it can influence the money supply relatively quickly and powerfully. If the ECB judges the water level too high, it does the opposite. It sells the government bonds that it already has on its ledger. It then takes the cash received and stores it away in its reserves. This way, it can keep lenders and borrowers of money happy, making sure there is enough liquidity in the system.

The ECB has a number of other instruments to adjust the supply, each with their own advantages and disadvantages. It obliges European banks to set aside so-called 'minimum reserves' for each investment that they make. When a bank injects money into the economy by lending out money, it automatically lays aside a given percentage of the money in the form of a deposit with the central bank. By monitoring the level of these reserves, the ECB is alerted to ebbs and flows of money in and out of the economy. This instrument is an early indicator of what is happening to the overall level of the reservoir. One disadvantage, however is that minimum reserves are a relatively expensive tool for private banks. The central bank only pays a small amount of interest on the reserves deposited with it, and so the banks make little or no profit from the arrangement.[6]

Equipped with a sophisticated tool-kit, the ECB's job is knowing exactly how it should manipulate the level in its new giant reservoir. For months before the euro's launch, ECB

---

[6] The buying and selling of bonds is usually in the form of so-called 'reverse transactions'. The bank agrees to carry out a transaction with a private bank and then to reverse the transaction within a very short period of time. These transactions do not only include the buying or selling of government securities. They also include direct collateralized loans. Other ECB instruments used to adjust the money supply are outright transactions, which refers simply to direct loans; the issuance of debt certificates; foreign exchange swaps; and the collection of fixed-term deposits. In its standard operation, the ECB performs the reverse transactions weekly, with the maturity on the transaction being two weeks. The bank also engages in monthly transactions with a maturity of three months, for the purpose of providing longer-term financing to banks. As a rule however, the ECB does not intend to use these long-term transactions as signals to the market, and therefore will act as a 'rate taker', that is, taking market rates at the time of its transactions. For fine-tuning, the bank uses any of its instruments it wants to deal with unexpected liquidity fluctuations, which might have adverse effects on interest rates.

researchers were trying to find the best answer. Making their task more difficult was the increase in money flows that the larger money reservoir was likely to create. If the US Federal Reserve lifts its interest rates, European investors shift money out of European bonds and invest in US bonds, where they can benefit from higher returns. Conversely, if the US lowers rates, money will cascade into Europe. Before, this effect was moderate because Europe's many separate national supplies of money were too small and controlled. This tended to dissuade US investors, who found they were unable to invest or withdraw money quickly enough.

ESCB

The ECB in Frankfurt is the command and control centre for the fine-tuning of Europe's central banking reservoir system, seated at the heart of an overall network that includes twelve central banks. The ECB executive board holds a running discussion of how much money should be funnelled into the system through the refinancing operations it conducts every two weeks. But the twelve national central banks are relied upon by the ECB to execute the decisions. In effect, they operate the reservoir's twelve key locks. The overall operation – the ECB and the national central banks – is called the European System of Central Banks (ESCB).

ECB board member Eugenio Domingo Solans, a Spaniard, is responsible for ensuring efficient communications between the command centre in Frankfurt and the lock operators down at the reservoir. Reporting to him is Jim Etherington, who is in charge of the ECB's information systems division. Etherington, originally from the Bank of England, is in charge of the day to day functioning of the computer hookups. The ECB acquired a Siemens teleconference system to link ECB headquarters with the national banks in case the governing council or other officials wants to consult them. British Telecom provides the ECB system with an integrated communications system. Etherington says one of the ECB's biggest challenges is overcoming the language barrier. Many of the problems with the ECB's preliminary tests in its payment system over the course of 1998 stemmed from simple misunderstandings between workers at the various national banks who were still learning English as a language of communication. 'At the end of the day, the problem is links between places like Portugal and Finland. You have to have people who can talk to each other in the same language. If you don't, you could have a spanner in the works.'

The ECB in Frankfurt provides the national banks with the terms of its open market operations through this computer link. At least twice a month, for instance, the ECB issues to the national banks the rates at which it will sell government bonds, which mobilizes the banks to start a bidding process with the private banks in their respective countries. As the bids are received from private banks, they are registered in the computer, so the ECB can see at a glance the various prices bid. It directs the national banks to sell allocated numbers of bonds to the highest bidders. If Irish private bankers bid a higher price than private banks in Spain, for example, the bonds go to the Irish. Usually, however, the private banks in the various countries make a range of bids so that money is injected sufficiently into each economy. The bidding process assures that more is injected into those countries where there is more demand.

The Italians

While Solans and Etherington make sure the technical means for the operations are up and running, it is two Italians who are the bank's front-line managers implementing the directives handed down by the ECB, making sure that they go through smoothly, and keeping in touch with the market's pulse to ensure there are no liquidity bottlenecks.

Chief of the operations division is Francesco Papadia, who joined the ECB after over twenty years of experience at the Italian central bank, the Banca d'Italia. Papadia directed the Italian bank's international operations, which effectively schooled him in one the most innovative, skilful and clandestine of missions. The Banca d'Italia didn't enjoy the comfort of the German Bundesbank, which controlled the rock solid anchor of the EMS system – the mark – and was therefore able to slumber most of the time, taking little action in the markets. Rather, the Banca d'Italia had to manoeuvre constantly to out-trick speculators wanting to knock the lira out of the system. This required sharp intervention in the currency exchange market in order to keep the lira pegged appropriately to the mark. Rome's short-term and chaotic borrowing habits kept the central bank constantly on its toes, deflecting it from any stable regularity in operations.[7] In addition, Rome's large budget deficit meant that the government borrowed large amounts of money from the markets, which interfered greatly with the system's overall liquidity.

At the ECB, by contrast, Papadia oversees a very 'controlled' set of operations. Exchange rate interventions are not part of the bank's regular portfolio, since the bank will not be pegging the euro to another currency. Papadia explains: 'Here, monetary operations are transparent and regular. We make sure that everyone understands what we're doing. This is our bread and butter task.'[i]

But if Europe ever decides to agree to an exchange rate mechanism in which the euro is pegged to say, the dollar or the yen, it will need to intervene cleverly in the markets, buying or selling currencies at strategic times in order to achieve the desired goal. Exchange intervention is much more of a psychological game of bluffing, and bluff-calling than the bank's regular operations, and one that Papadia is the best prepared for, given the skills he learned in Rome: 'They're in stand-by mode,' Papadia says, smiling.

Decentralized command and control

One key difference between the ECB and the US Federal Reserve is the chain of command. The US Fed's chairman has

---

[7] There was no fixed date for the Banca d'Italia's repurchase operations, and no fixed duration for them.

more hands-on authority than the ECB's president. Take for example former Fed Chairman Paul Volcker who 'ran the Federal Reserve', according to William Greider, author of a book on the Fed published in 1987. Back in August 1984, for instance, when the Fed's decision making body (the Federal Open Market Committee, or FOMC) decided to hold rates steady, Volcker had only one vote within the FOMC, but he supervised the daily operations of the Open Market Desk in New York. He had disagreed with the decision, having voted in the minority. In defiance of the FOMC decision, Volcker told the Open Market Desk to ease. Anthony Solomon, president of the New York Fed at the time, said:

> I knew what instructions he was giving the New York desk, and I thought he was not faithfully observing the instructions of the FOMC. He got the desk to take major actions that went way beyond the framework of the directive. He was taking too much leeway personally.[ii]

Things are different in Frankfurt. The governing council, Papadia says, is a collegiate body, and there is a strict division of labour that keeps the system decentralized. While the president is in charge of the bank's overall representation, he does not directly communicate with Papadia or the leaders of other divisions. The bank's procedures call for him to go through Sirkka Hämäläinen, the Finnish board member responsible for operations. Hämäläinen then contacts Papadia with instructions.

> The entire system is set up so that collegialism is ensured. The governing council makes the policy decision. The board then implements that decision, by communicating directives to the ECB staff. We then communicate the decisions to the staff of the national central banks. They then implement the policy. It's a very decentralized system. The president is much more a *primus inter pares* than a policy czar.

What would Papadia do if Duisenberg were to march into his

office and command him to sell 10 billion dollars to buoy the euro? 'I must admit, I've never thought of that scenario,' he says. 'I suppose it could happen, but it's unlikely.'

The ECB is not dependent on decentralization for efficiency in its operations. Technically, notes Papadia, the ECB in Frankfurt could take over the function of the national central banks. This would cut down on superfluous staff, and help Papadia and his colleagues in Frankfurt keep more direct contact with the pulse of the markets. But shutting out the national central banks would be highly controversial. Thousands of jobs are at stake, and understandably, the national banks are jealous of giving up their territory. The US Federal Reserve and the German Bundesbank, however, had their operations centralized over time, and Papadia can only conjecture whether the same will happen at the ECB. 'The frank answer is, I don't know,' he says.[8]

A more important requirement, Papadia says, is that Europeans change their mentality. They no longer belong to medium-sized countries with little financial clout. Operating without consideration of continental and world responsibilities is the way the Bundesbank operated for decades, and is what the Europeans have become accustomed to. Rather, there is an international political dimension to the bank's activities, and Europeans must learn to think in those terms. This vision of a greater, more powerful Europe is something Papadia says his bosses at the Banca d'Italia had long envisioned. Among those were Tommaso Padoa-Schioppa, now an ECB board member. Papadia explains:

> The Federal Reserve is our standard of comparison, which is a taxing standard ... It also has to do with a vision of Europe. It's something that carries you. I've been working with Padoa-Schioppa for many years, and with (former Banca d'Italia governors) Carlo Ciampi and Guido Carli. The three of them clearly had in mind that Europe is a project that

---

[8] Another Italian central banker, Lorenzo Bini Smaghi, left the ECB shortly after it opened its doors in 1998. He had headed the policy division of the EMI, and criticized the decentralized nature of the ECB's operations.

goes beyond money, beyond economics. It is a broader, more ambitious project.

Reporting to Papadia is 30-year-old Roberto Sciavi, the Italian director of the operation division's crucial 'front office', so-called because it is the office most engaged in the markets, actually arranging the buying and selling of bonds and other instruments, albeit indirectly through the national central banks. It too tries to stay in constant communication with market players, keeping a watch on markets to locate potential liquidity crises or other important developments.

Sciavi is the youngest director at the bank, having served three years in the trenches of the EMI's 'financial markets' division, which prepared the way for the ECB's operations division. Pacing the highly secure 'operations' room on the Eurotower's ninth floor, Sciavi looks more like a nervous private trader than a bureaucrat for a supranational European institution on an EU salary. Dressed in a dark suit, he stops to hunch over computer terminals, quickly scanning incoming data. Sciavi still has the air and instincts of the private banking world, where he worked for four years in Luxembourg for the subsidiary of an Italian bank, IMI. His job there was on the capital markets desk, responsible for trading of eurobonds and derivatives, mostly denominated in lira. His days lately have been 13-hour ones, which has meant giving up his gym visits. 'You have to keep up with the views of the dealers, so you have to keep the same schedule,' he says.

The market players with whom he keeps in regular touch are mainly the friends and contacts he made in Milan, Rome, New York, Frankfurt, London, Paris and Scandinavia, while working at the Italian bank. 'You never forget your contacts,' he says. Sciavi assumes his former colleagues are making more money than he is, but says he has the satisfaction of being part of an experiment that will lead to a stronger, more self-confident Europe. 'In the long run, we in Europe cannot stay as we are, small and divided. If we unite, we will be bigger and stronger. We can't do it overnight, but we can achieve it in small steps.'

E-day

During the first week of operations after the euro's introduction on January 1, 1999, there were a series of glitches, mostly in the system's payment settlement system, in which euro accounts are settled between private banks. If one private bank buys bonds from the ECB denominated in euros, and turns around to sell some of these bonds to another bank, it uses the payments system, called Target.

Again, it is an Italian who is ultimately responsible for this system: board member Tommaso Padoa-Schioppa. The initial glitches during the system's launch were caused by individuals working at private banks who had not been adequately trained to use the Target system, he says. They had typed in the wrong codes on their computers. Padoa-Schioppa likens the problems to those of a new airport, in which a control team needs to be trained to help land planes smoothly. If they aren't trained correctly, the planes will be backed up, and there will be delays. Indeed, after the bank's first few operations, the problems appeared to be over.

The German-Italian 'regulators'

The governing council of 17 decides on the level of Europe's interest rates each fortnight, but they leave it to the board to make proposals on the operations needed to regulate the reservoir's money supply. On the six-member board, it is Sirkka Hämäläinen who is technically in charge of operations. Papadia and Sciavi report directly to her. But the type, amount and duration of the operations are proposals voted upon by the entire board, and she has only one vote. Though on the surface, operations look more like a 'technical' issue, there has been quite a bit of disagreement on them, and they proved the bank's most controversial issue in the early months of 1999. The first operational disagreement came as a result of a traditional ploy by German banks that outmanoeuvered other banks, for example those based in Spain. Under the German system, banks were forced to overbid to be assured their share of central bank financing. Because of its penchant for control of the money supply, the Bundesbank stringently controlled the amounts of money it pumped into the economy during operations. If private banks bid more than the allotted amount, the Bundesbank awarded only a percentage of these bids. Over time, banks learned to bid for more than they really wanted.

During the ECB's first two operations, the bank issued only 8 per cent of the money that the European banks had bid, which bothered Hämäläinen and some others on the council, who weren't used to the practice. Many German banks bought up the money offered by the ECB at the tender rate of 3.0 per cent, and then turned around and sold it on the open market at a higher rate, about 3.2 per cent – just below the ECB's overnight lending rate of 3.25 per cent. That overnight rate sets a ceiling on interest rates, since it is the rate at which the central bank guarantees private banks needing financing.[9]

Combined with some initial problems in the ECB's target system, which obstructed the Frankfurt-based banks funnelling loans out to other countries, the bidding process meant that much of the money that the ECB had offered had been swallowed by German banks in Frankfurt, and that regions which were used to getting 100 per cent of the bidding – for example, Spain – had not received an adequate amount in the bidding. Spanish banks in Madrid, therefore, were being forced to buy the money from the other banks in order to get their liquidity, but in the process ended up paying a higher rate. The overbidding banks were earning a tidy profit at the expense of Spanish banks. To be sure, the custom was endemic in Germany, Austria and some other European countries. For instance, German banks would often bid high for central bank money and then sell it at a higher price on the open market.

With the changeover to the euro, however, this practice became a focus of dispute. Some central bankers, like Hämäläinen, believed such practice was outmoded, that it

---

[9] The overnight lending rate creates a ceiling because no bank has the incentive to take out loans at a higher rate – since the ECB guarantees them loans at this particular rate.

created distortions, and they feared that the ECB might lose control if it miscalculated the needs of the market. Hämäläinen believed that the bank should either move to a 100 per cent allotment system, that is providing banks with the exact amounts that they bid, or pull down the overnight rate to match the tender rate, and so remove the incentive for the banks to overbid. That would base the ECB's operations more on free-market forces, helping the bank to judge how much money the market really needs. This free-market approach is one practised by the Bank of Finland and some other central banks. Indeed, Hämäläinen's compatriot, Matti Vanhala, now governor of the Finnish bank, backed her up in council meetings, criticizing the in-built overbidding:

> It seems absurd to have banks make bids which, if they were accepted, would put the banks in difficulty . . . Banks should be encouraged to act responsibly and be willing to accept the consequences of the bids if they are accepted. We in Finland changed our system overnight. We said 'Okay, in fixed rate auctions, whatever you bid, you will be forced to honour them.' At which time all overbidding disappeared overnight. There's no reason why this can't work . . . But some people at the ECB are aspiring to control both the price and quantity of the tenders at the same time, which you can't do, neither in practice nor in theory . . . Issing thinks that if you don't set the quantity, and cut the bids to fit that total, then monetary aggregates get out of control . . . That's not true. If we tell the banks: 'Whatever you bid for, we will push it down your throat, even if you bid twenty times beyond your need,' the problem would disappear overnight.

In effect, the Germans wanted to keep setting rigid prices on a limited amount of money, even though some shoppers – the bankers – were willing to pay much more for the financing than others. The market forces of supply and demand were not being allowed to work efficiently. In council meetings in January and February, Hämäläinen and Vanhala began pushing for a resolution. If the council could not agree on 100 per cent allotment, then the ECB should move to a 'variable rate' tender. A variable rate allows market forces to play more of a role, since the refinancing rate offered by the ECB would be bid up as the banks demanded more. The challenge was to provide the banks with enough information for them to be sophisticated in adjusting to variable rates.

But in board discussions about the overbidding, Hämäläinen found herself out-manoeuvred. Issing argued that banks could get used to the tradition of overbidding. More important, he said, was a strict control of the price and quantity of the ECB's operations so that the bank can better estimate the amount of money needed by the economy. Close monitoring of market reactions would put the ECB in a better position to forecast how much to offer in subsequent operations. 'If we are going to control and target money, we have got to control operations,' he argued. The first two operations had seen overbidding but the bank should try to iron out those problems in subsequent tenders.

During the board discussions, Issing forged a fragile consensus, relying on the support of Padoa-Schioppa. Noyer had so far been passive during the board and governing council discussions, and Domingo Solans was not particularly opinion-ated on the issue, so Duisenberg – eager, as is his way, to cut off debate before it gets bogged down in long theoretical dis-cussions – closed the issue swiftly by siding with Issing and Padoa-Schioppa. One council member complained about the German-Italian axis view on operations:

> There is a tradition which thinks it knows better and wants to control everything, for example prices and quantities of operations. But if you control things, you very easily get distortions in the market. It seems to exist in those countries where the banking sector is oligopolist. But when you take the whole Euro-area, you can use a more market-oriented system.[iii]

In early 1999 the issue was heatedly discussed by the national banks, within the governing council and within the ECB committees. One central banker from Belgium remarked:

It's an issue that reflects two different traditions. Hämäläinen represents the tradition that says that if you set the rate of tender, don't worry about the quantity, because the market will take care of that. But in the process, you get much more volatility. When the banks make their bids, they don't know what their share is going to be of the total amount. For example, they might bid for a large amount. But then, if market interest rates go down, these banks are stuck with much more money than they need. They have to get rid of it through the sloppy and expensive way of taking it to the ECB's overnight (deposit) facility.[iv] Issing represents the tradition which says it's better to have a fixed-rate tender. You fix the amount to make sure that the market is fed how much it needs, and if you find you are off in a given tender, you readjust it slightly the next time. You keep making forecasts about how much to adjust for the next operation.

But if the council members were divided in their views according to their national traditions, it was the bigger banks that seemed to be dominating the discussion, with the Bundesbank in front, despite it not being the one most in conformity with market principles. Hämäläinen explains:

This is one of the basic problems we experienced during the evolution of this project. It existed at the EMI. The big central banks have an easier time of sticking to their own traditions, even if the traditions are not the most efficient. Small countries have a difficult time selling the benefits of their systems, even if they are more modern . . . Sometimes I have the feeling that big countries are listened to more.

The Scandinavians have found themselves sticking together on some major issues, in the belief that this is the only way to counter big countries like Germany. National differences, they say, make for a more variegated debate at the ECB, but also a slower decision-making process. In the ECB's policy toward banks, for example, the Bundesbankers insist that every bank, no matter how small, should be treated as an equal by the

ECB, even if it means incurring extra costs to cater to them. Scandinavian ECB staff members complain that Germany's banking sector is inefficient and should be forced to modernize, arguing that significant consolidation is necessary to strengthen European banks, allowing them to compete globally.

Differences between the various central banks exist on a number of other issues. For example, the Bank of Finland and the Bank of England abolished their 'international relations' divisions on the grounds that they are now superfluous, given the highly international nature of modern banking activities. Their argument is that each banking division – operations, monetary policy, banking supervision – has its own international concerns, and therefore should supply and represent its own international analysis. However, an international relations division still existed at the Bundesbank and the Banca d'Italia when Euroland was constructed, which is why one was also created at the ECB.

Other misunderstandings have occured. Under the EMI, a set of committees was created to handle special issues, for example monetary policy, banking supervision and payments, each chaired by a member of one of the national central banks. The understanding was that these chairs would revert to officials within the ECB once the bank was up and running in mid-1998. But several national banks, namely Italy, France and Germany – the ones giving up the most influence – suddenly became aware of the power that could be lost, and decided that the chairs should not automatically revert to ECB officials. Belgian central banker Jean-Jacques Rey kept to the understanding, purposely limiting his contract as chair of the monetary policy committee so that it would be timed to end when the ECB started operations in June. But he found to his surprise when stepping down that other national bank representatives were not doing so. Hervé Hannoun, the Banque de France vice governor, for example, is chairman of the international relations committee.

During the Maastricht negotiations, it was the Bundesbank that had been the most adamant about making the ECB as powerful as possible. It had stubbornly resisted a clause granting executive tasks to the national banks 'to the extent possible'. Says one banker who was active in drawing up the statues, and who is now a high-ranking official at a national central bank:

> The Buba [Bundesbank] felt that there was nothing for national banks to do. The Bundesbank was basing their views on their own experience, remembering the tension-filled relationship they had between the centre in Frankfurt and the Länder. They said 'we need a strong position in Frankfurt vis-à-vis the provinces.' Ironically, things have changed. Over time, the Bundesbank has become one of those jealous central bank branches. They've come closer to the French and Italian views.

There are an array of other jealousies created by the desire of national banks to hold onto power. For instance, monetary policy is formulated and debated in the bank's monetary policy committee, where membership is made up of national central bank representatives. Yet, in parallel, an ECB professional team led by German national Hans Joachim Klöckers, runs a monetary policy division. This overlapping of jurisdiction existed earlier at the EMI, the ECB's predecessor, and there were often rows when one group kept a particular strategy paper from the other. It is no secret, for example, that heated arguments occurred between Klöckers, who at the time was the deputy of the monetary policy committee secretariat, and the Frenchman, Philippe Moutout, who was the head of the EMI's unit responsible for monetary policy.

Iron lady

Hämäläinen was baptized in the vicious world of currency markets when she became governor of the Finish central bank in April, 1992. The Finnish currency, the markka, was not part of the EMS at the time, but the country had recently plunged into recession, a result of the collapse of the Soviet Union,

ECB Executive Board. © Photographer: Claudio Hills.
Standing, from left to right: Tommaso Padoa-Schioppa,
Otmar Issing, Eugenio Domingo Solans.
Sitting, from left to right: Christian Noyer,
Wim Duisenberg, Sirkka Hämäläinen

Finland's main trading partner. The government had pegged the markka to the mark, but market speculators ganged up on the currency, selling the markka in vast amounts on the hunch that the government wouldn't be able to hold its line. In September 1992 the Finnish government was forced to float the markka, after only fifteen months of pegging. The currency instantly plunged by 13 per cent.

The failure was the first in a series of developments which would partially damage the EMS in 1992, and then destroy it a year later. The Finnish debacle put pressure on the Swedish krona, as markets began to doubt whether Finland's neighbour would be able to withstand an attack. From there, the markets went on to assault the British pound and the Italian lira, and they too were knocked out of the EMS.

Hämäläinen, 60, looks younger than her age. She is slim, has cropped blondish hair and a ready smile. She has been called the 'iron lady' by the German and Swiss media,[v] because of her time at the head of the Finnish bank. Despite the markka's float, she stubbornly helped bring inflation down to the low levels of Germany. Hämäläinen is temperamentally tough. Wim Duisenberg told a fellow central banker: 'The firebrands on my board are Padoa-Schioppa and Hämäläinen,' because of the passion the two showed during board meetings. When the ECB first began operating in mid-1998, the two contended that the board should have the right to set the agenda in council meetings. Padoa-Schioppa sought to uphold a proposal for the rules of procedures which said that the board would have sole responsibility for the agenda, but the governors in the council batted it down, insisting that they be permitted to place items on the agenda too. They saw it as a power grab by the board, and they suspected Padoa-Schioppa in particular of being a euro-visionary set on centralizing power at this new European institution at their expense.[10] At a board luncheon, Padoa-

---

[10] Indeed the governor of the Italian central bank, Antonio Fazio, was the biggest sceptic of all the governors. Fazio, a staunch Christian Democrat and traditionalist, was selected as the central bank's governor when Padoa-Schioppa, who had been number two, had also been a running for that job. Not surprisingly, Padoa-Schioppa, who has a different vision from that of Fazio, soon left the bank.

Schioppa expressed frustration at the council's reaction. He insisted the Maastricht Treaty – which he had helped negotiate – gave the board the right to set the agenda. He even suggested that Duisenberg take the issue to the council of ministers, if necessary. 'We have been rather eager to defend the idea of Europe,' admits Hämäläinen. 'Especially Tommaso. It has been his vision for a long time.' Responding to Duisenberg's comment about her and Padoa-Schioppa being firebrands, she adds: 'Maybe its true. We are both very eager in our own areas of responsibility. I am rather outspoken. When I have a view, I let it be known.' Hämäläinen has irked some governors with her conviction that money markets and central banking operations should concentrate over time on a few financial centres. 'Some are afraid of centralization, they think it means political union. I've realized it's useful not to discuss these things too openly early on' she says.

But Padoa-Schioppa and Hämäläinen disagreed over other issues within the board, for example, the bank's representation at international fora. Hämäläinen felt that it was her job to represent the bank when operational issues were to be discussed, even though Padoa-Schioppa oversees the ECB's international relations directorate. Duisenberg's solution was to divide assignments. He takes vice-president Christian Noyer to the Group of Ten (otherwise known as the G-10) meetings in Basle, the most prestigious central banking meeting. Padoa-Schioppa has been given jurisdiction over IMF and Group of Seven (industrialized countries, otherwise known as the G-7) meetings.

The Old Boys' network

For Hämäläinen, the biggest battle has been to breach the 'old boy' networks. She finds offensive the stories whispered around the bank that she obtained her position because the ECB board needed a token female. In Finland, Hämäläinen had become accustomed to a society which took equality between the sexes for granted. Finland was the first country in Europe to grant women the right to vote. For two decades at the Finnish central bank, Hämäläinen, who has two children and two grandchildren, did not encounter sexism in the workplace. But at the ECB, a difference was immediately apparent and not just because there were fewer women:

> I sometimes have the feeling that I have gone back twenty-five years in history. Twenty-five years ago, I had the feeling no one listened to me. I knew that my ideas were good, but people didn't find it easy to listen to them. I have a similar feeling now . . . At first, I thought maybe it was my own imagination, the result of the new situation here, and because of the stressful work, and that I was a little tired. I thought it might be my poor English. So I tried telling myself that I was seeing shadows where there were none. But then I realized no, this is the same thing I experienced in Finland a very long time ago . . . I have the feeling that sometimes, when I say something, there is no reaction. When someone else, one of the gentlemen, says the same thing, the reaction is: 'Oh, yes, that is a very good idea.' . . . Of course, when I was governor in Finland, some people were in a way compelled to listen to me. Now I am just an ordinary board member, and I come from a small country, and I am a woman. I have the feeling that these boys have their own way of thinking and believe I can't understand them . . . Once, during a discussion, someone told me: 'You just don't understand.' Once I talked to Tommaso about the general atmosphere. He said no, he didn't sense it.

Only a third of the ECB staff is female, and woman are employed mostly at the lower levels. To be sure, the ECB is not as backward as the US Federal Reserve was in the 1980s, when Nancy Teeters became the first woman on the FOMC, the Fed's decision-making council, and evolved into the 'conscience' of that body, speaking out for a monetary policy which she believed would be more humane.[11] The Fed had to build a

---

[11] At the Federal Reserve, Teeters became recognised for her ability to bring in alternative viewpoints at FOMC meetings. She argued that the high interest rates being supported by the Fed at the time – in order to bring down inflation – were

woman's cloakroom for Teeters, since one hadn't existed before. At the ECB, female cloakrooms already existed because the predecessor institution, the EMI, had secretaries and female professionals who worked on all of the floors. 'The only thing I asked for was to have a locker in the ladies' room for personal possessions,' says Hämäläinen with a smile. She is also the only one of the board members to have curtains in her office, and like Duisenberg, also has several palm-leaved plants.

Hämäläinen is aware of Teeters' arguments within the FOMC, but believes there are no 'female economics. Facts are facts and you have to follow the basic rules.' But on the other hand, she says there are 'limits to the logic of economic theory'. Hämäläinen may well become a balancing voice *vis-à-vis* the hawkish views of men like Otmar Issing and Jean-Claude Trichet.

Banking supervision

In the year running up to 1999, a record number of mergers and acquisitions were taking place in the financial sector, as companies sought to increase in size so as to be better able to compete. They were encouraged by a slew of EU directives which helped harmonize Europe's financial sector laws. Banking supervisory agencies, however, have become increasingly strained by these developments. The German banking supervisory authority in Berlin finds it difficult to oversee the activities of recently acquired Italian subsidiaries of the Deutsche Bank without co-operating with Italian supervisory authorities. Moreover, many national supervisory agencies are

---

too stifling for the economy, and exacerbated unemployment. Her voice within the FOMC became one of conscience, speaking out for a monetary policy which she believed would be more humane. She too favoured low inflation, but she thought the Fed could be gentler its approach to hiking interest rates. By closing themselves off from society, and perusing statistics and economic models, the FOMC members were in danger of giving too little attention to the immediate social hardships that their policies were creating, and too much attention to what theory suggested was better for the long run. Teeters challenged the board to think in a different dimension, even if she found herself in a minority. The result, however, was that she was not taken seriously by the men on the board.

splintered, having jurisdiction over only slivers of the financial sector – banking, for example, or insurance. There is no overall watchdog authority to sound a warning alarm when problems occur. With no fire-walls between countries, and no unified system of defence, a crisis that breaks out in one bank or sector of the market could easily spread throughout the entire European financial system.

It is a question that concerns Alexandre Lamfalussy, the Belgian central banker who was president of the EMI – predecessor of the ECB. 'We are moving very quickly toward a basic shaking up of the entire banking and financial sector,' he says.

In a study released in February 1999, the ECB argued that the system of national supervision was sufficient, with some officials actually ruling out a move toward a united body immediately. But the Italian board member Padoa-Schioppa, in a speech shortly after the study was released, said he is in favour of moving forward to a united supervisory body eventually, and that more cooperation between supervisory bodies is needed.

Lamfalussy blames the Maastricht Treaty negotiations, which decided to keep banking supervision agencies under national jurisdiction – a result Lamfalussy calls 'sheer madness'. While many at the time, including Lamfalussy, voiced support for a centralized supervisory agency, national negotiators couldn't agree on whether to locate such a body within the ECB or outside of it. In many EU member states, the supervisory agency was a function carried out by the central bank (for example Spain, Italy and France). In others, the agency was located outside the central bank (for example Belgium and Germany). Because each country held jealously to tradition, the negotiators couldn't reach a compromise. In the end, they decided to leave things as they were.

At the bottom of Lamfalussy's fears is the cut-throat competition within Europe's financial sector that the single currency has unleashed. Comfortable profit margins that were once protected by regulation are now disappearing. Worse, these developments coincide with turbulence arising in other areas of the global economy, for example the currency crisis in Asia, which

The Bank

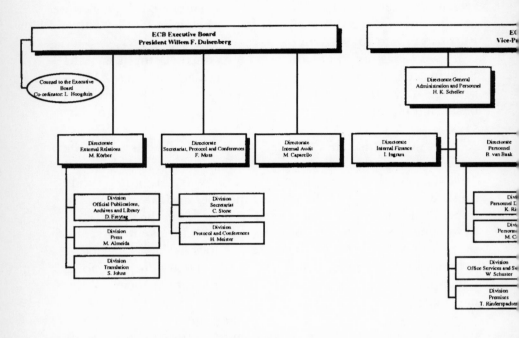

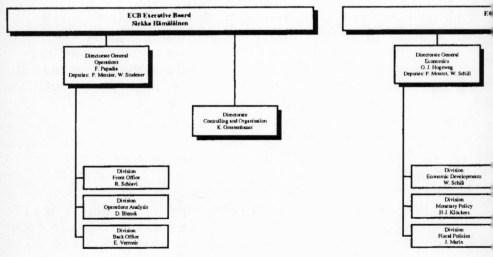

P.O. Box 16 03 19, D-60066 Frankfurt am Main
Kaiserstraße 29, D-60311 Frankfurt am Main
Phone: 00 49 69/13 44-0   Fax: 00 49 69/13 44-6000

8 February 1999

B A N K

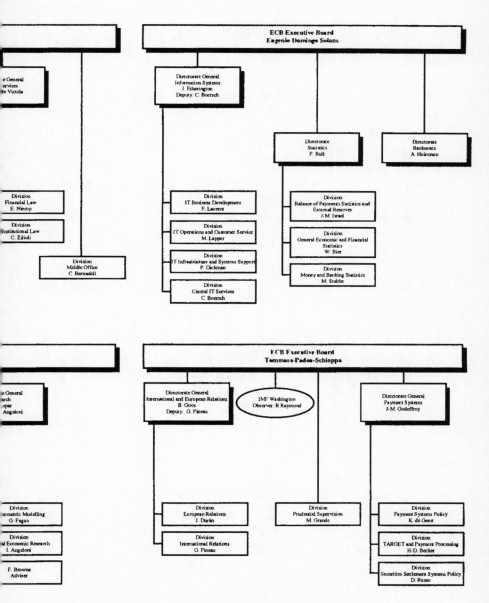

buffeted European and US economies over the course of 1998, and caused a general slowing of economic growth in 1999. These developments caused liquidity bottlenecks and also hurt the profits of Europe's financial companies. At the moment, national supervisors meet regularly for consultations under the aegis of the ECB in Frankfurt. European central banks insist that this solution is workable. For Lamfalussy, however, such cooperation won't suffice in hard times:

> In a situation of this kind, you must build up a strong supervisory system. It doesn't mean you have to meddle with the risk-taking decisions of banks. But you must have rules. You have to have an overview of the whole banking sector . . . we need to do it now. It's fine to say that cooperation is working when you've got peaceful times and nice weather. But there's a world of difference when you get the kind of developments in the global economy that we did in 1988, and when on top of that, Europe is going through vast structural change.

The US Federal Reserve, in contrast, has an extensive mandate for banking supervision, and Fed Chairman Alan Greenspan has even been seeking to expand its jurisdiction. However, in the US, the trend toward a 'universal' type financial system – in which a single company performs all financial tasks ranging from retail banking, investment banking, to insurance – is running behind Europe. The supervision question in Europe, therefore, is all the more pressing.

But there is a key difference between the Federal Reserve and the ECB in that the Federal Reserve benefited from the substantial private experience accumulated in the careers of its governors and regional bank presidents. Chairman Alan Greenspan was a private Wall Street economist before arriving at the Fed. Eurozone central bankers, on the other hand, do not have the same type of background. Most of them have spent the majority of their careers in central banks.

Moreover, the EU member states with the most experience in banking supervision and banking failures, Sweden and Britain, are not included in the Eurozone. The huge losses run by the French public bank Crédit Lyonnais, which had operated under the supervision of the Banque de France and the Trésor while Jean-Claude Trichet and Christian Noyer, respectively, were heading those institutions, suggest that the continental Europeans still have a way to go in efficiently supervising the banking sector during difficult times. The German experience in handling banking crises has also not been stellar,[12] although until now, it has been less challenged by crisis because of its conservative financial culture. Duisenberg, who oversaw a banking crisis in the Netherlands while he was central bank chief, has demonstrated the nerve to handle such a mandate.

Lender of last resort

Without a supervisory mandate, the ECB will be hampered in its ability to act as a 'lender of last resort', that is, bailing out financial institutions with emergency credit during times of crisis. The Federal Reserve, because of its supervisory functions, is equipped to act in such a capacity, and has been able to bail out ailing banks successfully in the past. During the failure of the hedge fund LTCM in 1998, the Fed invited the various creditors of LTCM together for negotiations. The Fed's help lent credibility and confidence to the negotiations and the creditors cooperated with each other. No taxpayer money was spent to bail out the ailing fund – that is, except to pay for the coffee and doughnuts the Fed supplied as the host of the discussions.

Europe and other parts of the world, however, do not have a credible 'lender of last resort' for crises that have international implications. Lacking the intense dialogue with banks that a banking supervisory agency would have, the ECB is a step behind in its intimacy with the financial system. To be sure, it can rely on the store of knowledge within the national central banks in the ECBS that do have a supervisory role, such as Italy, France and the Netherlands. But indirect reliance on scattered agencies might not prove sufficient.

---

[12] See Bernard Connolly, *The Rotten Heart of Europe* p.357 and pp 398–9.

Domingo Solans, the Spanish board member of the ECB, is the only one of the 17-member governing council to have had extensive private banking experience, but even Solans has had no hands-on experience in day-to-day banking operations. The lack of qualified personnel is why Solans believes the bank should remain without the 'lender of last resort' mandate.

Duisenberg, Hämäläinen and Tietmeyer are more cagey on the issue. They don't like to admit that they will be less capable of acting as a lender of last resort, fearing this could reduce the ECB's credibility. In sum, financial markets will tend to look to the Fed, or the US-dominated International Monetary Fund, for help in times of crisis, and by extension, to the dollar when they are looking for a secure reserve currency. Bill McDonough explains the difference that the US Federal Reserve made during the Asian crisis in 1998:

> Take South Korea. The American banks were not as heavily exposed there as banks from Japan and a number of European countries, and yet when someone had to get the banks in the same room, and focus on what was needed to restructure the loans, it was the Federal Reserve bank of New York and American banks that sat down and hammered out a deal within five days. The US has the experience of bringing people together and making things happen. When you have a crisis, that is when experience and tradition should be used. Of course, we were in contact with key European countries which were heavily involved in Korea. We did a lot of coordination behind the scenes.

Sometimes, German officials grumble about this. Jürgen Stark, the former state deputy finance minister, was critical about how the Americans would hear ideas put forward by the German delegation, then apply them during negotiations, and declare the resulting success as their own. But if Stark was content to remain in the background, others complained openly of America's strong-arm tactics. Jörg Asmussen, finance ministry official in charge of the IMF and G-7 portfolios in the international economics section, complained about how the US government negotiated compromises during the Asian crisis in 1998, while at the same time the US Congress couldn't agree to raise funding for international aid efforts. This, he believed, was hurting US leadership, and might force European countries to demand more say within international organizations like the IMF, especially now that the Europeans together make more of a financial contribution to that institution than the US. In Europe, central banks are usually in charge of deciding on how much to fund organizations like the IMF, and so the public and parliaments rarely have a chance to obstruct such aid. When the US took charge in coordinating the Seoul negotiations to re-structure South Korean loans, Asmussen explained, the decision by the US delegation to stay in the same hotel as the IMF delegation was 'not wise . . . It made it look to the European people as if the IMF is an American program.'

Bill McDonough responds:

> There are occasions when we Americans are a little careless and give the impression that we're figuring out how to manage the world and then let people know afterward what we've decided. . . . My impression is that it's a role that we try to resist most of the time. But why in the world would you care about whether the American delegation was staying the same hotel as the IMF? Most of the hotels in Seoul are within a two-block stretch. Do you go out into the dark, nasty weather and get cold, or do you stay in the same hotel and talk with each other? It's rather practical.

Regulation of the world financial system

Shortly after the LTCM fiasco in mid-1998, Christian Noyer gave a speech at the branch of Dresdner Bank in the wealthy north-Frankfurt suburb of Bad Homburg. He told the German audience that the French had long advocated more regulation for such risky hedge funds, and said that the Americans had refused. His comments emphasized the large on-going differ-ence in approach between the Americans and Europeans toward regulation. The Europeans are clearly more hands-on, actively seeking ways to control the turbulence that afflicts the global financial markets. The US, by contrast, has lacked a passion for regulation. They believe a minimalist approach will let business thrive more efficiently, and argue that Europe's heavy regulatory hand is partly responsible for the continent's higher unemployment rate and less impressive profit performance among businesses. They also point to the massive losses run up at Crédit Lyonnais as an example of the danger created by too much government involvement in industry. In his Frankfurt speech Noyer argued that banking supervision needs to be improved on the international level:

It is interesting to know that only a few weeks before the crisis of the hedge fund LTCM, we had informal meetings in which we had strong discussions about this issue with our partners around the world. The Americans seemed to be extremely hesitant about agreeing to any supervision of hedge funds, saying 'We think these are private institutions, they don't belong to the banking sector supervision. If private investors want to make risky investments, it's up to them. They are well managed. There is no problem at all. There is no need to ask for transparency. There is no need for supervision. No need for rules. No need for anything.' You saw what happened. The Europeans at the same time, were saying 'We think this is dangerous. This should be looked at, we should have more transparency. It is something that has to be worked out.' We saw the result.[vi]

William McDonough, president of the New York Reserve bank, and US central banker with the most intimate contacts with the Europeans over recent years, responds:

. . . Of course, we'd all like to come up with a way of dealing with highly leveraged institutions so that no such institution in future could create the possibility of systemic risk. The most effective way we can do that is through indirect rather than direct control over the leverage funds themselves, through counterparties, banks and securities firms.

A high-ranking US official dismissed Noyer's comments as another example of a European tendency to over-regulate:

> Ask the French why their unemployment level is at 12 per cent if they are such geniuses. There's always this heavy breathing, this 'we told you so' attitude. How would they like it if we compared the handling of the LTCM with the brilliant handling of Crédit Lyonnais. ... If you've got a hundred banks, the French *dirigiste* approach is to regulate all one hundred of them, including when each of the bankers goes to the toilet. If the banker breaks a leg on the way to the toilet, they'll say 'see, if we'd have regulated that, it wouldn't have happened.'

The differences are not only with the French. The US views on regulation differ from those of the Europeans on many issues. Ernst-Moritz Lipp, board member of Germany's second largest bank, Dresdner Bank, spoke alongside Noyer at a private talk at one of the bank's Frankfurt branches. He said the Europeans and Americans have a completely 'different ideology' on regulation.

Another example of these differences was seen during the Asian currency crisis. During that crisis, the IMF was criticized by Europeans for contributing to the contagion by creating a so-called 'moral hazard.' Investors put large amounts of money into high-risk ventures in Asia even though there were increasing signs that the currencies in the region were becoming overvalued. They were spurred on by the region's governments and companies who could not resist borrowing dollars to pay for expensive infrastructure projects. All sides were under the belief that the IMF would rescue them with loans if the regional governments and companies began to default. When the crisis finally erupted, and the regional currencies burst, governments and businesses were unable to uphold their foreign commitments. The ensuing contagion eventually overwhelmed the resources of both the foreign investors and the IMF.

In the aftermath, German officials grumbled about the IMF's loaning activities, and Tietmeyer and the Bundesbank dragged their feet on German participation in the IMF restructuring programmes for east Asia.

The US government has the largest quota of votes within the governing structure of the IMF, and clearly has the most at stake during international financial crises, since most of the speculative capital involved in Asia originates from US mutual funds and pension funds. Former Bundesbank President Hans Tietmeyer criticised the US for failing to augment its financial contribution to the IMF, in contrast to Germany, which had quickly agreed to top up its own contribution.

With the traditions of the German Bundesbank and the Banque de France merging into the ECB, the European criticism of the IMF has the potential to grow more vocal. Still, a co-ordinated response during the Asian crisis did not emerge. By the time the contagion had hit Russia, the Germans took the lead in criticizing the results of the IMF programme, but they failed to co-ordinate a common European solution.

If anyone could have exerted influence in Russia in 1998, when that country was threatening to default on its loans, it was Chancellor Helmut Kohl, leader of Russia's largest creditor and trading partner. Kohl had developed a strong personal relationship with Boris Yeltsin. The federal elections in September, which resulted in the defeat of Kohl's government, contributed to Germany's lack of leadership at the time.

The Europeans are sceptical about whether the US really has a genuine interest in regulating international finance, given that Wall Street investors have such a powerful lobby in Washington. Former German chancellor Helmut Schmidt criticized the US as 'the land of origin of speculative predator capitalism', adding that, because of its system, the US would not be able to provide a sensible initiative to deal with the problems. He recommended that Germany's new government work together with Paris and London to implement a three-point plan. He called for 1) states threatened by crisis to implement capital controls against short-term money inflows from abroad, 2) advanced industrialized states to widen the jurisdiction of bank and financial supervision agencies, and 3) the end of the IMF as a global lender of last resort. Finally, he stated, Germany and

France should work together to set the global agenda. Germany and France, after all, had first come up with the idea for a world economic summit to find ways to contain fallout from the oil crisis in the 1970s.[viii]

Even Trichet, the guardian of conservative orthodoxy in France, admits he finds himself holding different views from the Americans. In 1995, invited to an elite French leftist intellectual group, Phares et Balises, to discuss economic policy, he admitted: 'You know, when I discuss things with the Americans, I'm also very Phares and Balises.'[ix]

The penchant of Europeans for intervention and order was also manifest in the debate about how to create a more stable international financial system. The G-7 asked Hans Tietmeyer to draw up a proposal to do just that.

In February 1999, Tietmeyer proposed to create a Financial Stability Forum, to improve cooperation between the supervisory agencies of the G-7 nations and the major international organizations. But Tietmeyer's proposal was only the starting point in a movement that Tietmeyer hopes will lead to more supranational institutions. The problem with the financial architecture at the start of the twenty-first century, he believes, is that all of the international economic organizations – the Bank for International Settlements, the World Trade Organization, the IMF and the World Bank – cooperate very little with each other. They are weak because they do not possess any independent authority of their own. Tietmeyer's ideal world would be one where power is vested into supranational institutions, a world that is still far away:

> Abstractly, I can imagine an economic order where there would be one valid legal system, one court, and where there would even be one central bank. But a common order would also have to be geared to freedom and leave room for productive competition. In the world that we live in, such an ideal world won't come about perhaps for another two hundred years. So we are left to deal with an imperfect world, in which an economic problem in a developing country can spark a crisis throughout the world. The decisive question is:

Do we have enough of a common order? My task was to see how supervisory authorities could be brought together on the international level so that they could cooperate, know what the others are doing, and more easily see where problems are arising. Gradually, the whole order [*Ordnung*] will be built up. It will be very slow, but it will never be perfect out of the institutions that we have now.

ECB's foreign policy

Most of these international regulatory issues are being discussed in international organizations like the IMF, the Group of Seven and the Bank for International Settlements, which hosts the Group of Ten. Nominally in charge of the ECB's international relations is Tommaso Padoa-Schioppa, the Italian board member. During the first half of 1999, Padoa-Schioppa was busy visiting global capitals in an effort to find a way to reform the international financial order.

A consensus has emerged that none of the institutions, neither the IMF, nor the G-7, nor the G-10 is an adequate forum for international crisis consultations. The IMF is too unwieldy, whereas the G-10 and the G-7 are too exclusive or European-biased.

Like Germany, Italy is a young nation, and has more recent experience in constructing political institutions. Its political tradition is less deep-rooted, and it is therefore more flexible and willing to consider radical institutional changes. Given Padoa-Schioppa's experience in designing the creation of new single currency and the framework of the European Central Bank, the Italian is well placed as the ECB's foreign minister at a time when international leaders are searching for a new architecture for the global financial system.

The ECB's foreign relations are characterized by three main forces. First is the vision propagated by the likes of idealist Padoa-Schioppa, who seeks more efficiency and unity within European institutions. Only then will Europe be able to project its true power, he believes. The second is the credibility premium that exists as a legacy of the German central bank.

The German focus on a long-term, stability oriented financial system offers a credible alternative to the short-term, more turbulent US version of capitalism. There are signs, for example in the statements of European politicians and businessmen in early 1999, that this European alternative might now have more influence upon the international debate, especially now that Germans can hide behind the European banner even more than before, and if differences continue to rise between Europe and the US about the need for more order and regulation in the international financial system.

Adhocracy

The third factor determining the ECB's foreign policy, and the most perplexing, is the ECB's status as a half-way house between an international and a supranational institution. In the past, Europe's central bankers have attended the G-7 and IMF summits together with their political leaders. Now that the central banks have merged, Europeans have become confused as to how to represent themselves at international summits. The EU member state finance ministers still act as the ECB's political counterpart, but they all insist on attending the international summits. In the G-7, for example, France, Germany and Italy all continue to attend the meetings as separate nation states. This justified the demands by the three central bank governors to attend the meetings also, even it could be argued that the single ECB President would be a more efficient representative. Instead of reducing the number of European voices at the table, therefore, the ECB has simply added another one (The ECB President represents the central bank in these talks).

At the G-10, which is solely a meeting of central bankers, there is a similar arrangement. Germany, France, Italy, the Netherlands and Belgium (and the non-eurozone countries of Switzerland, Sweden and the UK) still sit next to each other at the same table with the US, Canada and Japan. Here too, the ECB President attends.

Since the birth of the liberal movement in the eighteenth century, increasing numbers of economists have argued that economic affairs, commerce and investment should be operated according to market criteria, not by the nation state, where the government is beholden to special interests. But as Paul Kennedy has noted, the nation state has proved itself a jealous actor over and over again, and always seems to reassert itself:

> The cosmopolitan ideology of liberalism was joined (and challenged), later in the nineteenth century, by a transnational workers' movement called Marxism. Each of these viewpoints opposed the claimed authority of the nation state; yet whenever a grave international crisis occurred – as in 1914, and again in 1939 – they were thrust aside. Diplomatic treaties and institutions were similarly powerless to prevent egoistic sovereign states from going to war. World War I produced the passport – a proof of an individual's nationality but, interestingly, owned by the government, which could recall it when deemed necessary. World War II produced the 'gross domestic product', an economist's device to allow the state full scrutiny of productive activity. In both conflicts, governments steadily augmented controls over information . . . After 1945 these trends ebbed somewhat in the economic sphere but continued strong in political life. International financial trading arrangements such as the International Monetary Fund, the World Bank, and the General Agreement on Tariffs and Trade sought to check a recurrence of the damage caused by inter-war protectionism and autarky; foreign trade and investment flows boomed. But the rising tensions produced by the Cold War badly affected the climate of international relations and pointed to the continued importance of 'national' security.[x]

Europe's international representation, therefore, remains notoriously complex. It was Henry Kissinger, former US Secretary of State, who once asked in frustration: 'When I want to talk to Europe, who do I call?' That question still haunts Europe. For economic and financial affairs, the first call should go to none other than Wim Duisenberg. Duisenberg speaks not only for the most powerful organization in Europe, the ECB, but he also attends meetings with the Eurozone finance ministers – the so-called Euro-11 – and attends all other major regional and international meetings.

The lack of a satisfactory solution to the question of the EU's representation abroad will have negative consequences, not least for its effectiveness in international bodies. This will affect its ability to act as a successful counterweight to the US. On many decisions, the big EU countries will still be forced to consult exclusively among themselves, finding it too cumbersome to include the others. This has already led to an informal 'Gang of Four' within the EU: France, Germany, the UK and Italy. During the Russian crisis in September, for instance, the state secretary of the German finance ministry at the time, Klaus Regling, simply got on the phone and called his counterparts in France, the UK and Italy. Together, they drafted a letter to Russia's leadership, encouraging it to push through reform and to pay back its debts. Neither the European Central Bank nor the European Commission spoke out with a joint statement on the crisis. Regling says this *ad hoc*, informal grouping is the way European diplomacy will remain until a better solution is found.

The redundant European representation is increasingly bothersome to the US and other powers. Why should Alan Greenspan, the president of the Federal Reserve, be forced during G-10 meetings to speak (not only with the big four, but also with) the Belgian central banker? European central bankers react defensively. Not only do they fear the loss of their cherished status, they fear the breaking up of a cosy world order where Europeans have predominated for centuries.

The BIS and the G-10

The highest-level forum for central banking diplomacy is the G-10. The group meets in Basle, in Switzerland, just across the borders with France and Germany, at the building of the Bank for International Settlements. It has a thirty-year tradition, and attendees consider it, in the words of BIS general director Andrew Crockett, 'the most interesting, frank and useful of all' international organizations. It is an exclusive club, and a friendly one. It meets monthly. 'Everyone is on first name terms. You immediately get down to business, no one ever speaks from a prepared text, and usually not even from notes. They just launch in and talk,' says Crockett.

Hosting the G-10 meetings is just one of the many banking activities of the BIS, which is why it has become known as the 'central bank of central banks'. During Crockett's tenure, the BIS has enlarged its board and extended membership to non-Europeans for the first time, bringing in the US, Canada and Japan. Additionally, several more key developing countries were brought in as BIS members. In late 1998, the BIS opened an office in Asia.

Before the September 1998 meeting of the G-10, when stock markets were reeling as a result of increasing uncertainty in the wake of the Asian crisis, US Fed Chairman Alan Greenspan used his contacts at the BIS to arrange a teleconference among the governors to review what was happening. Together, the key bankers of the globe were immediately able to consult each other and keep tabs on developments in various regions. It was the first such call, and a sign of increasing communication and co-ordination between US and European central bankers.

Given increased globalization and the recent insecurity of global markets, some observers say that a wider forum than the G-10 is now needed, in order to bring bankers together from both emerging markets and industrial countries. Asked why the governor of the Central Bank of Belgium needs to attend the G-10 meeting, one European central banker responds bluntly: 'The answer is: you don't.' More diplomatically, the BIS's Crockett concedes that Brazil, Mexico, India and China are all clearly larger and more important nowadays, but says: 'Whatever the logic, the G-10 has been an effective and cohesive grouping. It has worked.'

Meeting politicians in the framework of the IMF or other meetings, like the G-7, is too constraining for the bankers, Crockett adds. 'The central banks have got concerns they would like to pursue just as central banks. If you're managing markets, you can't just meet once every six months at the interim committee [of the IMF].'

Crockett recognizes the aim of the US-instigated 'Willard Group' – a group of 22 nations which includes many South-east Asian countries, including Malaysia, Thailand, Indonesia, Singapore and Hong Kong – to broaden international participation. 'It's a legitimate objective,' he says, 'but very difficult to get general agreement. The trick is to find a grouping that is broad enough to be adequately representative, yet small enough to be manageable and efficient.' He notes that there are five South-east Asian countries in the group, yet none from the Middle East and only one from Africa. 'I don't think we've found the solution yet,' he concludes.

Meanwhile, some European central bankers have proposed expanding the G-10, although they haven't been ready to sacrifice their own weight in the new organization. No European banks would be dropped. At least five other countries would be added, including China, India, Russia, Brazil and Mexico, but even this solution would make the cosy Sunday evening G-10 dinners far less personal.

When he was appointed to the BIS position in 1993, Crockett was, like most British, a sceptic about monetary union. At the time, he was still under the influence of the anti-EMU legacy of Margaret Thatcher. But, like many of the European central bankers themselves, he has reconciled himself to the single currency project.

The BIS has long been European dominated. Its rotating presidents have almost always been European, and only under Crockett's tenure has it opened up to a wider membership. It manages about 7 per cent of the world's total foreign exchange reserves. Founded in 1930 to channel German war reparations to other European states, it then helped to clear cross-border payments after the war. Today it is the home to deposit accounts from over 120 central banks, including those of all of the major industrialized countries. In recent years, it has expanded its function as banking supervisor, recommending minimum standards for banks, such as the amount of equity capital they should keep aside in the form of hard reserves.[13] Partly because of its clearing-house status among central banks, perhaps, the BIS successfully warned of an Asian crisis months before it happened.

The personal network

It is also at the G-10 where bonds of friendship have been created between European central bankers. One of the closest was that between Duisenberg and Tietmeyer. Duisenberg respected Tietmeyer's clout. Tietmeyer admired Duisenberg's coolness. A fellow central banker watched them grow closer:

> Tietmeyer and Duisenberg obviously get along together. They both have the same brand of teutonic conservatism. After all, the Dutch are seen by Germans as being the next best thing to being German. And during this whole EMU process, they needed each other. Between them, they were two important bankers. They were very close to each other in views, but they also knew that if they were together, they were stronger than if they were separate. Tietmeyer was shrewdly aware that a Dutchman would be sellable to German public opinion as the president of the ECB in a way that no other nationality could be. Forget about the individual, but you can sell the Germans on a Dutchman. A Frenchman would be hard. A Spaniard, an Italian or a Portuguese would be impossible. Tietmeyer just didn't have quite the same relationship with the other bankers. The Germans have always felt suspicious of the French, they're too *dirigiste*. The British, well, in the early stages, they only

---

[13] The BIS publishes the amounts of border-crossing bank loans for individual states, and it is seeking to increase the speed with which these reports are released. It has had twenty years of experience, and while the IMF at the beginning of 1997 seemed to be trying to compete with the BIS in formulating 'best practices' for financial oversight, the BIS recently seems to have succeeded in protecting its leadership. Later in 1997, the BIS released 25 minimum standards for an effective banking oversight that were to be incorporated by October 1998. These received the blessing of the G-7 and the G-10, which recommended that the IMF incorporate the standards within its own work on the supervision issue.

gave you the Thatcher line, although that changed with Eddie George, who Tietmeyer respects. But Duisenberg was an important ally. For Tietmeyer, the Dutch were as solid as gold. He never challenged Duisenberg in meetings. But he did challenge the Belgian.

In BIS meetings, both Duisenberg and Tietmeyer made common cause on policy. Once, Duisenberg resisted a proposal to include Brazil and Mexico and other developing nations on the BIS board, and Tietmeyer supported him:

They're not convinced that countries outside of Europe – and we're not talking about the United States, but about countries with a tradition that is non-European – can have quite the same discipline, management and the confidence of European countries. Neither of them were great believers in the EMU. They came very late to believe in it. Both of them were reluctant to invite the US and Canada on to the BIS board. Their argument was if the US and Canada come anyway, why do we have to have them running the BIS. They worried about the loss of European influence. They're very European people. They also felt that they couldn't trust America, because Congress would ask for information that could threaten their privileges. And they do have certain privileges.

Few people know, for example, that the central bank governors receive separate fees as 'directors' of the BIS, and some, but not all, countries allow them to keep the fees. Fees that are paid to Alan Greenspan and Eddie George are returned to the Federal Reserve and the Bank of England respectively. But among the continental Europeans, most of the bankers are content to pocket the money themselves. The only country that has decided to make this fee public is Sweden, a country not in the Eurozone. This is not surprising, since the fee is a big one. The Swedish governor takes home a monthly fee of 45,000 Swedish Krona, which makes up almost half of his regular monthly salary. Not long ago, the BIS paid its members in envelopes containing thousands of dollars in cash, although this practice has since changed.

ECB Declaration of Independence

The jealous guarding of independence by the central bankers has so far created much more friction between the ECB and European politicians than between the US Federal Reserve and Washington. This was manifest, for example, in the US instigated communiqué of the G-7 on September 14, 1998. Under pressure from plunging stock exchanges in the U.S. President Clinton tried to co-ordinate a joint calming of the markets by issuing a communiqué suggesting that interest rate cuts were likely on their way. The Fed immediately concurred.

Clinton reportedly pressured Treasury Secretary Rubin to muster European co-operation. Rubin knew that Europe's finance ministers generally favoured lower rates anyway, since it reduces the cost of financing debt and boosts short-term economic growth, and he quickly won their support. But when the European ministers, in turn, put in calls to their governors to see if they would agree, the European bankers – who were meeting at the BIS at the time – balked. It was legitimate for the US to hint at lower interest rates, the bankers thought, but the European economy didn't need it. 'The US can do so if it wants, but we don't want to go along,' said one banker, at the time. 'We don't want to be lumped in the same basket.' They also didn't like the idea that finance ministers were drafting a communiqué that commented on monetary policy, which the bankers believed was their territory. With the euro being introduced in January, the bankers were also reluctant to be seen cutting rates under political pressure. 'They were saying "Here, sign this." Our natural reaction was: 'Look, it's our business, not yours.'

German finance minister Waigel called the G-10 secretariat, and demanded to talk to Tietmeyer, interrupting the bankers' meeting. Waigel argued that the Europeans needed to show at least some sign of co-operation with the US. Finally, the bankers caved in and signed a communiqué, but only after it had been watered down. The sentence that was supposed to hint at the possibility of lower rates among the industrialized world was vague, but clear enough for the markets. Referring to a weakening of demand, it said 'The balance of risks in the world economy has shifted' away from inflation – towards much slower growth.

The US pressure had worked, and the statement contributed to a recovery in the markets. 'The purpose was to try to affect the mindset of policy-making all through the industrial countries. Getting that . . . in a statement was a way of further promoting it,' said Rubin afterwards.[xi]

G-7

The euro has made the financial world a tripolar one. The euro, the dollar and the yen are the three main reserve currencies. Some leaders believe the G-7, or the Group of Seven leading industrial nations, should be reformed to a G-3, so that only those three currency regions are represented. The G-7 is the most important meeting of global leaders, first proposed by Valéry Giscard d'Estaing of France in the 1970s, mainly for informal discussion and co-ordination of economic policy. It includes the heads of state, finance ministers, and the central bankers from each of the seven largest industrialized countries: the US, Japan, Germany, France, Italy, the UK, and Canada. The countries use it as a big-boy's club, from which they issue general communiqués about their concerns of the day. It is also a chance for the leaders to iron out any policy differences and to co-ordinate joint strategies.

But with Germany, France and Italy having merged into Euroland, the three large European countries have a single central banking representative. Theoretically, they should also have a single head of state and finance minister representative. In a G-3, the UK and Canada would be ejected, leaving Japan, the US and Euroland to tend to bigger business. The three central bankers, if they needed to, could get together on the sidelines of these meetings, either beforehand, if they wanted to co-ordinate a joint strategy between them before talking with the politicians, or afterwards. However, a further concentration of power into a 'G-3' would generate significant protest from the excluded nations.

NOTES

[i] Interview with author, September 29, 1998.
[ii] William Greider, *Secrets of the Temple: How the Federal Reserve Runs the Country*. Simon and Schuster, 1987, New York, p. 641.
[iii] Interview with author, January 14, 1999.
[iv] The ECB's overnight deposit facility sets a floor for interest rates. It guarantees a minimum return to banks seeking to deposit funds overnight.
[v] See, for example, *Neue Zürcher Zeitung*: 'Finnlands eiserne Lady,' March 30, 1998, or *Die Woche*: 'Die eiserne Euro-Lady', October 2, 1998.
[vi] Speech at Dresdner Bank, 1998. Given the European scepticism of hedge funds, it was particularly embarrassing for the Banca d'Italia when it emerged that the bank had $100 million of its reserves invested in the high-risk LTCM through the Italian Foreign Exchange Office. The right of national central banks to manage their own reserves is another example of the ESCB's decentralisation.
[vii] *The Times*, London, 17 June, 1998. 'IMF received broadside from Basle'.
[viii] *Die Zeit*, 'Der Globale Irrsin', September 3, 1998, page 1.
[ix] Éric Aeschimann, p. 265
[x] Paul Kennedy, *Preparing for the Twenty-First Century*, Fontana Press, London, 1994, p. 125-6.
[xi] *Financial Times*, 'Cooling the global markets' meltdown', December 30 1998.

CHAPTER EIGHT

Monetary Policy

Hans-Joachim Klöckers, the ex-Bundesbanker in charge of drafting the ECB's monetary policy proposals for council discussions, sits in a corner office on the 25th floor of the Eurotower that looks out on to the winding Main River below.

In the distance to the north are the forests of the Taunus, the hilly area bordered on three sides by the rivers Rhine, Main, and Lahn, and favourite playground for Frankfurters. The Taunus is also where Klöckers lives, and where he rents out a local tennis court once a week to play with colleagues from the ECB. It is a half-hour train-ride to work, which Klöckers uses as precious reading time. From 8.30 am until about 10 pm each night, he and his small team of analysts toiled away to make sure the ECB enjoyed a smooth birth.

So far, he's pleased with the results. After all, there is evidence that Europe is already reaping the benefits of a more credible monetary policy than the US Federal Reserve: lower long-term interest rates. Beginning in late 1996, Europe's long-term interest rates 'decoupled' from those of the United States, dropping lower as markets became convinced that the Europeans are more serious about fighting inflation than the Americans. In the first quarter of 1999, the spread widened even further. 'The difference in the rates shows something about inflation expectations and the credibility of the central bank,' says Klöckers. 'The markets have the impression: "These people are doing what they're supposed to do."'

This market conviction results from the fact that European central bankers have a singular mandate to combat inflation. The Federal Reserve, on the other hand, has a broader mandate, which is not only to combat inflation but to ensure economic growth. During an economic recession, the Fed is quicker to cut rates to boost economic growth, even if it means a slight jump in inflation. The ECB will feel no such obligation.[1]

None of the ECB's monetary decisions are as important as those on interest rates. They can trigger the move of trillions of dollars worth of capital in or out of Europe within seconds, sucking billions of dollars worth of value from stock exchanges (and thereby from companies listed there). By raising interest rates too high or at an inopportune time, central banks can unwittingly cause millions of companies to go bankrupt and throw hundreds of thousands of workers into unemployment. By lowering rates too quickly or too often, they can spur so much lending that it overheats the economy and creates uncontrollable inflation – which eats away at family savings and wages.

The full social impact of interest rate policy, otherwise known as 'monetary policy', has only recently begun to be fully appreciated by political historians. History books are being revised to take monetary policy's effect into account. It has now been generally recognized, for example, that the fall of several chancellors in post-war Germany was directly or indirectly contributed to by disputes with the Bundesbank over policy. Most Germans are oblivious to this. Likewise, in the US, the prolonged period of economic expansion during the 1990s can be attributed to the deft handling of interest rate policy by Federal Reserve Chairman Alan Greenspan, and by his predecessor, Paul Volcker, as much as it can to the particular policies of presidents and their policy makers. Central bankers, quiet and secretive as they are, rarely stand up to take credit for their successes. But more often than not, they are used as scapegoats by governments if things go wrong.

A lack of appreciation for the full significance of monetary policy is especially marked in Europe. Most Europeans outside

---

[1] In an interview, Fed Vice Chairman Alice Rivlin conceded that the Fed's mandate allows it to take the need for economic growth into account in its decision-making, and that this does make a difference in policy results.

of Germany were not involved in the monetary policy debates throughout the 1980s and 1990s because the Bundesbank was indirectly conducting their monetary policy for them. The mark was the anchor currency in the European Monetary System. Other European central banks were concerned mainly with keeping their currencies pegged to the German mark, with little latitude to consider independent policies. Little did they realise that the almighty Bundesbank was continually reacting to economic developments, such as recession and periodic credit crunches, and was sometimes at a loss as to what strategy to follow. With the transition in Europe to a single currency, assumptions about appropriate monetary policy strategy have, of course, been revised.

In the room of one of Klöckers' colleagues – Vítor Gaspar, head of ECB research – there is a blackboard. On one half is scribbled a standard formula for money and its relationship to interest rates and prices – reflecting the tradition passed on from the Bundesbank. But on the other half of the blackboard, separated by a simple chalk line, he has written the words *ad hoc*. It is an admission that the ECB's policy will have to do more with improvisation than tradition.

To make sure that the market stays sufficiently liquid, the central bank does not usually have to change the interest rate as part of its daily or weekly operations. It simply feeds the market with the cash it needs. But sometimes the community's economy does strange things. Human psychology – unpredictable as it is – is usually the reason. A sudden wave of optimism, for example, can expand economic activity so much that businesses begin to use more money to invest in more production of goods and services. At first, the central bank lends this money to banks (and thus, indirectly to businesses that demand it) to keep the system liquid. But soon bottlenecks arise. Companies looking for workers cannot find them because they already have jobs. Workers, who soon begin to realise their value, bid up wages. Resources become tight, and raw materials become expensive. Inflation increases. In order to cool the economy, the central bank lifts interest rates on the money it lends to banks. Faced with rising costs, the private banks charge clients more for loans. Less is borrowed for investment, which leads to slower economic activity, and therefore lower inflation. If there is a recession, the central bank lowers rates in order to resuscitate the economy.

If the central bank tightens the tap too much – by raising interest rates too high or too quickly – it can tilt the economy into a deep recession, as companies are starved of the money they need to carry out normal transactions. Loosen the tap too much, and the money will be so abundant it will lose value, creating inflation.

Régime change

Klöckers takes over the monetary policy division at a time when the old way of conducting monetary policy is being discredited.[2] Time and again, the Bundesbank had been perplexed by economic developments. Almost every other year – in 1992, 1994, and 1996 – money supply rose above the Bundesbank's predicted level. But instead of tightening the tap by raising interest rates, the bank had been forced by other conditions to do the opposite. Economic recessions or credit bottlenecks had been present during each one of these years, meaning that raising rates would have been suicidal. Each time, Issing cited abnormal, exceptional factors. The truth, however, is that money was losing its value as a simple rudder for steering the economy. In the mid to long term, money was related to inflation, but within a given year, money could do bizarre things. A relative tax decrease in Luxembourg, for example, could compel billions of marks to flee to the Grand Duchy. At least Luxembourg would publish statistics that would make the Bundesbank aware of the haemorrhage. Alternatively, money could flee to tax-free offshore accounts and, effectively, disappear from the statistics.

When Klöckers took over the division in mid-May 1998, the ECB's governing council's debate over how to formulate the bank's monetary policy strategy was in full swing. The goal was clear. The Maastricht Treaty gave the ECB one primary

---

[2] See Chapter 5.

mandate: ensure price stability. It was the means that were more difficult.

Issing, the directorate member responsible for devising a draft of the bank's monetary policy, relied on research that Klöckers had conducted at the EMI. Together, they realised that recent experience confounded their strategy. But they couldn't bring themselves to ignore one stubborn fact: that inflation was strongly related to money supply. Instead of throwing in the towel, they preferred to keep their strategy focused on money and, when confronted with shortcomings, find out and publicly explain reasons why money was 'temporarily' acting erratically.

The problem, however, was that the Bundesbank's explanations for apparent erratic behaviour in money were by nature *ex post facto*. When Issing and the Bundesbank were confronted with signs of a recession, but money supply was growing rapidly, they would hesitate for months before taking action, believing that the money-supply gauge heralded an expansion. When it didn't come, and the recession only deepened, policy changes came late.

In recent years, other banks gained the reputation for being more swift in reacting to such conditions. The US Federal Reserve had abandoned a strict monetary policy, and has become more eclectic in nature, considering a host of factors when making its interest rate decisions. By 1993, the central banks of England, Canada and New Zealand had all introduced a new strategy of targeting inflation directly. Sweden, Finland and Spain soon followed with similar policies. As soon as wage and price increases appeared on the horizon, these banks would react by lifting rates. They did not consider the money supply first. However, by lifting rates when inflation had already set in, the banks were always slightly behind the curve. Their higher interest rates would make money more expensive, which would slow down business borrowing, yet it took up to two years for the full impact of higher rates to be felt. By that time, the economy might have already slowed down. Nevertheless, at least they were responding directly to the goal of managing inflation. Slowly but surely, these banks were undermining the perceived supremacy of the money-based strategy of the Germans. They were also more democratically accountable for their results. In New Zealand, the bank was bound by contract to produce a specific rate of inflation over a three-year period, within a range set by the government. The governor was free to act independently, but if he failed to produce the required results, he could lose his job.

Issing, and his policy guru, Klöckers, thought that these policy innovations by other countries were too short-term oriented. Monetary policy could not 'guarantee' a particular inflation outcome, since other factors also contributed to inflation (for example government spending policies or so-called 'asymmetric shocks', such as the great oil shocks in the 1970s or German reunification in 1990). Moreover, inflation targeting meant that the central bank was bound to change interest rates the moment the slightest hint of inflation showed up. Issing and Klöckers suspected a medium-term strategy was more sound. They agreed with monetarist, Jürgen von Hagen: 'Inflation-targeting is like John Wayne riding across the prairie and shooting every rabbit that pokes up its head.'

More importantly, money targeting acted as a convenient political cover. If the Bundesbank failed to keep inflation low, it could blame external forces. The bank could insist that policy performance – of maintaining low inflation – should not be judged in the short term, but over the medium to long term, and that this was best done by keeping money growth constant. The Bundesbank's statutes required that it maintain price stability but did not stipulate what that meant. In addition, because the Bundesbank had reliably kept inflation down for so long, the public did not question its logic. Its strategy could also be used to shield it from complaints that its high rates were causing needless economic pain. That cover was also used by the US Federal Reserve chairman Paul Volcker when he introduced money supply targeting in 1979 to control rampant inflation.

Drastic changes in money supply developments, caused by deregulation and other financial innovations, had forced the US Federal Reserve to abandon the strategy in the 1980s. But for the Germans, there had been an additional reason to hide behind money supply targeting. Because of the harrowing experience with hyperinflation of the 1920s, the Bundesbank feared holding itself responsible for meeting a specific inflation rate. Missing the target would expose it to harsh criticism from the German public. A money target shrouded its operations in an arcane and mysterious world that few people understand; it avoided direct accountability for an outcome. As Banque de France governor Jean-Claude Trichet notes, the Germans didn't even publish an explicit inflation target, although they made clear that they believed 2 per cent was an inflation ceiling:

> The Germans are less visible. They are more shy, more timid, in displaying what they have in mind as regards inflation. But if you asked them what they have in mind, they would say less than 2 per cent. I prefer the French system, in which we have an official display of an inflation target. For the year to come and in the medium run, we say that we are pursuing this specific target for the year to come. Then in the medium run, we say we want inflation of lower than 2 per cent. It's a little different from the Germans, and in my opinion, it is better. It's been extraordinarily useful in France to say any inflationary expectations superior to 2 per cent are not appropriate at all. The independent central bank is there to prevent that. To the extent that the economy is made up of psychology and anticipation and expectations, it's extraordinarily important to have the nominal anchoring of those expectations.[i]

For example, Trichet could use the target as a public relations instrument to exert pressure on labour unions and employers to keep wage increases moderate.

The rhetoric of monetary policy

As discussions picked up at the ECB, Issing was deluged with opposing views, both externally and internally. The day the Social Democratic Party won the German elections, the party chairman Oskar Lafontaine began pounding on the Bundesbank's poor record in recent years, saying that the success of the US economy was the result of a more intelligent policy by the Federal Reserve. He expressed publicly that the ECB was in danger of following the Bundesbank's mistakes. Within the ECB, there were also detractors. Peter Bull, head of the financial statistics department at the Bank of England for seven years before joining the EMI, is chief of the ECB's statistics division. A convivial man, with a professorial mop of wiry gray hair, Bull inhabits an office on the tenth floor. It is piled with papers, his desk no longer visible under tall stacks of statistic volumes and other studies – a sign of the sweat and toil he has put into harmonizing the statistical data of the eleven participating countries, some of which had only scanty back-data on important statistics like money supply. Based on his experience, Bull doubts the strength of money's relationship with inflation, especially during the initial few years after the changeover to the euro. EMU is accompanied by a host of financial deregulation laws, which frees up money to circulate in new ways – ways that Bull fears will be 'strange and unpredictable'. He refers to his experience at the Bank of England:

One of the most striking episodes in my professional life was in the early 1980s. It was soon after a rather radical, conservative government led by Mrs. Thatcher came into power. They swept away a whole lot of money controls. They abolished exchange control in Autumn 1979. And in the middle of 1980, they abolished various sorts of restrictions in the banking system. There had been an arrangement under which banks effectively paid a tax if their lending increased by more than some amount. When these controls were removed, for a time the money stock behaved extremely erratically. I remember the shock in the Bank of England when we discovered in August 1980 that the money stock had increased by 4 per cent in only one month. Of course, it was linked to the removal of controls. But the confusion in the Bank of England at the time, and the analytical difficulty of presenting this to the government, was just awful. We could experience something like that in

Europe. These are the biggest changes that you will perceive for many, many years . . . Money could remain stagnant. It could grow 10 per cent. It could even shrink. We are doing a dramatic thing in monetary union. Who knows what is going to happen?

At the Bundesbank, Issing had already conceded that a mixed strategy was needed – monetary policy and consideration of other economic factors. In effect, the Bundesbank had applied such a mix for years anyway, but the stew was made up more of money supply targeting and less of other factors.

The debate about monetary policy strategy had long been a subject of European debate even before the ECB governing council took it up in earnest in September 1998. The governors, as members of the European Monetary Institute council – the ECB governing council's forerunner – had released a publication outlining the options that were open to the ECB: monetary targeting, direct inflation-targeting or a mix of both. Tietmeyer, Issing and other Bundesbankers gave talks in which they stressed to audiences the need for money supply targeting as a prominent component of the ECB policy. Tietmeyer argued the importance of money supply developments as a forerunner, and thus a predictor, of inflation: 'Why is money supply the most important? Because it is always an intermediate target. It is not a direct target. Money developments always occur, normally, from six to twelve months before inflation developments.' Finally, after extensive discussion in informal lunches and formal sittings, the council decided to pound out a final decision during the meeting of October 13.

The governor of the Austrian central bank, Klaus Liebscher, recalls:

It was clear that there was a difference between those who had monetary targets, those who had inflation targets and those who had exchange rate targets. Everyone had completely different experiences, and proud traditions. All of us knew the experiences of our own system. So we didn't want to move backwards a single centimetre from our position. We wanted to have our own system because we were convinced it was a good thing.

Spanish ECB board member Domingo Solans agreed. 'In a way, it is normal that each member of the council identified with the strategy that they know in their own country,' he said. 'This is not a matter of saying "Well, I think my position is the best." The reason is that after deciding on a strategy to live by, there is a lot of experience, and years and years of learning how things work.'

A majority of the council supported Issing's proposal that money targeting remain a key component of the ECB's monetary policy. First, France and Italy had, at least officially, followed money targeting in their own countries, and at times had tried to swim freely from the German mark, basing policy on monetary developments. Money supply developments proved too unreliable, however, and they abandoned the effort. Nevertheless, they still claimed money targeting was part of their official monetary policy. Most of EU bankers followed an exchange rate targeting policy, simply buying or selling their currencies in foreign exchange markets to keep them in tight range with the German mark – the anchor. Many of the governors, seeing that the stability of their own currencies was based on the German mark, which in turn was guided by money supply, were willing to support the German demand. Recalls Belgian governor Verplaetse:

We and the Dutch had pegged our currencies to the German mark. In a way, we were borrowing the stability of the German mark, which was based on monetary aggregates. So we were behind money targeting, even though we were not convinced of the stability of the aggregates. A majority of the council favoured money supply aggregates, and only a minority favoured inflation-targeting.

That minority – mainly those members from countries that had introduced inflation targeting in their monetary policies – consisted of Hämäläinen, Vanhala, Domingo Solans and the

Spanish governor, Rojo. While they didn't object to using money supply targeting, they were against giving it a much more prominent role than other economic indicators.

After hours of discussion, despite being confronted with a majority which sided with the German camp, the Spanish members continued to insist that inflation targeting should at least be made a pillar equivalent to monetary targeting. Domingo Solans, the most ardent monetarist at the Banco de España before he was appointed to the ECB's board in May, had joined the Spanish central bank in 1994, and had participated in scrapping a money target strategy because it hadn't worked.

He illustrated his opinion on the relative importance of money to a visitor in his office on the Eurotower's 24th floor. He drew a large circle on a piece of paper, which he labelled 'inflation'. Within that circle, he drew a small circle, labelled 'money', which took up at most a tenth of the larger circle. He explained:

> My experience at the Bank of Spain has shown me that there is danger of instability in the demand for money. We don't know exactly what can happen in the future with money demand in the euro area. If there were stability in the demand for money, I would have no doubt that the monetary strategy is the best. The problem is that this doesn't work . . . That is why I was emphasising the idea of inflation targeting. My position was in favour of constructing it as a strong second pillar based on the estimation of future inflation through some relevant economic variables.

Since inflation targeting considers money supply growth as well as other variables, Domingo Solans saw no reason to single out money so prominently: 'In any inflation strategy, money and the evolution of M3, plays a prominent role. Therefore, I think it's a mistake to polarize the two strategies. I think they can be taken together.'

However, Domingo Solans and the other governors all agreed on one major reason for giving the money supply targeting strategy a high profile at the ECB: inheriting the Bundesbank's credibility. Granted, the changeover to the euro made money supply developments more uncertain than ever, but the bankers were holding on to money targeting tighter than they might have otherwise in order to lay claim to German credibility. The trick was to formulate this in a coherent policy. As Verplaestse recalls: 'It was a great discussion before we came up with the words 'reference value'. I don't know who suggested it, but it was quite an invention.'

In fact, 'reference value' had been thought up by Issing's staffers at the ECB, the ex-Bundesbankers Klöckers and Masuch, who had assembled a list of words in the search for a more vague word than 'target'. They had picked out 'reference value', and Issing, liking it, incorporated it into his revised monetary policy strategy proposal.

A 'reference value' was vague enough to soothe those who believed money was no longer reliable enough to justify being a target, but explicit enough to mollify the monetarists. Every one could read what they wished into the word. In many ways, the agreement resembled the outcome of a European diplomatic summit – months of preparation and policy trial balloons, a five-hour meeting to thrash things out, a search for compromises to make all sides happy, and a smoothing out of any difficult wording. It was European diplomacy late-night at the Eurotower.

In the end, Bundesbank President Hans Tietmeyer could say that the policy merely reformulated in more accurate terminology what the Bundesbank's real policy had always been: 'What we now have *de facto* in the ECB is the same philosophy that we in the Bundesbank and an increasing number of central banks in Europe have followed,' he said, with a wide grin.[ii]

In other ways – although it was partly coincidental – the carefully diplomatic conclusion, full of platitudes, was ideal for the central bankers. They did not want to straight-jacket themselves. Some of the governing council members explicitly argued in favour of ambiguity. Verplaetse says:

The monetary policy, especially when you are on the eve of

creating a new currency, has to have some, let me call it, 'constructive ambiguity' built into it. If you debate a monetary policy with the parliament or with the media, you're in danger of not being taken seriously. The financial markets will know all of your arguments, and then they become more powerful than you are.

Verplaetse says the Federal Reserve under Greenspan served as a good model in operating opaquely. 'Greenspan's best decisions have been the ones he doesn't hint at beforehand.' He is particularly enamoured of Greenspan's famous response to a journalist in January 1988, a few months after becoming chairman: 'Since becoming a central banker, I have learned to mumble with great incoherence. If I seem unduly clear to you, you must have misunderstood what I've said.' But with its monetary policy announcement, the ECB was doubly ambiguous. It not only announced a 'reference value' for money, it also said it wouldn't commit itself to an inflation target. It chose to define price stability as 2 per cent, but did not commit itself to meeting this goal. Verplaetse recounts the debate:

> We said, 'let's be prudent, we cannot be too pragmatic at the beginning. We have to have monetary aggregates if we want the credibility of past monetary policy. Then, for a limited time – as a measure of prudence – let's take a basket of indicators about future inflation. That way we will take account of both money supply and these other indicators. And if both are going in the same direction, there will be no problem. We have a problem, when one turns down, the other up . . .'

Tietmeyer disagreed with the argument, however, that constructive ambiguity was desirable:

> There is something to be said for the argument [that constructive ambiguity is needed to stay one step ahead of the markets], but for me it's too dangerous. I'm of the view that

it depends on the situation. Monetary policy must be clear and provide orientation. People should be able to understand it. But that doesn't mean that we'll say in advance what we're going to do.

Still, the most vigorous defence of a strong monetary component came from a surprising source: Jean-Claude Trichet, the governor of the Banque de France. More incessantly than even the Germans, Trichet argued that monetary targeting should be the predominant pillar. For years, Trichet had professed that he followed a monetary targeting strategy at the Banque de France, but in reality he'd been frustrated by the need to stay pegged to the mark. His money supply figures were chaotic, and too unreliable to be used as prominently as the Germans did theirs. In 1994, the year the bank became independent and announced its money supply target, Trichet set a corridor for money growth of between zero and 5 per cent, a spread so wide that it would have been almost impossible to miss. The year before, money had actually declined by 1.6 per cent, far below the target of 5 per cent growth.[iii]

But Trichet was now a member of a council that could decide monetary policy freely, without the constraints of exchange rate co-ordination. Though money supply targeting had failed him, he had long envied the German tradition: targeting money was a bold step, a declaration of independence from outside forces. Most of the central banks that had introduced inflation targeting – those of England, Spain, New Zealand, Finland and Sweden – governed currencies that were heavily dependent on outside factors – buffeted for example by the effects of external trade and of the fluctuations in the value of their currencies against the German mark or the US dollar. Trichet had never wanted to admit that same dependence. The Germans had gained credibility and the mark had become one of the world's major reserve currencies. Trichet wanted to embrace the monetary targeting method that had underpinned the stability of the mark.

Trichet had been appointed the next president of the ECB, to take over after Duisenberg retired. His support for money targeting was also a way of gaining credibility among his colleagues.

Notably, Trichet did not argue for money targeting exclusively on economic grounds. Rather, he argued, it should be adopted primarily to ensure credibility:

> It has to do with confidence, how you accumulate confidence, how you provide confidence. I have to say that the French franc and the German mark have accumulated more confidence than the sterling or the dollar. The long-term rates are lower in France and Germany and the euro area than they are in the other countries. To the extent that one of our major challenges is to give the euro the full legacy of confidence that has been accumulated in Europe, it would have been extremely dangerous to suggest to global markets that we were departing from policy that proved over time to create confidence.

Trichet rejects Peter Bull's assertion that the link between money and inflation might be completely severed, for years to come:

> His viewpoint doesn't surprise me, because the Bank of England is in the other camp. You have three camps, the Bank of England, the US and the Continental camps. The Bank of England is based upon a very complicated equation for direct inflation targeting, which includes a great number of variables, including monetary aggregates. The US is totally pragmatic. On the Continent, we have our own vision . . .

Trichet's use of the word 'continental' by definition excludes two countries in the Eurozone, Finland and Ireland, both of which are less adamant about the role of money supply in their strategies. Finland's central bank governor Matti Vanhala notes that the larger continental countries such as Germany and France carry more ideological baggage, having justified their monetary policies to large populations. It is harder for them to change than for a country with only five million inhabitants like Finland. Vanhala wasn't the only one. Yves Mersch, central bank governor of Luxembourg, had noticed it too, but respected Trichet's style:

> He is very Gallic, with all that an Englishman can understand in such a word. He is truly French. My wife sometimes says, 'you're thinking like a Frenchman,' meaning that I think the world is upside down. But if you look at who has the most merits for stability in Europe, it might not necessarily be Tietmeyer, but Trichet. To turn around a country like France with 80 years of free lunches, is of course, no small accomplishment for a civil servant. It would have been easier to do what your masters would like you to do.

Meanwhile, Germany's Tietmeyer was also insisting on money supply targeting. A G-10 central banker, speaking of a meeting in early September, 1998, recalls:

> Tietmeyer has got this way about him, a lecturing fashion. He wags his finger at people and says 'this is precisely the point.' It is one of his phrases. But you never quite know precisely what his point is. It's a kind of filler from one sentence to the next. Tietmeyer speaks three times as long as everyone else. He said that Germany was the model, and he advocated monetary targeting, of course, and said that the euro had to build on it. He was being so much his typical self that people were smirking a bit at each other across the table. Even Hans' allies, Duisenberg and Verplaetse, were looking at the ceiling . . . Tietmeyer led a particularly egregious attack on inflation targets and how terrible they were, and he said that inflation shouldn't be allowed to go above 2 per cent, it didn't matter how low it went. Gordon Thiessen, who is the Canadian governor, said 'Oh, I can't let this one go by. Oh Hans, come on!' Thiessen started giving the Canadian view of inflation, that you had to have a lower limit to inflation as well as a higher limit.

The Becket Effect

But if his colleagues sometimes poked fun at Tietmeyer, none could deny the influence that he and his German colleague Issing wielded upon the culture of the European central bankers. Before the 1990s, most European countries had no experience of independent central banking. It was the Germans who gradually fostered a growing sense of self-awareness and common cause and, above all, pride in independence from political authorities. Take for example the experience of the Spanish member of the ECB board, Eugenio Domingo Solans. He began learning German in 1985 as a researcher during economic seminars held annually in the northern German city of Kiel and was impressed by the standard of debate about monetary issues there.

> The idea of an independent central bank comes from Germany. It is not a Latin tradition, nor is it an anglo-saxon one. I began to admire the idea. Hans Tietmeyer once made a statement that stuck with me: 'In spite of all the demands from government for lower rates, in spite of all the demands from business for lower rates, and in spite of all the demands from labour unions for lower rates, we are going to lower rates.' At that moment I understood what independence means.

What was happening among the European bankers at the ECB was the same thing that had happened at the US Federal Reserve and the German Bundesbank decades before. An independent dynamic influenced outsiders coming into the bank to conform with the bank's norms, beliefs and rituals – even if the outsiders had not previously been part of them. In fact, the Bundesbank had its own name for this conforming process: the 'Becket effect.' As David Marsh wrote in his book on the Bundesbank:

> Bundesbank insiders, with grim historical relish, draw on the saga of Henry II's chancellor Thomas à Becket, who opposed the King after he was made Archbishop of

Canterbury [and became a true adherent in the church]. He was murdered for his pains. The process under which outsiders brought into the bank often end up conforming far more than expected to the straight-and-narrow principles of *Stabilitätspolitik* is known within the Bundesbank as 'the Becket effect'. Like the erstwhile archbishop, the Bundesbank normally expects to win its tussles with the government: and, like Becket, too, its self-confidence can sometimes be over-stretched.'[iv]

At the Federal Reserve, too, there is an expression 'taking the veil', which compares the initiation of sometimes left-wing thinkers into the board's mainstream conservative ways to nuns entering a convent. As William Greider recounts in his book about the Federal Reserve:

When Nancy Teeters, a left of centre economist of the House Budget committee was appointed to the board in the 1970s, [Fed Chairman] Arthur Burns reportedly told her: 'Don't worry, Nancy. Within six months, you will think just like a central banker.' She reportedly said later: 'Arthur was right. I think I'm very much a central banker now. You're in a position where your views on money, credit and banking are not really a reflection of your political party or your positions on economic issues. It's not really a political job. I understand the whole milieu of what we are doing, the continuous decisions, the mystique of central banking.'[v]

Similarly, the ECB has also come to resemble the working of a Church, with an orthodoxy passed on by the the Bundesbank. The ECB has a pope, Duisenberg. It has a college of cardinals, the board members and the national bank governors, the most influential of them being Tietmeyer and his ally, Issing; it has a curia, the senior staff, led by Klöckers. The equivalent of the laity is the commercial banks. It even has different orders of religious thought like the Jesuits, Franciscans and Dominicans, only at the ECB they are different orders of orthodoxy: the creative orthodox (Trichet,

Wellink, Rojo, Padoa-Schioppa), assertive orthodox (Mersch, Liebscher, Verplaetse) conformist orthodox (Noyer, Domingo Solans, O'Connell, De Sousa) and the independents (Vanhala, Hämäläinen). Finally, there is the naughty parishioner, Fazio, who is overdue to confess his euro-sceptic sins.[vi]

The ECB's secrecy makes it all the more like a priestly order – as though the rituals are so sacred and powerful that the public eye must not be allowed even a glimpse of them.[3] The religious metaphors evoked during the debate on the ECB encourages this analogy. When Germany's Lafontaine called repeatedly called for interest rate cuts in late 1998, he accused the central bankers of 'absolutism' and living in a 'pre-democratic age', for their religious pursuit of price stability. But the more politicians criticize the bankers, the more stubborn the bankers become, responding that the calls for interest rate cuts are a threat to their independence. Jean-Claude Juncker, the Luxembourg prime minister, called the response of the bankers 'hysterical.'

As in a church, a central bank can function well only when there is capable leadership - something that both the Bundesbank and the Fed have been blessed with over the past two decades. But when William Miller was chairman of the US Fed in the late 1970s, he was considered too responsive to the White House and too complacent about fighting inflation. His weak leadership caused months of confusion and infighting at the Federal Reserve. Despite charges of 'aloofness' at the Dutch central bank,[4] Duisenberg runs a tight ship at the ECB, say the council members. Criticism from within has been rare. His forté has been to spot and then recruit high quality assistants such as

---

[3] Besides the minutes-taker, Frank Moss, the translators, and if they decide to visit, the president of the council of ministers and the EC commissioner on monetary affairs, no one else is allowed in the room while interest rate decisions are being discussed. The governors are allowed to designate one person to sit by them during council meetings, but these assistants must leave the room when interest rates are discussed.

[4] 'Each time Duisenberg left the country to give a major speech,' one colleague recounted 'we became a little more panicked because he wasn't always prepared.'

Lex Hoogduin, to help prepare him. He has also relied quite heavily on the young French vice president, Christian Noyer. 'When he goes on a trip, he tells me to hold the fort,' Noyer says. Explains Mersch:

> Duisenberg has the necessary detachedness without being aloof. He has the ability to manage a team and keep it together and on course. He has the extraordinary ability to know how much leash to allow everyone on the team and when to intervene to round off discussion. He is the right man for the job, especially at the start, because if you had someone with a stronger feeling about how the power relationship between the centre [ECB] and the periphery [national banks] should evolve, the discussions might have degenerated into more conflict than they have . . .

Duisenberg has the advantage of coming from a country that is medium-sized and located strategically – both regionally and ideologically – closer to the north of Europe than the south. The Netherlands has a population of 15 million, putting it right in the middle of the Euroland spectrum – larger than Luxembourg, Finland, Ireland, Austria, Portugal, and Belgium, yet still identifying with the insecurities of those small states - and smaller than Germany, France, Italy and Spain, yet still large enough to be taken seriously.

Now that Tietmeyer and Verplaetse have both retired, no one rivals Duisenberg in central banking seniority. Tietmeyer's retirement signaled a significant change of psychology within the board. Tietmeyer's credibility made him the father figure on the board. It was Tietmeyer who, when he walked into the first ECB council meeting in June 1998, promptly walked out again in protest, saying he would not sit down until country name-tags around the table were replaced by the bankers' names. He also supported a move to seat the council according to alphabetical order, rather than seat the board at one end of the table and the governors at the other. Duisenberg sits at the head of the table, with Noyer at his side.

There was no one on the German scene in early 1999 who

could come close to filling Tietmeyer's shoes. The front-runner for the position was Ernst Welteke, a 56-year-old member of the Bundesbank's council, closer than Tietmeyer to the new social democrat-led government in Bonn because of his membership in the social democratic party. Welteke was a dove within the council, having argued regularly for lower interest rates. He was overruled by Tietmeyer and Issing when he proposed to lower rates in 1996. He was finance minister for the German state of Hesse, before becoming president of the Hesse state central bank, based in the state's capital, Frankfurt. Within the council, he was a strong proponent of Frankfurt becoming a major financial cenre, and so is expected to be a supporter of greater centralization of power at the ECB's head-quarters in Frankfurt. Within the Bundesbank council, he was also the most passionate supporter of European monetary union. However, so far Welteke has not exhibited the intel-lectual firepower of Issing or Tietmeyer.

Verplaetse, the bonhomous governor of the Belgian central bank for the last decade, was a staunch supporter of the German approach to monetary policy. He had an endearing habit of starting his conversation with a gasping laugh: 'Ya, ya . . .' His country lost some credibility in the early 1980s when the budget deficit reached as high as 30.4 per cent. In 1982, during a stint as the prime minister's chief of staff, Verplaestse pushed through a dramatic devaluation of the Belgian franc. Worse, he did so without first consulting Belgium's partner in their mini currency union, Luxembourg. His relations with Mersch, the Luxembourg governor, were stormy until the end.

Luxembourg's Mersch can appreciate Duisenberg's neu-trality within Europe. Possessing a keen intuition and sharp sense of irony, Mersch represents a tiny country tucked in between France, Belgium and Germany, which suffered the highest number of casualties per capita during the Second World War. Mersch's father became an underground resistance fighter in Germany, helping smuggle French prisoner-of-war escapees back over the border.

After the war, Mersch's father took him along for visits to Germany to instill in his son an understanding of the Germans and their culture. Mersch learned to read German, and says he dabbled in Marxism as a left-leaning student before turning moderate during his college years. He soon joined the finance ministry, and quickly moved up to the deputy minister position in Luxembourg. As such, he attended the EU's Monetary Committee meetings, and from there helped negotiate the move toward the single currency over the 1990s.

During Monetary Committee and other summit meetings, he met all of the ECB's ten other national central bank governors at one time or another. He calls it a 'club', saying that the only person on the ECB council he didn't know by first name on the first day was the Spanish board member, Domingo Solans. The career path among the bankers is remarkably similar. Of the eleven governors, eight of them once worked in their treasury departments.

Flying Dutchman & Co.

The continuous contact between the ECB governors over the past decade has reduced the role that political affiliation plays in debates. The Dutch governor, Nout Wellink, a Catholic, is not a member of Duisenberg's social democratic party, but he says there is no longer any difference in ideology between them. It wasn't always that way. While Duisenberg pursued the left-wing doctorate subject of disarmament, Wellink was a member of a Roman Catholic fraternity while studying at Leiden university. As the one story goes, Wellink became particularly enthusiastic during the birthday celebration of the Catholic university's chaplain, and jumped into the Rapenburg, the main canal at the university. He came down on an rusty underwater bicycle, permanently damaging one of his legs. Wellink moved up to the deputy finance minister position in the Netherlands, and then became Duisenberg's right-hand man at the Dutch central bank.

Matti Vanhala, the successor of Sirkka Hämäläinen as the Finnish central bank governor, possesses a wit and relaxed sense of humour rarely seen in Europe's staid central banking circles. He earned the reputation as being more of a 'hawk' than

Hämäläinen, even though the two say they have no difference in their approaches to monetary policy – only that Hämäläinen is more openly pro-European. Vanhala sprinkles his conversation with references to the different mindset of the 'continentals'. He is one of the few on the council who argues that a 'Becket effect' has not yet occurred, saying differences between the governors are still too great, and national interests still too strong, for the council to be considered an organization stronger than the individuals within it. At 53, Vanhala was the youngest of the governors except for Antonio de Sousa, the 44-year-old Portuguese central banker. De Sousa was always precocious. At 26, he was already chairman of the economics department at Lisbon college. After obtaining an economics doctorate from the Wharton School in Pennsylvania, he returned and entered the Portuguese government. By 36, he became the country's deputy finance minister.

Spanish governor Luis Angel Rojo, Austrian governor Klaus Liebscher, Irish governor Maurice O'Connell and Italian governor Antonio Fazio are all in their 60s, and thus have direct memories of the war. Rojo was vice president of the EMI under Duisenberg, and switched between academia, government and the Spanish central bank during his career. He studied at the London School of Economics, and along with Issing, was the most prolific on the council in terms of publishing books and papers on economic theory. He was fascinated with Keynes, though was as much a critic as a supporter of the famous economist.

Like Duisenberg, Austria's governor Liebscher is a chain smoker. Liebscher, a lawyer by training, has been in banking for most of his career. He admits to an alliance between Germany and Austria on most issues, but Liebscher is too intellectually independent to be considered an unconditional ally. Ireland's O'Connell is a cautious, withdrawn member – a relative newcomer to central banking. He started his career as a school teacher, and made a switch in his mid-20s to the country's finance ministry. Ireland has been overwhelmed by its recent economic growth, and O'Connell is likely to be more pre-occupied with adapting the nation's financial services regulatory infrastructure to cope with Dublin's burgeoning financial service sector than in taking a forceful role within the council. He is a devout Christian. 'I say my prayers in gaelic,' he says.

Italy's Antonio Fazio is also a devout Catholic, and part of a more conservative Italian school that identifies closely with Germany's social market economy. This distinguishes him from the more secular, free-market oriented school embodied by Padoa-Schioppa. Like Padoa-Schioppa, he studied at Massachusetts Institute of Technology in the US, and has spent his entire career at the Banca d'Italia, becoming its chief economist in 1973. Fazio is fiercely protective of national central bank jurisdiction, and has led the effort to curb the ECB board from further centralizing activities in Frankfurt. Born in 1936, just north of Cassino, Fazio recalls the anguish created by the German occupation and then the fighting between the Germans and the Italian liberation forces on the Gustav line. He witnessed the great battle of Cassino: 'I saw [the German general] Kesselring, corpulent and limping, reviewing the German troops. I'll never forget the day the Abbey of Monte Cassino was bombed – the daily runs of the flying fortresses that dropped their bombs on Cassino, the razed city with its cultural treasures reduced to rubble, and the great dismay of the population. Then came the liberation, great hopes and the desire to create and reconstruct.' Fazio has remained a eurosceptic despite developing close ties with his European colleagues. But even Fazio admits the need to coordinate policies more closely on the European level, particularly in tax matters.

The decision

By September 1998, the council had agreed on another issue: how to converge interest rates by the deadline of January 1, 1999.[5] The Asian crisis had worsened steadily over the course

---

[5] The single currency requires a single interest rate. If rates had continued to vary, investors would put all their money into the country with the highest rates, in order to get the highest return.

of the year, changing predictions of where European interest rates were going to converge. The troubles of South-east Asia had spread to countries disturbingly close to the borders of the industrialized west – Brazil, on the border of the US, and Russia, on the doorstep of Europe. In 1997, conventional wisdom held that rates would meet somewhere in the middle of the range across Europe, or at about 4 per cent. But by summer 1998, markets expected rates would more likely converge toward the German and French levels of 3.3 per cent – the low end of the range. Only Austria had a lower rate: 3.2 per cent.

Many countries didn't have far to go to get to 3.3 per cent, but Ireland, Spain, Portugal and Italy would be forced to reduce rates substantially. They were all either experiencing higher rates of growth or were at an advanced stage of their economic cycle, meaning that it was time to lift rates rather than lower them, since inflation was beginning to creep upward. Out of European solidarity, the bankers from these countries agreed privately with the other bankers that they would lower their rates in lockstep, each decreasing their rate a notch at the same time every few weeks – except for Italy. Because of the political turmoil Italy was suffering, Fazio argued he needed to keep the country's rates a notch higher to fend off any last-minute speculation against its currency.

Before November, the assumption was that 3.3 per cent – the rate in Germany and France – was the floor. Nout Wellink, governor of the Dutch central bank dismissed the need to go lower. 'The European economy is a robust one ... What contribution to stability would reducing European interest rates of a quarter of a percentage point have?' he asked rhetorically on September 8. 'This would not change the situation in Brazil.' But little did Wellink know, the economic situation in Europe was going to deteriorate significantly over the next couple of months.

By October, the Asian contagion and its influence on bank lending in Europe had intensified. There was a consensus among the governors to cut rates down to 3.3 per cent by the end of December, but developments were so volatile that they agreed not to bind themselves to a specific level. On October 6,

Issing, Duisenberg, and Padoa-Schioppa attended the IMF and World Bank meetings in Washington, DC where they were subjected to a message of doom by the Americans. In a speech, Bill Clinton declared that the world was experiencing the worst financial crisis in the post-World War II era. The US Federal Reserve cut rates in October, the first of three cuts over a period of several weeks.

On October 8, Dresdner Bank board member Ernst-Moritz Lipp invited ECB vice president Christian Noyer to give a talk at the bank's branch in Bad Homberg. Lipp had just visited Washington and, introducing Noyer, described the negative mood that had prevailed there. Lipp spoke a message of doom and of the need for a quick boost of confidence from central bankers in the form of lower rates. He said he was confident that an interest rate would come, careful not to glance at Noyer when he said it. But the message for the young vice president was clear. German banks, which had been exposed to the crisis, needed lower rates. Lipp emphasized that Europe's major companies were also feeling the squeeze, and matter-of-factly added that several French companies were included in this bunch. It was a jeremiad that stuck. During his own speech Noyer was careful not to let himself get pulled into a comment about interest rate levels, but he couldn't help but hear Lipp's message. It was one more call in favour of an early interest rate cut. Slowly, more voices would be added to that call.

At each of the council meetings between the bank's first meeting in June and the meeting on December 1, debate about interest rates picked up in intensity. Until late November, the bankers had assumed the final interest rate for the euro's debut on January 1 would be decided upon only in late December. Some countries were still converging downward to the 3.3 per cent target, and it was still too early to consider whether rates should move lower.

On October 27, Mersch argued that a convergence of rates was all that could be expected by the end of the year and that he expected Issing would then take the lead at the beginning of the year with a proposal about what to do with interest rates. On October 30, Maurice O'Connell still believed that the decision to go below 3.3 per cent would be staved off until January. But he already suspected that rates were likely to fall lower: 'From January onward, the focus will be very much drafted in Frankfurt on a European basis. We have reason to believe that the decision made will not always be to our liking. I won't be alone in that. But we have to get on and live with it.'

On November 5, Verplaetse didn't see a need for a cut either. Belgium, like France, had joined Germany in raising rates to 3.3 per cent from 3 per cent a year before, in response to increased signs of inflation. Verplaetse, for one, wanted eventually to consider a move to 3 per cent, but he recognized it was necessary to wait until the others converged. He sympathized with Ireland, which was going to have a hard enough time getting down to 3.3 per cent as it was. Private economists expressed concern that the Asian crisis was unnerving banks, and that they were withholding loans, risking the start of a recession. At the time, Verplaetse said:

> In Euroland, there is no credit crunch. There was a credit crunch in Japan after the bubble burst and there may also be one in the United States because some financial institutions took some risks which might materialize into losses. But in Euroland, that's not the case. When you look at economic growth and all the figures we have in Euroland, they are much better than we expected. We don't know how 1999 will be. The first priority is to harmonize the interest rates to the interest rates of the core countries. Our biggest problem is the incredible economic growth in Ireland. It will be a success if they can get their rates down to ours in time for the first working day of 1999.[vii]

But by mid-November, economic data deteriorated still further. The respected Ifo Institute in Munich released a survey that showed a fall in the busines confidence index in Germany. In late November, the EU's Eurostat office released a European-wide business index that confirmed this pessimistic outlook.

The deteriorating economy concerned Tietmeyer, and by early November he had been convinced that a cut below 3.3 per cent was necessary. On November 6, the Irish had made an important cut, down to 3.69 per cent from 4.94 per cent, and for Tietmeyer this was enough for that country and the others to be in striking distance of a cut down to 3.0 per cent.

On November 19, a majority within the Bundesbank's central council indicated a potential readiness to cut rates, but Tietmeyer knew he would have to coordinate the cut with the rest of Europe. Tietmeyer conferred with Duisenberg, and they talked about the pros and cons of moving early, before January. A cut could be made before late December, even as early as December 3, when the Bundesbank held its next central council meeting. Duisenberg warmed quickly to the idea. At the meeting of the G-10 in Basle, on November 9, Alan Greenspan had indicated that US interest rates were probably headed lower. The US Fed had already cut rates in September and October, and sure enough, the Fed had cut rates once again on November 17, all in an effort to stave off a downturn in business sentiment caused by the Asian crisis. A European rate cut down to 3 per cent would make total rate cuts in Europe – including those made by the periphery countries in previous weeks – approximately equal to those of the US.

Better yet, an early move would take the markets by surprise. After all, the surprise 'pre-decision' made on May 2 about the rate at which the currencies would be locked in with each other on January 1, had proved a success. Why not take the same tack again?

Tietmeyer discussed the issue further with Trichet. Trichet also quickly agreed. Both realised that the slow down in economic growth called for interest rate cuts, and their finance ministers, Lafontaine and Strauss-Kahn, reminded them again of the fiscal peril in which the bankers were placing Europe by delaying. Lower interest rates would help the governments meet their commitments to keep their budget deficits lower than 3 per cent, which had become harder with the economic downturn. However, under no circumstances must the central bankers appear to be lowering rates under pressure from politicians. In fact, in November, Lafontaine had gone out of his way to call upon the Bundesbank to lower rates, which made a decision to cut more difficult. But during a council discussion, the ECB agreed to ignore political debate entirely, and focus on the right decision from an economic point of view.

There was one snag, however. The council still hadn't agreed on the reference value for money supply growth, which it had promised would be a key yardstick for guiding the ECB's monetary policy. Initially, the ECB had publicly said the aggregates would be ready only at the end of the year, having assumed that a decision on interest rates would come very late in December. On November 5, for example, Verplaetse had said the reference level for the money aggregate would be ready 'as of January 1'.[viii]

Duisenberg and Tietmeyer knew they would lose credibility instantly if they cut rates before agreeing on that yardstick. They would have to hurry. They decided to set an informal council session for the evening of Monday, November 30, specifically to discuss the cut. No minutes would be taken. The next morning, during their formal meeting, they would have to agree on the reference value. They called the rest of the governors to give them the heads-up. Padoa-Schioppa recalls: 'Duisenberg acted as the link, or the crossroads, between all these bilateral talks.'

The governors who were not part of the inner circle of bilateral talks – those from Luxembourg, Austria, Finland, Spain, Portugal and Ireland – were called up a few days before the Monday meeting and forewarned that a discussion of interest rates was on the agenda. They reacted more coolly to the idea. In Spain, Portugal and Ireland, prices were increasing at a more rapid pace than in Germany, France and the Netherlands. Meanwhile, Duisenberg had briefed the board during a meeting beforehand, and had gained their support, including Issing's. Although money supply wasn't falling, Issing realized that sentiment and economic data had to play a bigger role: 'When growth developments are on the downside, and when you are convinced that price developments are actually tending downward, we had to ask ourselves: "Why not now?"' Issing recalls.

During the Monday night discussion, the debate was intense, lasting for several hours. Duisenberg, in his blunt style, casually made the proposal that interest rates be dropped on December 3. Tietmeyer explained the reasons for supporting such a move, and took the lead in arguing the case. Austria's Liebscher supported the idea from the outset; Austria's rates, after all, had been the lowest in Europe. Trichet also supported the idea, saying an early move would keep the newly established ECB out of the fire of controversy during early months of its operations.

But they met strong resistance from a majority of the council, which still believed an interest rate cut in January would be a forceful demonstration of new European cooperation after the introduction of the euro. Over the course of the night, Tietmeyer and Duisenberg tried to argue that, on the contrary, an independent decision by the national banks to cut rates in December would be a more convincing demonstration of European unity, precisely because it showed a voluntary co-operation.

By the end of the first evening, the issue wasn't resolved. A majority was still opposed to the idea, but Duisenberg insisted on keeping the proposal on the table. He realized that Germany and Austria badly wanted to cut rates, but were searching for support from the others. The endorsement of his plan by his chief economist Otmar Issing gave him the confidence to push forward. He wanted to create an early consensus, and saw that the other countries needed some persuasion. 'Many of us had gone in thinking that it would be better not to have a national move,' recalls Mersch. 'We thought we should move in January, as the European central bank, to show that it was the "Europeans" who were making the first move.' O'Connell, Rojo and De Sousa made it clear that a cut wasn't needed in their countries. Rojo, the senior of the three, took the lead in explaining their case. Spain was, like the others, in an advanced stage of its economic expansion. 'I don't see any clear reasons to reduce interest rates,' he told the others. 'I don't know if it's the right moment. Maybe we should wait until the economic indicators really tell us that we need to make a decision.' De Sousa backed him up using a similar argument. Money supply had given no hint of the need to lower rates and there were few signs that inflation was really falling. The Bank of Portugal had been surprised by the increase in food prices, which exceeded forecasts. The price of the national dish, *bacalhau*, or salted cod, rose 34 per cent in November, compared to the year before, which in Portugal's strong economy, pushed the country's overall consumer price index up close to half a percentage point. He saw few signs of a deflation. In fact, he argued, wage agreements had been higher than expected in some countries, which seemed to counter the fears of deflation that had unnerved the markets and the governors of the Bundesbank and the Banque de France. Rojo and De Sousa, however, said they were prepared to cut if the others thought it was necessary. Italy's Antonio Fazio took a peculiar positon. A euro-sceptic, he still joined the Duisenberg camp in agreeing that moves by the national banks before January was in Europe's interests. Recalls one council member: 'Fazio was right for the wrong reasons.' He said: 'You do what you want. I'll do what I want.'

The meeting broke, and the council convened on the following day for the formal meeting. Duisenberg, surprising many of the council members, made a formal proposal that interest rates be cut to 3 per cent immediately. 'I was struck by his insistence,' said one council member, recalling Duisenberg's argument: 'Are you really convinced that we should keep decisions based on national interests until the end?'

His determinedness began to chip away at the resistance. Belgium's Verplaestse initially believed a January move would be the best demonstration of European unity, and had opposed an early move. But now he began to soften up to the idea. Mersch also made an about-face. 'I admit it. I made a wrong judgement. They convinced me that an early move might be better.'

De Sousa also gave in, seeing the tactical benefits of the move, and said he too would go along with it. After all, a difference of three weeks was negligible for real effects. Finland's Vanhala, who had also originally supported a later move, was also won over. It was remarkable tour de force for the habitually calm, quiet Duisenberg: 'Duisenberg is a talented consensus-maker,' says Padoa-Schioppa. 'He is very determined to reach a decision, but at the same time, extremely light-handed.'

Duisenberg's talent is not in the firepower of his presentation, but in the hours of private thought devoted to the big picture and careful moulding of consensus. Duisenberg's former assistant, Dirk Wolfson, says: 'He told me how valuable it was to be able to just look out the window and think when he wanted.'[ix] Eduard Bomhoff, the Dutch economist who has also observed Duisenberg closely, said:

> There are two different types of philosophies of leadership. There is the type embodied by Alan Greenspan, who is a details person, immersing himself in an endless number of statistics and then getting monetary policy more or less right on average. Then you have the model of de Gaulle, the former French president, – who does not work hard, but ponders major decisions. Duisenberg fits the second type. He was not a hyperactive governor [of the Dutch central bank]. He did not give many speeches, but in the difficult crisis of the Dutch economy between 1980 and 1984, when we were the sick man of Europe and people were talking about the 'Dutch disease,' he got the main issues exactly right.

Besides Fazio, only O'Connell put the interest rate cut in national terms – indeed, he had good reason. Ireland had already cut rates to 3.69 per cent from over 6 per cent over the course of October. Its economy was growing at more than 10 per cent, and its credit growth was over 20 per cent. Housing prices were soaring by 40 per cent. Inflation could start spinning out of control. Duisenberg cautioned O'Connell. 'I asked him to judge things from a European perspective. He thought about things for a few minutes and then conceded I was right,' Duisenberg said.[x]

Finally, Duisenberg had a majority of the governors on his side. The decision could be made unanimously – almost. The only one to hold out was Fazio, the perennial pessimist, who argued that Italy could not afford to cut rates because speculators could be waiting in the wings to attack the lira at the last moment and throw years of hard work to waste. But some council members got the feeling Fazio – long sceptical of the idea of handing over power to the ECB – merely wanted to demonstrate national sovereignty until the new year. 'It was a disappointment,' said one council member. 'After all, this was supposed to represent a watershed.' By late Tuesday morning, the governors were busy phoning members of their central bank councils at home, seeing if they too would be willing to agree to an early rate cut. During the Tuesday meeting, discussions continued, and by the time it ended, it was clear that everyone was on board. Fazio, who alone was responsible for setting Italian rates, would cut rates to 3.5 per cent. The council later agreed that the 3 per cent level should remain for the 'foreseeable future'.

'There is one big disadvantage' of placing the council members in alphabetical order, Duisenberg joked afterwards. 'It means presidents Hans Tietmeyer and Jean-Claude Trichet always sit next to each other. Although there is one man, one vote, they are both big central banks, so although their vote is not bigger, it is sometimes louder.'[xi]

Trichet had taken up the issue of the interest rate cut with a passion. Before the Monday meeting, he called up a financial journalist at *Le Monde* and told him the reasons why an interest rate cut was desirable. *Le Monde* ran an article the next day, coinciding with the council's formal meeting. The only newspaper in Europe to carry the news, it explained:

The scenario of a lowering of interest rates in Germany and France before the end of the year has become, over the last couple of days, highly probable. 'After the meeting of the ECB on December 1, we will see if factors justifying a modification of rates exist,' said Trichet. A few days ago, Trichet explained 'it is not because it is being asked of us to cut already very low rates again that we're doing it. Neither is it because it is being suggested that we're too stiff-necked.' Bankers have everything to win tactically by reducing the rates. First, it wouldn't be inflationary. Second, it would prove that the ECB is not dogmatic. It would boost the confidence of the international finance community in the euro. It would help smooth the way for the ECB's start in 1999 by enabling it to avoid rapid monetary decisions. It would prove that it can be pragmatic like Greenspan.[xii]

Also during the formal meeting on Tuesday, the council agreed on a reference value of 4.5 per cent growth. The debate on monetary policy had taken longer than expected, and the press conference, which had been held regularly in the past at 6.30 pm, was delayed by almost an hour while the meeting ran overtime.

The cut

Two days later, on Thursday, the Euroland-wide interest rate cut was made public, with all banks making the decision within ten minutes of each other. All the national banks lowered rates to 3 per cent, except for Italy, which dropped rates to 3.5 per cent. The markets were taken by total surprise, and it was accepted widely as a favourable move. Only *Le Monde* seemed to have predicted it, again because of its access to Trichet. On Thursday morning, before the cut was announced, it had run a second article listing more reasons why a cut was probable.

Trichet told *Le Monde* that the dollar's recent decline against European currencies meant inflation from import prices were less of a threat. Cutting rates would also be a way of keeping the euro from increasing in value against the dollar, by making it less attractive as an investment opportunity. The dollar had lost ten centimes over the two previous days. Furthermore, stock exchanges had lost value, the French exchange losing 4.03 per cent on Tuesday alone. Cutting rates would boost investor confidence. Apart from Trichet's comments to *Le Monde*, there were no public hints at the cut. A day before, the only publication that had indicated that the cut would be coming was the *Wall Street Journal Europe*, which had picked up on Duisenberg's negative comments about sentiment and growth during the press conference on Tuesday evening.

Speaking after the rate cut, Duisenberg hailed the move as 'rather sensational'.[xiii] But the Irish weren't happy. The cut was 'just rubbing a bit of salt in the tail', an Irish central banking official told the *Financial Times*. Duisenberg justified the move, saying that the Asian crisis had caused business sentiment to decline considerably, economic growth was threatening to slow down and prices were otherwise moderate. He added that in response, governments must continue to cut their deficits. Tietmeyer stated that the cut reflected a worsening of economic assumptions. While the bank's internal forecasts showed a 2.4 to 2.5 per cent growth rate for 1999, some private economists had been reducing their predictions to even lower than that.

Such a small rate cut, some market analysts complained, would not have much more than a psychological impact, since short-term interest rates (the ones influenced directly by the central bank's financing activities) were already low enough. In addition, the decision didn't at first reduce long-term interest rates, which are more important for companies making investments, they noted. But their grumbling proved unfounded. Over the next couple of weeks, long-term rates declined steadily. By March 1999, they reached the lowest levels since the 1940s.

Notably, one fact was ignored by the ECB's public statements and accompanying media coverage: money supply developments were not used as a justification for the move. Euroland's money supply had been rising steadily in line with the ECB's reference value. Money supply developments implied that no cut was needed. The fact that the ECB cut rates anyway was the final nail in the coffin for money supply targeting.

There was also no clear evidence of a fall in prices. The consumer price index showed that prices rose at an annual rate of 1 per cent in October compared to the year before – right in the middle of the range the ECB had set for itself. Adam Posen, economist at the Institute for international Economics, warned the ECB against adopting a 'monetary masquerade'. Also, some Bundesbank members voted against the move when the German central bank made the decision, on the basis that neither weakening of economic growth nor money supply developments merited it.

New era?

There were other signs that the ECB had moved to an eclectic approach similar to that of the Federal Reserve. After the rate cut, Duisenberg had said the euro's exchange rate would be 'one of the main indicators that we watch'.[xiv] Before the cut, Duisenberg had said the euro's exchange rate was just 'one of a broad range of indices' that the bank would watch. After the cut Duisenberg said he didn't want an 'overvalued' euro to hurt European competitiveness. 'We don't want the exchange rate to unduly undermine the competitiveness of Euroland with the rest of the world,' he said.

The ECB's policy goal is price stability, but the means for achieving it have become more discretionary than those practiced by the Bundesbank. Ireland, Spain and Portugal had agreed with the rate cut, seeing a joint action as crucial for the interests of Europe. What will happen when the core countries want to lift rates and the marginal countries are suffering a recession? It is a question that remains to be answered.

Every central bank chief at the Federal Reserve seems to have ushered in a new era. Alan Greenspan, for example, introduced more of a focus on the global economy into the Fed's interest rate decisions, and a garrulous way of dealing with the public. Duisenberg is not like that. He is short, and sometimes even gruff, in his answers.

I am a great admirer of Alan Greenspan and the way he can express himself and at the same time leave open so much ambiguity. It is very much a personal style. I'm different. I want to be and have to be as transparent and open as I can, and it is in my nature to be rather direct. And I cannot, and will not, change that attitude. Sometimes it will mean that I cannot, and will not, answer questions. Alan Greenspan would resort to giving an answer which nobody would understand or which would be multi-interpretable. I would be inclined to say: 'Sorry, I won't answer that question.'

But as his record at the central bank in the Netherlands during the banking scandal in the early 1980s highlighted, Duisenberg doesn't like long analytical discussions, and this style has spilled over into the culture of the board and governing council meetings. While he was president of the G-10 meetings in Basle, he surprised some committee meeting participants by his speed to call meetings to adjournment as soon as there was a moment's pause, and before some attendees had presented their positions. 'The Dutch central bank board meetings were very short,' complains one ECB board member, 'just decisions, no discussions. At our central bank, our board meetings were really discussions. We had seminar-style meetings, where every-one could express themselves and we could actually change the proposal after much discussion.'

Still, that frankness doesn't mean that Duisenberg doesn't try to develop ambiguity of his own. One expression that Duisenberg toyed with after the December 3 rate cut was the pledge that rates would stay at 3 per cent for the 'foreseeable future'. By February, 1999, he had repeated this phrase several times, and the media began trying to pin him down on what he meant. On December 22, when he declared that 3.0 per cent would be the ECB's starting refinancing interest rate for 1999, he said he wanted to give a signal 'that markets do not expect a change in interest rates in the foreseeable future'. When he repeated the phrase after the next governing council meeting on January 7, one journalist asked him to explain just how far the foreseeable future was. He answered in classic Greenspan form:

> We do not put a horizon to our future that we can see. Contrary to you, I come from a very flat country where we can always see the horizon which is very far away. So it certainly does not imply any date as you indicated that will be the end of our foreseeable future. As far as we can see, now we see no tendency which would force us to change interest rates in the future, as far as we can foresee it.

The phrase began popping up in comments by other ECB council members, including those of vice president Christian Noyer during the same press conference. Noyer commented that European national banks would keep the proportion of gold in their reserve holdings for the 'foreseeable future'. Duisenberg broke in, saying: 'And in this case, the foreseeable future is much longer than in the earlier case'.

Transparency

Transparency at the Bank of England means the ability to have a clear look at the decisions and arguments within the main decision making body, and thereby let the markets be prepared for interest rate decisions when they are made. Duisenberg's definition of transparency differs, since it doesn't mean fore-warning the markets. In fact, it appears that Duisenberg's definition of success is taking the markets off-guard, which is why he declared the December 3 cut so successful. In response to criticism that the bank had not been transparent, he responded:

> As regards the so-called lack of transparency, don't you mean, rather, that it was so totally unexpected by the markets and the media? And that is what is now being called a lack of transparency? We are rather pleased about the un-expectedness of the move.

Before the bank had even started, it had created some taboos. One of them was talking about deflation. Though the ECB kept insisting in its public announcements that deflation wasn't a danger, it was deeply concerned about sinking prices. It was especially worried because it had reached what it had believed to be a floor in interest rates. If it were to go much further, it would be in danger of falling into a trap similar to the one Japan was in: not being able to go any lower if conditions got even worse. As a result, the ECB desperately played down the deflation danger. One memo on the desk of Klaus Masuch, leader of the monetary policy's 'strategic' section, dated December 15, 1998, specifically outlined a policy to downplay deflation: However, it concluded: 'Of course, we can't pull the wool over anyone's eyes if they [market players] understand the economic situation.' The memo said that the ECB should justify the monetary policy stance by referring to sagging business sentiment, not falling prices. Not one member of the ECB's council so much as whispered the words 'falling prices,' even though price increases had fallen for several consecutive months.

Inflation was to remain so subdued that on April 8, 1999, the governing council lowered its refinancing rate by half a point to 2.5 per cent. It also lowered the marginal lending facility and deposit facility by one point, and half a point, respectively. As it turned out, Duisenberg's 'foreseeable future' was less than three months.

NOTES

i Interview with author, September 3, 1998.
ii Interview with author, November 17, 1998.
iii *Le Monde*, January 29,1994.
iv Marsh, p.22.
v Greider, p.74.
vi This analogy of the Church is drawn from the words of the vice-president of a Federal Reserve bank, cited in Grieder, p.54.
vii Interview with author. November 5, 1998.
viii Interview with author. November 5, 1998.
ix Dagmar Aalund and Greg Steinmetz. 'Top Euroland Banker Finds Himself Sailing in Uncharted Waters,' in the *Wall Street Journal Europe*. Monday, Jananary 11, 1999.
x Duisenberg quote from *Die Zeit*, December 16, 1998.
xi *Financial Times*, December 7, 1998.
xii Le Monde. December 1, 1998.
xiii *Financial Times*, December 4, 1998.
xiv *Financial Times*, December 7, 1998.

CHAPTER NINE

United Europe

The independence of the European Central Bank is enshrined in the Maastricht Treaty, and there is little question that the bank plans to lead a hawkish, stability-oriented monetary policy, regardless of political pressure to behave otherwise. But all central banks operate within a social and political framework which cannot help but influence the bank's decison-making process. As Otmar Issing has emphasised in speeches, public support is just as important in determining the outcome of the bank's decisions as its statutes. The extent to which Europe can resolve a number of inconsistencies and inefficiencies in its political organizations, including the ECB itself, will determine the social climate within Euroland, and therefore the degree of support that the ECB has from the population. Ultimately, these reforms will also determine the sort of policy the ECB will run.

Irresistible force

In 1950, Jacques Rueff, the former Banque de France deputy governor, declared that monetary union would be a catalyst for more political union. At first, Bundesbank chief economist for most of the 1990s, Otmar Issing, and other Germans rejected this philosophy, obsessed with the need to agree on a structure for Europe before taking small steps in an unclear direction that could end up destabilizing Europe rather than strengthening it.

The history of monetary unions without political unions has been dismal, as evidenced by the Latin currency union in 1861, the Scandinavian union attempt in the 1920s and the German–Austrian attempts of the 1850s and the 1860, which ended in 1867, a year after the two powers went to war with each other. These failures resulted from conflicts arising from different macro-economic conditions.

During the Maastricht negotiations, however, Bonn politicians, faced with French and British resistance to a political union, reconciled themselves to the idea of a single currency as a forerunner. Frankfurt's central bankers remained sceptical for many years, but they too gradually began to tone down their criticism of the Maastricht result. Though they held to the belief that political union was a requirement for Europe, they conceded Rueff's point that economic and monetary union could help push that process of integration forward, and that political union could crystallize slowly thereafter. Issing, one of the more vocal sceptics and an ardent structuralist, admits that he has changed his thinking over time, and is no longer a pessimist. In an interview at his ECB office, he says he now believes European unity can evolve in a variety of different ways, that the state of relations between European states can be more complex than he had previously thought. The single currency union is destined to succeed, and the political side will have to work itself out, he says.

The rest of the ECB's council members are divided in their views on the degree to which Europe must unify politically, ranging from enthusiastic European visionaries to extreme pragmatists. But all concede the need to advance, even if many of them are vague in their prescriptions.

The main drivers of this process, because of their size and clout in Europe, will remain the Germans. It was Joschka Fischer, the German foreign minister who, during Germany's tenure of the EU's rotating presidency in early 1999, outlined a need to push forward an agreement on a new goal of political union by 2001. The centrepiece of his vision was to move to a system of majority voting within the European council on all major policy areas, so that member states would no longer wield a veto right, which in the past has been used to slow up agreement. The ECB's Padoa-Schioppa enthusiastically endorsed the proposal: 'I do not regard it as desirable for the Eurosystem to be in a kind of political semi-vacuum or semi-desert for very long.'

By the time Germany obtains the EU presidency again in late 2006, Europe will be putting the finishing touches on its final vision. EU member states will have agreed on a new constitution, which will regulate with more clarity which duties are under EU jurisdiction in Brussels and which duties are under national jurisdiction. This will forge the way for Eastern European countries to enter the union. Squabbles over the amount each country pays to and receives from Brussels will be set aside by reaching a compromise over a sensible way to regulate payments, based partly on the GDP *per capita* and perhaps other factors, such as the size of the country's vote in the council of ministers. Reform of the Common Agriculture Policy and regional development programmes is already underway.

Power shift to the centre

What exactly is propelling Europe towards further unity? One force is a negative one: fear. Consider, for example, the case that the bankers were debating in Basle in 1997: Italy. Though Italy had qualified for monetary union, many observers, including central bankers, had doubts about its commitment and ability to hold to the Maastricht Treaty criteria over the long run. Without more political glue, it was thought, Italy might feel justified in veering from its commitments to the Eurozone, and in the process, seriously disrupt European finances. It was this fear that led the Germans to propose the Stability and Growth Pact, which was eventually agreed to by other EU members in 1996. The pact threatened countries with concrete sanctions if they breached the deficit limit of 3 per cent of GDP set by the Maastricht Treaty.[1]

---

[1] This is also why the Italians weren't in the room when the final compromise was made on the stability pact. The group consisted of the Germans, French, Dutch and the deal-making Luxembourgers: Kohl, Waigel, Chirac, Artuis, Kok, Zalm and Juncker. Here again, however, the Germans, cheered on by the Dutch, took a hard line. The Germans proposed that automatic sanctions be slapped on countries that exceed the 3 per cent deficit limit if they have economic growth in the year of more than minus 1 per cent GDP. The French wanted it to be less, saying a country should be exempt from paying the fine even if its recession is only minus 0.5 per cent of GDP. Waigel recalls that Chirac made the first move, saying

But there were more than external forces pushing for more agreement on budget politics. There were internal reasons too. The Italians, for example, had become more loyal to Brussels than to Rome. The prosperous southern states of Germany, Baden-Württemberg and Bavaria, have increasingly complained about Germany's federal demands, saying they are transferring too much money to the poorer, northern states, and have even challenged the federal redistribution system in the nation's highest court. France has also been under popular pressure to devolve power from Paris to the regions.

The transformation of Italy's fiscal situation over the course of the 1990s, in which the government cut the deficit from 11 per cent to 6.7 per cent between 1990 and 1996, and then made a last-minute plunge down to 2.7 per cent in 1997 in order to get beneath the Maastricht limit of 3 per cent by that year's deadline, is a showcase of what can happen under this mix of external and internal pressure. Tietmeyer still doubts whether Italy will survive the exhaustion caused by its efforts. Ultimately, however, the Stability Pact would provide some protection against misbehaviour.

To be sure, there are no guarantees that Italy will abide by its

he was willing to move to minus 0.6 per cent. Then Kohl said, 'Jacques, I didn't go to an élite university like you did, and I got far lower marks than you did in mathematics, but you know that if you take the average of -0.5 and -1, you get -0.75, and not minus 0.6 per cent.' Waigel says he'll never forget how Wim Kok, the Dutch Prime Minister, was standing there saying: 'Helmut, be tough! Be tough!' There are a number of other ways a country can be considered exempt from the sanctions. It was in this way that the French, joined by the Italians, managed to water down the 'automaticity' of the sanctions. Now the punishment system relies on a joint decision by heads of state that could involve interpretations and political fudging. Trichet, however, argues that the stability pact 'must be considered *less* rigorous' than the Maastricht Treaty, since the Treaty already contained the 3 per cent reference. Though the Germans had wanted to strengthen discipline by setting concrete fines in the event of failure, this hard line forced the Italians and French to insist on special exemptions, for example in times of recession. This set a dangerous precedent. In other words, Trichet believes that by getting explicit, the Pact could backfire on itself: an inviolable spirit had effectively become an interpretable letter. 'The pact explains why you can overshoot the 3 per cent in instances when there are exceptional circumstances,' says Trichet.

commitments. During an economic slowdown, the government might give in to a temptation to pump money into the economy to stimulate job creation. Now that it was part of the Eurozone, it could 'free ride' on the rest of Europe, enjoying Euroland's low interest rates secured by the discpline of the other countries. Before, the money pumped into the economy inflated the lira, and the Banca d'Italia was forced to lift rates in order to slow the economy. Now, the money pumped into the economy inflates the euro across the entire Euroland, but because of the size of Euroland's economy, the inflation wouldn't be as noticeable. In other words, Italy's neighbours would be paying for its spending binges.

Italy could perennially dance on the edge of acceptability, testing the political will of its neighbours, running up its deficits to the Maastricht Treaty limit, perhaps even creeping over the 3 per cent ceiling. If other countries expressed dissatisfaction, and threatened to slap on fines, Italy could then scamper back underneath the limit for a time until tempers eased.

The Italians realize the Stability Pact has a credibility problem. They have shrewdly been sowing doubt about its interpretation, with prime minister Massimo D'Alema saying public infrastructure investments should be not be included in the measurement of the deficit. Mario Monti, the Italian EC commissioner, and other European leaders have expressed sympathy with this view. Italy knows it will be difficult for politicians to justify massive fines if the country is already struggling financially – out of fear that a fine would set in motion a vicious cycle, forcing Italy to borrow even more to afford the fine. Italy could theoretically retaliate by threatening to leave the single currency zone. This too would be un-acceptable to the Europeans, all too aware that Italian exporters would gain an advantage if Italy reintroduced a weak lira. With their production costs factored in cheaper lira, the companies could undercut European goods in foreign markets.

Regardless of circumstance, fiscal backsliding would cause significant political instability in Europe. This is what lies behind the concerns – again expressed mainly by German and Dutch economists – about D'Alema's 'interpreting' the Stability

Pact differently from the strict definition favoured by the Germans and the Dutch.

It is precisely this set of concerns that is pushing the EU to even deeper forms of co-operation and consultation on economic issues. The European Union finance ministers review each others' budget plans twice a year. In the newly created Euro-11, the finance ministers of the Euroland countries consult with each other even more often about budget plans. The President of the ECB, Duisenberg, and a deputy of his choice (so far, his vice-president, Noyer) attend these meetings, allowing dialogue between the fiscal and monetary policy makers. Any problems in the Italian budget will now come to light sooner, and the countries can decide to orchestrate a barrage of public and behind-the-scenes pressure to embarrass the Italian government into remedial action. ECB President Wim Duisenberg, an invitee to Euro-11 meetings, can also place pressure on erring governments. The intense communication also generates a collegial culture, which ties Italian leaders into a set of common rules of understanding, making it more difficult for them to extricate themselves from commitments or otherwise pursue independent policies. The Bank of Japan's representative in Frankfurt, Kunio Matsuda, and the president of the Federal Reserve Bank of New York, Bill McDonough, both believe that Europe's budget review process is exerting more pressure on the governments to co-ordinate their policies. 'Political leaders realize they can't go in all different directions without putting tremendous strain on monetary policy,' says McDonough.

Some bankers, among them Finland central bank governor Matti Vanhala, worry about whether the rules of the Stability Pact are clear enough. But others, like France's Jean-Claude Trichet, argue that Euroland's council of finance minsters already has unprecedented power, possessing the ability to fine erring member states – a power that even the US government in Washington doesn't have *vis à vis* its states. Trichet says that the German government and Bundestag or French government and National Assembly can be 'told by Brussels' that they are misbehaving and that they have to pass a new fiscal law. 'We often underestimate the power given to the centre of Europe.'

But in the move towards political unity, an important, although underestimated precedent has been set: the EU's payments to poorer regions, called 'cohesion' and 'structural' development funds. These funds come from the common pot of member state contributions to the EU. In effect, wealthy European nations, such as Germany and the Netherlands, are net contributors to the EU, because they get little back in the form of this development assistance. In early 1999, Germany's new chancellor, Gerhard Schröder, demanded a reduction in his country's burden of payments to the EU.[2] But he knew full well that Germany would continue to be a net contributor to the EU budget, and he did not protest against that. This is an important precedent because it is the first step towards an official transfer system of the kind that exists in the United States, or even within Germany itself, which is designed to even out unbalances between states. In the US and German federal systems, transfers operate automatically. A citizen of the state of Connecticut may pay the same percentage of their incomes to the federal government as a citizen from any of the other states, but because he is wealthier, the amount is more in absolute terms. Washington then redistributes some of that in the form of social insurance payments to states with higher rates of unemployment or a lower standard of living. Connecticut is a net contributor to the US system, but it knows it reaps benefits in the form of the overall national political stability.

Amsterdam

In June 1997, European finance ministers sought to make some headway toward the political union that had been so neglected during the Maastricht Treaty negotiations for monetary union in 1991. One of its main goals was to reform the EU's institutions to pave the way to admit up to ten new countries from central and eastern Europe.

Negotiators located 66 policy areas where the EU still

---

[2] See footnote 17 on page 92 of this book, concerning the introduction of the Deutschmark in the ex-GDR.

decided issues by unanimous decision making, meaning that any country – even tiny Luxembourg – could veto decisions if they didn't want to go along. These areas are the source of Europe's gridlock, and the Germans have pushed as aggressively as any country in Europe to move toward majority voting in order to make decision-making more swift. The talks resulted in some minor progress in simplifying legislative procedures, and strengthening the EU's environmental and judicial powers. But major breakthroughs, for example, strengthening the European parliament to improve Europe's so-called 'democratic deficit', or moving toward a common security and foreign policy, were not achieved. While other countries hedged in the negotiations, Germany showed that it too would stubbornly protect its veto in certain areas. Germany refused to move to majority voting in setting European-wide standards for occupational standards, for example. Germany's highly regulated guild system 'is a residue from the middle ages. It is a sacred cow for Germans,' says the foreign ministry's lead negotiator, Schönfelder. In foreign and security policy, efforts to submit decision-making to majority voting were again blocked by the French and the British. Another problem was the fact that new EU members like Austria and Finland had joined the EU primarily because they sought economic stability after the turbulence created by the downfall of the Soviet Union in the early nineties, including a steep recession in Finland. They simply lacked Germany's fervour for political union. The Europeans did agree to appoint a new European official to represent the EU in foreign affairs, however.

Bundesbank President Hans Tietmeyer, eager to see progress on political unity, says the Amsterdam Treaty failed to make a major breakthrough. He expresses doubt about whether Europe, in its current form, will survive the challenges ahead. Because of Europe's disparate languages and cultures, workers are less willing than they are in the United States to move to a different state to find work. Fixed exchange rates and a common monetary policy means economies that are struggling will need an alternative compensation mechanism. Euroland, in Tietmeyer's mind, will eventually need a common legal system which includes formal tax compensation, for example. He still has doubts about whether it was the right decision to begin the currency union in 1999, but adds that he couldn't give a stronger public warning in May about Italy and Belgium when the heads of states made their decision to proceed as planned, because, in the end, it was up to the politicians to decide. 'In the long run, without a greater integration in the political area, the monetary union will risk experiencing serious conflict,' he says.

The bank

Nowhere is this force towards more integration as a way of avoiding conflict more powerful than at the ECB. With the admission of Eastern European countries on the horizon, European leaders will be forced to consider reforming the ECB into an even more supranational institution. Take, for example, the technical problems with keeping the governing council's minutes under wraps.[3] The bank's minutes contain a summary of the council's arguments for and against an interest rate move, and can indicate if a majority appears to be forming over a certain decision, providing evidence that a rate hike or cut is pending. For example, after the council meeting on March 4, President Wim Duisenberg was notably more pessimistic about the economic situation than in previous months, given data

---

[3] Notably, the formulation of a single monetary policy has also taken place under heavy influence from the Germans. It resembles the same layers of strategy seen at the Bundesbank. There is a reference value for money, which enables the bank to avoid direct accountability for producing a certain rate of inflation, giving it room to manoeuvre not enjoyed by the Bank of England. This indirectness in ECB policy making, perhaps not surprisingly, reflects elements of Germany's democracy. Not only is Germany decentralized, its constitution is purposefully constructed to avoid the threat of populism reasserting its ugly head. No referenda are allowed, as in France, the UK and many other countries. Proportional representation means that the party system is splintered and any one party is usually forced to share power with another in order to govern. Unlike in France, there is no directly elected leader who claims ultimate responsibility for national concerns. In Germany, candidates for chancellor are nominated by the parties, and are selected on the basis of a majority coalition in parliament. These chancellors can be selected at the party's whim, regardless of public input. Not until the 1998 election did a German chancellor actually get

showing a contraction in the German economy. He announced that the council had decided to keep interest rates the same, and insisted that the bank still wasn't leaning one way or the other. But given Duisenberg's penchant for secrecy, the markets suspected that a cut might be in the works anyway. The minutes, of course, would confirm whether or not the council was edging toward a cut. Market actors, if they secretly gained access to such minutes, could make millions, if not billions, of dollars in profits by trading on inside knowledge.

As it stands, scores of ECB professionals, mainly the directors, have access to the minutes. Then they are circulated to each of the national central banks, each bank having the authority to set its own guidelines about who at the national bank has access to them. This means that dozens of additional secretaries, translators and bankers will see the minutes every fortnight.

The ECB has also made a 'confidential agreement' to fax a copy of the minutes to the secretariat of the European Council in Brussels, but supposedly only for access by the minister of finance who holds the presidency (which means that the fax must be then faxed again to the finance minister's office), and to the office of the EU commissioner in charge of finance, Yves-Thibault de Silguy. In the process, the Finnish director of the European Council secretariat, Sixten Korkman, will also be able to read the minutes. There are no explicit rules prohibiting the president of the finance ministers spreading the word among his colleagues.

---

voted out of office as a result of a public shift in voting behaviour. Until then, every new post-war chancellor had been brought to office as a result of a reshuffling of alliances between parties in the governing coalition. This 'removed' democracy, with layers of accountability – including the federal, state and local governments – insulates the government from violent shifts in public opinion. Political leaders, like central bankers, tend to last for long periods of time. It is no coincidence that Kohl was one of the longest serving leaders in Europe. With a new unified, more confident Germany moulding the shape of the EU over the past decade, it can be no surprise that the European Union – not only the ECB – is also strongly shaped by the German system. The EU, even when taking into account the reform proposals of 1999, will continue to resemble a removed, indirect, passive democracy.

Officially, there will be 'more than a hundred' people who see the minutes, confirms Duisenberg. With up to ten more countries likely to be admitted to Euroland in the next few years, the number of people with access to the minutes could reach 200 people. Control of leaks would become almost impossible. If anything, leaking would be probable at that stage, considering the sums of money that the market is willing to pay for such information. Because national differences over the ECB's monetary policy are also likely, the probability is not small that a disgruntled national bank official will eventually find occasion to share the information with a sympathetic journalist in hopes of mobilizing public opinion for or against a particular interest rate decision. Never before has there existed a central bank with such an unwieldy and secret structure.

Duisenberg appears not too concerned about leaks, however. 'The track record of central banks in keeping things confidential is extremely good. To my recollection, I don't know of any leaks. And so sometimes something may leak. Would that be a disaster?' Alan Greenspan's answer would be an unequivocal 'yes'. He takes leaks of the closed-door meetings so seriously that he once summoned the FBI to investigate one of them. Unlike at the ECB, the Fed doesn't release its minutes secretly to government officials. When it publishes the minutes of its FOMC – on the Thursday following the succeeding FOMC meeting – it releases them freely.

In a secret system, like that of the ECB, leaks could happen more often than Duisenberg would like to believe. Duisenberg speaks with the experience of presiding over the Dutch central bank, not exactly the focus of intense public curiosity. In fact there were several times that Bundesbank central council decisions were leaked. The minutes were supposed to be sent to the ministry of finance in Bonn, and twenty copies were made and circulated to the government's highest officials, for example ministers and deputy ministers. In the circulation process, however, the top aides of these officials and secretaries would also get a glimpse of the minutes. With so many potential leakage points, the source of the leaks were difficult to track down. 'There were leaks, of course,' recalls Manfred Körber, former head of communications at the Bundesbank, but now at the ECB. 'It was disquieting. We would do our best to trace them.'

The structure is quickly proving to be unwieldy in other ways as well.

With new eastern European members scheduled to join the ECB, the overlapping responsibilities of the various committees (made up mostly of national bank representatives) and ECB divisions will have to be dealt with in a more orderly way.[i] Clearly, policy managers at the national banks are not ready to accept a reduction of their status to mere 'technicians', for understandable reasons. But their participation in decision-making has become redundant and inefficient. The voices of logic are pushing to centralize these policy decisions in Frankfurt.

Parliament

But the forces pushing for a more supranational, more powerful Europe also stem from the ECB's endowment of credibility to the fledgling EU parliament. Until recently, the parliament has been considered too weak to be effective, the result of national parliaments unwilling to hand over power. The Maastricht Treaty entrusts the EU parliament with the job of holding the ECB accountable. The seriousness of this responsibility gave the parliament a higher profile overnight, as the ECB board members were forced to attend parliamentary hearings before they could be sworn in. 'For the parliament, it's a way to get a bit more publicity and some respect that it does exist for good reasons,' said parliamentarian Fernand Hermann, the most senior of the parliamentarians on monetary issues.

With the lack of alternative oversight of the ECB, the parliament has a window of opportunity to demand the respect and resources it needs to carry out that mandate. The EU parliamentarians are being supported by the central bankers themselves, such as Nout Wellink, governor of the Dutch central bank. Wellink desires a decentralized Europe, but even he speaks of the need for powerful, democratic European institutions, such as the parliament. It is one more sign that a stronger, more politically unified and coherent Europe is being moulded by forces sceptical of centralized power:

> I think that sooner or later we should rebuild the political infrastructure of Europe. For the longer run, it is quite clear that the ECB and EMU are just the first steps. Other steps have to follow. Otherwise you would get a very unbalanced structure in Europe. We have a parliament, but at the same time we do not have a European parliament. And when I read all the parliament's so-called motions, sometimes they are so trivial and ridiculous. They confirm the fact that it is not a serious parliament. But a strong Europe, that is to say, a democratic Europe, can go hand-in-hand with a large degree of decentralization. Giving Europe a more democratic structure does not imply that you centralize everything. Take Holland. It is a small country. In many respects, it is centralized. In many other respects, it is rather decentralized. Our provinces and local communities each have their own responsibilities.[ii]

Indeed, the parliament has a long way to go. The first meeting in May, 1998 was unimpressive. After their nomination by the heads of state at the Brussels summit, the six board members were required to attend a hearing at the parliament, for official endorsement. The conventional wisdom among commentators was that a refusal by parliament to endorse a candidate was not strong enough to kill a nomination. But since there was no other official screening of the candidates, a thumbs-down opinion on a candidate would obviously be taken seriously. However, to screen the candidates thoroughly, the parliament needs the power and resources to research their backgrounds and to ask courageous, aggressive questions.

This was not the case in May 1998. In a sign that the parliament was only too aware of the limits of its power, the members of the parliamentary committee responsible for monetary affairs (the Economics, Monetary and Industry Committee) even asked the candidates whether they would accept a thumbs-down opinion if one were given. The candidates, all possessing a healthy dose of ingenuity, answered vaguely, for example stressing that it wasn't up to them to decide that question. The parliament, they implied, would have to fight that issue out with the heads of states, not the candidates they were supposed to be cross examining.

There were other signs the parliamentarians simply did not have the resources or the political will to examine the candidates seriously. The office of Alman Metten, a Dutch parliamentarian, intended to take the process seriously, and planned to examine the French nominee Christian Noyer's relationship with the Crédit Lyonnais bail out. The action took place while Noyer was director of the Trésor and therefore responsible for oversight of the bank. Metten's office was aware of a French TV programme on the affair, and had called around trying to get a copy of the transcript, to no avail. In the end, Metten was forced to ask questions based on media reports. He had no access to the documents being accumulated by separate investigations proceeding in France on the issue. After putting a single question on the matter, and listening to Noyer's standard answer that he could not have done anything more to remedy the situation, Metten was forced to cede the floor to other parliamentarians to ask their own unrelated questions. There was no thematic co-ordination among the questioners. After the allotted time, the chairman firmly closed the session.

Metten later said he was disappointed. The five to ten minutes of drilling allotted to each of the US Senators on the committee that questions Alan Greenspan several times a year would have enabled Metten more opportunity to inquire into Noyer's handling of one of the most disastrous banking failures in history.

Furthermore, even at the EU parliament, national sensitivities abound, and these coloured the hearing of the ECB board nominees. 'There was this nationalist feeling that infected everyone,' said one parliamentarian, miffed at what he viewed as a sort of collusion among parliamentarians to handle the candidates with kid gloves. The Spanish candidate, Eugenio Domingo Solans, for example, didn't make a strong impression, an opinion shared by parliamentarians. He seemed to stumble over questions, and appeared unprepared.

'They decided to be soft,' said Bert van Riel, Metten's parliamentarian assistant. 'They didn't grill him. There was the closed front, almost a deal making: "If we don't bother the Spanish candidate, they won't bother the French candidate."' Metten was upset by the national horse-trading, and was the only one who dared question Noyer about the banking problem. Still, it was enough to generate headlines the next day. Even the left-leaning French newspaper, *Liberation*, decided to abandon criticism of the Crédit Lyonnais debacle and give space to a parliamentarian official complaining of the audacity of Metten in attacking the French candidate.

When asked why he let the Spanish nominee off the hook without further examination, Fernand Hermann, an unfailingly upbeat French-speaking Belgian representative, responded:

> The guy made a poor show. He wasn't sure of himself. He was totally disoriented. Apparently, he'd never gone through such an exercise in his life. It was externally visible. I took pity on him. Intrinsically, he's a good man. He's competent. You can be a relatively good manager, but a relatively poor show man. On the contrary, you can be a real crook and bad manager, and still bluff all of the members of the European parliament.[iii]

Domingo Solans, like his five colleagues, was affirmed by parliament without any opposition. But there was another interpretation of the events, more damning of parliament. Sirkka Hämäläinen defends Domingo Solans, saying the translations during his hearings were misleading.

> I was listening to part of his hearing, because I was after him. There seemed to be some problems connected with the interpretation. For example, a Finnish lady asked him, in Finnish, 'What do you think about fixed exchange regimes?' And it was translated into: 'What do you think of fixed interest-rate regimes?' He said he didn't understand the question, and

requested that it be asked again. And the Finnish lady asked again. It was translated from Finnish to English and from English into Spanish, and the question was again translated wrong. Instead of the 'fixed exchange regime,' it was translated the 'fixed interest rate regime.' . . . He tried to answer for fifteen or twenty minutes because he didn't understand. What can you say about 'fixed interest rates'?

Domingo Solans argues that he was not nervous nor ill-prepared. He too blames the translation problems, and was surprised by the criticism that emerged later. Indeed, many of the parliamentarians' knowledge of economic theory is not very sophisticated. Many of the questions regarding monetary policy reflected a misunderstanding of its workings. For example the committee asked every ECB board nominee whether they would push down interest rates if low inflation had been obtained, referring to paragraph 105 in the Maastricht Treaty which says the ECB must support other economic policy goals when inflation is under control. The Treaty clause is the product of politicians – not economists, most of whom understand that applying the clause isn't as simple as it might sound.

The parliamentarians, being politicians, obviously sought an affirmative answer, in the belief that both low inflation and growth can be sought at the same time. But according to widely accepted central banking thinking, if interest rates can be lowered without endangering low inflation, they were too high in the first place. Hämäläinen explains:

It was a very strange discussion we had in parliament. The Maastricht Treaty says when inflation is under control, the ECB must support other economic policy aims. But I cannot understand that. I tried to explain that if there existed some room for manoeuvre in the interest rates to support the other policy goals, then interest rates must have been too high. You should never keep interest rates higher than just necessary to keep inflation under control. It was a mess because they accused me of not answering the question. I responded: 'This is not an intelligent question. Analytically it is totally wrong.'

Then they became impatient and demanded: 'Answer yes or no!' I felt like answering: 'This is like asking when did you stop hitting your wife? Yes or no?' You can't answer yes or no. I gave up and said: 'It is a matter of semantics: I can say yes.' It had become too political. It had already taken up half the questioning.

If there is low inflation, this is exactly the goal the bank is trying to reach. It will not therefore veer from this central banking nirvana by lowering rates. Most of the nominees remained patient, and answered vaguely enough to assuage concerns among parliamentarians that the bank might try to keep interest rates too high in an overzealous effort to counter inflation. Duisenberg, for example, said he would support bringing interest rates down if inflation was low. But Hämäläinen, who doesn't like to mince words, angered many of the parliamentarians by refusing to bend. She lashed out at the British parliamentarian, Alan Donnelly, who said she was being 'extremely evasive', by getting personal: 'Your point of view is very much that of a country where there has been a history of unstable exchange rates and rather high average inflation rates.'

The committee's chair, Christa Randzio-Plath, a German social democrat lawyer and writer, was particularly incensed by Hämäläinen's answers. 'She didn't leave a very strong impression,' Randzio-Plath said afterward. She also criticized Domingo Solans as 'weak'.

Randzio-Plath wants the ECB to publish its minutes freely, and refuses to accept a confidential copy similar to the one that is sent to the EC president and president of the council of finance ministers, saying she prefers a 'policy of openness'. She and other parliamentarians criticize the bank for being too secretive. 'I'm opposed to the mystic diplomacy of the ECB,' said an aide of Greek EU parliamentarian Katiforis, a critic of the ECB. 'The Maastricht Treaty makes them a sort of god above everyone else.'

Randzio-Plath says the parliament is still feeling its way:

This is a new process for us. We are still gaining experience. But it's clear that we need more transparency in the ECB's decision making. We favour the US model of central banking, which is rather open. We have started a regular dialogue now with the central bank, but we're now trying to make this dialogue more subject to the democratic process. The ECB's monthly report, for example, doesn't provide enough transparency. It explains the reasons for the bank's monetary policy stance, but doesn't provide a description of the council's internal arguments for and against the stance.

The parliament is also being transformed into a body responsible for checking the power of national leaders to interpret the spirit of the Maastricht Treaty, for example lending support to Duisenberg's denial that he had made a deal with national (read French) governments on splitting his term as ECB president.

As if an omen of things to come, the parliament's profile was boosted significantly in early 1999 when it called for the collective resignation of the European Commission after the Brussels bureaucracy became embroiled with alleged incidences of fraud, mismanagement and nepotism. In January, when the Commission refused to step down, the parliament forced the issue, calling for an independent inquiry into the allegations. On March 16, the Commission finally resigned when a report issued by an independent panel of experts accused commissioners of irregularities in managing humanitarian aid, tourism, vocational training and other programs. Never before had the parliament launched such a challenge to the commission, been the centre of so much public attention, or shown that it was capable of such swift, resolute action.

The resignation was the impetus for Germany's deputy foreign minister Günter Verheugen to renew calls for an EU constitution to reform Europe's institutions, which would include the German wish for a two-tier parliament with the power to scrutinise the commission and also the Council of

Ministers. Increasingly, government leaders also see the need to overhaul the custom of appointing weak, compromise figures to the commission, in favour of political heavyweights with the mandate to implement major reform. Indeed, the new president, Italy's respected former prime minister, Roman Prodi, agreed to take the position on condition that he be given a mandate to run a 'strong European programme'.

The swan song of the national central banks

As already mentioned, there have been a few hold-outs against the centralizing tendency within the ECB, mainly bankers jealous of losing national power. But it is not easy to see how they will be able prevent such a loss. The history of the German Bundesbank and the US Federal Reserve, both federal central banking institutions, reveals a clear trend toward centralization over a course of decades. As such, comments made in late 1998 by the idiosyncratic Antonio Fazio, governor of the bank of Italy, about his desire to retain powers at the national level, were a sign of little more than frustration. Despite numerous interviews with journalists during which he cagily expressed a demand that ECB remain decentralized, he has failed to mention specific areas where discretion exists, or where more national power would be desirable. Still, Fazio says that the Banca d'Italia will keep a separate assessment of the European economic situation, and he is building up a 50-person economics department to do that. The new economists will be able to do nothing more than what the ECB economists already do in helping Fazio understand European economic developments. Perhaps they could arm him with the best arguments possible when he participates in the ECB meetings to push for interest rates that are in Italian interests, but that would be unproductive for Europe. He could argue that he needs to understand the Italian economy to adequately represent Italy's interests in the council meetings, but his bank's staff of 8,400 workers already conducts such analysis.

Similarly, several of the central bank presidents of the German states who are members of the Bundesbank central council, but who now have been stripped of any say in decision-making on interest rates, insist that their regional banks keep a significant role in the system. Under the Maastricht Treaty, they will carry out operational and technical tasks similar to the ones they performed before the EMU. Some of them, however, are more ambitious. They see a way for the Bundesbank to wield behind-the-scenes influence on monetary policy. Franz-Christoph Zeitler, president of the central bank of Bavaria, the conservative southern German state, provides an example of how the Bundesbank has already wielded such influence:

> In the past, the policy of most European central banks was guided by the need to keep their exchange rates pegged to the mark. But the Bundesbank has gathered experience in being the leader in increasing interest rates, with all the political difficulties this entails. Take for example the ECB's decision on monetary policy strategy. This decision was discussed first in the Bundesbank central council. Then it was discussed in the ECB governing council. [ECB chief economist Otmar] Issing is no longer a member of the Bundesbank, but our formal and informal contacts with the ECB are very dense. After seeing the outcome of the monetary policy strategy decision I can say that I am very satisfied. With the single currency, the Bundesbank won't be the centre of public opinion anymore. But internally, it will still have an important and necessary role in preparatory work and in imparting lessons learned from its experience.[iv]

As much as Zeitler holds out hope for input into the ECB's monetary policy decision making, any chance for significant input was quickly tailing off at the beginning of 1999. Issing has already boosted the number of his ECB staff. Many of his most trusted lieutenants from the Bundesbank are already working for him. It is highly unlikely that the Bundesbank will have any substantial say. So most of these comments arising from the national banks reflect adjustment pains in institutions that have lost a substantial amount of power, and any spats are likely to dissipate quickly as the reality of the new system sinks in.

The board

One more place where power will begin to centralize at the bank is within the governing council itself. The first interest rate cut on December 3, 1998, was orchestrated by national governors Tietmeyer and Trichet, with the aid of Duisenberg as the 'conductor', but this was because Issing and the directorate didn't yet have the authority to set interest rates. Duisenberg effectively asserted his leadership by winning this early agreement to cut rates. With regular formal board meetings and frequent informal lunches together, the board will quickly become the centre of power – even if the board is outnumbered by the national central bank governors. The national governors, though possessing a majority within the council, have no similar means of co-ordination. Neither is it really in their interests. They govern over national economies which will continue to differ in economic performance. The governors of slowly expanding countries will tend to prefer slightly lower rates than those from countries enjoying more robust growth. Indeed, the original opponents to the December cut were the governors from Ireland, Spain and Portugal, all countries bustling with strong economic activity.

From January 1 1999 onwards, the board has been slowly exerting its authority. Issing draws up a proposal which then becomes the basis for discussion. Even back in September 1998, Wellink had remarked to a fellow central banker that the Bundesbank's Tietmeyer no longer seemed so powerful in the ECB meetings as he once did during the meetings at the EMI.

One significant counter to the centripetal forces within the ECB, however, is the Group of Ten. Duisenberg, as head of the ECB, and five of the central bank governors on the ECB council (i.e. those from Germany, France, Italy, the Netherlands and Belgium) meet together ten times a month at the G-10 meetings in Basle, where they mull over monetary policy together, with the added benefit of being able to sound out colleagues from the US, Canada, Japan, the UK and Switzerland.[4]

---

[4] Swiss central bank governor Hans Meyer has said he was not surprised by the December 1998 rate cut. Asked why, he said that the bankers talk about a lot at the BIS. Meyer sees the possibility of Switzerland belonging to EMI within ten years if all goes well.

In this way, the six-member board in Frankfurt is set off against the six-member contingent at the BIS in the process of coming to early conclusions about the desirable direction of monetary policy. While the board has the advantage of meeting confidentially, without other bankers listening in, the BIS contingent has the advantage of insights from the powerful central bankers of the US and Japan. In other words, there is only a group of five at the governing council (Austria, Finland, Portugal, Ireland and Spain) who are left on the margins of the debate – and likely to be confronted with opinions at an advanced stage of formation when they attend the meetings. Indeed, even though it was the national governors who agreed to make the interest rate cuts during the meeting on December 1 at the ECB, some of them had not known about details of the proposal before they showed up.[v]

Unity brings might

The history of international relations has shown time and again that size has brought with it might. The United States, once a small collection of scattered and divided settlements on the east coast of the North American continent, grew in power only as quickly as they bound themselves together, first as a confederation, and then as a federation. They learned that they could only resist interference by the British crown by unifying. If they had remained separate, they would have been doomed to abide by Britain's commerce and trade laws. Joining together, they could oppose them and even offer alternatives. As the settlers moved westward over the course of centuries, states were formed and added to the union, and a single currency was also introduced.

Europe, of course, is full of examples of how unity brings power. It was the unity of the French nation created by the 1789 revolution that Napoleon exploited to whip up an army that conquered German territories and an array of other lands, which taken together were more populous and more powerful than France. The Soviets, united under a Stalinist regime, exploited the power of unity by setting up special trading privileges between the Eastern bloc countries and by cobbling together a military force – made credible by nuclear power capability – which together created a counter-weight to the United States. Ancient Greece and the Roman Empire were other examples of how power can be achieved through unity.

In the post-WWII period, Western Europe's countries haven't been oblivious to this. They too knew that they needed to unite if they were to pose an alternative force to the Americans. This was a key motivation for German Chancellor Schmidt and French President Giscard d'Estaing when they were pushing the single currency and a European Central Bank in the late 1970s. 'It is in our interest not just to be ruled by the American dollar,' said Schmidt. 'It is in our interest that a European currency be created. It must have a weight on the world's markets equal to the American dollar,' he declared. Giscard echoed: 'It will be the money of Europe. For business, it will be the leading currency in the world.'[vi]

There are plenty of other examples of the benefits of unity. By coming together, the Europeans can collectively fund technological projects more efficiently than alone. One example is the pan-European project, Airbus, which has steadily chipped away at the market share of the American company, Boeing.

Having a united military component is another part of this European power building, and one which the British and French are now considering more seriously, after years of preferring to maintain the independence of their military structures which include the ultimate weapon: nuclear warheads. In today's world, massive military might is less relevant than it was 50 or 100 years ago, given that competition between nations centres around boosting and ensuring economic prosperity rather than around grabbing land. The fading relevance of military power doesn't obviate the occasional need for a quick, efficient military mobilization to defend vital interests, as the case of the Gulf War in 1990 made clear when the West's oil reserves suddenly came under major threat by the Iraqi invasion of Kuwait.

The larger EU members have retained significant military capability, and progress has been made on improving their ability to undertake joint, 'European' action. The political will and determination to do so, however, are still lacking. The US is the lynchpin for NATO, as demonstrated by its role in mobilizing NATO's response to the conflict in the former Yugoslavia, for example.

Leaving the US to play world policeman is a solution only as long as the US is willing and able to do so.[5] Many European leaders, particularly those in France, have rejected this as a viable *modus operandi*. Europe is eventually headed towards agreement on a military component that is capable of quick and efficient mobilization without the participation of the US.[6] French President Jacques Chirac said in April: 'Europe has little choice but to knit itself together – and to expand to the east – if it's to be a great power.' With the euro, he added, Europe can 'become the No. 1 power in the multipower world of to-morrow.' The Americans, including the Federal Reserve, have also recognized this power element of Europe's search for unity. 'Political union will be driven by desires to do something on the geo-political and military levels,' says the New York Fed's McDonough.

Schmidt and Giscard d'Estaing couldn't realize much of their vision for a more united, powerful Europe, given the prickly national sensitivities of their day. But their successors, Kohl and Mitterrand, seized the opportunity to take more steps toward integration. They promulgated project after project, from the Single Economic Act, which called for the free movement of goods, services and labour, to increasing harmonization in competition and financial services laws. Mitterrand's support for, and Kohl's acceptance of, the nomination of Jacques Delors to head the European Community, enabled the Commission to

---

[5] Consider the case, unthinkable as it may seem, of Washington DC, being blown up by an nuclear bomb smuggled in by foreign terrorists. Washington's leadership would disappear, and though a command and control bunker in central United States would remain functional, it would have no one telling it what to do. If it is to be responsible, Europe must take into account such a scenario.

[6] Indeed, the British have even made a proposal for such a capability. See chapter 10. Opposition to an effective European military organization has come from those who question the desirability of a military power at all, not the idea of co-operation itself.

issue proposals on a single currency and economic convergence that gained widespread political support, even in part by Britain. Throughout the 1980s, these proposals accelerated.

In the 1990s, with the signing of the Maastricht Treaty, the move for unity entered a new intensity. The thinking was that only a stronger, more unified market, with harmonized standards for goods and services, would help European companies gain the size and efficiency to succeed in a global economy where competition was increasingly cut-throat. But on the eve of the euro's introduction on December 31, 1998, Duisenberg declared that the euro was more than just a medium of exchange: 'A currency is also part of the identity of a people. It reflects what they have in common, now and in the future. May the euro become a unifying symbol for the people of Europe.'

Critics

With more and more decisions being made in Brussels, the concern about a 'democratic deficit' has grown as citizens begin to feel too removed and shut out from the decision-making process. The move towards more political union has created a need for more democratic accountability. That means giving more power to the European parliament, which is the sole way European citizens can be efficiently represented in supranational decisions, and in holding both the European Commission and the ECB accountable. The finance ministers who meet in the Ecofin and Euro-11 meetings are indirect representatives of national populations, but the link is too far removed given the importance of their task. A strengthening of parliament would also answer the arguments of Europe's greatest critics.

Critics have long denigrated the European project, especially the movement to form a single currency. These voices have been most numerous in Britain. Oxford University historian Timothy Garton Ash calls EMU a 'bridge too far', because countries like France are being tied into implementing policies in order to conform with EMU requirements which they would not otherwise legislate as liberal democracies. Garton Ash argues that the constraints imposed by the Stability Pact (that a government deficit cannot exceed 3 per cent of GDP) and other Maastricht Treaty arrangements place a straight-jacket on member states, denying them the ability to exercise their sovereign right to self-determination, and thus the Maastricht limits can be considered 'illiberal'.

According to similar criticisms, a multitude of layers of government have created an intolerable, opaque society. There is no clear division of responsibilities between each layer, which results in a mishmash of jurisdictions and problems of accountability. The Catholic principle of 'subsidiarity' has been pushed publicly by Bavaria's Catholic leaders, for example its minister president Edmund Stoiber and former German finance minister Theo Waigel. According to this argument, tasks should be carried out, as far as possible, at local levels of government. Of those tasks that cannot be carried out at the local level, as many as possible should be carried out by the national government. Only those carried out more efficiently by a supranational body should be transferred to Brussels. But European leaders have rarely consciously applied this principle in constructing European institutions, and rarely does the principle really help in making policy decisions.[7] For a long time, nations argued that merging currencies at the European level was neither efficient nor rational. That idea gradually changed to a recognition that a single European currency would indeed be in Europe's best interests. In the real world, interests and vision have dominated decisions about what level of government gets which task – and this may or may not coincide with the principle of 'subsidiarity'.

The main complaint of critics is that the European Commission is increasingly proposing European-wide legislation, without adequate accountability. Now, they complain, the governing council of the ECB, also unelected, is determining another key aspect of economic life – monetary policy. While

---

[7] Consider for example the administration of a welfare programme in a federation of 15 regional states. It is almost impossible to calculate whether the *economies of scale* won by carrying out a welfare programme at a federal level outweigh the *efficiency* won by execution at a more regional level.

pro-Europeanists concede that a restructuring of European institutions is necessary to make the system more accountable, anti-Europeanists prefer to reject further moves toward political union until such reorganization has been made. But rarely do they grapple with the core issue underlying Europe's move toward more political union: whether Europe can be considered a united people. Aside from history, language is the single most important remaining difference between the nations of Europe, now that business interests, religion, culture and other forces are no longer dividing people along national lines. Is language enough to divide Europe?

The significance of language differences appears to be eroding, as English establishes itself as a pan-European language, particularly among the educated classes. The French efforts to defend the use of their language in European organizations is indicative of the ground already lost. Consider, for example, the practice of speaking in one's native tongue during meetings. For practical reasons, the house language at the ECB is English – a watershed for a European organization. Predictably, Trichet is the exception when it comes to discussions in the governing council, but solely because of domestic pressure. In 1995, he was reproached by one newspaper critic for having published the Banque de France's annual report in English. Trichet countered with an editorial in the same newspaper – the conservative *Figaro* – saying: 'I am attached to the defence of our language, and the Bank of France is itself profoundly conscious of its responsibilities in francophone matters.' Trichet added that the bank had created an informal club for francophone central bankers.[8]

Trichet, like the ECB governing council members, can speak fluent English. However, in the ECB's governing council meetings, he is one of the only officials who speaks his native language. The only other one is Fazio, who sometimes speaks

---

[8] At the group's first meeting in November, 1994, Trichet recounted, 24 institutions attended. Besides France, attendees were Canada, Belgium, Luxembourg, Switzerland, Bulgaria, Romania, Moldavia, and a multitude of French speaking countries and territories in Africa, Asia, the Pacific and the Indian ocean. Then, with apparent relish, Trichet added that, after the delegates at the meeting had discussing monetary policy, 'we paid a visit to the 'Académie Française'.

Italian. A commonly held interpretation of the Maastricht Treaty is that the governing council members do not represent their countries, but attend meetings as independent individuals. But this is not enough to dissuade Trichet. For the few hours of that bimonthly meeting, he refuses to speak English, even in this tightly-knit group of central bankers who have known each other for years – and even though speaking English would obviously facilitate discussion (those not understanding French have to switch on headphones for a simultaneous translation). As soon as he steps outside the meeting, however, Trichet resumes his perfect English. The same is true at the BIS. During informal gatherings before and after the formal meeting, and even at the evening dinners in Basle at the BIS, which for his benefit are called 'informal', Trichet allows himself to speak English. But as soon as the BIS meeting is labelled 'official', he calls in the translators and switches to French.

Clearly, the French – not even Trichet – will be unable to sustain this effort in the long-term. Indeed, Trichet's younger colleague on the council, Christian Noyer, has given up. He speaks English.

The historical tide is irreversible, even if there are temporary set-backs on the way. Europe is coming together. Its future, inevitably, rests in a structure similar to that of Switzerland, Germany and the United States, that is, a common foreign policy (albeit with a lively, open and fruitful internal debate about its direction), security policy, trade and monetary policy, and to some extent, even fiscal policy. It already has two of those five elements, and has arguably already taken on elements of the remaining three. In this light, Gorton Ash and other critics come to sound like the anti-federalist voices in the US, before the US constitution was drawn up. The American states were filled with populations from different nations and traditions. The northern and southern states once had such fundamentally different views about individual and political rights – take slavery, for example – that the supposed 'United States' plunged into a wrenching civil war. Within a decade, however, many of those ideological differences had been resolved. In Europe, the wars of nationalism have already been fought. A basis for another ideological war does not exist. The pro-European faction has so dominated the governing élite that the European train is no longer stoppable.

One particular example of the change in Europe's intellectual climate is illustrative here. Wilhelm Hankel, the witty Frankfurt economics professor, was one of the four signatories to a legal challenge to EMU filed at the German constitutional court. He and his colleagues compiled a volume, '*The Euro Suit*,' a compendium of all the arguments against EMU they could come up with. The book received nationwide attention, and was an instant bestseller. The German public was still sceptical, despite having been bombarded with the advantages of a common currency by German businesses. Yet, in the end, Hankel and his colleagues were unable to mobilize a credible political force against the EMU. It is thus symbolic that in January 1999, days after the euro's introduction, Hankel changed tack, arguing that now the currency is here, a fully-fledged political union is indeed necessary to make it consistent. Even Hankel, a supporter of an independent monetary policy for Germany, admits to having seen the writing on the wall.

Hankel's conversion is symbolic of a profound change within Germany and elsewhere in Euroland over the course of the eight months between May 1998, when the decision to move ahead with EMU was made final, and January 1999, when Joschka Fischer, Germany's finance minister, abruptly declared the need for a new step towards political union. With the introduction of the euro in January 1999, Germany finally relinquished the instrument that had helped ensure social control and stability in the years after its rebirth from the ashes of the Second World War. Those five decades were a weaning period. In 1999, Germany was at last prepared to relinquish the mark. Symbolically, it was also relinquishing the only legitimate symbol of its nationalism, and had accepted a supranational European institution to manage it.

Austrian deputy governor, Gertrude Tumpel-Gugerell, says the Asian crisis contributed to building up German confidence in the new Europe. Before EMU, such a crisis would have rocked European currency markets, as investors fled from risky

investments into 'quality' investments, above all those denominated in German marks. The mark's value would have soared
against other European currencies, hurting Germany's export-
oriented economy. However, during the Asian crisis, that didn't
occur. In other words, Europe is already reaping the benefits of
the euro.

The critics fall short of making the case that Europe is
illiberal. Europe is endowed with one of most confusing and
complex set of government layers known to the history of
mankind. But ultimately, democratically elected governments
do have the final say in legislation. National governments, not
the EC, sign legislation into policy. Elected heads of state
appoint the EC president. Similarly, under the Maastricht
Treaty, governments choose the ECB board members, just as
national governments choose the board members of their own
central banks.

Jacques Delors, the former president of the European
commission, proposed a major reform of the European
apparatus, including a direct election of the EC president during
parliamentarian elections. Other government leaders have
called for a more democratic European structure. But they are
reluctant to move forward, since this would mean a reduction
in their own sovereignty. The truth is that a majority of people
in France, and especially in Germany, are in favour of continued
integration, and governments are elected only if they pursue
pro-European platforms. There are exceptions, of course,
namely Britain, Denmark and Sweden.[vii] But even these populations do not question their membership of a larger European
community that offers them stability and which has at its aim
closer co-operation between states.

End of ideology

Over the past five decades, national sensitivities have coincided
with very different standards of living and economic ideologies,
as partially outlined in early chapters on the French and German
traditions. The French-German core was surrounded by a group
of other states, each having very different levels of economic

development. For decades, Spain was a dictatorship. Finland was a state with as many economic ties with the Soviet Union as it had with the West. Italy was run by a capital rampant with corruption, its southern tip partly under the control of the Mafia. Those differences have narrowed radically over the past decades. Economic and social differences between Euroland nations are much smaller than differences between Europe and other regions, say the United States or Japan. That consciousness of 'Euroland' as a distinct entity is increasingly being reflected in the European political debate, for example in the joint manifesto released by the then German finance minister Oskar Lafontaine and French finance minister Dominique Strauss-Kahn on January 14 1999, in which they outlined the need to seek common policies at the European level:

> The euro is a powerful symbol of European identity . . . We know that we will only be able to harvest this fruit if we are in the situation to fully exploit this new political instrument. . . . All this is made possible because our economies have converged during the run up to European economic and monetary union at a level never reached before in lower, stable prices and solid public finances . . . In addition, we have observed recently a new 'philosophical convergence'.[viii]

It is true, Europe's economies have converged to a remarkable extent. This process has accompanied a convergence in thinking about the way an economy should be organized. The basis of this ideology is inherited from the German model. This includes an independent monetary policy, a stable, long-term oriented fiscal policy, a strong anti-cartel competition law, and a strong social net – all policies that were propagated through Europe by Germany, and which have now been fully accepted. These policies have, in turn, been conducive to the growth of a certain type of economy, defined mainly by the existence of a stable, long-term oriented business culture (and therefore, a strong manufacturing sector), and a significant role for the state.

The ECB devoted the first chapter of its first monthly report, issued in January 1999, to an assessment of how Europe distinguishes itself from other regions. Compared to the US, the report stated, Europe has a stronger industrial sector but a weaker service sector, has a larger public sector, and is more reliant on world trade. Europe's consumers put much more of their wealth in banks, compared with the US, where more wealth is invested in the stock market. All of these traits are lasting, not subject to change from year to year. There are reasons for these differences, for example Europe's public sector is larger because it has a larger social services budget. It is true that Europe's bankers believe that Europe needs to reform itself by trimming back state spending, but they also believe that Europeans must move jointly. European nations are now locked into a common fate. Significant divergences would rock the system and endanger the smooth conducting of monetary policy.

The Netherlands's Wellink speaks of 'Europe' almost as he does of a category, a specific entity, reflecting this new ability to differentiate Europe as a region in qualitative terms. When Wellink speaks of Europe's direction, he says it will need to restructure, reducing state intervention and moving closer to the US model of a free market. At the same time, he says the US model is 'not sustainable' either.

In their speeches, European central bankers concede that Europe will retain a more generous social safety-net than the US, accepting that the social element will be more prominent, but also stressing its strong points, focusing on stability and long-term growth, as opposed to the more volatile, short-term finance culture of the US. When asked what distinguishes the ideology of German economists like Issing and Tietmeyer (both considered free-market oriented within Germany) from US mainstream ideology, Bernhard Molitor, who knows them both well, said the differences are really only visible in their support of a strong component of social solidarity, for example, free education.

The New Left

When the Social Democratic Party in Germany won the

elections in late 1998, and formed a coalition with the smaller Green party, the nation became the 13th EU country of 15 in which a socialist or left-leaning party was part of the governing coalition.

Commentators wondered whether the 'socialist' sweep of Europe would mean a radical departure from the conservative reform agenda that had been set by preceding conservative or Christian Democratic regimes. German chancellor Gerhard Schröder was elected on a *'Neue Mitte'* ('new centre') platform, which promised ambitious tax cuts and other pro-business policies, but Schröder's finance minister, Oskar Lafontaine, who was also SPD chairman, tried to obstruct ambitious reform. Instead of initiating major reform, the government simply stalled for four months, falling into disarray by February 1999 amid widespread criticism for doing nothing. Former finance minister, Theo Waigel declared: 'I don't know what socialism means.'[ix]

By March, Lafontaine had run into trouble within the government. His conviction that 'macroeconomic' solutions such as lowering interest rates and boosting wages were needed to solve Germany's problems made him one of the most left-leaning within the SPD. After appointing his deputy, a Keynesian economist, Rainer Flassbeck, Lafontaine made a series of statements that indicated the possibility of reversion to traditional leftist policies. For example, the repeated calls for the German central bank, and then the ECB, to lower interest rates. He called for more financial market regulations and controls on market speculators, and pledged of more generous social policies such as increasing aid to families with children and bringing part-time workers back under the social insurance system. His reluctance to agree to more ambitious corporate tax cutting and other pro-business reform, however, caused friction with Schröder, and finally, amid growing criticism of his views on regulation and interest rates, Lafontaine resigned on March 11. In a trembling voice, Lafontaine declared to journalists gathered outside his house: 'There's something you should never forget . . . The heart isn't traded on the stock market yet, but it has a home. And it beats to the left.'

Schröder replaced Lafontaine with Hans Eichel, the more moderate former prime minister of the German state of Hesse. Immediately, the German stock market jumped 6 per cent, and the euro jumped two cents against the dollar to above $1.10 – reversing slightly the worrying 8 per cent fall of the euro against the dollar that had occurred since the euro's introduction in January. The euro had weakened mainly because of the differences in performance between the American and European economies and the large interest rate differential between the two zones. But Lafontaine's calls upon the ECB to lowest interest rates had also contributed to the euro's weakness, since the markets considered them threats to the ECB's independence. Meanwhile, Schröder's chief advisor, Bodo Hombach declared a change in direction. As prime minister of Hesse, Eichel had worked closely with Welteke, the likely successor to Tietmeyer as president of the Bundesbank, which also consoled the markets.

For the time being, the German orthodoxy had returned to rule placidly across Europe. The Greens continued to force through a decision to end Germany's nuclear power programme, a key demand that the party had staked its reputation on. Aside from that, however, there has been little else of substantial change from the former government's policies. Even 'Red Oscar' Lafontaine, announcing his government's first budget plan in early 1999, pledged to keep public spending in check. Mario Monti, EU commissioner for monetary affairs, says changes of government in today's context means very little, given that ideology is so similar across Europe.

Lafontaine and French minister Dominique Strauss Kahn, in their joint January declaration, advocated that Europe needed to harmonize taxes. They also called for cooperation with the G-7 in 'coordinating' exchange rates, arguing that the sharp drop in Asian currencies against the dollar had worsened the economic crisis in Asia that began in 1997. The European proposal foundered upon US and ECB resistance. They said such intervention would be 'dangerous'. By seeking to hold the dollar, euro and the yen within a 15 per cent or so band of fluctuation, governments would be inviting speculators to challenge such a régime.

The European desire to co-ordinate fluctuation between the dollar, the euro and the yen is symbolic of an instinct for greater international co-ordination. Lafontaine insisted that action to lower unemployment is needed at the European level, not at the German level only, as Helmut Kohl had argued. Despite this tendency towards international co-operation and agreements, Lafontaine launched no ambitious domestic interventionist policies. This stemmed partly from a changed personal conviction, and partly from the threat of punishment by the financial markets (which could shift funds out of the German stock and bond market into other markets). There exists a new consensus in Germany and across Europe that while a large social state is now outdated, the social market economy, based on a more moderate social budget, is worth fighting for, and that a dynamic economy and a humane society are both achievable only if the international financial system has sufficient order, control and transparency.

German influence

Germany will continue to have the most to say about this developing ideology in Europe for three reasons. First, Germany is the largest economy, and is reinforced by the credibility it has built up through its record of economic growth and prosperity over the last decades. It was the Germans who pushed forward their idea of competition policy at the EU level, which European countries have since accepted as a better standard than their own. Germany has also exhibited a better record on price stability, and its central bank has become a model for much of the world. There are vast weaknesses in the German system, but most of them can be attributed to generosity with social benefits and to its workers. Over-regulation has often been cited as a German problem, but even here, there has been a steady effort to reduce that, with considerable success. The Germans have also boosted their credibility by taking a hard-line in European negotiations, for example, by pushing for automatic sanctions in the Growth and Stability Pact, that is, no exemptions for fines on countries breaching the Maastricht deficit limit.

But Germany has served as a role model in other ways, including at the central bank. Officials of the ECB's statistics committee say Robert Fecht, head of the Bundesbank's statistics division, was forced to play the unpleasant role of disciplinarian, insisting that the other central banks upgrade their efforts to furnish back-year statistics on money supply that the ECB's chief economist Otmar Issing needed to operate an efficient monetary policy. When Fecht realized that other central banks weren't furnishing the numbers, he wrote a note to Domingo Solans, the Spanish board member in charge of statistics, to ask that he put pressure on the Euroland governors to whip their banks' statistics divisions into shape. Instead of carrying out this substantive task, the French statistic official was busy keeping a tally on the number of Frenchman in the ECB's statistics division, and complaining that there weren't enough.

Another reason why Germans will continue to play a leadership role in setting up the new European order is their capacity to think in structural terms. It is the Germans who demanded that the Delors group arrive at an 'endpoint' of a single currency regime, rather than agree to taking the incremental steps that the French and Italians originally proposed. Ultimately, it might be that sort of ambitious vision that will help Europe find its path. The announcement by Joschka Fisher is a step in that direction.

Finally, because of its history, Germany is more comfortable with an integrated Europe than any other European country. Nationalism as a force in Germany was discredited by the Nazis, and today patriotism remains relatively weak in Germany compared to other countries. Germany sees in Europe an *ersatz* source of identity. Germany is also a decentralized federal state, much like the state of Europe.

The French threat

This German leadership towards further integration risks prompting France to distance itself from Europe, if it feels the project becomes too German in appearance. The danger will only grow as Eastern European states get closer to joining the EU and its single currency. Since Germany lies in the middle of Europe, and Germany's ties with Eastern Europe are closer than those of other EU countries, Germany's economy is more likely to be the barometer for pan-European economic trends, and thus the basis on which the ECB will judge monetary policy. The risk will become greater that France, on the western edge of Europe, will fall into a divergent economic cycle, and that the ECB's monetary policy will not coincide with its interests.

The question is just how much has French 'exceptionalism' faded? Political scientists have argued that this has been on the decline over the past couple of decades.[x] Political ideology has softened. Public attitudes have moved towards the political centre. Surveys show that the numbers of people who say they are 'proud' of being French has declined. The French are questioning their political leaders more often, and by extension, the role of the state. Movements to devolve power to the regional and local level have persisted.

However, these developments are limited in scope. Despite increased regionalism, a movement toward more federalism is not in sight. The major French political parties – the socialists and the Gaullists – both share a distinct French tradition of centralized *dirigisme*, but one that appears to be on the defensive in contrast to Germany's decentralized model, which more closely reflects the trend in the rest of Europe.

The signs of resistance are also shown in the reluctance of Trichet to argue as forcefully as his European colleagues for the need for political progress on European unity:

> We presently underestimate the level of political unity that we have already worked out. We have a European parliament which is elected by all the people in Europe. You see the starting of a European citizenship. The council of ministers, in American terms, is a super-senate, where state representatives have weighted votes. It also has a super-president. Then there is a representative chamber, which is the European parliament. It's a very subtle organization, but it might prove workable.[xi]

There are signs that the French are still chafing under the German-proposed Stability Pact. Villery de Gallhau, chief of staff for French finance minister Strauss-Kahn, argues that the German proposal amounted to revisionism, which effectively nullified German criticism that the French are unreliable because their history shows a tendency to change its constitutions at whim. Despite their obstinacy, the French also have a streak of pragmatism that might mean a smoother ride for Europe than is often assumed. Some radical socialists and philsophers complain about French compliance with moves toward more unity, but French politicians have fully accepted the German-oriented orthodoxy as written into the Maastricht Treaty and subsequent agreements.

The French philosopher André Glucksmann has been one of the rare Frenchmen to accept the fact that the Germans are stronger and that France is going to have to live with that:

> Sure, it is possible that the two countries will become increasingly ambivalent and drift apart. If it comes to that, France loses. We could survive only as a tourist attraction, a sort of giant Monaco . . . Germany, in contrast, which sits in the middle of Europe, has the option to extend its market to the east and to help the former communist states become democratic and prosperous. Germany can also play a global role as deputy of the USA in Europe, similar to Japan in Asia. France doesn't have this possibility.[xii]

But the real threat to Europe's move toward political unity may not be France, but Britain. When Fischer and Lafontaine stepped up their efforts in early January to seek a change in the EU rules to allow majority voting on things like tax harmonization, it was the British who howled in protest, not the French. Indeed, therein lies the dilemma of Europe. Majority voting will make Europe more efficient institutionally. By taking away the British veto, the path will be opened for a Europe to create more harmony and more consistency in its laws and economic organization. This is the paradox. Europe would finally find the unity and international power it is searching for. But on the other hand, the alternative British vision of less state intervention and more free-market dynamism could be lost in the process. Britain's veto on tax harmonization and other issues enables Europe to keep a semblance of variety in its economic models. But if Britain gives up its right to a veto – as the Germans are now proposing – the variety within Europe would be lost. Europe would increasingly take on the colour of a German-led orthodoxy.

Italy: An example of post-nationalism

A look at how Europe's states are dealing with the move toward unification in areas beyond monetary policy is incomplete without discussion of an often underestimated participant, Italy, and in particular Italy's main contributor to the monetary policy story: Tommaso Padoa-Schioppa.

Of all European nations, Italy is the most euphorically pro-European. As in Germany, nationalism was largely banished as a credible force in domestic politics after the Second World War. But unlike Germany, Italy does not have the pride that comes with having the continent's most powerful, well organized economy, solid currency and status as the largest nation in the centre of Europe. Unlike Germany, which was forced to engage in foreign policy to obtain peace and reconciliation with the east, Italy was able to neglect foreign relations. Former US Secretary of State Henry Kissinger wrote of his meetings with Italians: 'In discussions with either the Prime Ministers or Foreign Ministers, domestic politics remained the main pre-occupation . . . One could not sometimes escape the impression that to discuss international affairs with their Foreign Minister was to risk boring him.'

No European country lacks the proud, self-assertion typical of Western nationalism as much as Italy. Since the Second World War, Italy has desperately wanted to be a good neighbour. The Italian foreign minister, in the first visit by an Italian minister to Austria after the war in 1973, quickly moved to resolve a long-standing territorial dispute between the two countries over South Tyrol. In 1975, it renounced territory and the Italian population around Trieste, which also calmed a dispute with Yugoslavia. With France, however, Italy has a strained relationship, often feeling insulted by France's inclination to shut Italy out of high-level international diplomatic negotiations.

The Italians tend to grasp at consensus. They fall in line when other European nations are united on a policy. According to American political scientists Frederick Spotts and Theodor Wieser:

The maxim that every country seeks power, security, and glory has remarkably little application to Italy. Almost all Italians, political leaders and public alike, take for granted that their country has no appreciable role to play in international affairs and would be mistaken and frustrated if it tried to do so. They lack any desire to assert Italian influence in the world and feel little concern for their military safety. Even though Italy has a population of 57 million, lies in a strategic location, and has an economy among the world's largest, it takes a minor part in world politics. Italian diplomats and scholars not surprisingly complain that their country's foreign relations are singularly lacking in force, direction, and substance. Indeed, after forty-four years in the diplomatic service one of Italy's most distinguished ambassadors, Pietro Quaroni, concluded: 'An Italian foreign policy in the real sense of the word does not exist.'

But one of the sources of this Italian apathy in foreign affairs is a lack of pride in its own system. During the 1980s and 1990s, there were signs that popular allegiance in Italy to Brussels was beginning to exceed allegiance to Rome. Time and again, Italians had been disillusioned by the corruption of national politicians. Taxes were high, yet social services were poor. The nation itself was divided between vastly different socio-economic regions. The northern area around Milan was as wealthy as any European region, and business was modern and bustling.

The Mezzogiorno, or south, was mired in poverty. The north continued to channel trillions of lira to the south every year in taxes, and political resentment had grown. In the late 1980s, a secessionist movement rose up in protest. But notably, after the signing of the Maastricht Treaty, the movement has slowly died down. The north saw closer integration in Europe, and a single currency, as a way of shifting more power to Brussels and away from Rome, and with it, a better way to secure its regional integrity.

The south, too, saw Europe as a wealthy club of nations that would continue to send it aid in the form of development funds. All across Italy, companies knew that, if they were shut out of the Eurozone, they would lose the benefits of economic stability promised by membership. They would be racked by the costs of exchange rate fluctuations, and they might even be better off transferring their operations, and jobs, to the Eurozone. Thus, with many interests overwhelmingly in favour of political integration with Europe, Rome's politicians were encouraged, indeed pressured, by public opinion to make the sacrifices necessary to keep finances within the Maastricht limits. The EU, therefore has become the cornerstone of Italian foreign policy. Among the major European countries, Italy alone has cherished an idealistic vision of a genuinely united Europe, welcoming every step on the road to unification.

The banker who would be a diplomat

Tommaso Padoa-Schioppa, the ECB's foreign minister, embodies his nation's vigorous embrace of Europe. Within the ECB council, he is the most passionate Europhile, convinced that a quick push toward political union is in Europe's interests. Within council discussions, Padoa-Schioppa zealously argues on behalf of the Eurozone's interests, not those of his particular country, unlike Antonio Fazio, the Italian central bank governor, who continues to argue that national central banks should hold on to the remnants of their power.

The assignment of an Italian to be the ECB's 'foreign minister' might appear odd at first glance. Indeed, how can an Italian be taken seriously when talking about a need for a new stable financial architecture, when Italy's government itself has been notoriously unstable in the past, both financially and politically? The average length of a post-war era government in Italy is less than a year. Worse, Italy's government fell apart yet again just two months before the start of the euro project.

The truth is that Italy has reformed itself – at least economically – over the past decade. Padoa-Schioppa has been one of the leaders of that reform. His childhood and subsequent career development show how he quickly affiliated with the ideas and culture of Northern Europe, and as a central banker, with the Germans and Dutch in particular.

Padoa-Schioppa was born in a northern town of Italy, not far from the Austrian border, into a family that had long prospered from European financial ties. He is a slender man, with the Germanic look of many northern Italians. He speaks with academic erudition; his English is impeccable. He is known to demand strict discipline from his workers, and has a hands-on management style. But he complements that discipline with an agile, analytical mind. His writings during the 1980s and 1990s, especially concerning the single currency project, have been prolific.[xiii] 'In terms of sheer economic training and intellectual capacity, Tommaso has an edge. When he speaks I always listen' says Andrew Crockett, managing director of the BIS, who has worked closely with him. 'I'll see something in a new light.'

Padoa-Schioppa's father was a Chief Executive Officer for the large Italian insurance company, Assicurazioni Generali SpA, with postings in Germany and Austria. His parents spoke fluent German, and they encouraged the young Tommaso to learn German at school. Before starting university, Padoa-Schioppa even worked in Germany as an apprentice in an insurance company. On graduation, he again returned to Germany to work for two years for the Dutch-German retail clothing company, C&A Brenninkmeyer.

The Dutch-German contacts were to develop later in Padoa-Schioppa's professional future. But first he returned to Italy, and joined the Banca d'Italia, where he started at the Milan branch. He then went to the United States, and attended the Massachusetts Institute for Technology, becoming the first Italian to obtain a masters degree in economics there.[xiv]

Padoa-Schioppa returned to the Italian central bank after studying in the US, and stayed there, almost without uninterruption, for 27 years. In the mid-1970s, he began pushing for reform in Italy. Together with the Italian professor Mario Monti, he launched the first efforts to liberalize the financial markets in Italy.[xv] Monti, who was later to become the EU Commissioner responsible for single market issues, shared Padoa-Schioppa's views that Italy needed to reform in order to catch up with its European partners. The two also believed that the central bank should be independent from political forces, similar to the system practised in Germany, a minority view at the time among Italian economists.

Monti, also born in the far north of Italy, recalls: 'It was heretical at the time in Italy to be in favour of the independence of the central bank, to suggest that the setting of the discount rate should be transferred from the treasury to the Bank of Italy. Even those in the Bank of Italy were extremely hesitant to claim their independence.' He recalls how he was criticized in the Italian press for being 'a German economist'. In the last half of the 1990s, however, mainstream Italian economists have come to accept the German-led orthodoxy. Christian Noyer, the French vice-president of the ECB, even called Italy's transformation a 'change in culture'.[xvi]

Padoa-Schioppa took a four-year break from the Italian central bank in the early 1980s to work at the European Commission in Brussels. It was there that he developed his skills in political negotiation, and also his vision of a more integrated Europe. He headed the European Commission's economic and financial affairs directorate general, the department in charge of measuring the amount of economic and financial convergence that had taken place in Europe and making proposals on further progress in that direction. As part of his job, Padoa-Schioppa paid regular visits to the member state central banks. It was during his first year, in 1980, that he first met Duisenberg, who had just joined the Dutch central bank.

Padoa-Schioppa visited Duisenberg and his board, and even attended the board's daily lunch sessions. He found them so useful that years later, he proposed to Duisenberg that he start the luncheon tradition at the ECB. Duisenberg agreed, and the ECB board now has lunch together daily. But Padoa-Schioppa was also close with another member of the Dutch board at the time, Herb Müller. Müller was the board member responsible for banking supervision, and impressed Padoa-Schioppa with his tireless work for more European co-operation in the field. Müller took Padoa-Schioppa under his wing, recommending that Padoa-Schioppa be given the job of chairing the EC's banking advisory committee. Some years later, Padoa-Schioppa chaired the BIS committee on banking supervision. The job was crucial in preparing Padoa-Schioppa for his eventual international responsibilities at the ECB, for they gradually inculcated within him the conservative central banking orthodoxy that Germany was trying to encourage within its European neighbours. His BIS experience gave him the credibility necessary to be able to push forward his vision of a single currency and a European central bank. He recalls a conversation with the German Bundesbank president, Karl-Otto Pöhl, that took place in 1982:

> During the meeting, he told me 'If you pro-Europeans . . . you people in Brussels . . . propose a 100 per cent monetary union with a European Central Bank, with a treaty, I can accept it, what I do not accept are provisions which are not really clear in their legal foundation and which do not offer a clear indication of the direction that is being taken.' That is to say that the maximist line, which probably also served to propose an objective that was so distant and so demanding as to be impossible to achieve, nevertheless corresponded to a German intellectual stance that had always been, was then and is now, in favour of European union, and against half-baked measures such as a small step forward might have been.

After returning to the Italian central bank, Padoa-Schioppa rose to deputy governor, where he remained for several years. In 1997, four years after losing out to colleague Antonio Fazio in a bid to become Carlo Ciampi's successor as governor, Padoa-

Schioppa left the bank to head the Italian stock exchange, CONSOB, until May 1998, when he was appointed to the ECB's board.

The 58-year old Padao-Schioppa now occupies a corner office on the north-west side of the Eurotower, up on the 34th floor. Padoa-Schioppa enjoys the stunning view over the west side of the city. From the north window there is a view of most of the towers of the banks that make up Frankfurt's impressive skyline. They are the same German banks that have been busy gobbling up smaller banks in Italy and other European countries, in their desperate attempt to grow in size to match their US and Japanese competitors. Their hope lies in Frankfurt, and in the ability of Padoa-Schioppa and the other central bankers to keep Europe a stable and prosperous economy.

The ECB's Machiavelli

If Italy's foreign policy has been unremarkable, its diplomatic contribution within Europe has been crucial for the success of the European single currency project and the construction of the ECB. No other central banker has been as close to the fulcrum of the diplomatic process that formed the single currency in the early 1990s as Padoa-Schioppa. He and the Italians were so convinced that their European goals were right that they pursued them with an abandon and diplomatic shrewdness that were at times ingenious, and at others bordered on unscrupulous. As one political scientist said: 'While appearing to be manipulated, Italy may be manipulating. Such was its mode of survival in the past; such is its way of surviving in the contemporary world.'[xvii] Referring to the way the Italians shrewdly outmanouevred the British during the Maastricht negotiations, Delors' chief of staff at the time Pascal Lamy, says: 'The Italians are formidable negotiators. Unlike negotiators in northern Europe, they have their own way of doing things.'

It was under Italy's presidency, for example, that a vote was taken in the late 1970s to allow the direct election of the European parliament. It was an Italian prime minister that started the negotiation process that eventually led to more EU decision-making by majority decision. Finally, it was in Rome, again under an Italian presidency, that the recommendations of the Delors committee to create the ECB were transformed into concrete commitments by the European heads of state. If the major ideas originated with France or Germany, it was Italy that possessed the distance and the diplomatic finesse to pound out an agreement. 'These are examples of extremely forceful leadership in European affairs,' Padoa-Schioppa says.

In July 1987, a few months before Genscher would officially propose the single currency project, it was Padoa-Schioppa who was writing of the need to transform the ECU to a real currency.[xviii] Just after the Genscher memo, in early 1988, Padoa-Schioppa met Jacques Delors, an old acquaintance and then president of the Commission, and implored him to put the single currency project at the top of Europe's agenda. Delors had been reluctant to overburden the EU agenda, which was running positively at that point, and he didn't see much hope of success. But within a couple of months, the Germans and the French had already agreed to launch negotiations, and made the unusual decision to appoint Delors to head a committee including the governors of all the central banks, to draw up a proposal on how to implement the single currency. For the governors, it was unusual to be presided over by an ex-finance minister and EC president. Delors, moreover, proposed Padoa-Schioppa's name to be a *rapporteur* to the committee, that is, the person in charge of drafting a summary of the discussions and agreements as they unfolded within the group. This troubled the German and the Dutch bankers, who knew from experience that Padoa-Schioppa was a pro-Europe idealist. The job of *rapporteur* was highly important, since he had the job of interpreting the results of the meetings. The central bankers insisted, therefore, that they should choose a *rapporteur* of their own, and selected Gunther Baer, a German already in Basle working at the BIS, and thus well known to the governors. As Padoa-Schioppa described him, Baer had 'a good, firm relationship with the Bundesbank'.

The Delors report, which became the first draft of the single currency plan and the architecture that would make up the

ECB, was filtered through the pens – and minds – of Padoa-Schioppa and Baer. Padoa-Schioppa recalls:

> We had the great advantage of not being able to speak and of observing . . . and at the same time having a monopoly over the pen . . . I certainly was greatly helped by also having a very precise idea of how in my view the treaty should be . . . how the Delors report should be. So I had a point of reference in mind in the light of which I could filter what I heard during the discussions. Without this mental framework of my own it would not have been possible, at least not for me, to put in order what the governors were saying.

In the end, through clever negotiating skills, Delors obtained the signature of the central bankers for the report. Now it was up to the Italian diplomats to achieve the signature of Europe's politicians. The techniques of Italian diplomats are suprisingly risky at times. For example, Rome has been known to arrange bilateral ministerial meetings by telling both sides that the other minister had agreed to a meeting. In actuality, neither had agreed beforehand, but both felt obliged to attend.

Such manœuvring is not uncommon in Rome, and Padoa-Schioppa has become accustomed to playing hardball when he needs to. Sometimes, his colleagues say, he can be too political for his own good. One central banker who observed him as Chairman of the Basle Committee of Bank Supervisors put it this way:

> He tends to hoard information and is reluctant to share decision-making authority. Although he was scrupulous in referring decisions to governors, he didn't really want them to comment, just endorse the Committee's views. And he was very resistant when the IMF started getting interested in bank supervision issues. I think relations with the rest of the BIS were not very good at this time.

At a certain point during the Delors committee meetings, the *Financial Times* began to carry stories based on leaks from one of the committee members, but Padoa-Schioppa found the stories biased. So he called the journalist who wrote them, Peter Norman, and offered him information on the condition of anonymity that would help make Norman's stories more objective. At the time, Padoa-Schioppa didn't tell anyone on the committee about this, not even Delors.

A year and a half after the Delors report, it was Padoa-Schioppa and Umberto Vattani, the diplomatic adviser to Italian prime minister Giulio Andreotti, who did most of the work preparing the monetary part of the Rome summit which laid the groundwork for subsequent negotiations that would lead to the Maastricht Treaty. Vattani and Padoa-Schioppa came up with a novel strategy. In their contacts with negotiators from the other countries, they made sure never to provide a written paper or call a multilateral meeting. They explained to their colleagues what their view of the Rome conclusions could be, and worked on the phone for months to forge a consensus. The text, written by Padoa-Schioppa, never left Italian hands, but carefully recorded the bilateral discussions. Vattani, the diplomat, travelled to the various capitals and did the negotiating. Padoa-Schioppa, the central banker, helped him stay within the technical course already charted by the central bankers during the Delors report.

The Italians were particularly cunning with the British. When Vattani finally revealed the conclusions, the other countries felt obliged to agree because they had already chewed over it in previous stages. But Nigel Wicks, the British treasury's negotiator, finally realizing what the Italians had done, declared that Britain would not accept the text. Vattani, assured of his text's credibility, told Wicks to write his own text, insisting that the Italian text would remain the text of the eleven other countries. With little alternative, Wicks agreed, and wrote up a separate text. It was then that the British were first knocked out of the game in the negotiation process. During the Maastricht Treaty negotiations a year later, the British would stay marginalized. In effect, the Italians had broken the EU's stifling rule of unanimity and managed to push Europe ahead to the single currency project even though Britain remained opposed. As Padoa-

Schioppa proclaimed: 'Once again, Italy succeeded in this decision by avoiding the rule.'

The Italians were so encouraged by their success in Rome that they proposed the subsequent negotiations should have a full-time secretary who would remain the same from one EU presidency to the next, and they proposed that the *rapporteur* should be Padoa-Schioppa. But the Luxembourgers, who had inherited the six-month rotating EU presidency, saw this as a blatant power move by the Italians, and protested. Yves Mersch, a staffer for the Luxembourg finance minister at the time, but now Luxembourg central bank governor and member of the ECB governing council, was particularly incensed. He told Luxembourg prime minister Jacque Santer that if the Italian proposal was accepted, he would not serve during the presidency. Mersch still hasn't forgotten the affront, and it doesn't help that he and Padoa-Schioppa sit close to each other on the governing council. Mersch praises Padoa-Schioppa's 'extraordinarily intelligent mind' but argues that the Italian has become so politically motivated that he gives the impression that he doesn't care about economics during the ECB's council discussions. For Mersch, Padoa-Schioppa and Issing form the polar ends of the spectrum within the bank:

> Padoa-Schioppa has a nimble spirit. He is certainly one of those minds who tries to find compromises. He is not rigid. But this also has its drawbacks . . . You must also be able to see where the red light is, know what you stand for, what your principles are. That is sometimes difficult to see with Padoa-Schioppa. It is like a shade, a moving target. He will even give up principles for the pleasure of intellectual advance. It is difficult to trust someone after they have given the impression that they will compromise on everything. What do you stand for at the end? He sometimes moves so fast that his troops cannot follow . . . (In council discussions), he gives the impression he is moved by political principles more than economic principles, and that economics is always only a means for him, an instrument to achieve political results . . . It always boils down to the same question: How to obtain power? . . . And in that, he is certainly much, much

stronger than Issing. Issing is 100 per cent economist and he doesn't care about politics.[xix]

The result is that whenever Padoa-Schioppa proposes a policy, Mersch suspects that there is an ulterior motive, such as centralizing power at the ECB at the expense of the periphery, whether it be in foreign representation of the ECB, setting the council's agenda, or organizing the payment system.

The coup at Maastricht

Padoa-Schioppa's most decisive contribution to the Maastricht Treaty was supplying a formula of dates for the start of the euro project. On the flight to Maastricht, he was worried about the risk of not making a true commitment to the single currency. Both Mitterrand and Kohl had declared their intent to make EMU an irreversible process, but neither side had agreed on a date. One problem was that the countries were required to meet tough fiscal criteria on budget deficits and public debt, so that an early date might disqualify laggard countries. On the other hand, politicians were eager to push ahead. Padoa-Schioppa approached Andreotti on the plane to propose how such a date might be written into the treaty. He suggested two dates – that if a majority of the twelve did not agree on a date to start by 1997, then the project would begin in 1999. Andreotti was so impressed that he asked Padoa-Schioppa to write it down for him, since Andreotti would be meeting Mitterrand that evening for dinner. Andreotti then proposed the date to Mitterrand, who agreed immediately. The next day, Mitterrand sprang the idea on his European colleagues, and it was accepted – with only slight modifications.

Knowing his place

Niccolò Machiavelli, the 16th century political adviser counselled his master in his famous work, *The Prince* (1513), that a successful ruler must pursue his interests ruthlessly, indifferent to moral considerations. It is interesting to note that Padoa-Schioppa's writings contain an occasional reference to *The*

Prince, albeit in more benevolent forms, and only when he is pleading for new political powers to govern Europe's growing interdependence. In an essay about monetary union, Padoa-Schioppa writes:

> That the creation of money is and must be a prerogative of the prince is almost universally accepted ... Neither the international economy nor groups of sovereign countries have a recognized prince with powers similar to those of the public authorities in a nation-state. When commercial and financial relations create interdependence requiring at least a minimum of international monetary government, a remedy for the absence of a prince is sought . . .[xx]

Once Padoa-Schioppa remarked 'The single currency is only comparable to the single army . . .'

Despite the bravado of his diplomacy, he is modest in person. Indeed, he believes Italians are naturally inclined to be modest: 'You rarely find Italians in international circles who are arrogant.' Even Padoa-Schioppa prefers to justify his support of political union by referring to backing from others. 'German Bundesbank President Hans Tietmeyer has publicly said that political union is desirable,' he says. 'I'm certainly not the only one who holds the conviction.'

On the other hand, Padoa-Schioppa is the type of person who will refer casually to media reports that the Italian government had pushed through an agreement that Padoa-Schioppa be appointed ECB vice-president after the Frenchman, Christian Noyer, steps down after his term is over – only to forcefully declare later that the reports are erroneous.[9]

---

[9] Each of the board members was appointed for a different term length, in order to ensure institutional continuity when terms end. Padoa-Schioppa's term lasts longer than Noyer's. Italian leaders have not acknowledged that such an agreement (on the vice-president position) was made during the Brussels summit in May 1998. But given the fact that Italy is the third largest economy in Euroland, it would make sense that if the Italians had asked for such a payoff – in the form of a secret 'gentleman's agreement' – in return for support of the Franco-German agreement on Duisenberg and Trichet, they probably would have secured it. And given their knack for diplomacy, it is unlikely that they would have missed the opportunity to make such a demand.

Many Italians suffer from a sense of inferiority to Germany, partly due to Germany's more advanced industrial development. The German-Italian relationship was summed up by an official of the German foreign ministry as follows: 'The Italians respect the Germans, but don't love them. The Germans love the Italians, but don't respect them.'

German social democracy is considered a model of economic and political success, and is demonstratively more stable than the Italian system. In the past, hundreds of thousands of Italians have flocked to Germany to find work. Italy does respect Germany's accomplishments, but also resents the prejudices Germany holds about Italy. When Italy's finance minister Carlo Ciampi visited German finance minister Theo Waigel, and his state secretary, Jürgen Stark, in 1997, he tried to convince them that he was dedicated to reforming the Italian budget. Rather than receiving encouragement, however, Ciampi was admonished for not doing enough. Waigel and Stark showed little personal support for Italy's candidature for monetary union, still clearly supporting the idea of a core Europe (not including the so-called club-med countries, Italy, Spain and Portugal). Less than a year later, however, Italy whipped its finances into order, and looked set to meet the deficit criteria. Germany's finances, meanwhile, had deteriorated rapidly, and now Germany was in danger of not meeting the criteria. Moreover, Stark had been humbled by his failed attempt to revalue the Bundesbank's gold reserves in a desperate gamble to close the deficit.

NOTES

[i] See chapter 7.
[ii] Interview with the author. September 18, 1998.
[iii] Interview with the author. December 8.
[iv] Interview with author. October 21, 1998.
[v] Interview with Hämäläinen.
[vi] BBC. *The Money Changers*. Post Production Script. February 1998. Prog 1. Page. 1.
[vii] See chapter 10.
[viii] January 14, 1999. *Die Zeit*, page 7.
[ix] Interview with author. January 21, 1999.
[x] Safran is an excellent source on this.

xi Interview with author, September 3 at the Banque de France.

xii *Wirtschaftswoche*. June 18, 1998. 'Geist des Kindergartens.'

xiii Author's interviews with Padoa-Schioppa, Sept. 7/Sept 11, 1998

xiv Author's interviews with Padoa-Schioppa, Sept. 7/Sept 11, 1998

xv Author's interview with Monti, September 30, 1998.

xvi Noyer speech, Dresdner Bank, October 8, 1998.

xvii Spotts & Wieser, pape 265.

xviii Padoa-Schioppa, page 88.

xix Interview with author, October 27, 1998.

xx Interview with author, October 27, 1998.

CHAPTER TEN

The Second Wave

By 2006 or so, the ECB will, on paper, replace the US Federal Reserve as the most powerful central banking body in the world. The three remaining EU states that have not yet joined – the UK, Denmark, Sweden – may decide to enter Euroland.[1] The addition of these four states would bring the worth of the Eurozone's economy to 6.9 trillion dollars (gross domestic product), with 370 million inhabitants, compared to the US's 7.2 trillion dollar economy and 268 million inhabitants. With the ability to wield more economic power, the ECB will eventually have more impact on the world economy than the Federal Reserve,[2] and its decisions will be even more closely scrutinized by millions of traders and private investors. But its power won't stop there. Within the next several years, a range of Eastern European countries are also expected to join the EU, and gradually therefore Euroland. Many of these countries, and other countries in the Third World have already sought to duplicate the German-style social market economy, and have erected central banks on the model of the Bundesbank. After the first round of likely Eastern entrants, Euroland, or the region in which the euro is used, will have an estimated 430 million inhabitants, and an economy of 8 trillion dollars. This will be 11 per cent larger than the US economy.

As discussed in the last chapter, irresistible forces will by this

---

[1] Denmark has already announced that it will shadow the monetary policy of the Eurozone as much as it can.
[2] Because of the dollar's status as a world reserve currency, however, there will continue to be more dollars than euros in the world money supply for quite some time.

353

time have pushed Euroland further towards political unity, providing a more resolute political counterpart to the ECB. The group of Euroland ministers, now known as the Euro 11, will increasingly set the agenda on financial affairs outside pure monetary policy. It is the prospect of this political monolith that most troubled Britain as debate there heated up in 1999 on whether to join the EMU.

Irresistible euro

All of the so-called 'out' countries depend on Euroland for about half of their total trade, and it is assumed that this tie will eventually push them into joining. Officially, the UK, Sweden and Denmark have still not decided whether they want to join. All of them met the fiscal criteria for entry when the project began in 1999. Greece, on the other hand, wanted to join, but did not have the fiscal discipline to qualify in 1999. (It joined in 2001.) Two days after the euro was successfully introduced in the financial markets with no glitches, both Denmark and Sweden showed signs of a change of heart. Suddenly EMU looked much more interesting. Swedish Prime Minister Goeran Persson announced that he wanted his Social Democratic Party, which was backed by a strong parliamentary majority, to hold a special congress early in 2000 to discuss participation. His finance minister Erik Aasbrink suggested entry before Sweden took over the EU's rotating presidency in the first half of 2001.[i] Sweden was increasingly concerned about being marginalized on Europe's periphery. The corporate sector was being shaken by restructuring and mergers, events that were heightening a sense of insecurity. A day after Persson's proposal, a public opinion poll in Denmark indicated that for the first time an absolute majority of Danish voters supported entry into EMU.[ii] Though Denmark's ruling establishment has long favoured entry into EMU, the population voted against joining EMU in a national referendum. The swing of public opinion in favour of EMU indicates that a referendum outcome could be positive next time around, and suggests that Denmark could enter

354

swiftly thereafter, possibly even before the euro coins are introduced in 2002.[3][iii]

How different it was in Britain. The loudest voices during the changeover at the beginning of 1999 were those of the euro-sceptic opposition. 'It was inevitable that the *Titanic* was going to set sail, but that doesn't mean you had to be on it,' declared William Hague, leader of the opposition conservative party, boosted by surveys showing that 52 per cent of respondents were opposed to the new currency.[iv]

'Wait and see' Britain

For the ECB, the most coveted among the 'outs' is the most difficult one: the UK. London possesses the most vibrant financial market in Europe. Some 600,000 people work in the financial services sector alone, matching the entire residential population of Frankfurt. Its currency markets are more powerful than even New York's. Britain's 59 million inhabitants and economy of 1.1 trillion dollars[v] would alone push the Euroland economy ahead of the US.

The UK knows that its markets can help Euroland. Former German Chancellor Helmut Schmidt made that clear when he was planning the creation of a European currency that would match the dollar: 'I have always been convinced that it was urgently desirable to have England integrated in Europe,' he said.[vi] It was no consolation for the Europeans, however, when Bank of England Governor Eddie George assured them they

---

[3] A possible technical hitch for countries wanting to join EMU is whether or not Euroland countries force them to be members of the so-called 'EMS II' for two years prior to joining. A clause in the Maastricht Treaty required membership in the European Monetary System before participation in the single currency project. The EMS II, designed to be successor to EMS, would link the 'out' countries currencies to the euro in a new band. This requirement, however, may not be decisive. Britain has argued that non-membership in the EMS II should not impede its ability to join EMU, saying that the Maastricht clause became meaningless when the EMS nearly collapsed in 1993, prompting a widening of its fluctuation bands. Britain and Sweden have not joined the EMS II. Denmark has, and Greece did before it joined in 2001.

could profit from the City's markets even if London stayed outside Euroland. The euro 'needs well developed pan-European financial markets,' George told an audience in Bruges, Belgium in October 1998, 'and providing liquid, transparent, competitive and innovative, but well-regulated, financial markets is one of the things that the City of London does particularly well . . . The financial markets of the City are our wedding present to the euro marriage partners. They are not just a national – but a European – asset.'[vii]

Until 1997, the UK government had taken a 'wait and see' attitude, but over the course of 1997 investors and businesses became increasingly restless with this stance. Feeling pressured to give businesses more certainty about the future, the Chancellor of the Exchequer, Gordon Brown, told the British parliament on October 27, 1997 that the government was ready in principle to join EMU, but that any final decision hinged on five economic tests. Furthermore, a national referendum would be required to confirm public support. On February 23, 1999, Prime Minister Tony Blair went even further, saying Britain should join the single currency project, and announcing a 'National Changeover Plan' to prepare the country to join. His comments increased the likelihood that the country would decide to join after the next election, in 2001. He said a referendum could take place four months after a government decision to join, and if it were positive, that euro notes and coins could be introduced between 24 and 30 months afterwards. Besides repeating the need for a decision to be based on Brown's economic tests, Blair put the decision in more political terms, saying adopting the euro made sense 'if it enhances British power and British influence . . . This is a world moving together. Sovereignty pooled can be sovereignty, or at least power and influence, renewed . . .'

The first, and most important economic test, Brown said, was whether the UK economy had *converged* with the EU economy. For years the UK's economy had followed cyclical developments in the US economy more closely than those on the continent. Both the UK and the US economies are heavily focused on services, in contrast to the continent, which is more based on manufacturing.[4] Brown estimated that it would be 'years' before evidence showed the UK had converged with Europe and that things would stay that way. The assumption is that the British and continental economies will become so inextricably intertwined with global economic activity that any difference in economic specialities will fade in importance, and that their cycles will harmonize.

The remaining four criteria are innocuous enough to be declared fulfilled at any time: whether EMU would give the UK enough *flexibility* to adjust to unexpected economic events; whether EMU would help spur *investment* by creating better conditions; whether it would help Britain's *financial* services sector; and finally; whether it would help *employment*.[5]

Another reason for Britain's continuing divergence from the continent is short-termism in monetary policy. Like the US, it has been more prone to boom and bust than Germany and the continental countries influenced by Germany. These have traditionally sought long-term stability-oriented policies. By swinging up and down much more violently, the British economy has been continually out of step with the continent's development. Given a UK decision to adopt a more stable fiscal regime, another source of economic divergence has been removed, Gordon Brown asserts:

This divergence of economic cycles is, in part, a reflection of historic structural differences between the UK and other European economies, in particular the pattern of our trade and North Sea oil. These differences are becoming less distinct as trade with the rest of Europe grows and the single

---

[4] In the UK, 71 per cent of workers are employed in services, compared to 33.2 per cent in Germany.

[5] Even the first and most serious test – whether convergence had been achieved or not – could be seen as putting the carriage before the horse. As was seen on the continent, it was a firm commitment to the EMU project that helped Portugal, Spain and Italy converge their economies with the northern countries over the course of less than a decade. Ireland, an economy that was growing much faster than the rest of Euroland in 1998, did not experience the inflation that some critics had expected when it was forced to submit to the continent's lower interest rates.

market deepens. But divergence is also a legacy of Britain's past susceptibility to boom and bust: the damaging boom of the late 1980s and the severe recession of the early 1990s. Since coming into office, the Government has introduced long-term measures to ensure that we are capable of maintaining stability by giving operational responsibility for interest rates to the Bank of England ... We will need a period of stability with continuing toughness on inflation and public borrowing.[viii]

Brown's statement, in effect, opened the door to entry, but made no commitment to actually enter. Far from creating more certainty for markets, it created less. As one parliamentarian on the House of Commons' Treasury Committee put it to George during a hearing in early 1998: 'Everybody seems to be operating on the basis that we will join but we do not know when or how.'[ix]

The real problems, of course, lie in history and geography. Britain's historical experience and its cultural development have differed radically from those of continental Europe, not just in this century, but for most of the millenium. The result is that Britain is divided from Europe as much by its collective mindset as it is by the English Channel. Frequently, Europeans lament, the British seem much closer to their American Anglo-Saxon cousins than to their EU partners. Seen from Brussels, the English Channel often seems wider than the Atlantic Ocean. Indeed, Britain has spent much of the post-World War II era attempting to resolve a national identity crisis: Is it an Anglo-Saxon nation whose destiny is to be the junior partner in an Atlantic alliance with its super-power cousin, America? Or does its future lie as one of many nations in an increasingly unified Europe?

The choice has been an agonizing one. The British have repeatedly allied with America, and the Atlantic link has served Britain well.

Unlike France, Britain chose to develop its nuclear arsenal in collaboration with the US. Its nuclear submarine fleet today is equipped exclusively with American Trident missiles. Britain is a staunch, reliable American ally, both as a permanent member of the United Nations Security Council and within the North Atlantic alliance. While other EU member states are also American military allies, there is little doubt that the Anglo-American 'special relationship' is more than a cliché.

Without American communications, logistics and intelligence help, it is unlikely that Britain could have won the 1982 Falklands War. And when the United States needed a base from which to launch F-111s attack bombers against Colonel Gaddafi's Libya in 1986, it was Britain's Margaret Thatcher who offered it. (At the same time, French President François Mitterrand forced the American pilots to take a several-hundred mile detour by refusing them the right to overfly France. Meanwhile, German foreign minister Hans-Dietrich Genscher could only agonise over the American use of force.) The post-World War II era is sprinkled with such examples.

At one level, the debate seemed to be resolved in 1997 with the election of Tony Blair, the first British Prime Minister since Edward Heath who seemed genuinely convinced that the country's future lie in Europe. But then Blair found an ideological soul-mate in American President Bill Clinton, and Britain once again seemed more at home with an Atlantic link than with Europe. As American war planes and cruise missiles attacked Iraq in December, 1998, they were accompanied on their mission by aircraft from just one other nation: Britain.

Europe's other two major powers, France and Germany, never faced such a strong Atlantic alternative. For France, the dream of European unity was home-grown, a brilliant concept that served not only as a vehicle to harness and control Germany's destructive power, but one that extended French power in the process. With Britain out and Germany cowed by a sense of obligation to compensate for its earlier historical wrongs, the early decades of European integration were dominated and shaped by France. Only with the end of the Cold War, German reunification, and the addition of new members into the European Union has this French dominance been eroded. A small but telling symbol of this erosion came on a day in 1995, when European Commission authorities in Brussels agreed for the first time to take questions from reporters in a language other than French at the commission's routine daily briefing. It was a decision taken over the strenuous objections of French journalists.

Gradually, belatedly, reluctantly, the British are accepting the logic that their ultimate destiny lies as part of an integrated Europe. The result of this indecision is that Britain has had little influence in the shaping of crucial moments in Europe's unification process, giving rise to another emotion: the worry of being left behind or left out. So it was with community membership, so it was with participation in the European Monetary System and so it is with monetary union.

Part of Britain's distance from Europe has to do with history, but it is also a matter of culture. In fact, London's stance toward European monetary union is merely the latest example of an instinctive British wariness of grand European ideas and tendency to circle around them suspiciously before considering possible participation.

In this century alone, the British blood spilled in Flanders and along the River Somme in World War I, Chamberlain's humiliation at Munich, the Battle of Britain and the war in Europe that followed have all acted to reinforce the deep-seated, almost visceral, conviction of the British that the continent is somehow a different and dangerous place. In England, the initial popular reaction to Europe is still to push it away. Margaret Thatcher may go down as the most divisive and controversial figure in British history, but she had little domestic opposition as she pursued a months-long crusade to win a rebate of Britain's European Community budget contributions in the mid-1980s. And while she appalled her European counterparts with her bar room behaviour at a European Community summit meeting in Brussels in 1984 by slamming her fist on the table and declaring, 'I want my money back!', she was a hero to many at home.

No continental leader could ever have behaved as Thatcher did over a decade of European summits and survive at home politically. The combative British leader seemed to attend these meetings in the spirit of late-night TV wrestling: she went to enjoy the brawl. When outnumbered eleven to one (as she often was) on the issue of the moment, she radiated a special energy at her post-summit news conferences. 'There is no shame or embarrassment in being a minority of one if I am the one who is right,' she would declare. Embellishing the British reaction to the European leaders' latest initiative, in case the message was missed, Thatcher's long-time spokesman Bernard Ingham would gleefully trash the latest vision produced by Brussels as so much Euro-blather. While such antics played well for a long time in Britain, the traditional cycle of British emotion to European integration eventually came full circle. The allergy to things continental gradually gave way to worry about being left behind.

Still, the inner suspicions remain, resurfacing on such issues as the Channel Tunnel, a project repeatedly panned by the British media during its construction while London-based political satirists ruminated on what continental plagues would eventually find their way through the tunnel to Britain.

There is little argument that the British are different. Over the centuries, the country has developed a pragmatic political and economic philosophy. Partly because of its geographical position, separated from the continent, it is not susceptible to being swept along by the idealistic visions of a grand design often expressed by the continent's political leaders, who argue that monetary union is the best way to achieve closer integration in Europe. The British are more cool-headed, wanting to know what is in their economic interests. Unlike the German, French or Italians, they don't see a threat of war – or even the potential for a threat of war – from neighbours. 'Wars have usually ensued from hegemonistic ambitions on the Continent,' said John Wilkinson, a Tory MP and euro-sceptic in early 1996 when Kohl was pushing for closer integration on the continent. 'It has been Britain's duty to maintain a balance of power in Europe, and to do that we have got to keep our distance.'[x]

Proud Britannia

At the base of its relationship with Europe is Britain's claim of exceptionalism. Through thousands of years of bloody European history, the Channel has protected Britain from being a major battle ground. Eddie George explains:

> I don't see it as an unqualified 'us vs. them' psychology. There's a pragmatic approach about British diplomacy traditionally. Do we want to move ahead or not? Where I would say there is a difference is that continental Europe has been a battle ground for these European wars. There's a kind of sense that political integration for the continent has more to be said for it than for the UK. Though we were very affected by these wars, we were never actually the kind of battle ground that the continent was.[xi]

In Britain, history education in schools usually begins with the invasion of William the Conqueror in 1066. Then there is a long line of kings (and queens) that is traditionally memorized by rote, whereas there are few lessons about the complex intermingling of royalty through marriage, war and betrayal on the continent. Students are left with the impression that England, perhaps because of her nineteenth century glory, is special and apart from the rest: 'We are with Europe, not of it,' wrote Winston Churchill 70 years ago.[xii] 'We are linked, but not comprised.'

The result is that the United Kingdom protects its sovereignty more jealously than any other European country. Padoa-Schioppa, the ECB board member who helped negotiate the Maastricht Treaty for the Italians, recalls the exceptional approach of British diplomacy:

> The main problem was the position of Great Britain. As always throughout the history of the European Union, Great Britain negotiates twice. First it negotiates the treaty of the others and then it negotiates its own position. And here it was the same. That is, in the dialogue with our interlocutors in London they would say to us 'we don't know if we will be

able to agree this text or not, but if you want to improve the chances of our adhesion then it would be better to remove this and that' . . . and so they participated in the negotiations but without committing themselves to a signature. It takes the great diplomatic skill of a country like England to accomplish something of this sort, that is to say to have negotiating power while maintaining a position which is still half outside the negotiations. . . . There was certainly a strong political line which Mrs Thatcher expressed by saying that the Queen's head on the pound coin should not be lost, that is that the coin as a symbol of national sovereignty should not be abandoned. This was the position which inspired what was being said on the English side in these meetings.[xiii]

The jealous protection of sovereignty has continued, but has been most pronounced in Conservatives. Prime Minister Tony Blair's comments indicate that he would be interested in moving forward on Europe's political project, but he is restrained by the Conservative opposition, as well as by anti-Europeans within the governing Labour party. In November 1998, German Chancellor Gerhard Schröder spoke of a 'federal' European order. But William Hague, leader of the Tory party, underscored the 'risks' posed to Britain's independence. The British media thrive on headlines that pander to their euro-sceptic constituency and pounce on any opportunity to dramatize the link between Europe's push for integration and the supposed loss of sovereignty for the British parliament.

The British media is notoriously anti-European. In February 1996, Chancellor Kohl produced his famous line: 'The policy of European integration is in reality a question of war and peace in the twenty-first century.' He was speaking in visionary terms, conjuring up the massive anguish that Germany had suffered from century-long wars with France and other Europeans, and arguing that integration was needed to avoid the resurgence of national hostilities. It was not a specific reference to the British.[6]

---

[6] Rather, he was speaking to an international audience at the Louvain University in Belgium.

Yet, the next day, the *Daily Telegraph* headed its story: 'Europe must integrate or risk war, Kohl tells Britain.'[xiv] In mid-1998, when Blair's government indicated in principle its interest in joining the EMU project, the *Sun*, Britain's widest circulating daily, ran a front-page headline with a picture of Blair beside it: 'Is THIS the most dangerous man in Britain?' The *Sun* is owned by Rupert Murdoch, a staunch opponent of EMU, and Murdoch's sudden turn on Blair proved a shock, particularly since he and the *Sun* had endorsed Blair during the latter's campaign in 1997. Later, the *Sun* turned on German finance minister Oskar Lafontaine after he began pushing for more harmonization of taxes within Europe, saying in a headline that *he* was perhaps the most dangerous man in Europe.[xv] Lafontaine had failed to learn the lesson learned long ago by Chancellor Kohl. As Kohl often repeated to one of his foreign policy advisors, Karl Lammers: 'Germany must lead, but must never be seen to be leading.'

Britain's sensationalist anti-European headlines have no parallel in the rest of Europe. In certain instances, the media borders on an outright hate campaign against Europe, seeing the danger of a powerful Germany round every corner. In late 1998, a *Daily Telegraph* columnist nicknamed the German ECB board member Otmar Issing 'Hissing', commenting on his 'sheer bloody-mindedness'.[xvi] Though Issing has only one vote on a board of 17 members and the Germans have a total of only two votes – the same as Finland, France, Italy, the Netherlands and Spain, – the implication is that the ECB is a duplicate of the German model. The columnist goes on to call the ECB a 'Rottweiler.' One conservative shadow minister admitted: 'Attacking the euro is the main weapon in our armoury.'[xvii]

As already noted, the Germans have had profound influence on shaping Europe, and most recently, the ECB. This influence is to be expected, given the size of Germany within Europe, and is by and large accepted as not only benign but beneficial. German power is rarely quantifiable or easily visible. Rather it is leveraged and accumulated through a series of small, but continuous, diplomatic steps in European legislation through the application of an economic might – and political credibility – that is unique in Europe. The British media have whipped up *angst* by warping this into the spectre of a lurking force, a dark, all-pervading, visually imperceptible influence – a phobia Britain still suffers following its experiences during two world wars. Off-the-cuff comments by British leaders only bolster these fears. One of Thatcher's cabinet ministers, industry secretary Nicholas Ridley, described economic union in 1990 as 'a German racket designed to take over the whole of Europe'. The minister later resigned, but it created consternation in Germany. When Blair began to surge ahead of the Prime Minister, John Major, in public opinion polls during the 1997 election campaign, the Conservative party put up posters of a pigmy Tony Blair sitting on the lap of a giant German Chancellor Kohl.

It does not help that the British were humiliated more than any other country in their experience within the EMS, and that events in Germany were mostly responsible. It was the high interest rates in Germany after reunification that put pressure on the pound almost immediately after Britain entered the EMS in 1990. The pound was in for only two years before being thrown out, after coming under unsustainable pressure from speculators. George Soros made $1 billion from the Bank of England's efforts to support the pound before if finally surrendered in 1992.[xviii]

Padoa-Schioppa argues that Britain's financial markets played a powerful domestic role in rejecting a commitment to EMU during the 1992 currency crisis:

> The plethora of dealing-room professionals earning their living from exchange rate movements rebelled against the prospect of seeing their shops closed, 'irrevocably locked' by a decree that would cancel a whole set of rows and columns from the matrix of world exchange rates. The epicentre of this rebellion was London, where it interacted with the unresolved reservations of British circles and public opinion about relinquishing the exchange rate as a policy variable ... When sterling came under pressure, floating was preferred to any new parity.[xix]

History lessons

The potential damage to Britain caused by staying outside EMU, however, echoes events in the early nineteenth century, when Britain was on top of the world. It was the first to harness the power of the industrial revolution, producing goods many times more efficiently than its competitors, and even exporting them with the aid of new inventions like large, iron-hulled steamships. By the mid-nineteenth century, it was an unrivalled world power. Yale professor of history, Paul Kennedy, called it 'one of the great success stories of the human race'. In 1865, the English economist Jevons proclaimed:

> The plains of North America and Russia are our cornfields; Chicago and Odessa our granaries; Canada and the Baltic are our timber forests; Australasia contains our sheep farms, and in Argentina and on the western prairies of North America are our herds of oxen; Peru sends her silver, and the gold of South Africa and Australia flows to London; the Hindus and the Chinese grow tea for us and our coffee, sugar and spice plantations are all in the Indies. Spain and France are our vineyards and the Mediterranean our fruit garden, and our cotton grounds, which for long have occupied the Southern United States, are now being extended everywhere in the warm regions of the earth.[xx]

But the UK slowly lost power over the later part of the century, as the US and Germany caught up with, and then eclipsed Britain's industrial strength. For decades, however, Britain retained its illusions of grandeur, facilitated partly by its language as English spread across the globe, and secondly, by the power of its currency, which continued to dominate trade transactions. After World War I, the pound's power faded, as the dollar overtook sterling as the chief currency in global commerce. Even after World War II, the British government clung on to its outmoded policy of a strong pound, sacrificing the competitiveness of its economy in the process by making its products too expensive to sell in foreign markets. Britain retains elements of that egocentricity today, partly reflected in its interminable waffling about whether it makes economic sense to join the single currency. Ironically, it was the UK which, because of its wealth and strength, argued for an open world economy and no barriers. British foreign minister Ernest Bevin said in 1945 that the ultimate goal of foreign policy was to 'be able to travel anywhere from Victoria Station without being asked for a passport'.[xxi] Even though that dream of free travel within the EU has been realised, it was not Britain that pushed the process; it was the continent. Now, as it moves into the twenty-first century, Britain is the major country in a group of four that has accepted a position on the margins of the EU, forcing foreign companies to pay extra transaction costs to do business with it. 'If the English wished to stay out,' said former German Chancellor Helmut Schmidt, 'they would have to decide whether to become the 51st state of America.'[xxii]

Regardless of the UK's anti-Europe ranting, the continentals are convinced that the UK will join. 'In European affairs, it's the [German-French] duo which is important. The trio only follows later,' said former French Prime Minister Raymond Barre. 'The English get there late, once they are sure things work.' Barre recalls a lesson that French statesman Jean Monnet gave him when Barre took up a post in Brussels in the 1960s: 'You're going to have a lot of difficulties with the English,' Monnet told him. 'I'll give you some advice: don't pay attention to what they say. Do what you have to do. You will see that if you succeed – which you must – they'll catch up with you on the double.'[xxiii]

British pragmatism or obstinacy?

No one embodies the pragmatic culture in Britain more than Eddie George, the governor of the Bank of England. After the new labour government came to power under Tony Blair in 1997, one of its first moves was to make the bank independent, after the model of the Bundesbank, and as called for by the Maastricht Treaty. While continental central bankers have felt obliged to remain faithful to the political line of their governments, and thus not speak negatively about the single currency project, George was refreshingly honest about the risks during speeches at home and abroad. He expresses doubt about the hurried nature with which the European countries were pushing for the single currency. Their unemployment rates were in general worryingly high. Worse, their labour markets were inflexible. Most Europeans are unwilling to move to other EU member states to take up unemployment, even during recessions. Now, with a single currency, and a stability pact which prohibits governments from using monetary or fiscal policy to spark short-term shocks to revive their economies, George worries that rising unemployment could spill over into resentment against the European project itself. Unlike the US, he points out, Europe doesn't have automatic fiscal transfers from states enjoying boom times to those that are suffering stagnation.[7] Finding no way to help themselves out of an economic rut, governments might resort to trade protectionism and other negative measures.

Though his comments reflect scepticism, George admits that there can be huge advantages if the currency union project succeeds and countries are able to withstand any resulting discontent. It is George's way of remaining unfailingly neutral. 'This country will need to think very carefully about the pros and cons of going in, even though we think there is some risk in this whole venture,' he told the parliament in May 1996. 'Set against that are the potential risks of staying out. We are going to have to balance those things and it will not be easy.'

As a central banker, he says, he has no 'standing' to talk about the political side of the EMU, which he says is left to politicians. He will only comment on the economic pros and cons of EMU, and on that score, he still can't make up his mind. In the run-up to EMU, when continental politicians were pushing hard for EMU, and even some of Europe's central bankers were agreeing that it was in their nations' greater interests, George concluded that 'the process was being driven

---

[7] 'Structural' and 'regional' funds allotted by the EU to struggling, backward regions are an important precedent, and a sign that this deficiency might be solved in the future. See chapter 9.

by the politics of Europe with less emphasis on the importance of economic convergence.'[8] [xxiv] As for his own country, he declared in a Treasury hearing in the spring of 1998, 'we do things because we believe that they are in the national interest to do them.'[xxv] He disagrees with arguments that more political union is preferable to make EMU work best, for example, Bundesbank president Hans Tietmeyer's view that certain taxes (for example, capital gains) should be harmonized.[xxvi]

Such blunt public declarations of self-interest are seldom heard in Germany. Bundesbank former president Helmut Schlesinger was a rarity on the German scene for speaking out for the nation's interests.[9] Schlesinger had not worked in Bonn, so had not learned the sensitivity with which the politicians pursued their policies.[10] Tietmeyer, who spent more time in Bonn than in Frankfurt, was keenly political. For many years, he believed only a core set of countries should participate in EMU. He was sceptical that countries like Italy had enough political stamina to make the sacrifices necessary to maintain stability-oriented policies. He was therefore only too happy to let Eddie George initiate the bankers' meeting in Basle in early 1997 by questioning the wisdom of starting EMU on time.

An MI5 spy in Moscow?

George was born in 1938 in Surrey, England. He attended Cambridge University and joined the Bank of England upon graduation at 23. Banking ran in the family; his father worked as a Post Office Savings Bank clerk.

The night before George was interviewed at the Bank of

---

[8] In early 1997, George was confronted with this political side in Basle when Jean-Claude Trichet argued passionately to hold to the timetable for political reasons, not economic ones.

[9] So much so that former Chancellor Helmut Schmidt once called Schlesinger a 'nationalist'.

[10] Timothy Garton Ash's book *In Europe's Name* (Random House, 1993) is an enlightening book about how Germany has aggressively pursued self-interested political goals, but as its title suggests, while under the veil of European interests. Germany's post-war situation, made its interests unusually convergent with those of Europe integration.

England, the Bank's recruiting agent showed up at a Cambridge University club without revealing his identity and sat down with a couple of other people to play bridge with George. The agent made what is called a 'psychic bid', designed to throw the opposition, but George saw through it and went on to win the game. He got the job.

The bridge lessons were to stay with him as he began to see that central banking was an art, not a science. Often it was better to play conservative. He earned the nickname 'Steady Eddie'. He later told a British journalist: 'Sometimes you get a tremendously strong hand which turns out to be a disaster. Other times you have a modest collection of cards but it plays well. I think there is a great challenge in trying to make the best of a poor hand. Money market management is like that'.[xxvii]

He showed an early passion for international affairs, learning French and German on a scholarship he won to Dulwich College, and studying Russian during national service in the Royal Air Force before going up to Cambridge. After graduation, he was initially set on getting a job at the World Bank, but it required an advanced degree and some banking experience. As soon as he walked into the Bank of England, however, he 'fell in love with it'. He admits being swayed a bit by the patriotism that prevailed. He recalls a war-time poster hanging in the office of a colleague responsible for exchange control, which read: 'Freedom is in peril. Defend it with all your might'. At the time, the UK set constraints on the amount of money which could be borrowed and then invested abroad. 'Here was a man who was exercising control over the economy, and he was recognizing that the way you exercise control was extremely important,' says George. 'It was a positive attitude. It impressed me.'

Within two years, as part of its hunch at the time that the Soviet Union was destined to play a major role in the world economy, the Bank sent George on a nine-month assignment in Moscow to study central planning at the State University and give tutorials at the State Bank. After six months, he was allowed to travel freely, but was required to notify Russian authorities of any out-of-town trips. He soon ran into trouble.

He took a visit to the countryside with a Tanzanian friend, but didn't inform the police. The trailing Russians lost sight of him for an hour and got nervous. When they caught up with him, they berated him, expressing bewilderment as to why anyone would want to visit the Russian steppe. Anxious that he might be an MI5 spy, Russian agents watched him closely for the rest of his stay. 'To be fair to the Soviets,' one newspaper account later remarked, 'George has just the kind of anonymous looks that would make him Central Casting's choice for a plum part in a John le Carré novel. He is shortish, roundish and sports steel rimmed bifocals. He also has an unnerving way of avoiding eye contact, focusing instead on a point slightly below him in the middle distance while he talks.'[xxviii]

The Soviet sojourn only whetted his interest in international finance. After he returned, he specialized in east European affairs, but within a year he was seconded by the Bank to Basle, Switzerland, to work as an economist for the BIS for three years. He was then seconded to the International Monetary Fund between 1972 and 1974, during the implosion of the Bretton Woods system. The IMF was in the midst of reforming the international financial system. 'I learned more then than in my entire life,' he says.

George has many similarities with his Dutch colleague, Wim Duisenberg. He is a smoker, and like Duisenberg, he is known for being friendly with rank-and-file Bank employees. He and his staff of 200 charter a 40-foot yacht to use each year. There is some self interest involved. His own love of the sea stems from family vacations on a neighbour's boat.

At the Bank, George has earned a reputation for being a hawk, running a monetary policy that, according to critics, focuses too narrowly on inflation. Like most central bankers, he believes that curbing inflation is the best recipe for creating jobs and ensuring economic growth.

He also has a deep religious belief, and makes himself available when the Archbishop of Canterbury needs advice on economic or financial issues.

Eddie George, Governor of the Bank of England

The corporate test

British business is split on entering Euroland. The large exporting companies, with exposure to foreign currencies, strongly support joining, while domestic retailers and other companies fear increased competition, with good reason. Everything equal, however, the passion for a single currency among British businesses is nowhere close to that felt by continental companies. One reason is because the British have been content, at least until recently, with their standing in the global economy. Businesses are, on average, highly profitable, run by strong management, with weak union organization. During the 1990s, the German corporate model was on the defensive against the anglo-saxon model, with profit margins noticeably lower in many sectors. German companies launched a decade of corporate restructuring, designed to give more attention to 'shareholder' interests. Key aims were increased efficiency and a boosting of profits. Simultaneously, German and European companies saw EMU as a way to gain the economies of scale necessary to protect their corporate model, in which workers, by law, have much more say in investment and hiring decisions. This often tends to protect jobs over profits.

Germany's export-oriented businesses were strongly in favour of joining EMU, and its largest banks, which have stakes in large portions of German companies, were among the most active in supporting EMU in the public debate. It is symbolic that just as the final decision on EMU participants was taken in May 1998, the supervisory board of Daimler was putting the final touches on the merger with Chrysler Corporation to form the third largest motor manufacturing company in the world. This new conglomerate bolstered German corporate elements in the company, such as the right of workers to participate in major investment decisions. It was sanctioned by Germany's largest bank, Deutsche Bank AG, which was the largest single shareholder in Daimler, with 24.4 per cent of the shares, and which was also arguably the biggest single pro-EMU force in Germany from the beginning.

All the better for the ECB

In some ways, the ECB is relieved that the UK is not part of Euroland at the outset. The UK, with an economy only slightly smaller than France's, would have substantial weight within the zone, and therefore in determining ECB interest rate decisions. Yet in the latter half of 1998, when the ECB was starting its operations, the UK's interest rates were still at 6.5 per cent, compared to rates of close to 3 per cent in Germany and France. Its economy was in a different phase of its cycle from that of the continent. The UK was slowing down after a six-year run of robust economic expansion. The major continental countries, by contrast, were still assumed to be in the midst of economic expansion after years of slow growth. With the UK's economy out of kilter with the rest of Europe, the ECB would have found it extremely difficult to agree on a single monetary policy, George warned a parliamentary treasury committee in May, 1996.[xxix]

As it stands, Ireland is the only country with an economy even more out of sync with the rest of Euroland. Because of its economic ties with Britain, it is more in line with the UK and US economic cycles. Besides geographic proximity, it has structural similarities to those countries, sharing an emphasis on the service sector. These services, whether low- or high-knowledge intensive, serve customers that are more short-term oriented in their demands. Innovative software needs to go to market immediately to beat the competition, with profit rewards diminishing quickly if there are delays. Software manufacturing companies are willing to borrow heavily – even at exorbitant interest rates – in order to complete their projects on time. The continent, meanwhile, is more specialized in heavy engineering, projects which are based more on long-term contracts and therefore financed by long-term borrowing. Companies are thus more careful to lock into low interest rates to minimize costs. There is a greater demand for stability, and long-term low-level inflation. Together, despite the fact that a majority of their total exports go to Euroland, the value of the British and Irish currencies have followed the value of the US dollar more closely than they have the mark, the continent's anchor currency.

With the healthy number of euro-sceptics in the UK, a monetary policy that does not match the country's interests would be difficult to sell. As noted, France is also a proud nation, but by 1998, it was more closely converged with the German economic cycle than it had been at any time in the prior eight years. Neighbours, their economies are now unlikely to be sent out of whack like they were in the early 1990s after German unification.

The UK would have a more difficult time adjusting to Euroland for another reason: taxes. Traditionally, Britain has had lower taxes, and continues to favour low taxes as a way of stimulating economic growth. Lower taxes, on the other hand, means that the government spends less, which is manifest in a weaker social net. Like, the US, it is more *laissez faire*. Britain is convinced of its own model and does not want to give up the right to lower taxes, which helps Britain lure investment from the continent. Lower taxes are also attractive to companies wanting to invest in the EU to take advantage of the EU's single market. Thus, Britain is unlikely to give up its veto on tax issues in Europe. If it were to agree to majority voting within the EU on tax matters, the UK would be overruled on most decisions by Germany and France, which are desperately seeking ways to harmonize taxes. They want the UK to do away with its tax-free off-shore markets, seeing them as unfairly drawing capital that would otherwise reside in their own economies. Giving up such a veto would be suicide for any British government.

In early December, 1998, Chancellor Brown insisted that he was ready to use the UK's veto to stall attempts to set uniform rates of corporate or indirect taxes across the EU. Other European countries, however, are pushing proposals that will prohibit tax oases and tax interest income at the same levels. British pension funds have about £60 billion pounds invested in eurobonds, which would be affected by the introduction of the proposed withholding tax on offshore investments.[xxx]

Now that the single currency makes differences between national prices and tax rates more transparent for consumers and investors, the absence of the UK could only be viewed with relief by German finance ministry officials. In fact, one oft-heard argument is that the UK lost out on a windfall of benefits by staying out of the single currency project. Under a single currency regime, its lower tax rates would have drawn automatic attention. Companies and investors, able to transfer businesses and money with no transaction costs and few taxes, would have shifted resources to the UK in droves.

Big costs

Public scepticism about the single currency has meant little political benefit for British politicians in associating themselves with it. When Gordon Brown failed to attend the christening of the euro in Brussels on new year weekend, the *Observer* newspaper compared it to the decision by Anthony Eden's government to dispatch a deputy official rather than a minister to the Messina conference in mid-1955, when Britain's partners drew up Europe's future and agreed for the first time on a vision of broad economic integration. Rab Butler, the British chancellor at the time, dismissed the seminal event as an irrelevant 'archaeological excavation' in some small Sicilian town.

Meanwhile Blair is doing his utmost to make progress on European integration in areas where he believes the British are more accepting, namely those where sovereignty would not be compromised, such as co-operation in security affairs. In October 1998, for example, Britain proposed a common European defence policy. This could help Europe regain influence in its strategic hinterland: North Africa, the Balkans, the Caspian oil basin and the Middle East.

Without question, UK is losing business by staying outside the euro project, especially in financial services. The City of London had profited during the 1980s by upgrading its stock and bond trading infrastructure, and pulled large amounts of business away from the more regulated continent. In early 1998, however, Britain suffered its first setback because of EMU. The electronic Frankfurt-based Deutsche Terminbörse overtook the London International Financial Futures and

Options Exchange in the trading of Europe's most actively traded bond derivative, the German government bond future. EMU will further shrink the derivatives market – a strong point of London – by reducing currency and interest rate risks. It has also unleashed intense competition and consolidation among Europe's banks. In 1998, Barclays and NatWest opted out of the equities and mergers and acquisitions markets altogether.[11] When challenged on this point by the parliament, however, Eddie George was open in acknowledging that Britain's historic position of strength has been unusual:

> It was extraordinary, if you take the particular Bund contract, which was the only one which has really been repatriated, it was extraordinary that it should have been here in the first place. That was true of a lot of the international equity trading which is actually still very active in this country, and so to be able to hold on to that kind of business against the normal expectations is a pretty remarkable achievement.[xxxi]

In other words, Britain is shrinking back to its rightful size. EU countries, in preparation for EMU, have accelerated financial services liberalization and harmonization in recent years, and so Britain's competitive advantage is fading. Now that it is outside the eurozone, and financial transactions in pounds will require an extra transaction fee, Britain's advantage has even turned into a disadvantage in some respects. British banks will find it harder to compete for major lending in euros, since they will not have euro as their primary capital. They will be dependent on the money markets to finance themselves, together with the risk

---

[11] Because the US legal system has meant a division of banks into specialized fields, American banks have become adept at specialization, and appear to be profiting. American investor Henry Kaufman predicts 'a new colonialization by Anglo-American banks'. For example, in 1998, American banks (Morgan Stanley Dean Witter and Goldman, Sachs & Co.) occupied the top two spots in European merger rankings for the first time (replacing European banks Warburg Dillon Read and Lazard Freres & Co. *Wall Street Journal*, Jan 7. 'In Europe, US Banks top Deal Rankings.'

and added inefficiency that entails. For example, they will not have access to the ECB's lending facilities.

Britain could lose out in attracting the investment from foreign companies that was so valuable for British economic and employment expansion during the 1990s. In December 1998, Australia's government warned its companies that they faced a 'competitive disadvantage' by investing in the UK. The government warned that they would incur additional transaction, accounting and hedging costs compared with competitors investing within the eurozone. The statement was only one of a series of blows to the contention by British government that there would be little impact on investment.[xxxii] A survey of Irish companies using British suppliers showed that 42 per cent were considering using new suppliers inside the eurozone.[xxxiii] In late 1998, the German car manufacturer, BMW AG, was also pushing the British government to join EMU, fearing a loss of competition if Britain's stayed out. In 1997, Hiroshi Okuda, Toyota's chairman, threatened a removal of its factories, sparking an emergency visit to Tokyo by the British economics minister at the time, Margaret Beckett. Ultimately, Toyota chose a site in France to establish a new factory, giving France's membership in Euroland as a justification.[12] [xxxiv] One reputed think-tank estimated that the total cost to the UK of staying outside could reach 1 per cent of GDP by 2005.[xxxv] If anything, the UK is becoming more dependent on Europe for trade, not less. Trade with the EU has been steadily rising over the past two decades. By 1999, the UK's trade with the eurozone was 50 per cent and growing. George admits that involvement in the single market has been an important factor in attracting overseas investment into the UK.[xxxvi] He recognizes the risks of not joining:

---

[12] The *Wall Street Journal* provided a good example of the extra costs incurred by a Swedish wallpaper producer, Duro Sweden AB, by being outside EMU. A small business with 60 employees and an annual revenue of 65 million kronor (8.1 million dollars), Duro makes 30 per cent of its sales abroad. Adjusting to the euro will cost roughly 900,000 kroner a year that Euroland competitors will not have to pay, the company estimates. Included in its breakdown of costs are 185,000 kroner for euro-related bank fees; 175,000 kroner for transfer-related costs such as the three to five days in lost pay days for the time the banks will hold

Can we afford to stand aside? There are potential risks in doing so. We might be penalized by financial markets which would require an interest rate premium to protect themselves against the exchange rate risk of holding sterling rather than euro. We might become subject to discrimination in some form if the euro-area were to see a need to protect itself against perceived predatory behaviour by non-participants within the single market. We might find that the UK became a less attractive location for overseas foreign investment – including investment in the financial services industry in the City of London.[xxxvii]

Some people have argued that the City might do *better* by staying out. 'It could be a Hong Kong to Europe's China,' *The Economist* noted in early 1998, referring to the potential benefits that could be gained by poaching continental business and investments by keeping taxes low.

There are political costs at stake as well. The centre of EU decision-making, traditionally the group of finance ministers, could shift to the select group of ministers in the Euro-11. Though decisions will have to be agreed to by the 'outs,' the fact that the euro-zone finance ministers meet separately in the Euro-11 council means that they will discuss issues more intensively, and could arrive at compromises more in their own favour. Britain and the other outs will lose political sway. Ultimately, these economic and political pressures are likely to force the UK to join. The euro could even arrive through the 'back door', as major UK companies with business on the continent find the currency transaction costs too great, and start keeping their books in euros. Already, British Steel and ICI, the major chemicals company, have said they want to pay British suppliers in euros instead of pounds.[xxxviii] The Chancellor of the

the money; 190,000 kroner for actual exchange fees; and 150,000 korner for higher interest rates on loans. This didn't include the cost of possible lost contracts, caused by prospective clients being dissuaded by the extra currency risks of doing business with Sweden. 'When I realised the costs involved, I got a little queasy,' Duro's CEO told the newspaper. *Wall Street Journal Europe*, May 1998. 'Sweden and Denmark Weigh the Price.'

Exchequer, Gordon Brown, has said companies can keep their books in euros, and British Petroleum has already declared itself ready to do so.[13]

A positive force within Euroland

Britain would of course bring the ECB and Euroland certain advantages. Its financial markets have already been mentioned. Ireland, in particular, would benefit from the UK's entry, because of the common economic cycles of the two countries. Maurice O'Connell, governor of the Bank of Ireland, believes Britain would offer a welcome counterweight to the German and French dominance over ECB decisions. Together, France and Germany account for more than 50 per cent of the gross domestic product within Euroland. Along with Italy, they also dominate the ECB staff. But if Britain was a member of the euro core, Ireland would have an economic ally within the ECB governing council. Ireland, which makes up about 1 per cent of the Euroland's economy, has almost no weight in the ECB's interest rates decisions. Britain's economy, tied for third largest with Italy, would change that.

But there is a more profound influence that Britain could wield if it were to join EMU, O'Connell notes. Britain is the only country that is big enough and impartial enough to play the honest broker between Germany and France in disputes on currency issues. The only other European country which is not considered broadly affiliated with the southern camp (led by France) or northern camp (led by Germany) is Luxembourg. But Luxembourg is not large enough for its proposals to be taken seriously immediately. One classic example of Britain's constructive role was during the 1993 currency crisis, when the French and the Germans were at loggerheads about how to reform the EMS.[14] In the end, it was the British who saved the

---

[13] The same goes for companies in other 'out' countries. Swedish companies Astra, SCA and Stora have also said they want to report their balance sheets in euros. *Manager Magazine*, July 1998.
[14] See chapter 4.

day. Having made no progress over a gruelling weekend of negotiations, Philippe Maystadt, the Belgian finance minister who was chairing the meeting of finance ministers, had finally given up. On Sunday afternoon, he told the ministers that the markets in Asia would be opening in a few hours, and declared the suspension of European central bank efforts to support the EMS, effectively announcing the end of the talks. Suddenly Kenneth Clarke, the Chancellor of the Exchequer broke in. He launched into a passionate defence of Europe, saying that a lack of a breakthrough would mean an 'historical defeat'. His intervention allowed the French to save face and finally agree to a widening of the bands that it had been refusing until that moment.

Britain's pragmatic approach is what makes Yves Mersch, governor of the Luxembourg central bank, also keen for the British to join:

> I certainly want them in, not for economic reasons but for political reasons, and I mean for reasons that go much deeper than tax issues. The British way of thinking would add a dimension that is very different from the French or the German approaches. Their way of tackling problems and producing pragmatic solutions would be very helpful to us. They have an experience in financial matters that runs very deep. Of course, they have a tradition of dividing in order to rule which is maybe less positive and more dangerous. But all this is the British approach to institution building. It is closer to the American system. The drawback in my opinion is that their financial structure is too much out of line with the European structure. They are closer to short-term financing, closer to centralized policy-making in monetary policy. All of these are fundamental differences which we will have to overcome when they enter.[xxxix]

The continental model of more regulation has so far dominated the general direction of the European Union. If they were to partake in EMU, the British would have more credibility to push their approach. As long as Britain stays out, the German orthodoxy has the upper hand, since the French and Italian systems are too close to Germany's to be real alternatives. Europe has already become a model for supranational and international co-operation, and in the world's eyes, it is increasingly Germany that anchors the European system with a set of beliefs about the political economy: those that underpin the 'social market economy'.[15] Eastern Europeans have traditionally had a special respect for the German model. Not only has Germany exerted more political and economic influence upon these countries historically, but it will do so in future when they join Euroland. A more active British role within EMU would reduce this homogeneity within Europe. It would challenge the assumptions of the main rival to the US economic model, since it would prevent Europe forming a consensus about its political and economic identity.[16]

Monetary policy differences

Because of Britain's divergent economic cycle, George argues that the British economy needs a different monetary policy from that pursued on the continent. In late 1998, for example, Britain needed higher rates because of the advanced stage of its economic cycle. But the ability of small economies like Britain's to pursue an independent monetary policy effectively is being increasingly questioned, even by British politicians. The Bank of England held to a policy of steady interest rates in mid-1998 even though there were signs of an economic slowdown. The Asian crisis, which steadily worsened over the year, accelerated the negative trend, and in the second half of 1998 and early 1999,

---

[15] See chapter 3.

[16] The French, Dutch and Belgians, for example, are close enough to the German view on the provision of a more extensive social net to be able to say, in general, that there is a European orthodoxy on how society should be organized. Indeed, this is the substance of what French Prime Minister Lionel Jospin meant in January 1999, when he said France must do more to present an alternative to the 'penseé unique internationale', or the international singular way of thinking. The phrase carries a lot of political baggage in France, since 'penseé unique' was the derogatory description French politicians applied to Jean-Claude Trichet to describe what, at the time, was believed to be too much emphasis on low inflation

the Bank was frantically lowering rates to avoid a recession.[17] If it had been part of a broader economic zone such as Euroland, its currency and economy might not have been so buffeted.

Once, during a parliamentary hearing in January 1998, Eddie George admitted that the complexities of a modern economy meant that European central banks were often shooting in the dark with their policies. For example, it was impossible for central banks to distinguish between the unemployment that existed because of sluggish economic growth, and that which stemmed from so-called 'structural' inefficiencies, such as excessive labour regulation and high wages, which scared away employers. The difference is important, since sluggish growth can be helped by sparking economic activity, for example, by a lowering of interest rates. Structural unemployment, however, cannot be helped by the central bank, but is dependent instead on government reform. In drawing up any policy, a bank is dependent on its 'perceptions' about structural unemployment, George said.

Quentin Davies, a Conservative member of parliament, jumped on George's concession. If central banking was so vague, and the economy so complex, how could George insist that Britain needed to control its own interest rates and currency exchange rates, and not enter EMU, in order to fine-tune the economy? Davies argued that many British companies were so intertwined with the global economy, and therefore dependent on the global cycle in their particular sectors, that a 'national' policy was outmoded. Take a situation in which world paper prices are low but steel prices are high. British publishers would prefer low interest rates to ensure a lower value of the pound, thereby ensuring the export of books at competitive prices in foreign markets. If steel prices are high,

---

at the expense of jobs. Jospin was not explicit in what he meant by this term, but the French audience understood. The implication is that there is a mode of thinking about economics that is being propagated around the globe by the US, and that Europe, led by France, can, and has the moral obligation to, come up with an alternative.

---

[17] On April 9 1999 the Bank of England lowered rates to 5.25 per cent. It was the sixth cut in seven months.

however, a machine manufacturer for the domestic market would prefer to have a higher value of the pound. That way, it could afford to import the steel and other products needed for its assembly process. Davies questioned whether it was fair to adjust natural prices 'over the heads' of the companies:

> All the variables with which you are dealing . . . are very uncertain. You do not know what the money supply is. You know what the M3 or M4 figures are, but you do not know how much of that is held for transactional purposes. You do not know what the underlying rate of unemployment is. You do not know what the output gap is . . . You cannot have it both ways. You cannot say that monetary policy is a very uncertain science and you often get it wrong (which may be true) and then say this is a wonderfully precise mechanism for adjustment and we should have national monetary policies because they can perfectly well adjust to asymmetric shocks. I put it to you that any of these shocks will impact on different sectors in different ways. Indeed, demand and supply conditions are changing for different firms every day of the week in certain cases. No doubt some of the real prices should be adjusted up at any one time and at any one time other real prices should be adjusted down. Exchange rate adjustment is an extraordinarily crude weapon, is it not? . . . It is not reasonable in a single market to say all of our countries are not only so different but so homogeneously different that running monetary policy exchange rate policy on a national basis makes any sense.

George agreed that Davies' logic was sound in part, but insisted that there is still reason to believe that a majority of firms would benefit from a nationally-oriented policy. Many companies are still very strongly geared toward the domestic market. If national sentiment turned negative and economic growth slowed, a majority of British companies would be adversely affected. By lowering interest rates, the British central bank would lower financing costs, and thereby spark economic growth. There the debate ended, unresolved.

The merits of a go-it-alone approach are highly contestable. Many economists have argued that the British departure from the EMS system in 1992 was beneficial for the economy. The sharp drop of the currency against European currencies boosted British exports, and sparked an economic and employment boom that would last eight years. By late 1998, the British economy was boasting the lowest level of unemployment for twenty years. Still, continental bankers saw it as just more evidence of an anglo-saxon penchant for short-term, but ultimately self-defeating, frenzies. Jean-Claude Trichet, for one, pointed out how the pound's EMS departure actually back-fired in the form of higher long-term interest rates, which are key for influencing business investment decisions. He criticized British policy as a 'politique du chien crevé au fil de l'eau', or that of an exhausted dog that lets itself drift with the current.[xl]

Britain has other differences in its approach to central banking. Britain has become accustomed to a transparency in its decision-making that is unparalleled on the continent. The Bank publishes the votes of members of its policy making committee, and summarizes their arguments, a policy that horrifies the continental Europeans, accustomed to secrecy in their decision-making, and where minutes are often kept secret for thirty years or longer. George is unabashedly proud of this transparency:

The great strength of publishing the minutes is that it forces each of the nine members of the policy making committee to have personal responsibility. It provides a clear exposition of the difference of views. This helps the world outside to understand the nature of the debate on monetary policy, and it helps outsiders to make constructive comments. It adds credibility to the process. All of this is hugely important in the British context, which has a pretty spotty record on price stability in the past. And within the national context, view-points of the MPC members are not likely to be subject to national pressures, such as national media and so on, in their home countries.[xli]

George recognizes why the ECB would not want to publish the votes of its members, given national sensitivities. But Bank of England monetary policy committee member and economics professor, Willem Buiter, has been more critical:

> The attitude of the ECB is typical of a central banking tradition that views central banking as a sacred, quasi-mystical vocation, a cult whose priests perform the holy sacraments far from prying eyes of the non-initiates. This mystique of the central bank, and the excessive clubbishness and clannish behaviour it sometimes encourages, is both entirely unwarranted and a threat to the legitimacy of the purposes the central bank is intended to serve . . . council members will be able to hide behind the cloak of confidentiality and avoid having to justify yielding to local political pressures. The exercise of undue influence is not deterred by secrecy and confidentiality but by openness. Smoke-filled rooms and confidentiality are more likely to allow ECB independence to be perverted by national political pressures and the occasional short-term embarrassment this entails.[xlii]

Buiter also said the ECB's governing council was 'too large for serious and productive exchange of views, discussion and group decision-making'. Buiter is not alone in his criticism. The respected Organization of Economic Co-operation and Development (OECD) also harbours doubts about the independence of the ECB's council members. It fears they will continue to serve national interests, a behaviour that could be perpetuated by secrecy. Tietmeyer argues the OECD is 'wrong', and that the ECB will develop into a 'true supranational decision making body'.[xliii]

Finally, George and his committee fiercely defend the Bank's policy strategy of explicitly targeting inflation. He rejects the European criticism that the UK's policy is too focused on the short-term, especially Bonn professor von Hagen's argument that inflation targeting is like John Wayne riding across the prairie and 'shooting every rabbit' that pokes its head up. George responds:

It's quite the reverse. You'll find that inflation targeting explicitly obliges you to look forward. Monetary policy has its full impact over a two year period. That forces you into looking ahead, not reaching for the latest piece of data, except for when it's saying something that's likely to be happening over the two year period. It's exactly what every central banker is doing. At the ECB, they've set an inflation objective, and that's what it's about. All of this is terribly exaggerated. It would be delinquent if we didn't take into consideration every piece of information. I don't believe in shooting rabbits, but I do believe in looking at all the varied wildlife on the prairie.

NOTES

[i] *Wall Street Journal*, January 11, 1999. 'Krona Rallies as EMU Tide is Changing.' *Wall Street Journal*, January 8-9 1999. 'Initial Success of the Euro is Prompting Holdouts to Reconsider Outsider Status.'

[ii] *Financial Times*, January 8, 1999. 'Danish rates cut as poll backs the euro.'

[iii] *Wall Street Journal*, January 4 1999. 'Raising Touchy Issues among Holdouts.'

[iv] *Wall Street Journal*, January 8, 1999. 'Bank of England Cuts Key Rate Again.'

[v] OECD, 1998.

[vi] BBC. 'The Money Changers,' Post Production Script, February, 1998. Prog. 1. P. 24.

[vii] Bruges speech October 21, 1998.

[viii] Statement on EMU by the Chancellor of the Exchequer to the House of Commons. October 27, 1997.

[ix] Malcolm Bruce. Treasury committee. Minutes of Evidence. 28 January 1998.

[x] *Daily Telegraph*, February 3, 1997. 'Europe must integrate or risk war, Kohl tells Britain.'

[xi] Interview with author January 12, 1999.

[xii] *International Herald Tribune*, 'Britain Outside, Again,' January 4, 1999.

[xiii] Padoa Schioppa interview, 1997.

[xiv] *Daily Telegraph*, February 3, 1996. 'Europe must integrate or risk war, Kohl tells Britain.'

[xv] Cited in *Wall Street Journal Europe*, January 4, 1999. 'Raising Touchy Issues Among Holdouts.'

[xvi] *Daily Telegraph*, December 16, 1998. 'Euroland can't bank on the ECB,' by Ambrose Evans-Pritchard.

[xvii] *Financial Times*, December 30, 1998 'Pro-euro Conservatives press Blair.'

[xviii] See chapter 4.

xix Tommaso Padoa-Schioppa, *The Road to Monetary Union in Europe: The Emperor, the Kings, and the Genies*, Clarendon Press, Oxford: 1994, p. 13.

xx Cited in Paul Kennedy, *Preparing for the Twenty-First Century*, Fontana Press: London 1994. p. 9 and in R. Hyam, Britain's *Imperial Century* 1815-1914 (London, 1975), p. 47.

xxi FAZ, January 6, 1999.

xxii BBC 'The Money Changers'. Prog. 1. P. 27.

xxiii BBC 'The Money Changers'. Post Production Script, February, 1998. Prog. 1. P. 25.

xxiv Speech in Bruges, October 21, 1998.

xxv 2 April 1998.

xxvi Interview with the author, January 12, 1999.

xxvii 'City Profile: Russia's "spy" at the Bank of England', in the *Sunday Telegraph*, March 14, 1993, by Judi Bevan.

xxviii Ibid.

xxix Speech in Bruges, on October 21, 1998.

xxx *Daily Telegraph*, December 30, 1998. 'Rivals make their pitch on eve of euro launch.'

xxxi George hearing before Treasury committee on April 2, 1998.

xxxii *Financial Times*, December 30, 1998. 'Australia cautions against investing in UK after euro.'

xxxiii *Daily Telegraph*, December 30, 1998. 'Rivals make their pitch on eve of euro launch.'

xxxiv *Manager Magazine*, July, 1998.

xxxv A study by CEBR.

xxxvi Eddie George lecture at the Paolo Baffi Center for Monetary and Financial Economics, at the Universita Commerciale Luigi Bocconi, Milan. 14 May 1996.

xxxvii Ibid.

xxxviii *Financial Times*, April 20, 1998.

xxxix Interview with author on October 27, 1998.

xl Aeschimann and Riché, p. 249.

xli Interview with author, January 12, 1999.

xlii *Guardian*, December 29, 1998. 'Biting at the heels of the top dog.'

xliii *Der Spiegel* interview with Tietmeyer, December 28, 1998.

CHAPTER ELEVEN

The Twenty-first Century

'With the euro,' French President Jacques Chirac declared in early 1998, 'Europe can become the No. 1 power in the multi-power world of tomorrow.' The European Central Bank, as the first genuine supranational organization representing Europe and as the institution governing the euro, is the symbol of Europe's newfound power. Through the ECB, Europeans will be able to act, swiftly and powerfully for the first time, without endless consultations, compromises and delays.

On paper, the ECB has all the prerequisites to match the US Federal Reserve in performance. It is by statute independent of political authorities, meaning that it can make unpopular decisions even against the wishes of member governments. Its sole mandate is to keep inflation at constant low levels. Finally, its monetary policy strategy has been formulated by the best minds in European central banking after years of consultation and debate.

Yet there is one more 'soft' factor that contributes to a central bank's success, and that is the skill with which it interacts with the markets and wider public opinion in order to create a positive sentiment conducive to investment and economic activity. It is this last factor, which I have called the *psychological* factor, that at end of the day will determine whether the ECB will be as successful as, or indeed more successful than the Federal Reserve.

Psychology

Of all the components required for central banking success, the psychological factor is the most complex to analyse. When any central bank formulates monetary policy, it does so in a permanent guessing game about the direction of the economy. It makes its best educated guess by analysing a set of economic data, including money supply developments, the consumer price index, import prices, the levels of wage settlements and so on. But bankers can rarely see further ahead than a few months at a time. Interest rate policy, however, takes up to six months to reach the peak of its impact, and up to two years to have exhausted its full impact. So if an unexpected downturn occurs, a rate cut by the ECB to counter its effects will be ineffective in the short term. The degree to which the central bank can steal the initiative, that is, guide the psychology of the markets, is thus especially important. It is a skill that Chairman of the US Federal Reserve Alan Greenspan has mastered, and one which Wim Duisenberg has not.[1]

In the European context, psychology is especially important. (In Germany, there is a saying among economists that 'psychology makes up half of economic growth'.) First, steady economic conditions are especially important for European manufacturers. Stability and economic growth encourage investment and thereby create more jobs.

But more important, the ECB is deciding on monetary policy for twelve different nations, each with its own language and traditions, and therefore each engaged in its own public debate. Since the ECB can only implement one monetary policy, it cannot help but pursue a policy that inadvertently advantages some nations over others. In early 1999, for example, the ECB's initial policy stance – an interest rate of 3 per cent for the 'foreseeable future' – was geared to priming economic expansion, a policy clearly more in the interests of Germany, France and Italy, which had lower rates of economic growth, than of countries whose economies were growing quickly and whose inflation was higher or creeping upward, such as Ireland, Spain and Portugal. But lowering interest rates is never as

---

[1] As president of the German Bundesbank, Hans Tietmeyer was the only European central banking leader with extensive experience in guiding markets orally.

painful as raising them. Considerable domestic discontent could break out if rates are hiked at a time when some countries are still in recession, exacerbating negative sentiment among businesses and consumers. If the country suffering were France, the controversy could become serious, given residual French suspicions that ECB policy is guided by Germans, and the people's quickness to protest on the street. Political unrest, in turn, could spark further concern among investors.

Thus, the ECB is likely to be quicker to drop interest rates than to raise them, because of stronger opposition within the council from bankers representing countries with slow economies.

In the long term, the ECB must give its moral support to furthering a pan-European political debate about the economy, which would help foster greater understanding of its polices. Despite two decades of increasing unemployment, European politicians remain incapable of pushing through the necessary reforms for creating more jobs. The ECB can help in two ways: first by continuing to make clear to politicians that only a more flexible labour force and lower obligatory social insurance contributions will create jobs; second, by supporting further steps toward political integration within Europe, since a greater sense of European identity will quell public discontent within the various countries about perceived unfair treatment.

The governing council

The 18 members of the ECB's governing council are at least as qualified as the central bankers of the US Federal Reserve. Between them, they have an impressive amount of experience in the central banking profession, and they have the political sophistication to meet the psychological challenge described above. President Wim Duisenberg and national central bank governors Jean-Claude Trichet and Nout Wellink have all spent several years as leaders of their banks and as members of government. Board member Padoa-Schioppa gained considerable political experience during the negotiations for the Maastricht Treaty as deputy to the governor at the Banca d'Italia. Board members Sirrka Hämäläinen, Domingo Solans and Issing, and national governors Vanhala, Liebscher, and Fazio have spent their careers in central banking, but all have participated in the institution building of the ECB – by nature a very political process. Issing and Domingo Solans were professors for a number of years before devoting their careers to central banking. Yves Mersch spent most of his career in the Luxembourg finance ministry, helping negotiate the Maastricht Treaty, and was a long-time member of the Monetary Committee. ECB Vice President Christian Noyer is the only member of the council without any central banking experience at all. More notably, there is a distinct lack of private sector experience when compared with their counterparts at the US Federal Reserve. It is not obvious just how necessary private sector experience is, however. Bill McDonough, president of the New York Fed, spent the bulk of his career in commercial banking, but doesn't think such experience is crucial. He has met many of the European governors during regular G-10 talks, and was impressed by them during crucial negotiations in east Asia when the US and Europe jointly sought to help stem the currency crisis in that region during 1998:

> It's nice to have had 22 years to learn how bankers work and think, to know how the payment system works, because I've been a part of it. It's one of those things that is useful to have as part of my background. Is it essential? In my view, the people running the bank – Duisenberg, Tietmeyer, Issing, Padoa-Schioppa, Hämäläinen and Trichet –are experienced bankers. They have spent an awful lot of time talking with people in the private sector, learning their view of things. You're not dealing with theoreticians with little practical experience. What we're concerned about is: would they know how to deal with a banking crisis? I have enough experience in dealing with them – for example, in reconstructing the bank debt of South Korea last year – to believe they can manage. I know more about the technical stuff, but they know enough through the experiences they've had with the plight of their own banks.[i]

The great majority of the governing council members come from middle-class, non-privileged backgrounds, and succeeded by studying hard and rising to their positions on merit. In this respect, they resemble their counterparts at the US Federal Reserve. On the other hand, the Fed's board and regional presidents have had less political experience than their ECB counterparts. It is precisely this political nose that will guide the ECB governing council through the sensitivities and controversies that lie ahead of it.

A sharp political instinct is also needed at the ECB because of the relative distance between Frankfurt and Europe's political capitals. In Washington, the Fed and the US government seem to work in tandem. In Europe, however, the relationship between the president of the ECB, Wim Duisenberg, and European political powers has been somewhat tense.

The Fed is helped by the fact that there are few jealousies between regions in response to a particular Fed policy. Granted, in the past, there have been differences within the Federal Open Market Committee (FOMC) in terms of voting, but rarely was the debate carried on in public. In past decades, there have been some occasions when the regional federal reserve presidents voted in the interests of their local economies, and when there were clear lines of division between the views of the regional presidents and board representatives in Washington, but such differences have narrowed over the past twenty years.

Judging from the make-up of those within the ECB governing council, European bankers are likely to move in a similar direction. They embody a European tradition that is more prone to political management and institutional meddling than the American or British traditions. These individuals are mostly civil servants who, as Europeans, suffered under the Cold War division and learned that diplomacy through a group of multilateral institutions such as NATO, the International Monetary Fund, the Group of Seven, and the OECD, was the best way for Europeans to achieve their goal of uniting East and West. In their own careers, they have engaged in a decade of intense multilateral negotiations within Europe to construct the European Central Bank. Through that experience, they have learned to appreciate institutional cooperation and craftsmanship. In addition, their culture, upbringing, and career development have taught them respect for Europe's social-political commitments. They do not apologize for Europe's relatively generous social system compared to that of the US. They only argue that it should be reformed to be more affordable.

Milestone in Europe's integration

The establishment of the ECB marks one of the most significant steps so far in European integration. It sets a precedent for European cooperation without national representation. The members of the ECB council embody the makings of a new kind of European citizen. This precedent will make a key contribution to further political integration, thereby strenghtening Europe's place in the world during the twenty-first century.

With the rise of East Asia over the previous few decades – regardless of recent set-backs the region has experienced – and with the ongoing strength of the United States superpower, the required direction for Europe is clear: Only by coming together can Europe create a bloc of peoples more prosperous and even more powerful than any other state in the world. As Paul Kennedy writes in his 1993 work *Preparing for the Twenty-First Century*:

> It is in those realms [of controversial measures like a common currency, enhanced powers for the European parliament, and co-ordinated defense policies] that there lie both the greatest potential for transforming 'Europe' into something very different from today's geographical expression *and* the greatest cluster of obstacles to changing the existing structure of a continent of nation-states. If these obstacles are overcome, the EC might well develop the place in global affairs which federationists envision for it; if they are not, it could remain what one disgusted Belgian minister called it during the 1991 Gulf War – 'an economic giant, a political dwarf, and a military worm'.

Although organizations to promote regional co-operation

exist elsewhere in the world, none possesses the commercial importance or attracts the intellectual and political interest of the EC. It conducts one third of world trade. Collectively, its financial resources are enormous, since it possesses many of the world's largest banks, insurance companies, and finance houses. Of the globe's top ten trading nations, seven are European. In industries such as automobiles, pharmaceuticals, machine tools, and engineering goods generally, the EC countries together produce more than any other country in the world . . . The economic rationale for a harmonization of the tariffs, commercial practice, taxes, traffic legislation, and associated activities of these countries is simply overwhelming.[ii]

On paper, Europe has everything it needs to succeed. In 1988 Harvard political scientist Samuel Huntington suggested the 'baton of world leadership' in this century may pass from America to a European federation:

The European Community, if it were to become politically cohesive, would have the population, resources, economic wealth, technology, and actual and potential military strength to be the preeminent power of the twenty-first century. Japan, the United States, and the Soviet Union have specialized respectively in investment, consumption, and arms. Europe balances all three. It invests less of its GNP than Japan but more than the United States and possibly more than the Soviet Union. It consumes less of its GNP than the United States but more than Japan and the Soviet Union. It arms less than the United States and the Soviet Union but more than Japan.

It is also possible to conceive of a European ideological appeal comparable to the American one. Throughout the world, people line up at the doors of American consulates seeking immigration visas. In Brussels, countries line up at the door of the Community seeking admission. A federation of democratic, wealthy, socially diverse, mixed-economy societies would be a powerful force on the world scene. If the next century is not the American century it is most likely to be the European century.[iii]

Finally, in late 1992, American economist Lestor Thurow wrote in his bestseller *Head to Head* that 'future historians will record that the twenty-first century belonged to the House of Europe'.

This flood of optimistic predictions tapered off after the early 1990s, however, as European unemployment continued to increase and the US began a strong recovery, reached new lows in unemployment and showed clear dominance of the new future-oriented Internet and computer industries.

In response, more sceptical views about Europe appeared. Harvard University political scientist Stanley Hoffman pointed out early on that Europe was still hampered by a maze of border controls, government subsidies to national industries, closed national systems of procurement in military and other key public sectors and different regulations in industries such as manufacturing, copyrights, transportation, banking, insurance and health care. If Europe struggled to overcome regulatory hurdles in such elementary areas of the economy, it was asked, how on earth would it succeed in making breakthroughs in more ambitious areas such as creating a common currency and creating a federal central bank, goals which challenged the most profound elements of a nation's sovereignty? By the mid-1990s, many observers were calling the EMU project Utopian.

Within a few years, however, the euro was introduced, and successfully so. Simultaneously, a slew of other EU directives have been implemented by EU members, many of which tackle the problems mentioned by Hoffman. Border controls and government subsidies have been reduced significantly and progress has been made on harmonization of procurement legislation and regulations concerning copyright, banking and insurance. Granted, there are many great challenges ahead. The continental model is still plagued by high unemployment, a result of the unwillingness of European political leaders to make labour markets more flexible. But whether Europe tackles those questions is more of a question of *will* than ability. Otherwise, not even the greatest Eurosceptic can deny that the pace of progress over the past decade has been impressive.

Despite periods of doubt and serious political challenges to the EMU project, European leaders have proved how committed they are to the project of political integration by toughing out the EMU negotiations. It is that sort of commitment that will make the Europeans now turn to other areas on the integration agenda. There are irresistible forces pushing in that direction, among the most important of which is the need to change the way European legislation is implemented.

Under the plan of German foreign minister Joschka Fischer, majority voting would become the norm in all aspects of EU decision-making except for 'questions of fundamental importance such as treaty amendments'. That would mean that the EU member countries could no longer be held hostage by a single member, such as Britain wanting to veto a particular proposal. There would be advancement on creating a common foreign and security policy. Fischer proposed starting negotiations on the reforms by 2001.

Such a move would create a more politically efficient, more coherent and more united Europe. Fischer's proposal is eerily similar to the one made by his predecessor Hans-Dietrich Genscher exactly a decade earlier. In February 1988, Genscher proposed the creation of a single currency, and his proposal received little public attention at the time, perhaps because it seemed so idealistic. But it took on a momentum of its own, and the single currency arrived within a decade.

There might be set-backs or pauses for breath before launching into the next ambitious stage of integration, as when the complications arising from enlargement set in, for example, but it is bound to come. Issues such as tax harmonization have become the focus of considerable ideological polemic. Critics saying that tax harmonization would force tax rates to converge at higher levels instead of the lower levels. They fear that the Germans and French want to make Britain raise taxes in order to stop companies leaving the continent and relocating in the British Isles to take advantage of its lower corporate taxes.

This is a simplification of what the continental Europeans are

397

proposing. They insist they do not seek a rigid equalization of tax rates but merely to erase certain tax-free investment opportunities that have no real justification other than helping investors avoid a fair rate of taxes. It is often overlooked that the United States also has a unified tax code, but allows its states to raise different levels of taxes within that overall regime. This is nothing more than what the European proposal would do.

ECB President Wim Duisenberg, who has expressed scepticism about a politically unified Europe, also concedes that Europe is being pulled together, and that tax harmonization is inevitable. He explains:

> I find it a little bit vague and somewhat dangerous to talk about political union as such. One has to respect the cultures in this fragmented Europe. We have built up quite divergent cultures, and people want to feel that their cultures are safe. They want to preserve sovereignty over their own destiny. I very much support that ... Political union is a very vague concept. First you have to define what political union is. What politics are you talking about? Is it fiscal policies, foreign policies, defence policies, or general managerial policies? What I'm sure about is that economic and monetary union will act as a catalyst to achieve more unity or common decision-making in other areas, whether you like it or not. For example, this will happen in the tax field. To avoid tax competition, there will be a tendency toward more and more harmonization of tax structures. This does not mean that the result will be a completely egalitarian or rigidly unified tax system. Look at the United States. The tax regimes between various states can differ considerably, but they can differ only to some extent. As far as European taxes are concerned, I think that ultimately, tax structures will develop in such a way that differences between member states will no longer be a motive for people or capital to move from one place to the other. EMU will act as a catalyst in moving other national structures closer together as well, for example in the social security field, and co-operation in passing budgets. But that is inevitable ...

There is a set of irresistible forces and overwhelming logic pushing Europe towards more political integration, and the extent to which the UK will continue to be the main brake on this process remains unclear. If the UK opposes compromise too rigidly, self-imposed distance may gradually turn into isolation as Europe moves ahead without it.

Bi-polar world?

As the euro project lends Europe more confidence to move forward, one can't help but start questioning whether US triumphalism is misguided. Many economists have talked of a New Economy, a new era of continuous, unbroken growth fostered by unprecedented productivity gains in new technology and intelligent guidance of monetary policy by the US Federal Reserve. As US economist Paul Krugman has argued, the robust growth that the American economy was experiencing in the late 1990s was being sustained by temporary factors that were keeping inflation low, such as the Asian crisis and a switch to managed health care, which has squeezed worker benefits: 'Just as pronouncements of American triumph turn out, on close examination, to be overstated, so do the dismissals of European and Asian prospects that one now hears,' he wrote in a 1998 *Foreign Affairs* article.[iv]

Former under secretary of commerce for international trade Jeffrey E. Garten travelled frequently to Europe during the first Clinton administration, and he too believes Europe has more in store for the US than most Americans have been willing to admit. Saying the euro will turn Europe into a 'superpower', Garten argues:

Not only will EMU succeed but it will eventually pose a major challenge to Wall Street, corporate America, and Washington. After all, when America's boom ends, it will still be the world's largest debtor, whereas the EMU region will be a net creditor. The US will continue to run chronic trade deficits, while the European Union amasses large surpluses. America will not have reversed its super-low savings rates, while EMU members will have no such problems. American companies will also want to keep an eye on the emergence of European corporate goliaths and the long tradition of European governments helping their own businesses win big commercial projects in emerging markets. A lot of experts are pointing to the need for Europe to brace for the changes ahead. So should America.[v]

Europe has undoubtedly made as much progress over the past decade as anyone might have hoped. But the US has also enjoyed significant recovery. The effects of the so-called 'peace dividend' have been tremendous. Now that the Cold War is over, the US government has been able to channel tens of billions of dollars into the peacetime economy that were formerly used for funding its military. This has fuelled a US economic resurgence, and helped it regain the innovative lead in many high-technology sectors.

Regulation in the country's banking sector has allowed its banks to retrench and consolidate. US banks are now proving they can hold their own against competitors in Europe and Japan. In Europe they have increased their presence, and in some sectors are beating European competitors on their own turf. Financially, the United States is still by far the most powerful country according to a number of other indicators.

While the Euroland and US government bond markets are about the same size (about $1.9 trillion),[vi] Euroland's corporate bond market, valued at $160 billion, is one-sixth the size of that of the US. The value of Europe's stock market, about $3.6 trillion, is less than half the size of US equity markets, valued at about $9.5 trillion. This compares with a stock market value of $2.0 trillion in Japan. These are large gaps that will probably remain for quite some time, partly because of the different financial structures in the two regions and not necessarily because of inherent weakness in Europe. (In Europe, more money is invested in banks than in the stock market, and more companies borrow from banks than issue corporate bonds.) The US also enjoys some marginal advantages from the popularity of the dollar. Roughly 60 per cent of all US dollars circulate outside US borders. These holdings represent an interest-free loan to the United States, amounting to roughly $15 to $20 billion per year.

This seigniorage benefit, which the US has enjoyed for decades, will be slowly reduced by the incursions of the euro. But the reasons why foreigners hold dollars – its widespread use as a reserve currency, its use as the basis of billing in trade transactions, and so on – will continue for the foreseeable future, and the euro is unlikely to challenge the pre-eminence of the dollar within the next couple of decades. While nearly one-third of world trade is denominated in eurozone currencies, 48 per cent is denominated in dollars.

The US is therefore not about to decline in power as quickly as many critics had assumed a decade ago. Still, the euro's ramifications have yet to be fully realized. For one, after 1999, Europe suddenly faced $50 billion to $100 billion in excess dollar reserves, as economies of scale achieved by merging the national central banks into the ECB mean that Europe's central banking system does not require the huge amount of national bank reserves. These funds could theoretically be injected into the EU's economy – quite a free lunch. There's also an estimated $400 billion in private portfolio shifting from dollars into euros that is likely to occur over the next few years, as investors seek to diversify their assets. This is one reason why in December 1998, a survey of 240 fund management companies found that 60 per cent favoured the euro above other currencies over the next year. Only 20 per cent supported the dollar.[vii] Governments in developing countries could shift about $75 billion worth of their portfolios into euros. These are all conservative estimates.[2] Taken together, these effects will gradually influence the relative prestige of the euro and the dollar within the international monetary system.

Finally, the US economy is not without its weaknesses. Despite America's more favourable fiscal condition, its trade deficit is widening. In 1998, it was close to 3 per cent of GDP.

---

2 The Institute of International Economics in Washington, for example, reckons that up to a trillion dollars will shift from the US currency to the euro.

Euroland, by contrast, enjoys steady trade surpluses. Its share of international trade is 19 per cent, larger than the US share of 17 per cent.[viii] That is not to mention the array of other advantages that the euro will bring to Europe, including simplification and reduction of costs of accounting for companies engaged in cross-border business, the abolishment of $65 billion annually in currency exchange costs, and the production of a vast pool of capital in Europe that will invigorate the continent's stock and bond markets. All of this will bring greater competition and improve companies' competitiveness.

The real surprise, however, has been the set-back in Asia. Japan's economy remains on artificial respiration, buoyed only by a Keynesian government spending package implemented in 1999. The Asian crisis also affected many Southeast Asian countries. Recessions have thrown many people out of work, and many parents are unable to pay for schooling, thereby setting back countries like Indonesia an entire generation, according to some estimates. The exact cost of the crisis has yet to be calculated, but it has significantly reduced economic growth in the region. While many observers talked several years ago – during the euro's making – of an emerging tri-polar international financial system (with the yen, the dollar and the euro as the three poles), the status of the Japanese yen is looking increasingly wobbly. Though the yen will continue to serve a valuable function as a reserve currency, there is little likelihood that it will gain a following in Asia that would propel it to the status of a rival reserve currency. Asia is simply too divided politically. The lack of a regional pole worries the former US Federal Reserve chairman, Paul Volcker:

Asia is much tougher than South America [which has the dollar as a natural pole, because of trade relations]. The reason that Asian countries are more vulnerable is because they don't have a natural pole. Where, or to whom, do the Asian countries go during times of crisis? They have a lot of trade with Europe and with the US. They also have even more trade with Japan, and a pole might be the yen. But the yen can't be a pole for the simple reason that there are residual political misunderstandings and antagonisms between Japan and other Asian countries, and because the Japanese market isn't very open. This vacuum in Asia is a factor that contributed to the Asian currency crisis. The instability among the major currencies is a danger; it would make a difference if there was reasonable stability between the yen, the dollar, and the euro.

If you want to speculate, in 15 to 25 years, if the Chinese economy continues to develop and expand as it has been doing, China will become a natural pole in Asia. It has the potential mass, and an awful lot of relations, cultural as much as economic, with all of these other countries. There is potential for conflict too. Asia is a sea of political unrest.

For the next two decades, a bi-polar world looks likely, with the two major reserve currencies being the euro and the dollar, backed up by the economic and political strength of the world's two greatest powers, the EU and the United States. Latin American countries are increasingly linking their currencies to the dollar. Meanwhile, across the Atlantic, non-Euroland countries are linking their currencies to the euro. Explains Padoa-Schioppa, the ECB's foreign minister:

I regard the European time zone as the natural zone of the euro, namely the zone where the euro is either the currency or the anchor currency for other currencies. This area runs from the North Pole to Cape Town. It includes Africa of course. The whole of Europe, including central and eastern Europe is natural too. Russia is very special. It's half in Asia. I'm not saying that we should be actively promoting this. But in the end I regard it as a natural development.

Meanwhile China and India, with populations that are expected to reach around 1.5 billion by the year 2025, manage economies that, if they continue on their present trend, will catch up with the United States over the course of the century, with China catching up sometime before 2040. But in *per capita* income, these countries seem set to remain far behind for a longer period of time. Their financial systems remain very underdeveloped compared with the West, and heavy state involvement in their economies has meant continued inefficiency. The Chinese central bank has been reforming itself, but remains under heavy state control. What is more, the Chinese remain deeply suspicious of the Japanese, and there is no hope in the near future of a political tie between these two nations of the sort that has happened in Europe. A single Asian currency is a long way off, even for those countries outside Japan or China. If China does emerge as a regional pole by 2015, it will have to build much more political trust with its neighbours before its currency can emerge as a regional reserve currency. The probability is that disunity will continue in Asia, and that the region will lag in terms of its organized influence within the international financial system. At the height of excitement surrounding the euro changeover weekend at the beginning of January 1999, Joseph Yam, chief executive of the Hong Kong Monetary Authority, the territory's *de facto* central bank, called for regional discussions about the possibility of creating an Asian monetary union. This would be required to put Asia in a stronger position and make individual countries less vulnerable to speculators, he said. He conceded that concrete steps were a long way off, but that discussions needed to begin. There are few alternatives if Asia wants to be world player like Europe and the US, he implied:

> The fact that we are open, the fact that we are small, makes us vulnerable to manipulative play by market players with quite [sizeable] resources. How do we tackle that? We cannot close our markets. We cannot overnight enlarge our markets . . . How do we enlarge our markets? By unifying them in one way or another. One way is a common denomination.[ix]

All things considered, the currencies of China, India and other Asian powers will lack the international prestige and trust needed to make them reserve currencies. These countries will thus not threaten the status of the euro or the dollar for a good many years to come.

Europe's master plan

Europe stands alone among the world's regions in another way. It is the region with the most visionary, master plan approach. Unlike US leaders, the current crop of European politicians don't seem content to allow free-market capitalism to take things where it will. They are not happy with the 'muddling through' adopted by the US and other regions. Germany has been a crucial player here. After the Second World War, the nation lacked a sense of identity and has since been seeking to integrate itself into a Europe that is 'post-national'. Other European countries have been infected by this idea, and together, though the end design is not as explicit as some would hope, Europeans are clearly moving in the direction of a federation, based on free market principles and supported by a generous social welfare state.

The ECB has shown how effective this structural approach of the Germans has been. It was the Germans who insisted on an overall plan to construct EMU and the ECB before work was even begun – in contrast to the Italian and French desire to move forward in little steps without first determining the final outcome. It is this concern for the end goal, this laying of value on the long term that is one of Europe's main strengths. (To be sure, this search for perfection may also be one of its principal weaknesses, since it often results in inflexibility and slowness to respond to challenges.) The ECB is just the latest embodiment of that strength. The successful launch of the euro and the ECB has already infused Europe with renewed optimism.

That concern for international diplomacy and willingness to live by multilateral rules contrasts with increasingly uni-lateralist behaviour on the part of the US, a behaviour which is often inward-looking, and which comes at the expense of the international economic system. Adam Posen, analyst at the Institute for International Economics in Washington and an expert on European financial issues, told a German audience in 1998:

I do not exaggerate to say that American political support for the entire postwar economic system is weakening – the putting aside of the fight for the proposed 'Fast Track' trading authority is the tip of the iceberg. A far more important battle over the International Monetary Fund arising out of the Asian crisis is looming. Too often Americans and American politicians make conceptual mistakes in how they think about international issues. They see crises or conflicts in terms of specific countries' interests rather than as precedents and implementations of larger trends. They compare the direct costs of involvement to an imaginary baseline of no effect upon the US, rather than to the reality of potentially great costs of non-involvement.[x]

As Asian countries and nations of the developing world seek a mentor, a model currency for their own currencies, it is the greater sensitivity with which Europeans approach multilateral negotiations which could help the ECB and the euro pose a more credible alternative to American power. So far, Europe's playing of second fiddle on the world political scene has brought considerable benefits. Unlike the US, Europe does not pay the costs of overextending itself militarily or politically, but it does reap the economic benefits that are generated by the order maintained by the US policeman.

It is for this reason that the US has become adamant that Europe start pulling its weight on the international scene. In early 1999, for example, the US insisted that Europe play the lead role in resolving the Kosovo/Albanian crisis in the former Yugoslavia. Precisely because of the advances Europe has made in political and economic integration, there is likely to be continued friction between the US and Europe in sharing the costs of world leadership.

To date, the ECB has inherited the European habit of hiding behind US leadership. The US Treasury and the Federal Reserve continue to play the lender of last resort in international banking crises, and took the lead in trying to find solutions to solving the Asian crisis. The ECB and the Europeans were noticeably quiet. The Europeans piped up with calls for increased transparency in Asian business and lending practises, but the impression created was that they simply were not ready yet to deal with the problem as aggressively and assuredly as the Americans. Volcker worries about 'potential conflict' in a bi-polar world:

> It's true that the United States like to think that they're dominant, probably because they are. This is expressed through its actions within the IMF, the World Bank and through other ad hoc means. If the United States has a disagreement with a united Europe, it is going to be more of a problem than if they had a disagreement with a group of smaller countries. There's a potential danger of conflict. Unfortunately, I think that is going to be a reason why the dollar relationship with the euro is going to swing strongly between strong and weak.[xi]

Professor Martin Feldstein, a former chairman of the President's Council of Economic Advisors, is more fatalistic: '[EMU] will change the political character of Europe in ways that could lead to conflicts in Europe and confrontations with the US'.[xii]

Still, the official line from the Clinton administration, and, the conventional wisdom of most economists, has been that a successful ECB and a strong euro will actually *help* the US economy. A thriving European economy will buoy the world economy and make it easier for US companies to operate in Europe. Moreover, a more assertive Europe on the world scene would help take some of the costly burden of leadership from US shoulders.

The German question

While it has become obvious that further progress in political integration is desirable for Europe to realize its full potential, an important question remains: On what basis will it take place? Despite the convergence of ideologies, there remains a keen awareness that Germany continues to play a dominant role within Europe, which is of some concern to countries with proud traditions like France.

The role of Germany in the European integration process and establishment of the ECB is one that many Europeans, and even the Germans, do not like to talk about. From the beginning of the Maastricht Treaty negotiations, the Bundesbank was taken as the model for the ECB. There were several reasons. First, because the Bundesbank operated according to an ideology – the need for low inflation as a prerequisite for long-term growth – that proved superior to other ideologies within Europe over time. Second, the Bundesbank established a fine record of actually meeting its goal of maintaining low inflation. Third, unlike the Netherlands or other countries which also showed favourable records on low inflation, Germany's economic power within Europe was so decisive that its currency became the *de facto* anchor currency for the European monetary system. The Bundesbank therefore accumulated exclusive experience and proved itself in a leadership role throughout the political and economic trials of the 1970s, 1980s and 1990s – in a way that other central banks simply could not. Finally, the Bundesbank was already based on a decentralized structure, with a central directorate and a group of state central banks, which was exactly the sort of structure that the Europeans could duplicate as a draft for their own federal central bank. In personnel decisions, it was the Bundesbank's Hans Tietmeyer who gave his support to Wim Duisenberg in bilateral talks with Alexandre Lamfalussy, the president of the European Monetary Institute, before Lamfalussy proposed Duisenberg as a candidate for the ECB's first president. It was the Germans who stood by Duisenberg and the Dutch government when the French proposed their own candidate, Jean-Claude Trichet. There is a view in France – indeed, it is partly true – that Duisenberg was the 'German candidate' and is considered part of a 'German camp'.

The Germans also dominate the formulation of the monetary policy strategy for the bank. Otmar Issing, the former Bundesbank's chief economist, was appointed as the ECB's chief economist and drew up the final proposal for monetary policy strategy for the ECB's governing council. The council agreed to this proposal, almost without change. It was Issing's protegés, Hans-Joachim Klöckers and Klaus Masuch who did most of the legwork on the proposal in its draft stages. They are also the ones who continue to scour press releases and speeches of the board members – particularly when it comes to monetary policy comment – to make sure they conform with the ECB's monetary policy orthodoxy. In ECB governing council meetings, Otmar Issing gives his presentation of economic developments shortly after Duisenberg opens the meetings every fortnight.

At the same time, the Germans have been fair at the ECB. They have agreed to arrangements for an evenly representative staff. It is due to their influence and experience that that they have ended up in key positions. It is a German who heads the communications division. It is also a German, Hanspeter Scheller, whom both insiders and outsiders admit was the key person at the EMI in making sure that the entire project ran smoothly, who worked tirelessly from his office in the Eurotower helping advise other central bankers during their negotiations with governments over the drawing up of relevant central banking legislation to comply with the requirements of the Maastricht Treaty.

Observations of German influence, therefore, should not be construed as arguments that this influence is insidious and should give rise to concern about the merits of moving ahead. The credibility of Germany's actions is manifest in the positive direction Europe has moved in over the past few decades. It is precisely because of the fear of German power that German leaders have pushed for quick integration with EU institutions. This way, others can participate in joint decision-making processes, and Germans cannot be criticized for dominating by themselves. Nowhere is this more true than at the ECB. Before, the Bundesbank *de facto* dominated European monetary policy. Now, by sharing their power with Europeans, the other Europeans have a seat at the table. France, for one, has been exceptionally shrewd in its diplomacy. It has ensured that the next president of the ECB will be French for a full eight years – and the vice president of the ECB under Duisenberg is also French.

One crucial test of the ECB's success lies then in what I have described as the psychological sphere: the ECB's biggest challenge is to convince Europeans that, although it has been set up under heavy German influence, it serves the interests of Europe as a whole. Inevitably, one of the instruments it will have to use in that battle is transparency. The reason why the central bank must make its decisions behind closed doors and with no record of the protocol – there is a person who scribbles down the 'minutes' of the meeting, but those are inevitably subjective and only released after 30 years – is because the bank fears sensitivities might arise in EU countries over its policies. The ECB must help reduce these sensitivities if it is to win the psychological game. This can come only through intense dialogue with the national governments and through communicating with domestic populations. Only then will Europe be able to nurture the trust to proceed further in the direction of unity.

The factors of economic ideology, credibility, power, and institutional desirability that made the Bundesbank the model for the ECB have given Germany the ability to influence and shape the structure of the EU. As we have seen in this book, Germany's political-economic order in the post-war period – a superior monetary policy, a system of free market competition governed by a strong anti-cartel legislation and accompanied by a strong social insurance net, its dominant economic size, its constructive engagement in European and world politics through peaceful, careful diplomacy – have brought about its dominance of the European political integration process. Granted, the French-German tandem has been crucial for progress in Europe, since without France's approval, Germany would have been stymied in any move towards greater integration. But it is Germany that continues to be the lead architect of Europe's project of political integration, even if its influence is often wielded behind the scenes. Sometimes, this influence is less subtle. It was Germany's recognition of an independent Croatia in the early 1990s that many critics say was responsible for throwing Europe's southern rim into sudden turmoil as the Yugoslav nation disintegrated. The rest of the EU had little choice but to fall in line behind Germany. It was also partly Germany's instinctive reluctance to participate in armed warfare – because of its history – that hampered Europe from making a more decisive contribution after war broke out between Serbia and its neighbours – first Croatia, then Bosnia, and finally, Kosovo. Europe's other major powers (France and Britain) showed no ability to lead the rest of Europe forward to resolving the crisis. If the proposal for a European defence arm within NATO is achieved, it will be because Germany supports it and becomes a major – and most likely dominant – contributor to the project.

Germany's historical and trade ties with Eastern Europe will also put it in a commanding position to broker the final terms of agreement under which Eastern European countries are admitted to the EU, and similarly, to participate in the single currency project and the European Central Bank. Within the future economy of a wider EU, Germany will be at its heart, and the ECB's monetary policy will (again, because of Germany's size) inevitably be geared more to Germany's economic pace than that of other countries.

In conclusion, the further integration of Europe will take place under German leadership because there are few alternatives. The major risk to the ECB project remains the national sensitivities that can flare up if the ECB policy is not deemed appropriate to local needs. Germany will push vehemently for further political integration to avoid just this sort of dissonance. The question remains whether France and Britain will resist, or whether those two countries will gradually reinterpret and redefine their national interests as being synonymous with European integration.

NOTES

[i] Interview with author, December 10, 1998.
[ii] Paul Kennedy, *Preparing for the Twenty-First Century*. (Fontana Press, London: 1993), p. 260, 261.
[iii] S. P. Huntington, 'The US – Decline or Renewal?' *Foreign Affairs*, vol. 67, no. 2 (Winter 1988-89), pp. 93-94. Cited in Paul Kennedy, *Preparing for the Twenty-First Century*. (Fontana Press, London: 1993), pp. 258-259.
[iv] Paul Krugman, 'America the Boastful,' in *Foreign Affairs*. May/June 1998.

pp. 33-45.
^v Jeffrey Garten, 'The Euro will Turn Europe into a Superpower,' *Business Week*. May 4, 1998.
^{vi} *Business Week*. April 27, 1998. p. 28.
^{vii} Survey published by US investment bank Merrill Lynch. Cited in *Financial Times*, December 16, 1998.
^{viii} *The Economist*, November 14, 1998. p. 107.
^{ix} *Financial Times*, December 31, 1998/January 1, 1999.
^x Adam S. Posen. 'Agreement without Convergence: Some Guidelines for Translantic Economic Relations.' Remarks made at a conference sponsored by the Social Democratic Party of Germany in Berlin, January 19, 1998.
^{xi} Interview with author, in December 1998.
^{xii} *The Observer*, April 19, 1998. '*Emu* Crusader Conquers Wall Street.'

CHAPTER TWELVE

Learning To Walk

Alas, Europe! Since this book was first published in March 1999, the euro has fallen dramatically against the dollar. At one point, it was 30 per cent lower than it started, hitting 82.28 cents on Oct 26, 2000.

The currency's fall translates into lopping off almost a full third of the value of the European economy – and was enough in 2000 for California to overtake France as the fifth largest economy in the world. At times, the European media has castigated the European Central Bank for the fate of the euro. In particular, ECB president Wim Duisenberg has been the focus of blame: 'Dim Wim,' announced one British newspaper headline in 2000, after a gaffe last year in which he said the ECB wouldn't intervene to support the currency even as it hit new lows.

The euro bounced upward at the end of 2000, but floundered again over the course of 2001. It flirted briefly with its Oct. 2000 low, and then tried to climb upward again, helped by evidence that the U.S. economy was slowing. The terrorist attack in the U.S. on Sept. 11, 2001 nudged the euro over 92 cents, still much lower than when it started. In April, 2000, an association of German banks despaired so much for the ailing euro that it imported seven 'euro' kangaroos from Australia in an effort to win the hearts of Europeans (and, of course, to associate the euro with rebound potential). Not even that has worked. Reports that Americans have begun snapping up villas on the Riviera, aided by their new-found dollar wealth, have added to European angst.

The euro had already started falling as the first edition of this book went to press in March 1999. Then, differences in economic growth between Europe and the US, and political problems posed by Oskar Lafontaine – the German finance minister who was pressuring the ECB to lower rates – contributed to the euro's decline. These factors were mentioned in the first edition. However, no one predicted that the euro would keep falling.

This chapter recounts and explains some of the major developments since the single currency launched on 1 January 1999. Theories for the euro's fall range the gamut: from external factors beyond the control of policy makers in the ECB and European governments, to inexperienced leadership and inadequate policies inside the bank. The debate over the reasons for the euro's woes continues, but it seems clear that economic fundamentals are part of the picture.

One reason for the strong dollar mentioned by Federal Reserve Chairman Alan Greenspan has been the difference between US and European growth rates. This caused investors to flee to the US, thinking they would get a better return, and propped up the dollar because outsiders would have to buy dollars in order to make such investments – at the expense of the euro. But when US growth slowed in late 2000, it was widely assumed the euro would make a come-back. It didn't happen, and it left many policy experts, both inside and outside the ECB, befuddled. Within the bank, I am told there is no agreement on the reasons for the euro's decline.

Grasping for an explanation, many europhiles complained the market is distorted. For irrational reasons, they argued, currency traders were discounting the euro by 'up to 30 per cent,' as the European-dominated International Monetary Fund put it in a November 2000 report. Paul Krugman, an American economist who has watched euro developments, concluded in September 2000 that the euro was being driven by herd mentality, not economic fundamentals.

However, if the euro was truly undervalued, there'd be plenty of profit-seeking traders willing to bet big money on it. The prospect of an easy 30 per cent return on their investment would be too great to ignore. There must be some reason why the potential of huge profits didn't make them move. Blaming the markets would be letting the Europeans off too easily. True, markets can be wrong in the short-term, but rarely is that the case consistently over the course of years.

Some observers have pointed to other, more plausible reasons why the market has downgraded the euro. One is the perceived lack of trust in the ECB management capabilities, generated by a series of bungled policy pronouncements over the last couple of years. Another is a lack of faith in Europe's ability to restructure its business, labour, social and other laws that are perceived to hamper economic growth – and so returns on investment. Investors seem to believe that the unfettered US market was better equipped to handle change in an increasingly dynamic global economy.

Others point out that exchange rates closely reflect differences in labour productivity. America's red-hot economy at the end of the 1990s was partly fueled by growth in productivity, and many economists said this explained why the dollar had risen so strongly. They argue that in the short term, European productivity is likely to catch up, or even surpass, American productivity. However, views about future labour productivity growth differ widely.

Finally, some economists point to technical factors for the euro's decline, for example temporary bottlenecks in the liquidity of the new currency, bottlenecks that might be worked out as the ECB improves calculations about how much money supply the euro area needs, a process that will be aided after the world's other central banks finish consolidating their European foreign reserves. Though even that argument can remain valid only temporarily.

Bill McDonough, President of the New York Federal Reserve Bank, has given one of the most balanced explanations for the euro's weakness. Over the last few decades, exchange rates have generally trended along the rate of so-called 'purchase power parity,' or the rate at which users in regions can afford to purchase the same amount of goods and services with their currency. Between the euro and the dollar, that rate is approximately when 1 euro = $1 to $1.10, according to Fed calculations. However, history has shown that two other sets of factors contributed to divergence from that rate. The first is the difference in productivity. Just as the dollar was weak through the 1970s because of slower US productivity, the dollar rose strongly over the course of 1999 and 2000 because of higher productivity. The second is expectations for economic growth over the next six months. Falling expectations about European economic growth so far this year have contributed to a continued weakness in the euro.

In normal times, there isn't anything wrong with having a weak currency. A weak currency can help an economy by lowering the price of exported goods in foreign markets. A weak currency also helps attract outside capital, as foreign investors seek to exploit cheaper real estate and labour prices for their own production.

But the symbolic effect of a falling euro, at its birth, was devastating in one key respect: it pushed out the date at which Britain will join for at least two years. For the British, the euro's decline looked like a lack of control. The ECB's desperate, but unsuccessful, attempt to stem its fall – including currency intervention – didn't help. Denmark, another country that remained outside of the eurozone at its founding in 1999, voted against the euro again in a September 2000 referendum. The vote served to bolster British scepticism. At the euro's founding, the Brits had also chosen a wait-and-see approach, characteristic of its historical relationship with the continent. By 2001, opinion poll leaders predicted that a victory for a 'yes' campaign by Prime Minister Tony Blair in the current parliament would be a virtual impossibility.

The addition of Britain would have helped Europe equal the size of the US economy. By dissuading Britain from joining, the euro's decline has torpedoed hopes of that happening anytime soon.

Aside from the euro's decline, there have been four other notable developments at the ECB since the first edition – some of which are related to the euro's woes, some of which are not.

First, the euro's introduction has brought benefits to Europe, mainly in the form of a deeper, more liquid bond market. Second, the ECB completed the first half of an entire *interest rate cycle*. A full cycle refers to the period in which an economy moves from peak to trough and back to peak again – in other words, a full circle. During the slow down, a central bank first lowers interest rates in order to boost economic activity. When economic activity heats up again, the bank raises rates in order to stamp out the threat of inflation.

For the ECB, that cycle began in December 1998, when the ECB helped coordinate the first euro-zone rate cut because of slowing growth across the continent. In spring of 1999, the bank cut rates once more. However, later in the year, the bank switched tack, and raised interest rates seven times in a row. Finally, in May, August and September of 2001, it cut rates again, indicating the first cycle of *rate increases* had been completed. Taken as a whole, the ECB's record hasn't been as bad as its critics claim – at least until mid-2001, when the ECB embroiled itself in a major new controversy about its direction. Also notable is that the ECB's interest-rate moves during its first 18 months followed the US Fed's moves by about four to six months.

ECB interest-rate moves

Date:	Refinancing Rate
April 8, 1999	2.5
November 4, 1999	3.0
February 3, 2000	3.25
April 27, 2000	3.75
June 8, 2000	4.25
August 31, 2000	4.50
October 5, 2000	4.75
May 10, 2001	4.50
August 31, 2001	4.25
September 17, 2001	3.75

Third, the ECB, after much reluctance, chose to try to boost the euro artificially in the currency markets by buying euros and selling dollars, a so-called 'intervention' strategy that had mixed results at best.

Fourth, and perhaps most significantly, the ECB's leaders exhibited continued difficulty in communicating its policy to market actors.

This chapter outlines these problems and discusses some of the possible reasons for them.

1. The promise made true:

Despite the controversy surrounding the ECB, the euro's introduction has helped European financial markets, businesses and the economy in the ways it was supposed to. It created a bigger and more liquid European stock and bond market. This is important because small and large European companies can now more easily issue stocks and bonds to get the financing they need to grow quickly. Quick growth is essential for high-tech companies seeking to dominate their sector, or maintain market share against US competitors. By the same token, big companies in mature industries can more easily get financing for mergers and acquisitions during consolidation. Investors, too, will be lured to Europe by deeper financial markets. They'll be more willing to invest in stocks or bonds knowing that markets are more liquid, and thus less likely to fluctuate wildly by relatively small moves of capital in and out of Europe.

No longer will the US enjoy a strong advantage in its capital markets. The value of European mergers and acquisitions in 2000 was roughly double that of 1998, the year before the euro was born. The US saw no such increase.[i] Within 18 months of the euro's introduction, the size of the overall euro-denominated bond market increased by 16 per cent. The market for euro-denominated bonds issued by non-financial corporations grew 25 per cent.

To mention just a couple of the early examples:
- Fiat, the Italian auto maker, issued five billion euro's worth of bonds within the first two years of the euro's birth.

When it had last issued lira bonds in 1997, it had issued the equivalent of only 200 million euros;

- Buhrmann NV, a Dutch office supply company, issued a high-yield bond to fund the purchase of the even larger Corporate Express Inc of the US;
- Unilever bought American companies like Best Foods and Ben & Jerry's ice cream. Though the company used mostly cash at the time, it has since restructured its large debt by issuing euro bonds;
- Freddie Mac, the US government sponsored mortgage agency, announced it will issue 20 billion euros of debt each year;
- The Philippines has already issued bonds in euros, and Malaysia had plans do the same.[ii]

Interest rate cycle completed

The bank managed its first year and a half deftly. After the coordinated rate cut in December 1999, the ECB dropped rates again on April 8, to 2.5 per cent from 3 per cent, prompted by Europe's deteriorating economy. The half-point move was larger than the expected quarter-point move, and was taken as evidence of the ECB's desire to take the markets by surprise. Duisenberg said the move was meant to signal that the bank was done with cutting rates for the time being. 'That is it,' he said at the time.

However, conditions changed over the spring and early summer. Oil prices continued to rise, and the low euro was beginning to cause concern. By July, Duisenberg began guiding the markets for the first time, saying that a tightening bias was 'gradually creeping in' to the ECB's interest rate deliberations. In November 1999, the bank raised rates back to 3 per cent. Throughout 1999, the euro fell against the dollar, but the European bankers were steady in arguing that the fall didn't bother them. That changed in February 2000, when Duisenberg first indicated discontent with the euro's weakness. Later that month, the ECB raised rates again to 3.25, and Duisenberg said that the risk ahead for interest rate policy continued to be on the 'upside'. That was good guidance: The bank raised rates four more times over the subsequent nine months, finishing at 4.75 per cent. Each time, the bank's leaders openly said that the euro's fall was contributing to inflation because it led to the higher prices of imported goods, like oil.

However, there were bumps along the way. In March 2000, for example, the ECB raised rates on a day when it didn't have a news conference, the first time in its 15-month life to do so – again, seen by outsiders as a way of a catching the markets off guard. The markets had expected the ECB would act at their next meeting. In June, board member Otmar Issing recognized the irritation in the market, saying: 'The verdict among most, if not all, 'our watchers' seems to be that – broadly speaking – the ECB has done a good job but has not been very effective in presenting and explaining itself.'

ECB intervention

The exchange rate, according to economist and Nobel Laureate Robert Mundell, is 'one of the most important prices for its economy.' Beginning in late 1999, Mundell, professor of economics at Columbia University, began calling for Europe and the US to intervene to stop the euro's fall. In a 2000 article entitled 'Threat to Prosperity,' he argued that the biggest danger to world prosperity arises from wide swings in the exchange rates of the dollar, the euro, and the yen, that are not based on economic fundamentals. The central banks, he argued, should intervene and dampen these swings, and such steps should be reinforced by other steps by the US, Europe and Japan towards the ultimate development of one currency managed by a world central bank. Classical economists had been in favour of fixing currencies. John Stuart Mill, Mundell noted, deplored the nationalism that made currency union impossible in the nineteenth century. 'So much of barbarism . . . still remains in the transactions of most civilized nations, that almost all independent countries choose to assert their nationality by having, to their own inconvenience and that of their neighbors, a peculiar currency of their own.' Mundell lamented that

throughout history, the dominant country has rejected mean-
ingful monetary reform, fearing a weakening of its monopolistic
currency position.

In general Europeans are readier to intervene in their
economies than the Americans. And so, on Sept. 14, 2000, with
the euro still in a steady descent against the dollar, and inflation
on the rise, the ECB flirted with intervention when it began
selling $2.6 billion worth of dollars and yen, and buy euros. The
effect was minimal: the euro moved up slightly, but fell back
again. Publicly, Duisenberg said intervention was not the
motive, and that the assets sold were merely interest on the
ECB's foreign currency reserves. In hindsight, however, the
bank was just warming up for a slew of new intervention
attempts. A week later, on Sept. 22, the Group of Seven intervened jointly to support the euro, but again with minimal
success. That was the first and last time that the US participated.
Later, in November, the ECB intervened several times, after
data showed eurozone inflation rising to 2.8 per cent – far
higher than the ECB's accepted target of 2 per cent. The IMF
appeared to support the ECB's efforts, when it released a
separate report after the interventions saying it believed the
euro was undervalued by 30 per cent.

None of the interventions were decisive, although some
bankers argued that the temporary blips in the euro served an
important psychological function. 'First and foremost, it broke
the psychology of a one-way market that seemed to be
predominating since September,' said Peter Fisher, executive
vice president of the New York Federal Reserve, shortly after
the intervention. Duisenberg, too, stressed that intervention
was not to reach a specific euro-dollar target but mainly
designed 'to break the psychology that the euro could move
only in one direction.'

Europe-US relations

The Europeans will have to go it alone for the foreseeable
future. The Bush Administration is even more sceptical of
intervention than the Clinton White House. George W. Bush's

top economic advisor, former Federal Reserve Governor Lawrence Lindsey, criticised the US participation in efforts to boost the euro in September 2000.

Worse, diplomatic relations between the US and Europe have cooled since Bush entered the White House.

In fact, the US-Europe relationship has declined markedly, especially after the new defence secretary, Donald Rumsfeld, made a trip to Munich in February 2001 to address the allies for the first time and did not once use the words 'European Union.'

The lack of cooperation between the two currency zones has also created a leadership void for countries outside of the US, European or Japanese currency jurisdictions. Global financial forces are buffeting these countries, rocking their economies like small boats on a stormy sea. The ECB and the Federal Reserve did work closely in the wake of the 2001 terrorist attack in the U.S. They supplied $300 billion in liquidity to the financial system to head off a crisis in the world's bond and stock markets. It is not clear, however, how closely cooperation will be replicated by the regions' political leaders.

Economists like Mundell argue that it is not healthy that one of the only options open to smaller countries is to fix their currency to one of the G-3, a situation he says is reminiscent of nineteenth century monetary colonialism.

Roughly 40 per cent of the world's output comes from countries outside of those three economic zones. Their inability to ensure monetary stability threatens to disrupt economic activity – which could haunt the G-3's own economic prosperity.

The euro area, measured by the volume of transactions, will likely exceed the existing dollar area by the end of the current decade. However, the expansion of the euro area – to include a vast swathe of Eastern Europe and perhaps other countries on its periphery – is being accompanied by a simultaneous expansion of the dollar area.

Panama was the first country outside of the US to adopt the dollar, almost a century ago. However, in 1990, Ecuador shocked its neighbors last year by embracing the dollar as a part of a desperate effort to avert an economic crisis. In 1991, El

Salvador also joined the dollar zone. Meanwhile, Guatemala has passed a law allowing companies to pay salaries in dollars and banks to set up dollar bank accounts. Nicaragua, Honduras and Costa Rica are studying similar ideas. Argentina has pegged its currency to the dollar, and many of its stores accept dollars.

This trend of division into two, three or possibly four (with the rise of China) zones of influence is likely to continue.

Communication problems:

So why would the ECB get such a bad rap when it is trying its best to implement good policy, and by most accounts, was succeeding, at least until mid-2001? Indeed, before spring 2001, the delphic Alan Greenspan was getting more criticism for his handling of interest rate policy than the ECB was. And according to insiders, decisions at the bank have so far been made by consensus, not by vote-taking – hardly a sign of internal conflict under Duisenberg's leadership.

Clearly, one factor is that the ECB has no track record, and so has to try harder to explain its decisions. However, there was a more profound reason why the markets – and the press – became frustrated with the ECB. Put simply, the controversy surrounding the euro centres around one man: Wim Duisenberg. His verbal foibles began from the beginning, in 1998, when he announced he'd reached an agreement with French President Jacque Chirac: in return for gaining French acceptance for his candidacy, Duisenberg would step down as ECB president in 2002 – four years before his term officially ended. The markets saw this as a sign of giving into political pressure, however they reserved judgement, not sure whether the joke might actually be on Chirac (after all, Duisenberg could theoretically snub Chirac and stay on for the full term).

Almost immediately afterwards, Duisenberg seemed to retract his agreement, creating insecurity in the markets. The waffling seemed to reflect a history of other flip-flops in his career. From the birth of the euro, Duisenberg seems to have failed to learn from his mistakes. In April, 1999, when the euro was just four months old, and just as its fall against the dollar began to accelerate, Duisenberg announced that the ECB's policy towards the euro was one of 'neglect.' Again, he would retract the statement a year later when the ECB began desperately trying to prop it up through oral and fiscal intervention.

Watching-Duisenberg, an observer can't help but get the feeling that he is exhausted from work, and that his heart isn't really in the position. He once stumbled in late to a Frankfurt press conference in 1999 with his shirt unbuttoned and his tie askew. He is the absent-minded professor – charming enough, and distinguished with his thatch of white hair. A touch of the curmudgeon, and dangerously aloof when it comes to living up to the duties demanded of him.

It is understandable that the other European bankers trusted him with the position of president (they went back years together, and knew he would uphold the German orthodoxy), but they overlooked the amount of stamina and energy the job required. In September 2000, Duisenberg didn't show up at a twice-yearly meeting of eurozone finance ministers and central bankers in Versailles. Instead, he flew to Canada for a different conference. When Duisenberg testified that month before the European parliament, a French Gaullist member heckled him: 'Is anyone flying the plane? Is it a question of the plane being faulty or the pilot incompetent? Should you not resign?' Former French President Valéry Giscard d'Estaing added: 'I have always thought the ECB's first president should be a man whose international authority would be immediately recognized ... Whatever the personal merits of Mr. Duisenberg, it was a casting mistake.'[iii]

The irony is that Duisenberg means well for the euro. To understand why the markets are unable to tolerate his verbal gaffes is to appreciate the historical baggage built up between financial markets and Europe's political class. That baggage is what this book spends much of its time explaining.

During the decades of negotiations over currency alignments, European markets had remained unsettled by the prospect of a single currency. They feared that political disunity at the European level could endanger the independence of the central bankers. Specifically, they dreaded the *dirigiste* tradition of French bureaucrats. That suspicion remained even as the European political leadership agreed to market demands that an independent central bank be a cornerstone of their plan – one based on the successful model of the Bundesbank.

After the euro was introduced in 1999, pro-intervention sentiment remained strong in some segments of Europe's political circles. German Finance minister Oskar Lafontaine openly pushed for more intervention on exchange rates, called upon the ECB to lower rates, and generally sought to assert more political cohesion among finance ministers vis-à-vis the bankers – moves that in the end contributed to his downfall in March 2000. France's leading newspaper, *Le Monde*, wrote a wistful editorial at the time, saying that Lafontaine 'shared the concern of the French not to leave the management of the eurozone only in the hands of central bankers, and to accompany the creation of the single currency with a real coordination of European economic and social policies.'

Because of such periodic threats against the orthodoxy of independence, the markets had demanded a *quid pro quo*. The ECB was to provide clear, transparent guidelines on how it would conduct monetary policy, and it would write these guidelines itself – without political interference. These guidelines would based on tried and true maxims of the past, for example setting a rough ceiling for inflation, and using interest rate policy to get there. 'Independence' as it was understood by the markets, meant the ability to implement these goals without outside interference.

However, what independence didn't mean was freedom from any guidelines *per se*. The market wanted the ECB to be fiercely independent, cunning, and internally consistent. However, if the ECB veered too far away from its stated guidelines, questions could arise about its true motivations. Suspicions would arise about whether policy was being compromised because of political deals being cut. The market wanted affirmation that political or national differences between the members of the ECB's governing council, or pressure from outside politicians, wouldn't get in the way of sound monetary policy.

The problem, from 1999 through 2001, is that the ECB, in a number of instances, failed to deliver on these counts. Issing acknowledged that in his June 2000 comment. The first major mistake, however, came later, during the ECB's intervention to prop up the euro. When the euro continued to hit record lows against the dollar in the fall of 2000, ECB bankers began to back away from statement they'd made in 1998 and 1999 indicating a reluctance to intervene in the currency markets.

Oskar Lafontaine, the German social democratic finance minister during the year leading up to monetary union, had sought to gain support among Japanese, US and European leadership to intervene to set fixed exchange rates, and he was criticized by the bankers for wanting to intervene in currency matters. However, in late 2000, the bankers evidently became desperate to find a way to stop the euro's fall. Despite seven interest rate hikes, they'd failed to bring an end to the euro's fall. They expressed concern that it could cause inflation by making the cost of imported goods more expensive. Thus, the Bank slowly started preparing the financial markets with statements suggesting that intervention was a tool it might exploit after all.

The ensuing interventions had little success, however, and in October 2000 the euro was still struggling badly. So all hell broke loose when, on October 16, the markets learned how Duisenberg answered a question by a journalist at *The Times* of London, about whether it would be appropriate to intervene if the Mideast crisis sparked a sharp fall in the euro. Duisenberg's answer: 'I wouldn't think so.' It was the exact opposite of what the ECB had been priming the market for. The euro fell sharply after the statement, nearing a new low.

Germany's respected Süddeutsche Zeitung newspaper ran the headline: 'Deadly Sin of a Banker.' The UK's Daily Telegraph asked: Will Dim Wim ever learn? Has the president of the European Central Bank not noticed that every time he opens his mouth, the currency he is supposed to protect and preserve takes another sickening dive?' France's Liberation bemoaned:

'Duisenberg: No one would be sorry to see him go.'

It wasn't just the press. The market's respect for Duisenberg faltered too. When a rumor spread on October 17, 2000 that Duisenberg had resigned, the euro actually rallied briefly. And the German and Belgian members of the ECB governing council expressed differences with Duisenberg. The German banker, Welteke, in a thinly veiled slap, said intervention 'can be successful only if one does not talk about it.' On October 19, the euro sank to a low of 83.24 US cents. The euro was falling even though the US tech market bubble had been pricked, and the US economy was clearly slowing – factors that should have depressed the dollar, not the euro.

The next day, the embattled Duisenberg announced that he would heed the advice of colleagues and critics and stop answering questions about intervention: 'I accept the advice,' Duisenberg said.

However, the euro continued to reel, and hit its low thus far of 82.28 cents on October 6, or a level 30 per cent lower than the rate at which it started.

The lesson of consistency should have been learned by the ECB. To start with, millions of citizens scrutinize the ECB's every move for reasons other than mere verbal clarity. Europeans affiliate the ECB officials with the 'eurocrats' – the public servants that work in Brussels – and all of the perks and privileges that they are perceived to enjoy. Indeed, there are similarities. ECB employees are paid very well – paid more, for example, than the employees of the national central banks, and they enjoy special 'EU' tax levels and other perks of eurocrats – for example, an 'expatriate' supplement of 16 per cent of their salaries. Over the decades, public resentment of 'eurocrats' of the European Commission intensified because of such treatment, a resentment that was inflamed in 1999 when reports of corruption led to the firing of the commission's entire executive staff.

The ECB hasn't been able to shake such negative associations. Thus, when it comes to policy matters, any deviance by the ECB from its stated policy guidelines raises suspicions that it, too, might be abusing its privilege of relative political unaccountability. There arose a readiness among the public, and in the markets, to pounce as soon as Duisenberg or the other bankers appeared to exercise discretion that exceeded that vested in it by the EMU Treaty.

There was also a lingering suspicion that the bankers – in the run-up to EMU – had been too eager to focus on the inflation target to the exclusion of everything else. The bankers had given themselves a mandate to focus solely on battling inflation, to avoid political meddling. But at a time when Europe's economy struggled, markets began to wonder whether the bankers might begin to revisit their decision. Perhaps the rigid focus *was* too stiff, after all. Even the Bundesbank at times had begun to weary of its own strict monetary guidelines. And during the late 1990s, there had been widespread praise of the Fed's policy of making monetary policy decisions by mixing considerations of economic growth as well as inflation. The 1990s proved to be the longest period of expansion in US history.

All this was put under a magnifying glass in the spring of 2001, during the ECB's second major controversy. By March 2001, all of the major central banks, including Japan, the US, the UK, Australia and Canada had lowered interest rates to stave off slower growth. The ECB alone had resisted the trend, saying the economic outlook still looked robust and risks of inflation still existed.

In late March, however, some members of the ECB council began signifying a change, led by Otmar Issing. Issing announced in late March that over the course of the month, risks of slower growth had increased, and he stated that the inflation pressures were only 'a temporary phenomenon.' French banker Trichet seemed to express similar views. These statements came from two of the ECB's most resolute anti-inflationary hawks, and together they seemed to indicate that the bank was preparing the market for a rate cut.

The markets, meanwhile, assumed the comments reflected the feelings of the council as a whole. However, a few days later, Ernst Welteke, the Bundesbank president cautioned: 'It is not the time to speculate about changes.' After the March 29 meeting, it became clear the ECB was deeply split. Duisenberg appeared to be part of a contingent that was resisting a rate change, along with Welteke, and apparently Klaus Liebscher of Austria and Vitor Constancio of Portugal. This group prevailed over a group consisting of Trichet, Issing and Noyer. Because of the sensitivity of their decision not to reduce rates, Noyer proposed that that council jointly jot down a script for Duisenberg and others to follow in public speaking engagements – the first time the council had taken such a measure.[iv] In it, the memo outlined a 'wait-and-see' policy.

However, the ECB's appointed spokesperson, Wim Duisenberg, wasn't effective in crafting and voicing his opinion or that of the majority. Duisenberg did signal a difference with Issing, that is, that 'some factors still argue for caution' on inflation. And while Duisenberg predicted growth of just under 3 per cent, Issing was suggesting growth closer to 2 to 2.5 per cent – perhaps reflecting his concern about the German economy, which appeared to be cooling quicker than other European economies. And Belgium's central banker, Guy Quaden, announced that business sentiment fell across the euro-zone in April to the lowest level since June 1999. That came after a leading sentiment index in Germany also slumped to the lowest level over the same period. However, at no time was there any sign of consistent guidance by one person, as there is in the case of the Federal Reserve.

The ECB's internal debate was made more difficult in April by the exhortation of outsiders. First, the International Monetary Fund called upon the bank to reduce rates. Then Germany's new finance minister Hans Eichel, called upon the bank to 'consider the slowing economy' in its decision making. That, in turn, was followed by a pledge by Didier Reynders, the spokesman for the euro-zone's finance ministers at the time, that the ministers would 'repeat concern about the economic slowdown for the central bank to draw its own conclusions.' The Austrian finance minister, Karl-Heinz Grasser, did so twice in mid-April. Duisenberg's response: 'I hear but I do not listen.'

After Duisenberg's wait-and-see statement, it took only a month for that stance to be severely tested. On May 9, a report showed that the German construction industry contracted sharply, and was bringing Germany's manufacturing sector down with it. Meanwhile, the country's unemployment rate had risen four months in a row. Dieter Kübacher, a Bundesbank council member, said he believed a recession was possible, and other economists echoed his concern. Still, none of this changed a simple fact: The ECB's mandate was to check inflation, and inflation was still on the high side of its corridor of acceptability. Simply put, inflation was above the ECB's ceiling target of 2 per cent.

With no preparation of the markets at all, the ECB, meeting on May 10, cut interest rates by .25 of a percentage point. Duisenberg tried to spin: 'It's not our policy to surprise the markets, but sometimes its unavoidable,' he said. He also said: 'It can now be concluded that there is no threat to price stability over the medium term.'

The markets were caught off-guard, with one poll showing that 19 of 20 economists had expected rates to stay steady. They were perplexed by the bank's move: In fact, Christian Noyer had effectively ruled out a change only a week before: 'We have kept and are keeping interest rates on hold,' he had said.[v] Similarly, Ernst Welteke, president of the Bundesbank, had told reporters: 'For now, its wait-and-see – on hold.'[vi]

The markets were also displeased because the bank's expressed mandate was not to lower rates to support economic growth. Rather, it was to hold strictly to its inflation target of 2 per cent or lower. Inflation was running at 2.6 per cent, and while that was expected to taper off with the signs of slower growth, it was still high enough to expect the bank to to implement means to make sure that it was contained – not threaten to push it the other way with a monetary easing. Sure, inflation was below 2 per cent once the gas and food components were factored out, something the bank also pointed out. But inflation didn't seem to be tapering off yet.

The markets were specifically unhappy with two of the reasons the bank gave for the easing. One was that union wage negotiations remained moderate, which Duisenberg said was a 'very positive factor,' and so now was no longer an inflation threat. But as recently as May 3, Issing, the chief economist, described the risk of inflationary wage deals as 'the main upward risk to price stability over the medium term.' There had been no apparent change between the two dates that would signify such a radical difference in views.

Second, the ECB said that its money supply growth data had been overestimated by a full half-percentage point. Once money market fund units held by people outside the euro-zone were excluded, the bank announced, M3 holdings ran at an average annual rate of 4.3 per cent between January and March, instead of the 4.8 per cent originally estimated. Suddenly, the money rate growth was below the ECB's reference value, or loose target, of 4.5 per cent. Lowering rates, which helps inject cash into the economy, would help the ECB get M3 back to its target. However, this came with little warning. On May 3, only a week before, Issing had said that the ECB might possibly revise downward its growth estimate because of distortions, but had indicated that the decision might take some time: 'The ECB is trying to better identify such factors and hopes to be able to eliminate them from the data in the course of the year,' he said. But why, if the bank was really attempting to be transparent, would the changes be made secretly and then suddenly released as a reason for a rate cut? And also, why would a reference value of slightly below 4.5 be used as a reason for a rate cut when the bank had been relaxed about long periods of M3 growth rates above the target range?

These were questions that seemed to grate on the market, and raised the suspicion that monetary targets were being wheeled out as an excuse for cutting rates. It was a blow to the assumption that the bank was sticking to clear, transparent policy guidelines. It was an 'object lesson in how to give people what they want and offend them at the same time,' said Nigel Anderson, of the Royal Bank of Scotland, at the time. 'It shows that you cannot believe anything they say before or after a meeting,' said Robert Prior-Wandesford, European economist at HSBC Investment bank.[vii] 'We have to seek reasons for why the ECB has shown a certain amount of flexibility in interpreting its mandate of price stability,' chimed in a study by the respected London-based Centre for Economic Policy Research.

It didn't help that after the rate cut, evidence of increasing inflation seemed to grow. Less that two weeks later, for example, data was released that showed German inflation growing at 3 per cent or more in April. Europe's inflation, meanwhile, rose to 2.9 per cent, from 2.6 per cent in March. In May, it soared to 3.4 per cent, an eight-year high. Duisenberg argued that the rise was triggered mainly by the rise in food and energy prices, and by the weakness of the euro. However, in May, for the first time, even 'core' inflation, excluding food and energy prices, climbed at a rate of 2.1 per cent – above the ECB's ceiling of 2 per cent. ECB officials argued, however, that a slowing economy would reduce inflationary pressures in the coming months.

One concession that the ECB has made in its communication policy, after two years of resisting, has been to publish its internal forecasts of inflation and GDP growth – something the Finnish banker, Matti Vanhala, had pushed for as a way to make the bank more transparent.

However, quantity of transparency isn't the same as quality. The OECD, in a critical report in April 2001, recommended that the governing council should meet less often than every two weeks, cutting meetings to 10 to 12 times a year, which it said might help simplify communication with the markets. It also suggested the ECB could do better if it explained more about the policy debate in its written documents and relied less on speeches and Mr. Duisenberg's press conferences. Economists at the Centre for Economic Policy Research added: 'The ECB has shown overall good judgement in its action. If there is a problem it is the link between what it says and what it does.'

Despite the gaffes, the damage is far from irreparable. The odds are that within two or three years down the road, Duisenberg's blunders will appear as a mere footnote on the ECB's record.

First, ECB has done a better job than the Fed at keeping core inflation under control. Second, disagreements about policy are not shortcomings: Indeed, over the course of 2000, Greenspan was criticized from within the Fed for being too slow to raise rates – and then later, too slow to lower them – a criticism that in retrospect looks quite astute. Two notable hawks, Larry Meyer, a Fed Governor and Jerry Jordan, president of the Cleveland district Fed, both gave the impression in speeches that they thought interest rates should have been increased more rapidly.

The ECB's main problem is not internal dissension, it is communication. The bank will likely change its format of conversing with the outside world. If anything, the internal pressure within the ECB has made it possible for Duisenberg to step down in 2002, as he promised back in 1998. The new President, be it Trichet or someone else, will probably announce that the bank will be holding fewer press conferences. From the very beginning, Duisenberg admitted that he had a problem of being too frank and blunt with words. It will help if the new president, like Greenspan, is passionate about the subtleties of policy and strategy, energetic about forging consensus, and preemptive in directing the markets.

At base, Duisenberg is responsible for the image of disorder in Frankfurt. He has served out his initial mandate, that of moderator and consensus builder among a disparate group of headstrong council members. As such, he created solidarity within the bank at the sensitive starting point – something a Frenchman like Trichet would have had a harder time doing if only because his intentions would have always been held suspect by the Germans. As one German banker told me back in 1998, shortly after Duisenberg was chosen: 'Duisenberg is good because he's a diplomat. But Trichet is really the better man.'

Britain mulls it over

For Britain's prime minister, Tony Blair, the euro has been a like a girlfriend that he doesn't want his acquaintances to know about. He has twisted and turned in public statements concerning the euro, but one gets the sense that underneath he wants Britain to join.

In February 1999, Blair first signaled a desire to prepare Britain for potential entry into the EMU. In March 1999, a group of pro-euro Tories registered as an independent party, laying down a challenge to the leader at the time, William Hague. That was the high-water mark of British support for the euro. A year later, in May 2000, the euro had fallen sharply and political support began to ebb – so much so that the Liberal Democrats declared that there was a 'void' in political support for the euro. They moved to form a high-level group to examine what was required for Britain to join the currency. The group included Willem Buiter, a member of the Monetary Policy Committee that sets interest rates for the Bank of England, and several other economists with high profiles in the UK. Liberal Democrat leader Charles Kennedy said he wanted to reverse the 'bunker mentality' in the UK regarding the euro.

Since then, however, opinion polls have showed growing opposition by the British public to the idea. In an ominous sign, Blair reportedly said during a trip to South Korea in late 2000 that he would vote 'no' in a referendum on euro-membership under the circumstances at the time. Polls showed that a high percentage of British respondents were against joining, while just over a quarter were in favour. Pollster Bob Worcester said a 'yes' campaign victory was a virtual impossibility, even in the new parliament.

In February 2001 – perhaps because of the heat of the then-upcoming election – Blair relented somewhat. He announced that he would decide within two years of the elections (held on June 7, 2001), whether even to call a referendum. However, he affirmed in the days before the election that he felt Labour could win such a referendum and stated that cooperating with Europe was in the national interest. Hague, who opposed the euro, cast the election as a decision on whether or not to join. Blair's decision to support the euro apparently stemmed from the belief that British voters do not have deep-seated objections to the euro, even if they are sceptical.

The day after the election, the British pound slipped to $1.377, a 15-year low against the dollar, on assumptions that Blair would eventually move to hold the referendum. Later, it slipped to further lows. Then, on Sep. 11, the day terrorists attacked New York and Washington, D.C., Blair made his strongest statement yet in favor of joining the euro. In a statement at Brighton, Blair disagreed with the view of naysayers that the euro would be a disaster: 'I think they're wrong. And a successful euro is in our national interest. So provided the economic conditions are met, it is right that Britain joins.'

A series of job cut announcements by Japanese manufacturers in Britain including Matsushita, Sony and Hitachi, suggested that parts of the British manufacturing industry were being hit by exclusion from the euro-zone. However, the reasons weren't clear: In fact, some of the Japanese were relocating to Eastern Europe. Meanwhile, British unemployment was at just over 5 per cent, compared with 9 per cent in euro-zone.

In June 2001, British central banker Eddie George ruled out Britain's participation in the euro at the exchange rate at the time. The euro was floating between 3.15 and 3.20 euros to the pound, a rate he judged as much too low against the pound for it to make sense for the Brits to join. A low euro meant that British goods would be expensive in foreign markets, and could hinder British imports. When asked about what was an 'acceptable rate' against the euro, he suggested that anywhere between 2.40 and 3.00 would be reasonable.

Looking forward.

The European Union is negotiating the accession of a host of Eastern European states. They include 12 mainly eastern and central European countries, and Turkey, which has yet to begin negotiations. At the EU summit in Gothenburg, Sweden, in mid-June, the EU leaders agreed that the most advanced candidates would complete negotiations for entry into the EU by the end of 2002 with the objective of becoming full-fledged members by 2004.

That means that 2006 will likely be the earliest that any of these countries will be admitted to the euro area (two years of currency pegging to prove discipline has become the accepted norm among eurozone leaders). However, with 30-odd members on the ECB's governing council, it will become difficult to hold monetary policy discussions around a single table, let alone decide upon policy by consensus. This raises the prospect of the ECB undergoing institutional reform, perhaps giving the four big countries – Germany, France, Italy and Britain (if it joins) – permanent seats on the governing council, and then rotating the other, smaller countries on an annual basis. That is what happens at the US Federal Reserve, with the New York Reserve Bank governor having a permanent status, and other regional banks having rotational status. In March 2001, Duisenberg gave indications that the ECB will likely opt for a rotation of voting members on its policy-making committee.

Many challenges remain. The central bankers still haven't divided responsibilities clearly between the ECB and the national central banks. One major area is the supervision of banks.

The bankers will continue to face challenges from Europe's politicians too. French Prime Minister Lionel Jospin repeated the French call for an 'economic government' in a highly-publicized speech in May 2001, again reminding the bankers that the French remain discontent about the lack of a power that the national finance ministers have vis-à-vis the ECB.

There have been few important personnel changes at the bank. Duisenberg will soon make up his mind whether to step down in 2002, a date he originally agreed to at the time of his appointment. That seems likely, given the criticism of his tenure.

However, the planned successor, Trichet, has legal problems. He is under judicial investigation in connection with the near-collapse of Credit Lyonnais SA in the early 1990s. A protracted investigation by Judge Jean-Pierre Zanoto is looking into whether Trichet condoned understated losses by Credit Lyonnais at time when he was active in supervising the bank. The consensus is that Trichet has a better than 50-50 chance of putting these problems behind him.

The decisive body at the ECB is the governing council, which has 18 members. They include six board members, who sit in

Frankfurt, and 12 national central bank governors. Here's a look at who has picked up influence at the ECB since its founding in 1998.

Without question, Otmar Issing remains the next most influential banker after Trichet. He still dominates the monetary policy agenda at the council meetings through his position as chief economist. He was the first to signal that the ECB would cut interest rates in the spring of 1999; he articulated why the bank would raise rates in 2000; and ultimately, he was the first to indicate that rates would be cut again in 2001. Two days before each meeting, Issing sends his 'orange' book to each council member outlining his view of the economy. He also drafts the ECB's monthly communiqué.

However, he is already on the ECB's executive board, and so is ruled out from becoming president.

Most of the other board members have boosted their stature with the markets. Christian Noyer, the vice-president, has surprised many bankers who feared his youth and lack of experience could bring him under sway of political influence from Paris. Of all the bankers, Noyer has enhanced his reputation the most, insiders say. And Padoa-Schioppa, another intellectual heavyweight on the board, has done well. As chief of international relations at the ECB, Padoa-Schioppa negotiated the intervention with the G-7. Despite worries by some observers that his pro-EMU zeal might get the better of him, he has managed to keep his mouth zipped when it comes to spontaneous comments about the euro.

Sirkka Hämäläinen, meanwhile, fought early on from within the ECB for a switch to so-called 'variable-rate' refinancing operations, which she said would help avoid volatility and ensure adequate liquidity in the financial system. Issing and others on the board opposed the move, saying that 'fixed-rate' operations were a better way of controlling money supply and short-term interest rates.

With its fixed-rate operations, the ECB set the price for market funds in the form of a fixed interest rate, and banks requested the amount of funds they wanted. But this fixed-rate method kept smaller banks disadvantaged because they were less skilled at negotiating the tenders. Helped by the bank governors from some of the smaller countries, Hämäläinen was able to overcome opposition. In June 2000, the ECB made the switch to 'variable-rates.' Under this method, banks name both the volume of funds they want and the interest rate they are willing to pay. The change helped boost Hämäläinen's reputation in the markets.

There have been a few newcomers, but they hail from smaller countries and it is still too early to say whether they will yield significant influence. In 1991, Greece became the euro's 12th member – doing away with Europe's oldest currency, the drachma. Greece's central banker, Lucas Papademos, joined the council, thereby expanding it to 18.

Papademos, 54, spent much of his career as an economist in the U.S. But he has extensive experience at the Bank of Greece, making him a full-fledged member of the banker's 'club.' He took over as central bank governor in October 1994, and enhanced the central bank's position in Greece by negotiating its legal independence from the government in December 1997.

Greece's membership increases the euro-zone's population by 11 million to 302 million, and its total gross domestic product by 2 per cent to about $5.6 billion.

There was some opposition to Greece's accession, mainly from the German Bundesbank. In April, 2000, Hans Recker, member of the German central bank's council, tried, but failed, to delay Greece's entry by arguing that it didn't meet fiscal and inflationary criteria.

Since 1999, four other bankers have joined the ECB council. They are the bankers from the national banks of Germany, Belgium, Portugal and Spain – who have replaced bankers who have stepped down. Welteke, as expected, replaced Tietmeyer to become the Bundesbank president. Guy Quaden, governor of the Belgian central bank, is seen as a passionate supporter of Europe. He has called the euro's weakness 'excessive and unjustified.'

Spain's Jaime Caruana, has remained relatively elusive. In his first six months in office, he gave no interviews with the press. Before his position at the head of Spain's central bank, he was head of supervision for the bank.

Vitor Constancio, the 58-year-old governor of the Portuguese central bank, became a major ally of Hämäläinen on the switch to variable-rate operations, and a report from his bank played a role in convincing the ECB board to make the switch. Meanwhile, he's had a tough job keeping his government in line. Portugal has the highest inflation rate in the EU, not helped by excessive public spending – something that has brought stern warnings from Brussels. Portugal is not expected to balance its budget before 2004. There is a growing angst in that country that it is falling behind rather than catching up with Europe.

The orthodoxy of the European Central Bank remains firmly intact. Despite criticism, the bank retains one chief mandate: the control of inflation. It has done a relatively good job in attaining this goal, largely neglecting the euro's exchange rate to pursue it. Even Britain's central banker Eddie George has come to the ECB's defense. Since the euro's birth, he said in a Paris speech in October 2000, the eurozone had shown 'impressive' results: strong economic growth, falling unemployment and a low inflation rate. 'I find some of the popular criticism I read in the media....greatly exaggerated if not wholly misplaced,' he said. Then, in a London speech in May 2001, George said that the ECB's success can only be measured by consistently low inflation: 'Against this criterion, the ECB has been relatively successful,' he concluded.

The Fed's McDonough agrees. Duisenberg has had a steep learning curve in dealing with the media. But by mid-2001, he seemed to be hitting a more confident stride.

One example was Duisenberg's interview with the New York Times in June 2001,[viii] when Europe's growth rate seemed to slow sharply, and optimism flagged across the continent. Duisenberg stated that monetary policy could do nothing about Europe's poor economic and productivity growth rates. Rather, these problems required eliminating many of the structural rigidities in Europe, including government regulations on goods and labour.

Sitting in his office atop the Eurotower headquarters of the ECB, he vocalized the motivation that has been a political driving force behind the European project from the beginning: Europe, he said confidently, would soon grow faster than the United States for the first time in many years.

NOTES

[i] *Wall Street Journal*, November 6, 2000. 'The Euro: A Dismal Failure, a Ringing Success – Yes, It's Sunk Like a Stone, But It Has Cracked Open Europe's Capital Markets,' by G. Thomas Sims and David Wessel.
[ii] *Wall Street Journal*, November 6, 2000.
[iii] *Financial Times*, Oct. 18, 2000.
[iv] *Wall Street Journal*, April 26, 2001.
[v] *Wall Street Journal*, May 11, 2001.
[vi] *Financial Times*, May 11, 2001.
[vii] *Financial Times*, May 15, 2001.
[viii] *New York Times*, June 14.

Index

441